The Chinese
Entrepreneurship Way

The Chinese Entrepreneurship Way

A Case Study Approach

Julia Pérez-Cerezo

business**expert**
Press

The Chinese Entrepreneurship Way. A Case Study Approach
Copyright © Business Expert Press, 2013.

First published in 2013 by
Business Expert Press, LLC
222 East 46th Street, New York, NY 10017
www.businessexpertpress.com

ISBN-13: 978-1-60649-764-7 (paperback)
ISBN-13: 978-1-60649-765-4 (e-book)

Business Expert Press Entrepreneurship and Small Business Management collection

Collection ISSN: 1946-5653 (print)
Collection ISSN: 1946-5661 (electronic)

Cover and interior design by Exeter Premedia Services Private Ltd.
Chennai, India

First edition: 2013

10 9 8 7 6 5 4 3 2 1

Printed in the United States of America.

To David & Gabriel, my beloved nephews,
with the hope that, when they grow,
they will become themselves—
extremely clever innovative entrepreneurs.

Abstract

China is the second largest economy in the world, and it stands poised to become the largest. China's geo-political power is also developing at a stunning pace. It has been predicted that China will have more impact on the world over the next 20 years than any other country. The world order as we have known it is changing, and China is becoming its leader.

But, contrary to the belief that China's economic "miracle" is solely due to its government, the reality is that it has been fuelled by its people's enormous ambitions and entrepreneurial spirit. Private-owned companies account for about 60% of the country's gross domestic product (GDP) and about 75% of the country's jobs. The real secret to the Chinese economy's outstanding development had most to do with the nature and attitude of the Chinese people.

This book is about models of Chinese entrepreneurship. It tells the stories of fifteen women entrepreneurs, but dealing with them just as entrepreneurs. They have been chosen because in today's China, women are closer to the *junzi* ideal of Confucius. The book shows that Chinese entrepreneurs' good performance is based on principles and values shaped over the millennia. It sheds light on the approaches and rationale of the entrepreneurial paths that Chinese follow.

A striking feature of Chinese entrepreneurs is how they all seem to go with the flow of things. So, they are not afraid to face risks or to start all over again. They do not panic when adversities arise, for they know that success will always follow adversity. For Chinese entrepreneurs the world is a place where anything is possible. This makes them creative and able to persevere, willing to try what for others may seem impossible or unrealistic. They are brimming with a unique inner strength, self-motivation, and self-control. Chinese entrepreneurs have a tremendous emotional intelligence and are experts at generating new ideas and strategies. They regard their employees and the building of an internal corporate culture as the soul of their business. For them a crisis is an opportunity to improve and learn, to focus on working hard and being efficient today in order to succeed tomorrow.

Chinese entrepreneurs operate in "the Chinese Paradigm," a paradigm that overlaps very little with our Western paradigm. But, while the

Chinese are very familiar with Western modes of business, we Westerners are unaware of how the Chinese operate. This book is aimed to throw some light on this.

Chinese entrepreneurs think they can turn the world around and re-establish the order that for over eighteen centuries placed them at the center of the world. And they probably will. It is only a matter of time. By learning from their achievements, we should be prepared for it.

Keywords

Chinese entrepreneurship approaches, Chinese principles and values, Chinese business culture, Chinese business attitude, Chinese business behavior, Chinese leadership styles, the Chinese paradigm.

Contents

"[L]ove of kindness, without a love to learn, finds itself obscured by foolishness. Love of knowledge, without a love to learn, finds itself obscured by loose speculation. Love of honesty, without a love to learn, finds itself obscured by harmful candor. Love of straightforwardness, without a love to learn, finds itself obscured by misdirected judgment.

Love of daring, without a love to learn, finds itself obscure by insubordination. And love for strength of character, without a love to learn, finds itself obscured by intractability."

—CONFUCIUS

Foreword

Scott Shane, one of the world's leading scholars of entrepreneurship, recently said that China is becoming the world leader in entrepreneurship. So what is it that we can learn about becoming better entrepreneurs from China?

This book examines individual Chinese entrepreneurs and provides an unusual window into the attitudes, behavior, and experiences of leading entrepreneurs operating inside China's economy today. Basically, it examines the roots of contemporary Chinese entrepreneurial style, exploring, describing, and explaining them via fifteen case studies of Chinese entrepreneurs.

From an academic standpoint, Chinese approaches to entrepreneurship may vary from those elsewhere, including the West. First, entrepreneurial theory and practice in the West may not explain entrepreneurial behavior in China. This has implications for the development of theory on Chinese entrepreneurship. Second, taking the comparative approach, we face the possibility that Chinese entrepreneurial attitudes and behavior may vary from those in the West. How much does it differ and why and how does that matter become the interesting questions at this point.

Julia's focus in this book is that there is a difference in Chinese entrepreneurs, especially in the entrepreneurial approaches and entrepreneurial styles they adopt. This is rooted, not in Chinese institutions or the Chinese economy, but at the level of the individual entrepreneur. That is, Chinese entrepreneurship is rooted in the "soft aspects" of their entrepreneurial orientation (that is, in their individual attitudes and behavior, as based in a common culture).

One perspective common to the study of management and entrepreneurship in the West is the contrast between the Normative (what entrepreneurs should do) and the Behavioral (what entrepreneurs actually do in the "real world"). In the Chinese cultural context, according to the author, these two perspectives should converge, at least from the point of view of the Chinese entrepreneur. The logic of this convergence, however,

may be obscured to the foreigner's eye because he or she does not understand Chinese culture and therefore lacks an understanding of, in Julia's
phrasing, the micro dynamics of Chinese entrepreneurial behavior.

In this book, Julia largely adopts the Narrative mode. In fifteen case
studies, we hear the story of entrepreneurial intent in the entrepreneur's
own words. The facts are told as stories, revealing both the cognitive and
attitudinal aspects of how entrepreneurs approach their tasks dynamically,
fluidly, that is, what the process is like of being entrepreneurial while also
being Chinese. In a cross-cultural sense, the "cultural baggage" we bear
with us as individuals throughout our lives is never unpacked, wherever
one goes in the world. This is as true for someone Chinese as for anyone
else, no matter where their home culture may be. Yes, the entrepreneurial
story cannot be separated from the storyteller, but paradoxically, the lessons learned from each story should still prove universal in application.
In other words, you don't have to be Chinese to learn from these stories
of entrepreneurial learning.

Another perspective worth considering, but one that the author rejects
in this book, is that the difference in entrepreneurial contexts (China vs.
elsewhere in the world) matters. Here, the issue is how we should look
at China. Do the differences in China's social, economic, and political
institutions change the entrepreneurial story or experience, rendering
the "lessons learned" to a minimum since they cannot be transferred or
applied elsewhere in the world? Hardly. As individuals, we can learn from
others' experiences, and reshape our own attitudes and behavior. Education and learning have this principle at heart. Here, we can learn from
our peers or counterparts who happen to operate in the Chinese context.
Certainly, entrepreneurs in China face a different set of opportunities and
threats; indeed, each case study involves a different entrepreneurial context from the other as Julia has chosen her interviewees from a variety of
organizational contexts in China, as well as differing individual histories
or backgrounds.

One interesting question, relative to Scott Shane's statement, is how
these entrepreneurs got interested in becoming entrepreneurs, despite facing an often unfavorable business environment and/or a lack of supportive institutions and/or resources along the way. Julia's discussion of the
general optimism of the Chinese today, including Chinese entrepreneurs,

in the face of seeming global economic uncertainty and adversity is a central element to this book.

From the Western perspective, we may lack an understanding, or even a direct experience, of how these entrepreneurs in China could disbelieve the "facts" like these they face all around them. If the global economy looks bad here, why should it look any different there? But the argument here is that, culturally, the Chinese interpret the situation differently because they do not perceive the same "facts," let alone interpret them the same way as the non-Chinese do. The cultural perspective matters, and perceptions of the facts differ. The Chinese, like most entrepreneurs everywhere, are made, not born, through a lifetime of learning, in school, on the job and through their daily lives. Some of us who have spent years living in China learned this directly from our experiences there. For readers elsewhere, however, her argument and books are necessary correctives. We may live in the same world, but we see opportunities and threats differently. Perhaps there is an advantage in that difference.

Julia's argument is that the cultural perspective is more persuasive, and therefore, more insightful or "truthful" than the alternative explanations.

So, how have these entrepreneurial actors succeeded in an environment that reopened to entrepreneurship 25 or 30 years ago, even though China itself may not have been ideally the most hospitable environment for entrepreneurial activity, let alone entrepreneurial success?

Ultimately, of course, the payoff from reading this book for the non-Chinese reader falls in two areas: competitive aspects and negotiations. Less obvious, however, is that the payoff for all readers (non-Chinese and Chinese) should be in reflecting on these questions: Are there one or more common Chinese entrepreneurial styles? That is, is there a typology of Chinese entrepreneurial styles? This book won't answer that question, but it suggests the possibility that there may be several styles, and not just one. Indeed, how many styles are described from the case studies in this book? I'll leave the answer to you, the reader.

A related question: in reading each case study, can we individually learn to distinguish the individual entrepreneur from the "typical" entrepreneur, or the "stereotypical" entrepreneur we carry in our own mind's eye? This is true not just for China and Chinese entrepreneurs, but in general.

Finally, the "big question" worth reflecting on here, in my opinion: if we are to borrow from the successes of Chinese entrepreneurs, what is it exactly that we should be imitating or emulating from Chinese entrepreneurial practice?

Two classic examples from global exposure to Japanese management practice over the past 30 years might provide guidance to what we should do here.

First, 20 or 30 years ago, one lesson adopted in the West from Japanese managerial practice was the use of vision or mission statements in corporate strategic planning (Komatsu's "Encircle C" vision for challenging Caterpillar's dominance of the global construction equipment industry). Back then, no one put a vision or a mission statement into their annual reports or business plans except the Japanese. Now, it is a recommended standard practice globally, for large publicly held corporations and individual entrepreneurial ventures. Second, the Harvard Business School case study on Honda's entry into the US motorcycle market provided another, more controversial, discussion on the nature of Japanese management styles and strategies, including much debate over the actual strengths exploited in their managerial practices successfully entering the US market. Opinions on the lessons learned here continue, years later. The answer here, like beauty, may lie in the eyes of the beholder.

Julia's premise is no less than this: there may be aspects to Chinese entrepreneurial practice that are no less important, not just competitively or for negotiating purposes, but for emulating. In other words, if you are an entrepreneur or businessperson, it is time to learn from the Chinese.

What could, or should, entrepreneurs elsewhere learn from the best Chinese entrepreneurial practices? For this last reason alone, this book is worth reading, and reflecting over.

I recommend this book to you as another route to learning more about Chinese culture and Chinese entrepreneurs. These Chinese entrepreneurs, all of them women, coincidentally, have an entrepreneurial story to tell. Each has at least one moral to their story, and each account carries at least one potential lesson for you as an entrepreneur or businessperson, no matter where you are from or where you call home.

Ultimately, entrepreneurial behavior everywhere is rooted in individual action, but is embedded in a social and cultural setting. It's a dynamic process because there is give-and-take, with feedback in the system, if the entrepreneur is paying attention. What is happening here may be interesting to some, but it's the how and the why of the stories that, to my thinking, hold the real promise for learning, and for practical application to real-world businesspeople.

Enjoy!

David S. Shaw, Ph.D.
Member of the faculty, Business
The Evergreen State College
Olympia, Washington, USA

Preface

Today, China is the second largest economy in the world, and it stands poised to become the largest. The country is on track for a transformation to an economic model based largely on domestic consumption and on services. China has more than US$ 3.2 trillion in foreign reserves. By the year 2025, the Chinese government plans to build 221 cities with more than one million inhabitants, and another eight hyper-modern megacities which would be home to more than 10 million people. It has been estimated that by 2020 the Chinese middle class will rise to 600 million people, with total consumption of US$ 4.8 trillion, making it the second-biggest consumer market after the US. Like the US, China has three domestic companies included in the top 10 of the Fortune Global 500. It has launched its first aircraft carrier and runs one of the world's most ambitious space programs. In 2011, there were 157,558 Chinese students in US universities, many of them pursuing or intending to pursue PhD degrees. China's geo-political power is also developing at a stunning pace. "Knowledge, Networks, and Nations," a recent study by the UK Royal Society, concluded that China would overtake the US in published scientific output by 2013. US national intelligence sources have predicted that China will have more impact on the world over the next 20 years than any other country. The world order as we have known it is changing, and China is becoming its leader.

During the last three decades, China has experienced around 10% annual economic growth. Much of this has been due to the government's funding of massive infrastructure projects and its powerful influence over the country's biggest companies. State-owned companies dominate China's banking, energy, telecommunications, health-care, and technology sectors. Overall, they account for about 40% of the country's gross domestic product (GDP) and about 25% of the country's jobs. However, contrary to the belief that China's economic "miracle" is solely due to its government,[1] the reality is that China's growth has been fuelled by its people's enormous ambition and entrepreneurial spirit. When one spends time living in China among the Chinese, the expression most often heard is *zuo shengyi*—literally, "do business"—and everybody offers a foreigner plenty of theoretically potential opportunities to *zuo shengyi*. The Chinese people are so highly entrepreneurial that they are always trying to find ways to develop business and make money, everywhere.

When doing the field work for my first book "China's New Leaders" ("Emprendedoras Chinas," in Spanish), organizing the information gathered, and completing the writing for the book, I was sure that the real secret to the Chinese economy's outstanding development had more to do with the nature and attitude of the Chinese people, more so than any of the other issues commonly raised in the Western world (for instance, unfair competition, poor labor conditions, undervaluation of the yuan versus foreign currencies). I was also quite certain that the unique nature of the Chinese people had much to do with their traditional cultural principles and values. These had been in place for many centuries before the Communist system came into place in 1949 when many elements of Traditional Chinese Culture, including its philosophical and religious schools of thought, namely Taoism, Buddhism, and Confucianism, were officially restricted.

Despite Mao's fervent efforts to erase Traditional Chinese Culture, however, he himself incorporated it into his rule, reflecting how deeply rooted it was in the minds of the Chinese people. As a result, even if today's young urban residents may have to learn more about Chinese philosophy and values,[2] the reality is that they have been raised with the same set of values and principles as their parents, grandparents, and great-grandparents.

Since my first book was published, I have been questioned many times about the subjectivity of my observations of Chinese women entrepreneurs' values and principles, even though I had attempted throughout to let them speak for themselves. We are seemingly obsessed in the West with defining what China and the Chinese are not. As a result, we always find excuses to "turn things around" when what we read does not fit the preconceptions we already hold.

This book is about models of Chinese entrepreneurship. My hope is to prove that I have imagined or invented nothing in conveying that Chinese entrepreneurs perform well. They do so by following models based on principles and values shaped over the millennia. By combining these principles and values with entrepreneur's own individual innovative approaches, collectively these Chinese entrepreneurs may well end up conquering the rest of the world commercially.

Many books have been written explaining how Chinese people negotiate and behave in business situations, sometimes linking these behavioral patterns to their historical conditions, beliefs, and cultural traditions. But not much has been written so far shedding light on the approaches and rationale of the entrepreneurial paths they follow. Why do Chinese people act the way they do? Why it is so difficult for a Westerner—even one accustomed to being among Chinese business people—to anticipate their tactics or strategic moves? In my experience, Chinese business people are experts at generating new ideas and strategies. The perception elsewhere that they do not innovate is flat out wrong, for these entrepreneurs have extremely creative minds, and are constantly generating new ideas and alternative ways of doing things. For instance, when it comes to the management of human resources, they apply models for motivating employees which are not necessarily in line with Western approaches, but that have proved to be more successful with Chinese employees. Chinese entrepreneurs operate in what I like to call "the Chinese Paradigm," a paradigm which overlaps very little or not at all with our Western paradigm. Hence, the famous phrase typically used for Joint Ventures (JVs)—*hezi*—with foreign companies: "same bed, different dreams."

In fact, without being familiar with "The Chinese Paradigm," it is very difficult to understand how the Chinese approach their relationships with foreigners. It is also very difficult to understand Chinese attitudes toward entrepreneurship, business development, and management, and how they are able to maintain a positive attitude in the midst of today's global uncertainties. The Chinese are very familiar with Western modes of business: our professionals, our entrepreneurs and business managers, and our companies. If as foreigners we remain unaware of how the Chinese operate, our economies may well remain at a competitive disadvantage, not only today or tomorrow, but also in the more distant future. As a result, we may well remain trapped in our pessimism for a long time, unable to see any way out of it, while China continues moving at a faster pace, exploiting our relative ignorance. Thus, it is my hope with this book to shine some light on Chinese entrepreneurial paths and the rationale behind them, so that in the West we can gain a better understanding of how the Chinese lead and manage their businesses, learn from their experiences, and incorporate their techniques into our own business and entrepreneurial culture.

As in my first book, I look at China taking a micro (not a macro) approach. Traditionally, most foreign observers have taken the macro perspective when referring to the country, its politics, and business. As explained in my first book, an entrepreneur in China is today not only a person who has started his or her own business, but also a person who has helped guide and transform a government-owned company into a competitive—and sometimes even a global—firm. It is important in this respect to mention that many of China's government-owned companies have proved to be relatively efficient. This contradicts the experience of what typically happens in many countries in the West and elsewhere. Furthermore, in China the relationship between state-owned enterprises (SOEs) and private firms is not only very close, but also unique. I refer to these as "Chinese Public–Private Partnerships," for they are commonly seen throughout China whether in a JV form or merely where both organizations are merely complementing each other's business functions (for instance, as supply chain partners). For me, these partnerships show us that both growth and global leadership are possible following this alternative model.

This book tells the stories of fifteen women entrepreneurs, but it deals with them primarily as entrepreneurs, rather than focusing on their gender as in my first book. So, why have I chosen to look exclusively at women entrepreneurs instead of both male and female entrepreneurs? There are several reasons for this decision, the most important being that, in today's China, women are closer to the *junzi*[3] ideal of Confucius. Chinese women are closer to giving a good account of their professional and social duties and to living up to the *junzi*'s standard of social justice. Over the years, I have observed that Chinese women have been more successful at keeping the positive traditional Chinese values intact. In today's China, women entrepreneurs nearly always seem spontaneously to emphasize and practice the need for internal equilibrium and peace with oneself, which then allows the generation of sustainable external wealth. In contrast, this trait is not as often found among their male counterparts. Since this idea of the need for a happy interior life in order to perform well in business is receiving more and more attention over time in the Western world, it made sense to focus on the inherently Chinese values of these Chinese women entrepreneurs. Moreover, women entrepreneurs have been playing a major role in the Chinese economy since the beginning of its reforms. They are what I like to call "a precious hidden source of energy that disseminates everywhere," starting at the household level (still very important in China), continuing at the professional and business level, and extending throughout all of Chinese society.

Although it is not well known in China or in the Western world, women have played a significant role in Chinese history, despite being placed at the very bottom of the family hierarchy by Confucius. Ancient China had some matriarchal societies. Archaeologists and historians have shown that these matriarchal societies played significant roles in their communities, in some cases extending their influence over time and in ways that continue to be evident today. This is the case with Feng Shui, which archaeologists and historians believe was validated by a group of women who were advisors to the chief of the ancient matriarchal tribe *Fuxi* who lived in what is today northwest China. A living vestige of China's matriarchal societies remains on the shores of Lugu *Hu* (Lugu Lake), on the North West Yunnan plateau, where the Mosuo people live. In fact, Mosuo's ancient family structure is considered a kind of "living fossil" for researching the marital development history of human beings, as well as the last "Realm of Matriarchy." Because of the dominant role women play in their society, Lugu Lake is called the "mother lake" by the Mosuo people. The marriage rites of the Mosuo people are known as the "*azhu* marriage" ceremony. The unique aspect of their social culture—in which women exercise the right to choose and change their husbands at will—has given the name of "the Exotic Land of Daughters" to the area. *Azhu* in the local Mosuo language (which does not have a written form) means "intimate sweetheart." *Azhu* marriage is the way of life among the Mosuo people; it is an arrangement of convenience in which the partners come and go as they like. Women have the rightful ownership of land and houses, and full rights to the children born to them. The children carry their mother's family name and pay greatest respect to their mothers, who in turn enjoy high social status. The male companions are known as "axias," and work for the women.

Additionally—and quite often forgotten—is the fact that, unlike other countries in which women played no role in political affairs, early on China had an Empress: Empress Wu Zhao, who in 690 proclaimed herself *huandi* (Emperor) and founded her own dynasty, the Zhou (周), which succeeded the Tang Dynasty. Despite the polemics surrounding her life and behavior, Empress Wu Zhao held great power and strongly supported the development of Buddhism in China, which she made the official state religion in the year 691. She is said to have made interpretations of Buddhist doctrines that gave legitimacy to her reign.

The Chinese Constitution of 1954 includes a clause recognizing the equality of men and women. Today, 45% of the Chinese labor force is women and 38% of the Chinese Communist Party members are women. Women occupy 18% of the positions in China's Central Government and 10% in its Provincial Governments.[4] In the universities, they occupy 16.7% of the managerial positions. At the business level, women today occupy 27% of managerial leadership positions in China.[5] When focusing on entrepreneurial and family-owned businesses, the percentage rises to 31% in Mainland China and 35% in Hong Kong.[6] Chinese women entrepreneurs are present in every sector throughout China, from real estate, construction, manufacturing, energy, technology, agriculture, and livestock to finance, commerce, services, health, education, and culture. About 68% of Chinese women entrepreneurs are over 40 years old and generally do not speak English, while 30% are between 31 and 40 years old. Eighty percent of them established their enterprises after 1990, and two-thirds of them after 1996. About two-thirds of the companies run by women have developed their own trademarks and about 40% of them their own brands. 17% of women entrepreneurs' companies own international patents and 24% of them domestic patents. Most of these women work between 8 and 12 hours a day and, according to their own statements, in 95% of their situations they have consistently made a profit.

Chinese women entrepreneurs' influence today extends well beyond China, since more than half of the richest women of the world are Chinese. Both the "Top 200" Forbes' 2012 list and *Hurun* Rich List 2012 show Wu Yajun (185th richest person in the world), General Director of

Longhu Real Estate Development Co, a developer in the south western municipality of Chongqing, as the richest Chinese woman, with an estimated family fortune of 38 billion Yuan (US$ 6.12 billion). Including her, there are 156 women among China's 1,000 richest people, accounting for 15.5% of the list. The average wealth of the listed women is 13.7 billion Yuan and the average age 48 years old. The real estate industry remains the biggest source of wealth for the richest Chinese women, with 30% coming from this industry as well as six of the top 10 women. Guangdong province is home to the headquarters of 10 listed women's companies, more than any other region in China, followed by Beijing with nine and Zhejiang with six. Thirty-three of the 50 richest Chinese women are self-made billionaires. On the list of the world's richest self-made women, 18 who have more than US$ 1 billion come from China.[7]

This book is based on the information gathered during my in-depth interviews with 15 women entrepreneurs, in August 2009—in the midst of the financial crisis—and again in October and November 2011, during the turmoil about the future evolution of the global economy and the world as we have known it. Most of this information was shared through personal interviews, although supplemented in some cases through written communications. Since the global economic situation began changing so much in 2009, it was my decision not to write this book until a second run of in-depth interviews could be completed two years later, so that a broader perspective of the entrepreneurs' businesses and their management approaches could be gained. I wanted to use this two year break to see the changes both in the entrepreneurs' businesses and in their lives. I considered it especially important given the fact that, when the first in-depth interviews were done in 2009, the companies led by women entrepreneurs still largely relied on exports. According to the "2009 Development Report for Women Entrepreneurs of China" (see the bibliography), 20% of women entrepreneurs received at least 70% of their income from exports while an additional 28% gained between 31% and 70% of their revenue from exports.[8] In 2009, 17% of Chinese women entrepreneurs reported that their exports were already decreasing (although in only 2% of the situations was there a risk of bankruptcy). As a result, by 2009, 61% of these women had already said that they would seize the opportunity to expand their presence in the domestic market, while 22% of them had already entered less developed regions in China, and 17% had entered the service sector. In the 2009 scenario, 10% of women entrepreneurs saw new opportunities in the global market—including mergers and acquisitions, but most of them stated that they were going to rely on innovating in their core business and in the domestic market in order to deal with the economic crisis.

Between 2009 and 2011, several important changes took place in the Chinese economy: the continued decrease in its exports and industrial output; the shift by Western companies' sourcing activities from China to cheaper fast-developing economies; the continuing rise in prices, faster than the corresponding increase in quality; and the clear emphasis by the government on the domestic market, the green economy—*lusi jinji*—and the development of the service industry. Together with the deterioration in the world economy, this has, in a way, made China more Chinese and more economically differentiated from the West; in turn the Chinese people have become more chauvinistic and more certain of the idea that they are destined to lead the world.

Both in 2009 and 2011, I was struck by the contrast between the positivism and pro-active attitude of the Chinese entrepreneurs and the negativism and passive attitude of the Western world's citizens. This is particularly true among the generation that has made China's development possible. The new young generation, while better educated (sometimes holding degrees from the world's best universities) and with a better command of English (in some instances close to perfect), do not always face such a positive attitude.[9] But even so, most young people do not have a negative attitude; most would say "*hai keyi*" when asked about how they are doing, meaning that they are doing fine (although this literally translates as "so, so"). As a matter of fact, many of these young Chinese have thought about starting their own business, even if their families have no entrepreneurial background and they themselves lack the most adequate or innate entrepreneurial attitudes (a situation somewhat akin to how the US used to be).

According to the same report mentioned above, in 2009, 97% of Chinese women entrepreneurs said that they were optimistic about their economic prospects, and felt certain they could find a way to survive the crisis and move ahead through it. They said so even though they faced substantial competition—58% of these women claimed their competitors were well established brands that were not easy to defeat, especially because the women entrepreneurs could not afford bigger marketing and advertising budgets to do so. In fact—and contrary to what many people in the West think—competition in China is paramount. There are so many Chinese people innovating and enterprising, precisely because of the many opportunities in China's big markets. There is competition from domestic companies and there is competition from international companies. As for the export-oriented consumer product companies, there is also competition from other developing and fast-growing economies, such as Vietnam and Indonesia. However, none of this really matters to Chinese entrepreneurs who, contrary to what we may think, do not expect their government to provide them with any help. They know they must rely on themselves to keep the strength to move ahead, to continue living, and to be happy no matter what the circumstances are.

In addition to these in-depth interviews, this book is also based on my observations, my education about China, and notes I have taken over the years since 2004, when I lived in China for three years straight and managed to make friends with a generation of Chinese entrepreneurs who made possible the transition to what China is today. These friendships (together with the in-depth interviews) constitute the most important source of information for this book, which has been further complemented by extensive analysis and reading—a small sample of which is represented in this book's bibliography.

There is a vast spectrum of cultural and industrial variation across China's geography. Beijing is the center of Traditional Chinese Culture's revitalization today, and there are certain economic activities that are focused in this city, such as services, banking, and culture. Eight of the fifteen women entrepreneurs included in this book are based in Beijing. Two more are in nearby Tianjin, one of the five "national central cities" of the People's Republic of China, the center of the pharmaceutical industry (and home of Tasly), and a prosperous metropolis. The remaining five entrepreneurs are based in Qingdao, a pleasant smaller city (with a population of over 8.7 million) in eastern Shandong province, which is home to Haier and the world-famous Tsingtao beer.

The women entrepreneurs discussed here represent a varied array of profiles and operate in a variety of economic sectors. Their firms[10] range

from small 100% family-owned business to listed companies (or companies that are in the process of being listed) (such as Tasly) to global groups
(such as Haier), for which inevitably a great deal of written information
was also provided. The entrepreneurs' ages range from around 35–40 to
about 70 years old, with the majority of them being over 40 years old.
There are entrepreneurs who have started their first and only business from
scratch; entrepreneurs who, after having built a successful business, started
all over again in a completely new area multiple times; women who became
entrepreneurs by acquiring shares in the previously government-owned
company they were managing; entrepreneurs who have remained in the
same sector and others that operated businesses in more than one industry; entrepreneurs who explicitly place Traditional Chinese Culture at the
core of their business and others who acknowledge it and, when managing, make use of it, but do not consider it so relevant; women entrepreneurs who started with partners (whether family or friends); entrepreneurs
who did not consider it necessary to have the support of any partner and
took full managerial responsibility; and entrepreneurs who decided to
enter Joint Ventures (JVs) and have been successful in their relationships
with their JV partners.[11] In some cases, women joined with a male business partner—sometimes a husband—becoming like *yin* and *yang*, linking their success with that of their complementary partner's. All of these
women entrepreneurs occupied top positions in a number of professional
associations, but to avoid repetition and to make the reading easier, these
affiliations have not been mentioned. Neither have I included the extensive
list of awards that these entrepreneurs and their companies have received.

Although I conducted all the face-to-face interviews in Mandarin Chinese without the assistance of an interpreter, grasping the entrepreneurs'
main ideas and summarizing them has not been an easy task. First, there
was the difficulty of arranging and managing the interviews themselves,
in particular the second set of interviews in 2011.[12] Second, there was the
issue of the figures which, though highly valued in the Western world,
were not always provided[13] or coherent—if not sometimes contradictory.[14]
Third, there was the understanding of how the shares are distributed in
the company, when and how JVs—*hezi*—or associations—*hezuo*—are
established, the nature of their relationships with state-owned enterprises,
and how these have all evolved over time (Chinese business-people can

be particularly obscure when approaching these issues). Fourth, there were my efforts to understand their business structure[15] and their business models, which do not follow a straightforward Western logic. Fifth, there was the organization of the information gathered, so that it would make sense in the Western paradigm. Finally, there was the issue of not distorting what these entrepreneurial women said while attempting to explain (and interpret) it through a Western prism. Due to our different cognitive and behavioral paradigm in the West, we are used to applying "biased filters" to everything happening in China; as a result, we just see it with our framing. This is like looking at a white piece of paper through a colored lens; we will not see the paper as white but instead as the color of the lens. This is why, as a Westerner myself, I have tried as much as possible to transcribe what the entrepreneurs said themselves and present what they said in the same order, so that the reader can discern the direct meaning of their words and the real essence of their thoughts. The result, thus, is a kind of "documentary" book, since judgments, interpretations, and opinions are avoided. In some cases—and in particular, when referring to their corporate culture—I have chosen the style of letting them talk, since their wording means a lot. Sometimes, in a particular chapter, there may be ideas that seem repetitive, but I decided to leave them this way, because it reflects the emphasis made by that particular entrepreneur. To have presented this information in a different way would have been to apply my own colored lens to what they said, distorting my attempt to expose the reader, to the extent that it is possible, to what I have called "the Chinese paradigm." Only those familiar with China can imagine how much perseverance, effort, time, and money has been invested in getting the information and materials for this book and in interpreting and making sense of them.

This book is not about describing the commercial implications of the different economic sectors covered in China. It is also not about how these sectors and companies are transforming to adapt to the new economic situation. The book includes a lot of information on each of the companies, as this cannot be avoided, but the focus is not on the company itself, but instead on the entrepreneur managing it. As such, it focuses primarily on the entrepreneurial and leadership styles in particular areas of operation, which vary from person to person.

To the extent possible, this book details the entrepreneurs' approaches to working with family, friends, or both, as well as the eventual involvement of their children in their businesses. The book also includes descriptions of the context in which the women entrepreneurs were raised and have remained since adulthood, as well as any other elements of their environments which have made a significant impact on their lives and values (for instance, religious beliefs). It was interesting to observe how religion in China has become increasingly relevant over time, sometimes playing a central role in entrepreneurs' lives and their managerial style. This is explicitly shown in the book which, in each individual chapter, provides a glimpse into the evolution taking place in China's domestic market.

Of course, if would have been a dream come true (in fact one I still look forward to) to have the opportunity to focus solely on Yang Mianmian—President and Executive Vice chairwoman of the Board of Directors of Haier Group Company, and a role model for so many Chinese entrepreneurs—and write a book on her life and her business, not unlike the biography Walter Isaacson wrote about Steve Jobs—even more so because Haier benchmarks itself against Apple—but it was not possible for me to do this in China, until now.

The book includes a chapter on the so-called "Three Doctrines" or "Three Teachings"—Confucianism, Taoism, and Buddhism—at the root of Chinese behavior. Without some awareness of these three doctrines, it would be impossible to gain a fundamental understanding of how Chinese people behave in business (including their negotiation processes), or to learn from them and eventually incorporate these practices and insights into our own business and entrepreneurial culture. Only by doing so, will we be able to share some of their competitive advantages.

My own experience in China began in the urban areas, which attract today's global attention, as they represent the modern China. From there I began to develop an interest in understanding the so-called Traditional Chinese Culture, so that I could begin grasping "the Chinese Paradigm." What I have found as a result is an interesting paradox.

Currently in the West, Eastern philosophy and its spiritual approach are seemingly necessary, so much so that it is a long-standing fashion. Many people turn to meditation; there are courses on meditation and

Zen philosophy for managers, business, and general leadership, to name just a few examples. We diligently absorb the theory, but have difficulty with its application in everyday life, since our minds are used to very different habits. In contrast, we have the Chinese: today, they may know nothing about meditation, or about the intellectual history of their traditional values, but these qualities are so deeply rooted in their culture that they define how the Chinese behave as individuals, both in their personal and their professional spheres. The Chinese people do not look for Enlightenment (it has been said they never did), but when it comes to "living in the here and now," they are in some ways spontaneously enlightened through their social and cultural historical environment. Even Sun Tzu in "The Art of War" emphasizes how important it is—for the commander and the troops—to have peace of mind (by which he means self-control over one's emotions) in order to achieve victory: "to enter into conflict men shall properly be trained and prepared emotionally, mentally, and spiritually."

Writing such a chapter was, then, a must for the pages that follow in this book, briefly summarizing these complex philosophies and their many different dimensions (including religion). This has proved such a challenge that I must apologize for any mistakes I have made, since I am far from being an expert on the subject.

The book also includes a chapter on what I have called "Understanding the Chinese Paradigm," in which I make an attempt to relate the underlying principles of Traditional Chinese Culture—and other traditional concepts that are deeply rooted in Chinese people's minds—to the main features of Chinese entrepreneurship and business managerial behavior and attitudes. Again, any conceptual or interpretational errors are exclusively my own.

It should be noted that, although the entrepreneurs whose stories are described in this book are all women, all the quotes concerning Traditional Chinese Culture were made refering to men, for this is the way everything was written in the ancient past and transmitted over the centuries.

Since this book examines the strengths of Chinese entrepreneurs—in particular, those of the generation that participated in China's great economic transformation—at some point when reading this book, one should ask the following questions: what about managerial weaknesses, mismanagement and abuse of power?; what about deception, subterfuge, and misinformation to consumers for example, in order to make as much money as possible in the shortest feasible timeframe?; what about all the scandals that the China media constantly shows and the corruption that follows?[16] I have only this answer to those questions: If we go back to Chinese history, all these issues were also present when Lao Tzu and Confucius aimed to restore the natural order, and also when Buddhism was brought to China. Despite how hard he tried, Confucius did not succeed in eliminating them. The traditional symbiotic relationship between the merchants and the mandarins continues: officials clear the way for business, while business people pave the way for officials to accumulate assets (for instance, the introduction of opium in China by the British). Of course, all of this is also part of China, of that "continent" (much more than just a country, considering its population size, its unique history and cultural background) full of contradictions, which is also of great size and diversity. In a country the size of a continent, what even Confucius could not eradicate, may just have to be accepted as an additional dimension of its unique and contradictory features.

When Westerners go to China—whether for business or for pleasure, they quickly and easily grasp that China is not just one more country they visit, and they often find it difficult to understand. In contrast, the Chinese people now understand the outside world much better than the outside world understands them. Up to now, this has played to their competitive advantage. Let us hope that a more equal and harmonious scenario can be built, in which the outside world can understand Chinese entrepreneurial approaches and fully apply them. This will be beneficial for everyone, including the Chinese.

Acknowledgments

Many people contributed to the achievement of this project but foremost I have to thank my great friend, Shi Qingqi, who kindly introduced me to all the entrepreneurs of this book except Xu Xiaoyu who I knew since 2004. Shi Qingqi was Executive Vice-president and Secretary General of the Chinese Association of Women Entrepreneurs (CAWE), at the time of my first set I conducted interviews and remained there until her retirement in 2011, when she became advisor of the Chinese government in its "Green Economy" area. Unfortunately, Shi Qingqi will not be able to see this book published since, due to a fulminant brain cancer, she passed away in September 2012. But her warm and helpful personality and her unconditional friendship will remain with me for the rest of my life. I would like this acknowledgment to be a kind of a last public homage to her.

I also have to thank the fifteen women entrepreneurs of this book for their time and dedication (in some cases during weekends) to this book project, as well as for their hospitality and patience in listening (quite often for the very first time) to an occidental person talking in Mandarin. Without them this book would have not been possible.

I also want to express my gratitude to these entrepreneurs' secretaries, assistants, and closer employees for having supported me logistically throughout my project and having helped me to better understand their bosses' environment and managerial approach.

I am also very grateful to all those Chinese entrepreneurs, friends, acquaintances, or just simply people I met over years, since I moved to live there back in January 2004. They helped me not only to understand Chinese business culture, but also to be exposed to Chinese Traditional Culture and understand the basics of it. By doing so, they helped me to go beyond the current materialism of Chinese society to find the more profound human and spiritual side that guides Chinese entrepreneurs' determined behavior.

On the occidental side, I have to thank David S. Shaw, who not only wrote the foreword for the book, but also contributed enormously to its editing. Without his editorial help and that of professional editor Jhaleh Akhavan this manuscript would not have come to light. In this respect, I do also have to thank Simon Wan, Chairman & Chief Executive of Cornerstone International Group www.cornerstone-group.com, with whom I have been working together since 2004 and that financially supported the professional editing work. Cornerstone International Group is a leading well-established executive search trademark, with approximately 100 offices in key markets on six continents.

Finally, but not less important, I want to offer very special thanks to my parents, Julia and Angel, my brother Ángel, my nephews David and Gabriel, my sister-in-law Ute, and my cousin Mari Carmen and her family, all also my cousins—Diego, Jesús, Juan Carlos, Laura and Lourdes—for being there, providing me the necessary strength to keep living, and moving ahead to make my dreams come true, in this over time more challenging world.

CHAPTER 1

Chinese Behavior's Roots

Confucianism, Daoism, and Buddhism constitute the essence of Traditional Chinese Culture—*RuDaoFo*. Historically, the relationship among the three has been marked by both contention and complementarity, with Confucianism playing the more dominant role. These three philosophical traditions—known as the "**Three Doctrines**" or the "**Three Teachings**" since the Tang dynasty—have played an enormous role in shaping the mindset of the Chinese people, affecting their aesthetics, architecture, literature, and other forms of art, politics, astronomy, and medicine. In fact, it is evident that China owes its long-standing survival to two factors: the community of values and principles fostered among its population and its government of scholar officials. These values and principles constitute the basis for China's progress, from its developing status at the end of the 1970s to becoming the world's second largest economy in just three decades and are at the root of Chinese entrepreneurship and the Chinese style of business management; it could even be said that, without a basic familiarity with these principles and values, it would be impossible to understand either Chinese entrepreneurship or Chinese business culture.

An interesting feature that still permeates present—day China (and not just because of the Communist revolution) is the secular nature of what we could call "the pure Chinese values." These are Confucianism and ancient Daoism, leaving aside for now Buddhism and the later religious approaches of Daoism. At the time when Buddhism and Jainism appeared in India (as a reaction to Hinduism) and monotheism was proclaimed by the Jewish, China generated two strong philosophical (or we might even refer to them as spiritual) currents—Confucianism and Daoism. However, these are not religions in the traditional Western sense of the word. Moreover, when Buddhism—which has important philosophical and spiritual dimensions and shares many basic principles with Daoism—spread across China, it blended with Daoism to produce the *Chan* School. This Buddhist school of thought provided a practical approach to living everyday life, valuing every present moment (indeed, this very moment) rather than focusing on roadmaps to the afterlife.

Both Lao Tse (571–490 B.C.) and Confucius (551–479 B.C.)—Chinese philosophers—lived at the end of the Spring and Autumn period (770–476 B.C.), a time of political upheaval that led to the brutal struggles of the Warring States period (475–221 B.C.). The ruling House of Zhou was in decline and all under Heaven was in disarray. Lao Tse and Confucius tried to restore the natural order, reinvigorate the principles of harmony, and re-establish continuity.

The most important characteristic of the Chinese world view (as shaped by Daoism and Buddhism)—or, its essence—is the awareness of the unity and mutual inter-relatedness of all things and events, the experience of all phenomena in the world as being manifestations of the same basic oneness, emptiness or Dao. Dao is not a thing in itself, but rather a background, an infinitely open "space" that allows for anything to appear, change, disappear, or reappear. All things are seen as interdependent and inseparable parts of this cosmic whole, or as different manifestations of the same ultimate reality. Adding to this is the principle of impermanence—of every thing and every thought and every life's manifestation being in constant flow, always changing. There is no solidity or singularity. Forms, concepts, thoughts, and feelings are all just projections—but not the essence—of our mind.

Understanding these three doctrines is a basic requirement for an insight into Chinese behavior in business (including, but not restricted to, behavior in negotiations). This understanding can partially offset the unique but not easily replicable competitive advantages of Chinese business people. Further, one can learn from these doctrines and eventually incorporate their elements, as appropriate, into any business and entrepreneurial culture.

This is of great relevance because China has historically remained a world unto itself, never obliged to deal with other countries or civilizations that were comparable to it in scale or sophistication. China has never been tempted to acquire overseas colonies or venture abroad to convert the Barbarian into Confucian, Daoist, or Buddhist principles and virtues.[1] As a result, their paradigm and ours have remained quite separate.

Historically, when one party approached the other, it was Westerners who travelled all the way to China. This isolation encouraged the Chinese to restrict themselves to their own ideas and, over time, to judge everything by the benchmark of purely Chinese conventions—a tendency which has persisted even in recent times. A good example of this is the tradition of China referring to itself as *Zhongguo*—the "Central Country"—which could also be translated as the "Middle Kingdom." These translations accurately describe the understanding of the Chinese with respect to the position that their country assumed throughout history—China is the center of the universe (or, more generously, the center of the known universe). Without doubt, China and the Chinese people are unique, and very Chinese in character (or by definition). This has a strong influence on the way they do business and practice entrepreneurship—but what exactly does this mean?

The Great Harmony

A special feature of the Chinese civilization is that it seems to have no beginning.[2] When the Yellow Emperor—revered as the legendary founding ruler of China—appeared in myths, Chinese civilization was already in chaos. The new hero pacified the realm and was acclaimed as emperor. However, he re-established the empire and technically speaking, it was not founded by him. This paradox of Chinese history repeats itself with Confucius and Lao Tse, who looked back to reinvigorate the principle of harmony which had previously existed in the "golden age," but had been lost due to political chaos. The good ruler guided his people with humility, not seeking to interfere with the rhythms of social life conducted within the larger patterns of the natural world and the entire cosmos.

Featured in the Chinese history are many periods of civil war, interregnums, and chaos. After each collapse, however, the Chinese state has reconstituted itself as if by some immutable law of nature. At each stage, a new uniting figure has emerged (following the precedence of the Yellow Emperor) to subdue his rivals, reunify China, and re-establish continuity.

Another interesting feature is that it supported the conception of the Emperor as a figure of universal consequence, presiding over *tianxia*—all under Heaven—and hence combining the spiritual as well as secular claims of an orderly society. It could be said that the Chinese Emperor was both a political ruler (the Emperor of Humanity) and a meta-physical concept (The Son of Heaven), who intermediated between Heaven, Earth, and humanity. The Emperor was perceived as the linchpin of the Great Harmony of the Universe. If the Emperor personally strayed from the path of virtue, *tianxia* would fall into chaos. The current dynasty would be perceived as having lost Heaven's mandate, and a new dynasty would appear (indeed, must appear) to restore the loss. So important has this Great Harmony concept been for the Chinese that even today it is at the core of Chinese strategies and actions, whether at the geo-political, macro-economic, or micro-economic levels.[3]

Yi Jing

One relevant tool for achieving this overall great harmony, which in fact can be considered as the departure point for both the Daoist and Confucian perspectives, is the *Yi Jing*. The *Yi Jing* (rendered as "I Ching" in the Wade-Giles system)[4] is frequently called the "Book of Changes." It, views the world in a dynamic way—that in the eyes of time, the world is just an endless cycle. It is a divination book, what in present times may be called a decision-making tool (which in effect makes it an Ancient Chinese decision-making tool). It can be said that, *Yi Jing* gives people a practical framework for evaluating their personal and professional environments, make decisions that affect their lives, and work toward improving their relationships, careers and businesses, thus helping them achieve greater overall harmony.

This was the most popular book among Zhou dynasty scholars, including Lao Tse and Confucius. In fact, Daoism is heavily rooted in the *Yi Jing;* its teachings are also enriched with the ideas of *Yin Yang* co-existence and the exchange cycle. Daoism was the first philosophy in China to record in written form the opinion that there is no absolute good or bad. Many Dao philosophers moved to the mountains, and Daoism further split into scholarly secular philosophy and religious practice. On the other hand, Confucius, inspired by the idea of the great harmony, dreamed of building a perfect government through the process of building perfect human beings. Confucianism became the mainstream philosophy at the beginning of the Han dynasty in 206 B.C.

The Concept of Yin Yang

The concept of *Yin Yang*, developed initially by Daoism and often referred to in the West as "*Yin* and *Yang*," is used to describe how polar opposites or seemingly contrary forces are interconnected and interdependent in the natural world, and how they give rise to each other in turn. *Yin* and *Yang* are "two polar energies that, by their fluctuation and interaction, are the cause of the universe." They are deep-rooted in Chinese culture and without a minimum understanding of their meaning, it is almost impossible to grasp Chinese entrepreneurship or its business culture.

Yin and *Yang* appear in the commentaries on *Yi Jing* and *Spring and Autumn Annals*, both written over 2000 years ago. *Yi Jing* states that the Dao itself seems to be composed of these principles—it is made of *Yin* and *Yang*. In the *Annals* (mentioned later) it is written that *Yin* and *Yang* separate and merge again. "When they are separated they merge, when they are merged they separate..."

Thus, opposites exist only in relation to each other. The concept lies at the origins of many branches of classical Chinese science and philosophy and provides the primary guidelines for Traditional Chinese Medicine. It is also a central principle in different forms of Chinese martial arts[5] and exercise—such as *baguazhang, taijiquan* (Tai Chi)[6], and *qigong* (Chi Kung)—and of the *Yi Jing*. Many natural dualities (such as, dark and light, day and night, summer and winter, female and male, low and high, cold and hot, right and left, strong and weak, and so on) are thought of as manifestations of *Yin* and *Yang*. Thus, *Yin Yang* is defined as complementary opposites that interact within a greater whole as part of a dynamic system. Everything is regulated by the ever-lasting interaction of *Yin* and *Yang*. Everything has both *Yin* and *Yang* aspects, but either aspect may manifest itself more strongly in particular objects. Each can also ebb or flow over time. The concept of *Yin* and *Yang* is often symbolized by various forms of the *Taijitu* that literally means "diagram of the supreme ultimate." This is probably the best-known aspect of Daoism in western cultures.

The *Taijitu* is one of the oldest and best-known life symbols in the world, but few understand its full meaning. It represents, perhaps, the most fundamental and profound theories of ancient Daoist philosophy.

At its heart are two poles of existence, which are opposite but complementary. The light white *Yang*, moving up, blends into the dark black *Yin*, moving down. *Yin* and *Yang* are dependent opposing forces that flow in a natural cycle, always seeking balance. Though they are opposing, they are not in opposition to one another, as they are merely two aspects of a single reality. Each contains the seed of the other, which is why we see a black spot of *Yin* in the white *Yang* and vice-versa. They do not merely replace each other but actually become each other throughout the constant flow of the universe.

What is the meaning of the Taijitu? In terms of the Daoist cosmology, the circle represents the Dao (Tao), the undifferentiated Unity out of which all existence arises. The black and white halves within the circle represent *Yin-qi* and *Yang-qi*—the primordial feminine and masculine energies, whose interplay gives birth to the manifested world: the Five Elements (metal, water, wood, fire, and Earth) and the Ten-Thousand Things (all of phenomenal reality).

The Taijitu

The curves and circles of the *Taijitu* imply a kaleidoscope-like movement. This implied movement represents the ways in which *Yin* and *Yang* are: mutually arising, interdependent, and continuously transforming, one into the other. One could not exist without the other, since each contains the essence of the other: night becomes day and day becomes night; birth becomes death and death becomes birth; and friends become enemies and enemies become friends. Such is the nature of everything in the relative world.

The smaller circles nested within each half of the symbol serve as a constant reminder of the interdependent nature of the opposites (black/white).

It reminds the Daoist practitioner that all relative existence is in constant flux and change and that a relaxed attitude can be maintained around the creation of opposite pairs. This is because each side always contains the other, as the mother "contains" the infant that she will, in time, give birth to.

"Existence" and "non-existence" is a duality that can be understood in the way suggested by the *Taijitu*—mutually arising and interdependent "opposites" that are in constant motion, transforming from one into the other. The things of the world are appearing and dissolving continuously, as the elements of which they are composed go through their own birth-and-death cycles. The appearance of "things" is considered to be *Yin* while their resolution back into their more subtle ("no-thing" or "not-thing") component, *Yang*. To understand the transition from "thing" to "no-thing" is to access a profound level of wisdom.

In the Daoist philosophy, shade and light, *Yin* and *Yang* appear in Chapter 42 of the *Daodejing* (*Tao te Ching*). It becomes sensible from an initial quiescence or emptiness (*wuji*), sometimes symbolized by an empty circle, and continues moving until quiescence is reached again. For instance, dropping a stone in a calm pool of water will simultaneously raise waves and lower troughs between them; this alternation of high and low points in the water will radiate outward until the movement dissipates and the water in the pool is calm once more. *Yin* and *Yang* are thus always equal and opposite qualities. Further, whenever one quality reaches its peak, it will naturally begin to transform into the opposite quality: for example, a seed that germinates, develops and reaches its full height in summer (fully *Yang*) will produce seeds and die in winter (fully *Yin*) in an endless cycle.

It is impossible to talk about *Yin* or *Yang* without some reference to the opposite, since both are bound together as parts of a mutual whole, just as one cannot have the back of a hand without the front. A way to illustrate this idea is to postulate the notion of a community with only men or only women; this community would disappear in a single generation. Yet men and women together create new generations that allow the community they mutually create (and come from) to survive: their interaction gives birth to things. *Yin* and *Yang* transform each other: like an undertow in the ocean, every advance is complemented by a retreat, and every rise transforms into a fall. Thus, a seed will sprout from the Earth and grow upward toward the sky (an intrinsically *Yang* movement); then, when it reaches its full potential height, it will fall (a *Yin* movement).

The relationship between *Yin* and *Yang* is often described in terms of sunlight playing over a mountain and in the valley. *Yin* (literally means the "shady place" or "north slope") is the dark area occluded by the mountain's bulk, while *Yang* (literally means the "sunny place" or "south slope") is the brightly lit portion. As the sun moves across the sky, *Yin* and *Yang* gradually trade places with each other, revealing what was obscured and obscuring what was revealed.

Yin is characterized as slow, soft, yielding, diffuse, cold, wet, and passive and is associated with water, Earth, moon, femininity, and nighttime. *Yang*, by contrast, is characterized as fast, hard, solid, focused, hot, dry, and aggressive and is associated with fire, sky, sun, masculinity, and daytime.

The relativity of *Yin* and *Yang* and the dynamic tension of their interaction are the basis of thought and expression in Daoism. Maintaining a balance between *Yin* and *Yang* will result in perfect health of the body, mind, and soul. In Chinese classic medicine, *Yin* and *Yang* refer to energies and functioning modes of the human organs and of the human body. It is said that the healthy state is brought by the right balance between *Yin* and *Yang*. Thus, man must choose the right food and nurture a psychic equilibrium in order to acquire health and longevity.

Daoist philosophy generally discounts good/bad distinctions and other dichotomous moral judgments in preference to the idea of balance. Confucianism (most notably the philosophy of Dong Zhongshu, c. the second century B.C.E.) did attach a moral dimension to the idea of *Yin* and *Yang*, but it has been said that the modern sense of the term largely stems from Buddhist adaptations of Daoist philosophy.

Confucianism

Confucianism is an ethical and philosophical system based upon the teachings of the Chinese thinker and social philosopher, Confucius.

Confucius (Kong Zi) lived from 551 to 479 B.C. in Qufu, the state of Lu (in modern Shandong province).[7] He came from a family of officials and his concern was with the restoration of the "Way" (*Dao*) of the just and harmonious societies of the ancient past. His teachings were therefore related mainly to society and its governance. He advocated strict conformity, and thought that fostering correct behavior, within the context of the family, would produce an ordered society. He was not particularly interested in religion, except insofar as it related to social life. Spiritual fulfillment was a task not of liberation but of patient recovery of forgotten principles of self-restraint; its underlying goal was rectification. His philosophy sought the redemption of the state through righteous individual behavior. His thinking affirmed a code of social conduct, not a roadmap to the afterlife.

Confucius stressed *Ren*-benevolence (compassionate love) and *Li*-rites (the performance of the correct rituals), referring to respect for the system of social hierarchy (what he expressed as "know the place"), as well as filial piety. His philosophy emphasized personal and governmental morality, correctness of social relationships, and justice and sincerity. Confucius sought to inculcate a sense of responsibility and obligation in the educated class. He believed that humans can achieve self-realization through devotion to their family, community, and country, while encouraging them to adapt and accept social norms. Junzi (君子) or nobleman was a term he used to describe his ideal human being, someone who has gained inner peace through being virtuous. The Junzi will always think of the consequences of his actions. By contrast, the Xiaoren (小人)—literally means small person or petty person—seeks only immediate gains, is egotistic, and does not consider the consequences of his action to the overall scheme of things. Confucius said: "*Respect yourself and others will respect you. What the superior man seeks is in him; what the small man seeks is in others. When anger rises, think of the consequences. Wherever you go, go with all your heart.*"

Confucius spent much of his life travelling around China to promote his ideas among the rulers. Eventually, he became involved in teaching disciples, attached great importance to education, and was a pioneering advocate for private schools. He is particularly famous for teaching students according to their intellectual inclinations. Confucius' thoughts have been developed into a vast and complete philosophical system known in the west as Confucianism. His teachings were later recorded by his students in "*The Analects*."

In *The Analects*, Confucius presents himself as a transmitter who invented nothing. He said: "*I am not one who was born in the possession of knowledge; I am one who is fond of antiquity, and earnest in seeking it there.*" His greatest emphasis is on studying. In this respect, he is seen by Chinese people as the Greatest Master. Far from trying to build a systematic theory of life and society, he wanted his disciples to think deeply for themselves and relentlessly study the outside world. For almost two thousand years, *The Analects* has also been the fundamental course of study for any Chinese scholar, for a man was not considered morally upright or enlightened if he did not study Confucius' works.

In 59 A.D., during the Han Dynasty (206–220 A.D.), it was decreed that sacrifices should be offered to Confucius. This initiated a process, which would make Confucian philosophy the foundation of the Chinese political order. Confucius himself had only accepted the legitimacy of offering sacrifices to one's own ancestors, but from this time an official Confucian cult emerged, with its own temples. It gradually became linked with the state cult of the Emperor; *The Analects* simultaneously played the role of a government constitution and a religious "holy book."

Mencius also contributed greatly to Confucianism. He lived in the Warring States Period (389–305 B.C.) and advocated a policy of benign government as well as the idea that human beings are good by nature. Confucianism became the orthodox ideology in feudal China. Over the long course of history, it drew on both Daoism and Buddhism.

From the fifth century A.D., Confucian orthodoxy retreated before the growing popularity of Buddhism and Daoism. But a "renaissance" of Confucian through took place during the Song dynasty (960–1276 A.D.), when Confucianism developed its own meta-physics. This new trend is known as Neo-Confucianism, and its main advocate was Zhu Xi (1130–1200). By then, Confucianism had evolved into a rigid philosophy that called for preserving heavenly laws and repressing human desires. It subsequently became the main orthodoxy of the scholar-officials until the demise of the imperial system in 1912.

In contemporary China, the Confucian cult has disappeared, but the Confucian approach to government and society still retains a powerful hold on educated people, manifesting itself in politics, businesses, and everyday life.

Daoism (Taoism)

The origins of Daoism are obscure, but it was first seen as a rival to Confucianism. The teachings of early Daoism are ascribed to Lao Tse (571–490 B.C.), although some people believe he is just a mythical character. It is said that, after many years of study, Lao Tse became enlightened and travelled far and wide across China. His insights and thoughts on self-transformation were practical, and he documented them in the *DaoDeJing* (Tao Te Ching)—loosely translated as something like "The Classic of the Way and the Power," or "The Canon of the Way of Virtue and Power," in any case the most influential Daoist text.

Dao (Tao) can be defined as "path," "road" or "way." The way of the Dao is the way of Nature and of ultimate reality. Dao is often described as a force that flows through all life. A happy and virtuous life is one that is in harmony with the Dao, with Nature. The philosophy of Daoism understands Dao as the One Thing that exists and connects the Many Things. Dao, Nature, and Reality are One. Matter and spirit formed a continuum within a cosmos that is self-generating and impersonal. Where Confucianism stressed ethical action, Daoism spoke of the virtue of WuWei (non-action or non-doing), of just doing as part of the natural flow of things. Where Confucianism sought to inculcate a sense of responsibility and obligation in the educated class, Daoism preached that humans must learn to appreciate nature and the cycle of seasons, and learn to be in harmony with it, rather than go against it. Lao Tse wrote:

"There is a thing, formless yet complete. Before heaven and Earth it existed. Without sound, without substance, it stands alone and unchanging. It is all-pervading and unfailing. We do not know its name, but we call it Tao. Being one with nature, the sage is in accord with the Tao."

Zhuang Zhou, the main advocate of Daoism during the Warring States period, called for skepticism, given the limitations of a human life-time and limitless bounds of reality that can be known in a life-time. Daoism has greatly influenced Chinese thinkers, writers, and artists.

In 440 B.C., Daoism was adopted as a state religion of China, with Lao Tse honored as a deity. Many emperors, generals, and relevant Chinese statesmen were also honored as deities and, in many cases, hold the title of "immortal", since Daoists were concerned with achieving "immortality"—which they saw as a transmutation of earthly existence. This also led to the development of alchemy and to methods of meditation aimed at reaching material immortality.

As time passed, Daoism found itself in direct competition with Buddhism's teachings. It borrowed Buddhist practices and also drew on folk religious traditions to create its own religious form and ethos. It secured an essential place in popular religious life, but in this form it ceased to bear much resemblance to the philosophical precepts of its early teachers. The earlier, more philosophical Daoism continued to inspire Chinese painters and poets through the ages, while its teachings appealed to many scholar officials who adhered to a strictly Confucian ethic in public life. State support of Daoism ended in 1911 with the end of the Qing dynasty, when much Daoist heritage was destroyed.

The so-called "Eight Pillars of Daoism" (these are mentioned later) that cover every aspect of a person's daily existence were designed to satisfy completely the basic physical needs in a manner that allows the realization of one's full potential as a human being. Among these "Pillars," the most relevant from a business perspective are the first—the "Dao of Philosophy" and the last—the "Dao of Success." The "Dao of Philosophy" includes, among other things, guidelines for attaining success in the following spheres: political, family, love, military, economic, and business. The "Dao of Success" helps to adjust a person's everyday strategies and actions in accordance with the "universal law," to be more capable of successfully dealing with future adversities and uncertainties.

Daoism is described as being at the root of Traditional Chinese Medicine (TCM)[8] and many Chinese health practices—for instance, reflexology[9] around 5,000 years ago, and also at the root of *Feng Shui*,[10] whose practice still has a strong influence in the daily life of the Chinese.

☰	Represents the Dao of Philosophy, which comprise political, family, military, economic, business, amour, and many other sciences or philosophies.
䷀	Represents the Dao of Revitalization (exercises for the internal organs).
䷀	Represents the Dao of Balanced Diet (regular or daily food diet).
䷀	Represents the Dao of Forgotten Food Diet (Daoist herbology).
䷀	Represents the Dao of Healing Art (acupuncture, acupressure, and other spiritual healing methods).
䷀	Represents the Dao of Sexology (sexual wisdom and techniques).
䷀	Represents the Dao of Mastery (Personology, Fingerprint system, Numerology, Astrology, Directionology and Symbology).
䷀	Represents the Dao of Success (secrets of true success revealed).

The Eight Pillars of Daoism.

Buddhism

Buddhism is the only foreign religion that has been widely accepted in China. It is a moral philosophy and religion based upon the teachings of Siddhartha Gautama (566–486 B.C.). Siddhartha Gautama became known as the Buddha—also Buddha Sakyamuni. "Buddha" (from the ancient Indian languages of Pali and Sanskrit) means "the awakened one." It is derived from the verbal root "budh," meaning "to awaken" or "to be enlightened," and "to comprehend." At the age of 35, meditating under a Bodhi tree, Siddhartha reached enlightenment, awakening to the true nature of reality, which is Nirvana (the Absolute Truth).

The Buddha offered meta-physical knowledge into the nature of reality as well as a moral way of life. The Middle Way is an important idea in Buddhist thought and practice, which means to seek moderation and avoid the extremes of self-indulgence and self-mortification. The Buddha taught that the nature of reality was impermanent and interdependent and that an individual does not exist apart. We suffer in life because of our desire for transient things. Liberation from suffering may come by training the mind and acting according to the laws of karma (i.e., cause and effect), which means that with the right actions, good things will come. At the core of his teachings are the Four Noble Truths:

- Dukkha: Suffering is everywhere.
- Samudaya: There is a cause of suffering, which is attachment or misplaced desire (tanha) rooted in ignorance.
- Nirodha: There is an end of suffering, which is Nirvana. The possibility of liberation exists for everyone.
- Maggo: There is a path that leads to the end of suffering, known as the Noble Eight-fold Path (right view, right intention, right speech, right conduct, right livelihood, right effort, right mindfulness, and right concentration).

Inherent "Buddha-nature" is the source of wisdom, but it is obscured in most people because of their attachment to thoughts, desires, and other mental phenomena. By detaching oneself from such phenomena—which is not the same as suppressing them, the Buddha-nature reveals itself.

Buddha stated: *"All (mental) states have mind as their forerunner, mind is their chief, and they are mind-made. If one speaks or acts with a defiled mind, then suffering follows. Liberation of the will through love will develop, we will often practice it, will make it vehicle and base, take our stand upon it, store it up, thoroughly set it going. Hatred is never appeased by hatred in this world; it is appeased by love. This is an eternal Law. By endeavor, diligence, discipline, and self-mastery, let the wise person make (of himself) an island that no flood can overwhelm."*

Buddhism was introduced to China, through the Silk Road, in the third century B.C.E. during the reign of the first emperor of China— Qin Shihuang. In the middle of the second century, the Kushan empire under King Kaniska expanded into Central Asia, and at its peak taking control of Kashgar, Khotan, and Yarkand, in the Tarim Basin, modern Xinjiang. As a consequence, cultural exchanges greatly increased, and Central Asian Buddhist missionaries became active shortly after in the Chinese capital cities of Loyang and Nanjing, where they particularly distinguished themselves by their translation work. Central Asian Buddhist monks from the Tarim Basin and East Asian Buddhist monks appear to have maintained strong links until around the tenth century, as shown by frescoes in the Tarim Basin. The vigorous Chinese culture progressively absorbed Buddhist teachings until strong Chinese characteristics developed. From the fourth century onward, with Faxian's pilgrimage to India (395–414), and later Xuanzang's (629–644), Chinese pilgrims began travelling on their own to northern India in order to get better access to the original scriptures. The Silk Road transmission of Buddhism began to decline around the seventh century with the rise of Islam in Central Asia. The Buddhism that established in China followed the Mahayana (literally, from Sanskrit, the "Great Vehicle") tradition—the larger of the two major traditions of Buddhism existing today, the other being that of the Theravada[11] school. Mahayana, also called the "Bodhisattva[12] Vehicle," refers to the path of seeking complete enlightenment for the benefit of all sentient beings.

When Buddhism came to China, there were three divisions of training: training in virtue and discipline in the precepts (Skt. *sila*), mental training through meditation (Skt. *dhyana*) to attain deep states of meditation (Skt. *samadhi*), and training in the recorded teachings of Buddha (Skt. *Dharma*). As a result, three types of teachers with expertise in each training practice developed: Vinaya masters specialized in all the rules of discipline for monks and nuns, Dhyana masters specialized in the practice of meditation, and Dharma masters specialized in mastery of the Buddhist texts. Monasteries and practice centers were created that tended to focus either on the Vinaya (training of monks) or on the teachings, which typically focused on one scripture or a small group of texts. Dhyana masters tended to practice in solitary hermitages, or were associated with Vinaya training monasteries or Dharma teaching centres. The later naming of the *Chan* School has its origins in this view of the three fold division of training. After several centuries of assimilation, Buddhism evolved into many sects in the Sui and Tang dynasties and became localized.

By the Tang dynasty, Buddhism was the most dynamic and influential of all religions in China. However, it's very success led to a severe curtailment of its activities during the late Tang, as officials began to see its growing influence as a threat, both to their own power and to the order and prosperity of society. After this, it remained an important element in

Chinese life, ideology, and art, but took its place alongside Daoism and a revitalized Confucianism and blended with the two.

During the long process of adaptation, various Chinese schools emerged, such as the Pure Land and the *Chan* schools, which were more congenial to traditional Chinese thought. The Pure Land (with its stress on faith in the Amitabha Buddha[13] as the way to salvation) and *Chan* (with its meditation techniques) became the dominant forms of Chinese Buddhism. These teachings, with their focus on sudden enlightenment and salvation through grace rather than through ascetic practices, appealed to many ordinary Chinese, since they fitted well with their practical approach to life. Both these Buddhist schools were influenced by Daoism. Because of its on-going influence in the Chinese approach to life—in particular the *Chan*'s idea of taking life as it is and the *Linji*'s teaching approach and principles—both schools are described in some detail below.

Buddhism today is still an important force in some parts of the country, particularly in the villages, and the extent of its influence is growing in the cities. Temples and monasteries are re-opening in many places, and new monks and nuns are being ordained.

The Pure Land School

Pure Land Buddhism is based on the Pure Land sutras, which describe Amitabha and his Pure Land of Bliss, called Sukhavati.

The Pure Land teachings played a role in early Mahayana Buddhism in India, but first became prominent in China with the founding of a monastery upon the top of Mount Lu by Huiyuan in 402 C.E. As a young man, Huiyuan practiced Daoism, but he felt its theories of immortality were vague and unreliable, and unrepresentative of the ultimate truth. Instead, he turned to Buddhism and became a monk studying under Dao An. Later he founded a monastery at the top of Mount Lu and invited well-known literati to study and practice Buddhism there, where they formed the White Lotus Society.

The Pure Land teachings and meditation methods quickly spread throughout China and were systematized by a series of elite monastic thinkers. The main teaching of the Chinese Pure Land tradition is based

on focusing the mind with the Mindfulness of the Buddha through reci-
tation of the name of Amitabha Buddha, so as to attain re-birth in his
pure land of Sukhavati.[14]

The Pure Land Path has been popular among both commoners and
elite monastics as it provided a straightforward way of attaining awakening. Although much emphasis is placed on the centrality of Amitabha
Buddha in Pure Land Buddhism, he is not considered a supreme god
or a deity. The concept of a supreme being as a world creator deciding
the fate of beings is contrary to Buddhist teaching in all traditions. In
Mahayana Buddhism, there are many Buddhas, and each Buddha has a
Pure Land. Though there are various traditions devoted to various Pure
Lands, Amitabha is by far the most popular.

The Chan (Zen) School

The establishment of *Chan* (禪) is credited to the Persian or South Indian
prince-turned-monk Bodhidharma, who came to China around 470 C.E.
to teach a "special transmission" outside scriptures, not founded on words
or letters. The emergence of *Chan* as a distinct school of Buddhism was
first documented in China in the seventh century C.E., during the Tang
dynasty. The word *Chan* is derived from the Sanskrit word *dhyana*, which
means "meditation" or "meditative state." The *Chan* tradition emphasizes
meditation and "direct pointing into the mind," or the direct experience,
over study of the sutras and philosophical discussion. The historical records
required for a complete, accurate account of early *Chan* history no longer
exist. Theories about the influence of other schools in the evolution of
Chan are widely variable and rely heavily on speculation rather than written records or histories. Many scholars have argued that *Chan* developed
from the interaction between Mahayana Buddhism and Daoism. Some
scholars instead argue that *Chan* has roots in yogic practices, specifically
kammaṭṭhana, the consideration of objects, and *kasina*, total fixation of
the mind. A number of other conflicting theories exist.

Bodhidharma settled in the kingdom of Wei. Shortly before his
death, Bodhidharma appointed a disciple named Huike[15] to succeed him,
making Huike the first Chinese-born patriarch and the second patriarch of
Chan in China. Bodhidharma is said to have passed three items to Huike

as a sign of transmission of the Dharma: a robe, a bowl, and a copy of the *Lankavatara Sutra*. This transmission then passed to the third patriarch Sengcan, the fourth patriarch Daoxin, and the fifth patriarch Hongren. The sixth and last patriarch Huineng (638–713) was one of the giants of *Chan* history, and all surviving schools regard him as their ancestor.

In the centuries following the introduction of Buddhism to China, *Chan* grew to become the largest sect in Chinese Buddhism, and produced the largest body of literature in Chinese history of any sect or tradition. The teachers claiming Huineng's legacy began to branch off into numerous schools, each with their own special emphasis, but all of which kept the same basic focus on meditation practice, personal instruction, and personal experience. The proliferation of the *Chan* School during this time of the Tang Dynasty is described in a famous saying, *"Look at the territory of the house of Tang, the whole of it is the realm of the Chan School."*

During the late Tang and the Song periods, the tradition continued, as a wide number of eminent teachers, such as Mazu, Shitou, Baizhang, Huangbo, Linji, and *Yunmen,* developed specialized teaching methods, which would variously become characteristic of the Five Houses of *Chan*: *Caodong, Linji, Guiyang, Fayan*, and *Yunmen.* The Linji School was established by Linji Yixuan and ultimately became the most successful and widespread of the Five Houses of *Chan.*[16] For centuries his followers were the leading *Chan* Buddhist masters of China.

Linji's method of teaching was straightforward, blunt, and rough. He did not hesitate to use the stick on his disciples, if he thought they needed to be knocked out of their attachment, or conventional reasoning and logic. In some ways, this style actually reflected the national spirit of China, which was warrior-like and fierce; China was constantly at war with the invaders from the West (for instance, Tartars and Turks). Linji's style of Buddhism, (later known as Zen in Japan), was a way of opening up the mind beyond all conscious thought.

Philosophical or meta-physical questions were answered by Linji with a swift blow. Students and disciples were required to step out of their paradigms and habitual patterns of thinking. When Lin Chi asked a question, the response could not be based on logic, traditional teachings, or reason. The disciples could not lean on any model or pattern of thinking. Linji pulled the rug out from under everyone. Ordinary models of thinking were unacceptable and there was nothing to hold on to. When students wanted to know the truth sincerely, whole-heartedly, an abandonment of all former thinking was necessary, so that the mind would open up to the direct experience of its own nature.

Linji rejected the dogmas of the Buddhist religion and the philosophical and scholarly approach of Buddhism teachings. In his approach, he stressed spontaneity, absolute freedom, and emptiness:

"Friends, I tell you this: there is no Buddha, no spiritual path to follow, no training, and no realization. What are you so feverishly running after? Putting a head on top of your own head, you blind idiots? Your head is right where it should be. The trouble lies in your not believing in yourselves enough. Because you don't believe in yourselves you are knocked here and there by all the conditions in which you find yourselves. Being enslaved and turned around by objective situations, you have no freedom what-so-ever, you are not masters of yourselves. Stop turning to the outside and don't be attached to my words either. Just cease clinging to the past, and hankering after the future. This will be better than ten years' pilgrimage."

Linji's teachings encourage people to have faith that their natural spontaneous functioning is the true Buddha-Mind. In this pure state of being, one does not obstruct, block, withhold, or repress anything. In this state of being, freedom from attachment does not mean to be without feelings, but rather it means: entering into all activities with the whole heart, not holding anything back, being at one with any situation. This is the enlightened way to live an ordinary life. Linji said:

"When it's time to get dressed, put on your clothes.
When you must walk, then walk.
When you must sit, then sit.
Just be your ordinary self in ordinary life,
No concerned in seeking for Buddhahood.
When you're tired, lie down.
The fool will laugh at you but the wise man will understand."

Linji stressed that a true human being should not search for what he can get out of life, but for what life is in itself. A true human being sees things as they are, is free from wrong ideas about reality, and acts in harmony with the universe at all times.

Over the course of the Song dynasty, *the Guiyang, Fayan, and Yunmen* schools were gradually absorbed into the *Linji*. During the same period, the various *Chan* teaching methods crystallized into the gongan (koan)[17] practice, which is unique to this school of Buddhism, although it was also employed on a more limited basis by the *Caodong* School.[18]

Chan thrived in the post-Song period, with a vast body of texts produced up into the modern period. While traditionally distinct, *Chan* was taught alongside Pure Land Buddhism in many Chinese Buddhist monasteries. In time much of the distinction between them was lost, and many masters taught both *Chan* and Pure Land, which is also the situation today.

Chan Buddhism enjoyed something of a revival in the Ming Dynasty with teachers such as: Hanshan Deqing, who wrote and taught extensively on both *Chan* and Pure Land Buddhism; Miyun Yuanwu, who came to be seen posthumously as the first patriarch of the Japanese Obaku Zen[19] school; Yunqi Zhuhong; and Ouyi Zhixu. After further centuries of decline, *Chan* was revived again in the early twentieth century by Hsu Yun,[20] a well-known figure of twentieth century Chinese Buddhism.

Spiritual awakening was always the goal of *Chan's* training, but what distinguished the tradition as it developed through the centuries in China was a way of life radically different from that of Indian Buddhists. In Indian Buddhism, the tradition of the mendicant (begging or reliance on charity for survival) prevailed, but in China it turned to the development of a temple and training-center system, in which the abbot and monks all performed everyday tasks. These included food gardening or farming, carpentry, architecture, housekeeping, administration (or community direction), and the practice of folk medicine. Consequently, the enlightenment sought in *Chan* had to stand up well to the demands and potential frustrations of everyday life. The Chinese *Chan* master Baizhang (720–814 C.E.) left behind a famous saying which was the guiding principle of his life: "a day without work is a day without food."

How much of the *Chan* culture penetrated Chinese people's minds over the centuries is difficult to say, but the fact remains that their practical approach to everyday life, their acceptance of life as a constant, ever-changing flow, their understanding of the concepts of interdependence and their lack of a concept of individuals living independent from others, their readiness to work, their willingness to act instead of reasoning or thinking without reacting are all features that can be found today in their culture of entrepreneurship and business management.

From the Tang Dynasty to Today

During the Tang dynasty (600–900 C.E.), the so called "Three Doctrines" or the "Three Teachings"—Confucianism, Daoism, and Buddhism— were an important part of Chinese people's daily life. In those times, a man would honor his ancestors by following the rigid rules of social behavior as dictated by Confucianism, attend a Buddhist pageant, and practice Daoist breathing exercises, all in the same day.

People saw no contradiction in attending both Buddhist and Daoist worship, or in incorporating a diversity of gods into the local pantheon. The Confucian state, dominated by Confucian thinking, was generally tolerant of the various religions that contended for the hearts and minds of the people. Other religions were allowed to flourish provided they did not challenge the fundamental Confucian order. Both Buddhism and Daoism inspired heterodox religious systems; so, from time to time, these broke out in social rebellions, leading to state intervention and attempts at suppression.

The Communist revolution sought to break these ancient connections. In 1949, *Feng Shui* practice was officially forbidden in the People's Republic of China, along with other "feudalistic superstitions." However, the success of these efforts was limited. Despite all attempts at re-education by the Communist Party, the family cult associated with Confucianism and popular religion still flourished throughout the countryside, as did the so-called "superstitious practices" and structural principles of Chinese Traditional Culture. Mao Zedong himself was a student of Sun Tzu's "The Art of War"[21] strategies and applied them, during the Chinese civil war, for instance. He also used historical (millennium-old) strategic principles in delicate and potentially dangerous situations of conflict, such as the 1962 war with India over an area of border between the countries under dispute. These were all manifestations of how deeply rooted the "Three Teachings" were in Chinese culture and among the Chinese people.

Today *Feng Shui* is no longer forbidden in China. Yi Jing research is now openly applied to *Feng Shui* and can even been seen in governmental publications. Religious practices are being reintroduced and there is a growing interest in communicating and applying Traditional Chinese Culture—based on The Three Teachings—in all spheres of life, including business. The entrepreneurship models that follow in this book have all these cultural principles as their background.

CHAPTER 2

Understanding the Chinese Paradigm

In the midst of the economic, financial crisis and the turmoil about the future evolution of the world, the Chinese, not just as a nation but as individuals as well, remain positive and active and hold hope for the future. In fact, 91% of the Chinese hold this view.[1] How can this be possible? Are the Chinese not sensitive about the decline of exports, the closing of factories, and the loss in their country in recent years? Is it the situation that the country is so big that this negative side of the economy is not that relevant in their overall picture? Is it the case that there are still so many opportunities in the Chinese economy (and abroad) that they need not worry about the restructuring of their domestic economy, a big challenge ahead for them? Are the Chinese largely insensitive to the other major economic challenges the country faces (for example, too much dependence on infrastructure investment, the latent bubble in its real estate market)? Are they ignoring the many social challenges the country is facing (for example, the level of corruption, the weaknesses in its social welfare system)?

Or maybe they are, but in a different way than we would. Perhaps they are approaching these issues with a completely different attitude and/or framework than the way we might typically follow in the West. This attitude about life and about business is what has most affected me since I first came to live in China in early 2004. Over the years, I have come to the conclusion that this attitude comes from historical wisdom, from a historically wise understanding of how the world (and the universe) functions and how we, as human beings, are placed in it. This wisdom is based on "The Three Teachings"—Confucianism, Daoism, and Buddhism—that share so much in common that one could say that the three have merged, forging the Chinese character and culture we see today. Together they constitute what has been named the Traditional Chinese Culture (TCC).

Certainly China is huge—it is like a continent in terms of its expanse, its population, and its diversity. Roughly 50% of its population is still rural,[2] and it is clear when travelling within China that this wisdom and understanding of how the world works cannot be extended to its entire population. For instance, we may see physical violence in the street (generally toward someone who has not been able to repay a debt), despite the fact that TCC advocates the avoidance of violence and the use of persuasion instead in confronting an enemy. But these contradictory expressions are also manifestations of how uneducated Chinese have traditionally dealt with life in a country where they have never held individual rights. Instead, they have had to solve their problems directly, that is, in the most practical manner they could. Pragmatism is certainly a prime feature of the Chinese population.

Today, China is rapidly strengthening its geopolitical and economic power internationally, and it is doing it using "subtle power," a variation of American scholar Joseph Nye's "soft power" concept. To a certain extent, "subtle power" is an application of some of China's highest philosophical principles in the field of strategy. Less spectacular than hard power, but more intangible than soft power, subtle power aims to shape the context, thus maximizing the effectiveness of the two traditional dimensions of power. Where hard power acts directly—including by force—to impose itself, and soft power attracts and co-opts, subtle power reconfigures the environment in which hard power and soft power operate, thus creating more optimal effects. The efficacy of subtle power lies in the permanent interplay of five elements:

- Nonconfrontation: This not only helps to satisfy one's needs, but also elevates one's status and avoids the need to make enemies.
- Noninterference: Over history, the Chinese have never been agitated by a desire to convert the world toward its norms and beliefs.
- A permanent readiness for change: This applies even while following the approaches that are opposite to those that the Western world follows.

- Restraint: The Chinese are well aware that the capacity to limit oneself and to avoid any kind of excess is, in the long term, the best way to preserve one's relative strength. In fact, Sunzi (Sun Tzu) stressed that the best generals prevail without a fight and that only those that are less skilled are forced to learn how to navigate the "fog of war."
- Ambiguity: "Subtle power" is also the cultivation of ambiguity and vagueness, which are often misinterpreted as mystery or obscurity.

Subtle power is not a set of predetermined rules or procedures to follow mechanically but rather the art of creating a favorable context. It should not be confused with a sense of self-proclaimed indispensability, superiority or grandeur; instead, it should be thought of, in a constantly changing configuration, as the capacity to maintain centrality, or positioning oneself in the center. China's name—*Zhongguo*, "the Central (or Middle) Country"—certainly refers to a given and fixed geographic location, but it has also been interpreted as a position gained by intelligent strategic moves in the dynamic complexity of the power game. Chinese entrepreneurs and business leaders have an extraordinary ability to contextualize and to take a holistic approach to business affairs. This is often interpreted as a refusal to take a clear position on any singular question, but it should be understood as a desire to take a prudent approach, to consider carefully how actions on one particular issue might affect the entire equilibrium of the system. This reflects the moderation and peace embodied in the character *he* (和) or harmony. Chinese business leaders say: "Rules can cheat people, people can mislead people, but concepts can lead people."

In the pages that follow, and based on my relationships and in-depth interviews with Chinese entrepreneurs and business leaders (including those I have mentioned in this book), I have tried to relate the main underlying principles of TCC and other traditional concepts that are deeply rooted in Chinese people's minds. This includes the main features of Chinese entrepreneurs' and business managers' behavior and attitude (including negotiations), the most common (and perhaps the only) aspect that most foreigners are exposed to. Because of its particular relevance in the field of strategy, references to Sunzi's (Sun Tzu's) "The Art of War" are often made.

It is important to make it clear that what follows may be applied to two types of relationships: how Chinese relate to other Chinese, and how Chinese relate to foreigners. A common misunderstanding among foreigners is to believe that Chinese only treat foreigners poorly while, in reality, and judging from my own perspective as being a foreigner, we could say that the Chinese actually treat one another in an even worse manner. It has been said that, from the first time Chinese military strategies were formally laid out, they were not fundamentally of a military nature, but instead aimed at the psychological dominance of the opponent. In this respect, it is also important to bear in mind that the Chinese have always behaved in unique ways throughout their history. To cite two examples: what other country has built a Great Wall (or in fact several Great Walls as recent archaeology discoveries have uncovered)?[3] And which companies, outside of China, have acquired manufacturing companies in developed countries, dissembled their complete manufacturing facilities, transported them to their home country, and rebuilt the plants for operation there?[4]

Harmony

The need for harmony and for a harmonious society can be considered the main root of TCC. In fact, Chinese political and business leaders often refer to it. It is based on the idea that nature and the world can be understood but not completely mastered. As a result, the best that can be accomplished is to adapt into harmony with them. The idea of harmony is pretty much in line with the YinYang (*Yin Yang*) concept. Human beings and the universe are the products of interdependent, harmoniously orchestrated relationships. For China's classical sages, the world could never be conquered. Wise rulers could only hope to harmonize with its trends. As such, in their approach to business management, the Chinese:

- Respect superiors: What we may interpret as hierarchy and paternalism is not perceived this way within the culture.
  In fact, the Chinese consider it essential to maintain the chain of command, for without it nothing will function in harmony.

- Respect authority: When the superior gives orders with fairness and authority, all will be in harmony with heaven, and all will prosper. The superior does not hesitate to take advantage of a favorable circumstance that heaven has presented him.

- Avoid direct confrontation: One can and should put others into confrontational situations with other parties, but one should avoid putting oneself in situations that are directly confrontational.

- Practice instead flexibility and strategic encirclement: Historically, to avoid direct all-or-nothing conflicts, Chinese instead developed elaborate manoeuvers based on subtle indirection and the patient accumulation of relative advantage. It has been said that by looking at how *weiqi*⁵ (wei ch'i) works, one can begin to understand the way Chinese operate, by seeking victory not in a single quick battle, but through the accumulation of competitive advantage. This is rooted in the use of flexibility to increase one's relative position and to decrease the one of the other party with the aim of encircling the opponent. *Weiqi* teaches the art of strategic encirclement; in fact, this is what Chinese often try to do in their negotiations. If conflict cannot be avoided, before going into it, a person should be properly trained and prepared emotionally, mentally, and spiritually, and should retain their peace of mind.

- Avoid violence: "The violent man shall have a violent end" wrote Laozi (Lao Tzu). "When he is not in danger, the warlord does not fight if he can use alternate methods to destroy the enemy".⁶

- Always show equality and mutual respect in negotiations. Look for stability and trust, but keep one's distance. Do not look for intimacy or real friendship, even if the word *pengyou* (friend) is being used at the very initial stages of any business relationship. (This is often misunderstood by foreigners).

- Always adopt a position of being nice and looking out for the benefit of the other party and not just for one's own benefit.

- Do not provide information that may give rise to conflict. The fewer cards that are shown to the other party, the better. Instead, the negotiator should play "dumb", as this is a more beneficial approach. Sunzi (Sun Tzu) counseled: "When able, feign inability; when deploying troops, appear not to be; when near, appear far; when far, appear near."
- Go around finding ways to disarm the opponents' arguments instead of directly facing the issue. The truth is always shaded to maintain harmony. So, realize that the negotiator may act one way, but think another.
- Avoid situations that may mean a loss of face.
- Do move persistently but silently. Sunzi (Sun Tzu) said: "The skilled warlord moves and strikes like a poisonous snake, sinking his fangs deeply into the enemy, bringing about the enemy's downfall and subjugation. This is the mark of an enlightened warlord."
- Try to move with the flow, not against it. The Daodeqing (Tao Te Qing) said: "The human being follows [the laws of] the earth, the earth follows the heavens, the heavens follow God, and God must follow nature."

Impermanence

The impermanence of every thing, thought, and phenomenon; the fact that everything is in constant flux; that life is like a river that flows; that nothing lasts forever; these concepts are not difficult to understand. We just have to think, for example, about how our physical bodies are undergoing constant change and how—in pure metaphysical terms—the molecules, atoms, and subatomic particles that make up this book are always shifting and changing, moving around. However, it is not as easy to accept or internalize that everything is in constant flow, and that we need to adapt to ongoing changes in the marketplace, or to the fact that Europe and the United States are no longer the economic paradise they used to be. For some reason, most likely cultural, through their understanding of the YinYang (*Yin Yang*), Chinese are better adapted to deal with the reality of impermanence, to accept that there is only the flow of

Dao (Tao). They perfectly understand that every situation is in essence evolving and that the strategist must capture the direction of that evolution (the *shi*) and make it serve his or her ends. Thus, in their approach to business management, the Chinese:

- Accept that thoughts and actions happen as naturally as the wind blows and the rain falls.
- Are almost always ready to start all over again without any regret over what was left behind.
- Accept adversity and grow from it (for example, a natural disaster, an economic crisis) since, by doing this, success will come.
- Keep trying without giving up, because the circumstances will change and sooner or later they will turn favorable. "You have to keep trying, there is no other way to get things done in this world" is a phrase often repeated by Chinese entrepreneurs.
- Are not afraid to take risks, and not afraid of anything because, if something goes wrong today, it will be all right tomorrow. They accept that there is the possibility of losing everything, but that this situation will not last forever, since failure is always followed by success.
- Are fully aware of the fact that it is never too late to start a business, or to mobilize one's creativity. They always keep in mind that, as Laozi (Lao Tzu) said, "A journey of a thousand miles begins with a single step."
- Accept that nature and the world can be understood but not completely mastered, so ups and downs are an intrinsic part of life and business. If something goes wrong or does not go as well as it was planned, they do not feel desperate, but try to learn and build up from there, knowing that adversity will be followed by good luck.
- Are very flexible. They follow the flow of events, the path of least resistance; they go with and not against the current. If necessary, they wait a bit before following the flow. In fact, flexibility in adapting to any situation and understanding that "the world is a great theatre"[7] are two of Chinese's main

competitive advantages. Daoism calls for flexibility and creativity. Buddha said: "Be still like a mountain and flow like a great river." Flexibility is implicit in Sunzi's (Sun Tzu's) idea that the strategist mastering s*hi* is akin to water flowing downhill, adapting to the terrain, following the swiftest and easiest course. Chinese understand the need to be flexible and down-to-earth to adapt to different situations, since nature and the world can be understood but not completely mastered. One should accept the natural flow of life and move with it to serve one's ends.

- Do not see contracts as fixed documents. Many Chinese today advise not doing anything in China without a properly signed contract but in fact, they do. However, as important as the contract itself is its evolution over time, that is, the amendments that will follow. Sunzi (Sun Tzu) stated that, if there is room for re-negotiating a situation, it should be evaluated in order to protect the overall condition of the pre-established plan. If not, then, conditions must be re-thought to restore the situation to one's advantage. In fact, with the Chinese it is normally the case that the relationship built during the negotiation of a contract has more permanence than the contract itself.

- Are very resilient, knowing how essential it is to make changes in the management of a business. Without it, the sustainability of the business is not possible. Sunzi (Sun Tzu) stated that "the man who would be warlord knows of the inevitability of change in the administrative practice of maintaining the state."

- Do not trust what cannot be touched, since immaterial things many be different the next day—for example, people may change their minds tomorrow about what they said today. How can any thing, or any person, be trusted if they cannot point to anything as solid, singular, or unchangeable, if the idea of permanence and singularity is just an illusion and if everything has an empty nature? This helps explain the Chinese systematic attitude of working with immediate family or a circle of close friends. This also explains why it can take time for them to build trust and confidence in other people.

This also helps explain why, in decision-making processes and negotiations, the Chinese keep gathering and contrasting information, asking over and over again the same questions.

Non-Attachment

Linked to the acceptance of impermanence is the Chinese approach to non-attachment, the ability to live in the present moment, the now, without constantly turning their head toward the past or too much into the future, as people tend to do in the West. In the Chinese approach to business management, this is seen because the Chinese:

- Think short term: They are concerned with today, not with eternity. This is shown, for instance, in their desire to make money quickly. This does not contradict the fact that large companies prepare and implement detailed multi-year plans.
- Are narrowly focused on their interests, not expending energy or resources that are not necessary to achieve their goals.
- Are not afraid of taking risks because the past and the future do not exist, only this very moment counts.
- Understand the futility of attachment, by accepting the relativity of everything. Even the truth is not absolute, which may partly explain why they follow different ethical patterns, a Chinese ethics code, which does not necessarily match the Western ethics code.
- Do not dwell upon a choice or decision made, since these are part of the natural flow of life. According to Taoism, choices and decisions happen on their own. Once a conscious decision about something has been made, that is natural and should not be thought through after the fact.

Inter-dependence

Nothing in this universe is independent. Human beings are all related to each other as well as to the cosmos. Everything is relevant and connected; each factor influences the other, giving rise to subtle shifts in momentum and relative advantage. Even a simple object like a chair does not inherently exist, but rather emerges from a combination of causes and conditions. The realization of the concept of interdependence helps the Chinese in shaping their business strategies and negotiations approach; in particular, to:

- Understand that even thoughts and feelings are not things in themselves, but occur through a variety of causes and conditions; and that, by playing around with these, peoples' thoughts and feelings may change; and that, sooner or later (because nothing is permanent) they will in fact change.

- Take time for decision making: In negotiations, Chinese tend to turn third party's attitudes and opinions to their advantage, for they normally need time to allow for causes and conditions to change the other party's thoughts and feelings. Also, since the Chinese understand that what they think and how they feel today may change tomorrow, depending on the causes and circumstances, they also need time to see how they will evolve. Sunzi (Sun Tzu) says that the spirits of most warriors vary with time and that there are signals to be understood before an attack, all of which require time. Moreover, "it is essential for the enlightened warlord to understand the differences in the distinct states of mind and body. Great care should be given to planning for all possibilities when entering into conflict."

- Not enter some places—mentally and physically—that must not be entered into until the proper control of thoughts have developed the proper strategy. According to Sunzi (Sun Tzu), "the astute person must consider avenues of penetration and escape with equal reasoning. All avenues of escape are cutoff when entrapment is intelligently employed. They shall be prudent and cautious and shall never be caught in an area where they can be taken by surprise." The Chinese are extremely pragmatic people and they do not like to waste their time and energy. So, if they do (for example, in a negotiation), it is always for a reason: because they are not yet prepared to decide or act.

- Alternate some of the negotiation team's members, since causes and conditions may operate differently with each, and keep the best human resources for the special moments, always keeping the flow of information. "Your own elite troops are to be used only when situations call for it and at no other time," says Sunzi.

- Diffuse decision making through many layers and listen to other people's thoughts. Confucius said, "Three people's opinions are better than one person's." This also has the effect that no one person can be blamed, which the Chinese sometimes do.

- Be patient, since the quickest route may not be the shortest. "The most difficult terrain to overcome may not be the most disadvantageous." The Chinese believe that careful timing, preparation, and patience allow them to become superior; that all things related to an action should be well thoughtout prior to its beginning; and that it is important to spend time observing and cultivating changes in the strategic landscape, studying the opponent's preparation and morale, playing on his opponent's psychological weaknesses, until at last perceiving the opportune moment to strike him at his weakest point. Part of this preparation goes toward understanding the reactions of the opponents and of those not yet taken into consideration in the ultimate plan. Sunzi said: "warlords would be wise to analyze the conditions of war before entering it. They would be wise to consider all aspects of an alliance prior to making one. They would be wise to consider the reasons for another's wishing to associate with them. They would be wise to attend to their own needs before entering into agreements. They would be wise to seek council from their generals and rulers. They would be wise to think twice about a request for the assistance of troops and supplies. Then they should make their decisions."

- Never repeat any successful action in the same manner, for it could be learned by an opponent. Instead, always use new methods of attack. Sunzi said that "wise landlords always diversify their attack when necessary. Failure to see new ways to do things causes sloppiness in thinking."

- Understand the importance of having as much information
  as possible from all types of sources, including, for instance,
  competitors' employees, or employees from the firm they
  are negotiating with. Sunzi stated that "stalemates in battle
  are caused by a lack of information (and supplies). Agents
  are invaluable and must be treated accordingly when they
  provide information that can foster victory. Only the warlords
  that are intelligent and enlightened can use agents properly.
  If the information proves to be valid the informer must be
  rewarded."

- Manipulate circumstances, creating difficulties, along the way
  for the adversary. This is accomplished by proper planning
  and is based on all the information that has been gathered, as
  well as on a good understanding of the principles of action
  and inaction. The Chinese can mobilize tremendous capabilities of emotional intelligence to influence others (partners,
  employees) to achieve goals that are only of benefit to them,
  sometimes without the third party's realization of the fact.
  They fully grasp the idea that nothing is as it appears and they
  have mastered how to utilize the tactic. In fact, the Chinese
  are great masters at managing their emotions and taking the
  time to understand the opponent's psychology to be able to
  influence him. This partly explains why they do not trust
  others, since they think others may end up doing the same
  to them. "Even after winning the battle you should not think
  that you are invincible. The strength of your victory also
  depends on the weakness of your enemy, which you must
  have determined." It also partly explains their historically
  rooted "zero-sum" mentality: for somebody to win, somebody
  else has to lose. The concept of "win-win" is only occasionally
  implemented by the Chinese when dealing among themselves or with very close cultures (for example, Koreans and
  Malaysians).

- Use deception, subterfuge, and misinformation with the
  opponent, by appearing where they are not expected, and
  never leaving any trace of where they have been. Their plans

are well thought out, but should be unfathomable to the opponent, making him believe that he is being befriended while the plan is to defeat him. They understand that it is best to have the opponent align with them, making their takeover much easier. They see victory in creating difficulties for the adversary. They like to foster divisions among the other parties they are negotiating with, using them to check themselves, to act against themselves and, when necessary, to attack themselves. "It is always best to let the enemy kill himself," says Sunzi. He added: "Even with a smaller force, if adequately organized and using hit-and-run techniques, victory can be achieved. By constantly harassing the large force, a warlord can determine where its strengths and vulnerabilities lie. When the hit-and-run tactics are efficiently used, the main forces of the larger army disperse. And it is easier to disrupt a large group when it is done from inside."

- Get a good sense of when it is time to act and start an offensive or defensive attack, so that it will destroy the morale of the adversary. When the time arrives, any method can be devised to accomplish these ends, and all the resources shall swiftly and suddenly be deployed along the path of less resistance. When convenient to reach a reasonable agreement with the other party, shortcuts should be taken. They truly believe that men of worth see victory where most men see nothing.

- Keep trying until the situation turns to their advantage: The Chinese believe that persistence always pays and hence really practice it. They believe that Heaven—the nature of the universe—will always cooperate with a person of true belief, with a person whose timing, reasoning, resources, and desires are perfect; with a person whose attack is complete and who is relentless until the goal is achieved. This partly explains why, regardless of the circumstances, the Chinese have so much confidence in the future of their businesses. They know that challenges coexist with opportunities.

- Be great human observers who can analyze the psychological and personal elements in any business situation, within their own companies and in negotiations with third parties. Their tactics are always aimed at psychological combat and at getting concessions from the other side. The Chinese can remain inactive—*wu wei*—and silent, as if paralyzed or pretending to lack understanding of a particular situation, until the right moment for action arrives; until the circumstances are favorable for heaven to help them. Even if they do refer to it this way, the Chinese are great believers in emotional intelligence.

- Understand how to maximize their competitive advantages by smartly exploiting the interactions between the public and private sectors, by sagely complementing government-owned companies' functions with those of private firms—for example, the government-owned company manufactures and packages the products (which guarantees quality) and the private firm (more efficiently) distributes them in the market.

- Not see any great difference between their personal and the business lives, since both are interdependent.

Many Chinese may not have this philosophical background today, but rooted in their minds somewhere (without their consciously realizing it) is the idea that nothing is permanent, singular, or independent.

Love/Compassion

The Chinese have the profound belief that you receive what you give. This is illustrated by the practice of starting a relationship by always giving a present to the other party or, for instance, by their understanding of the need to give money in the temple in order to receive grace. The concept of compassion is at the core of Mahayana Buddhism, and it is being manifested in China today through philanthropy. At the entrepreneurial level, its influence is fully present in the area of human resources. For Chinese entrepreneurs, it is important not only to choose the right employees, but also to nurture and care for them, so that they behave in line with the company's goals. In the West, we may interpret this as paternalism, but this is far from the truth in terms of how Chinese employees feel about these practices. In fact, the turnover rate is much lower for Chinese companies than for foreign companies operating in China. Indeed, today, more and more young Chinese executives prefer to work for Chinese companies, both state-owned and private. Sunzi said that "a warlord that considers the needs and desires of others before himself should be praised to heaven; he marches with his men when they are marching, he eats only when their food is cooked, and he drinks only when they are not thirsty. He treats his men as he prefers to be treated. He respects them and they respect him. They both love him and fear him."

Chinese entrepreneurs let each member of their staff know they are valued for the performance of their role, but they do not allow them to think they are their equal. Chinese entrepreneurs delegate with intelligence and authority, knowing they have to assign the correct tasks to their staff, based on their capabilities and limitations. They know they have to delegate in light of the overall situation, while dealing with the inevitability of change. Women entrepreneurs, in particular, show their love for their employees and make sure they are told that their tasks are important, even if in many cases the tasks are largely meaningless. They know the importance of communicating what is expected with their employees and of rewarding them, administering reward and punishment with the same force and intent. Women entrepreneurs often like to maintain personal control over their employees, helping maintain their high morale. They make sure that their employees are constantly employed because, if they are not kept busy, they might have time to devise additional ways of not doing their duty. They know that they will lose credibility and authority if employees feel that they have not been led with discretion and intelligence, thus they try to remain serene and calm at all times. They know that leadership means constantly communicating to their employees their worth and value to the enterprise so that they will come to see their worth and value in themselves. They know that it would be foolish to know the market well, but not their employees, whose personal needs must be given their full attention. Chinese entrepreneurs know that by managing their employees with wisdom and love, their employees will follow the companies' goals without question. They know that for heaven and the universe to cooperate with them for their personal success, as entrepreneurs they must show their concern for their employees openly and care for their greater needs.

Learning

Confucius attached great importance to education and studying. Sunzi also emphasized the need to study deeply and to learn to manage "all types of territories and personnel" to prepare for war. Zhuangzi[8] stated that life is limited while the knowledge that can be learned is unlimited. Deng Xiaoping also called for education, setting the basis for making technology transfer and training as key components in any business relationship with foreigners. In fact, Chinese entrepreneurs never stop studying, learning and—perhaps most important of it all—applying what they learn. When the "reform and opening up" of China's economy began, the Chinese entrepreneurs knew that they did not need to reinvent the wheel; all they had to do was use Joint Ventures (JVs) to diligently study and learn from foreigners. Several stories related in this book are examples of this process.

Work Ethics

The Chinese are known to be hard workers. In fact, most Chinese entrepreneurs would claim that what helped them to be successful was *nuli gongzuo* (working very hard). They have the firm belief that nobody can get anything done without diligence and hard work. They firmly believe that work is good for health. They often state that "a person who seeks success will never give up, because the meaning of life is to work diligently to achieve prosperity." This working ethic is deeply rooted in TCC, so much so that the Chinese still remember that "a day without work is a day without food." Confucius said: "Wherever you go, go with all your heart." Buddha's last words were: "All materials things pass away. Strive for your own liberation with diligence." "The Art of War" is itself a manual of how to achieve victory through hard work, mobilizing the troops the proper way and maintaining their morale to defeat the enemy; this is accomplished by simultaneously studying, designing, and re-designing strategies and tactics to defeat the enemy psychologically. Sunzi states that "in the ancient days, warriors made themselves unbeatable through constant practice, knowing there was no other way they could make the enemy vulnerable."

Equanimity

Perhaps the main manifestations of Chinese entrepreneurs' equanimity are their inner strength, self-motivation, and self-control. They do whatever is necessary to accomplish their goals, irrespective of the feelings of others, who might otherwise wish them misfortune or harm. They remain strong enough to confront those who seek to pull them down. They try not to be affected by external influences; they truly believe in their own ideals. They remain true to themselves, which they know will allow them not to lose face or power socially. They always remember and stress that "at the end of the day, there is only me." Without equanimity, they will not achieve anything in this world. Instead of being affected by external circumstances or people, they focus on using their emotional intelligence and everything at their disposal to survive in this world. They constantly strive to become stronger. They know that if they are weak, their orders will appear ambivalent; employees will lack leadership and fail to respond properly. The result will be chaos. Confucius said: "Respect yourself and others will respect you."

Chinese entrepreneurs know how important it is to have internal equilibrium in order to generate sustainable external wealth. But they never get dizzy from their own success. They know that anger prevents the greatest of leaders from acting intelligently. He or she needs cold-blooded planning to be successful, and to be favored by heaven. To compete in the market and to manage the internal conflicts that may arise, leaders have to be, not only properly trained, but also prepared emotionally, mentally, and spiritually. They must have peace of mind. Only when this happens and they work very hard, can they be successful. Most Chinese entrepreneurs would claim that they started their businesses because they knew they could accomplish things that others could not. To earn money was not the main motivation when they began, but they knew that, by remaining strong and working very hard, material success would follow.

Buddhism says that "he who defeats the other is strong; he who defeats himself is powerful." Sunzi said that "the pressures of being a great leader are not understood by lesser men. He does not permit the alleged power of his enemies to influence him, and will always issue the final order: good, bad, or indifferent" and that "a hard-nosed, cold-blooded mentality is essential to personal development, both on the field of battle and at the negotiation table." He added that "to perform an attack, men have to be properly trained and prepared emotionally, mentally, and spiritually."

Pragmatism

Perhaps it was not a coincidence that *Chan,* with its practical approach to life, originated in China, for it called for the integration of spiritual practice into every aspect of daily life: "Take life as it is and enjoy every single second of it," is the main message. Perhaps this was how TCC was applied over time. It has been said that, throughout history, the Chinese have focused on gods of wealth and kitchens, not on spiritual enlightenment. If anything fully characterizes the Chinese population, it is their extreme pragmatism and creativity. The Chinese people are 100% result-oriented, always seeking truth from the facts. They certainly believe that the biggest problem is not seeing the problem, but they also believe that nothing is fixed and that every situation can be turned around. And so, they always try. They use physical and material displays as a surrogate indicator of worth. They use whatever is necessary to get the best possible results. Historical proof of this is the famous story of McCartney (mentioned later), who finally received the opportunity to make an informal courtesy call on the Chinese emperor, but was required to kowtow[9] which he, of course, refused to do. As a solution, the Chinese suggested that, when McCartney entered the emperor's presence, there would be a curtain hanging behind the emperor and that, behind that curtain, there would be a portrait of King George III. This way, instead of kowtowing to the emperor, McCartney could make his kowtow to the king's unseen portrait.

An explanation of where this extreme pragmatism comes from may be found by looking back at China's history. Ancient China was mainly populated by farmers bound to their ancestral plots. The mandarin elite earned their positions through mastery of the Confucian classics and refined arts such as calligraphy and poetry, not through displays of martial valor. On the other hand, because of China's vaunted centrality and material wealth, barbarian invasions from over a dozen neighboring states hung over China as a permanent threat.[10] Thus, the only option left for the Chinese was to rely on a rich collection of practical, diplomatic, and economic instruments to draw potentially hostile barbarians into relationships the Chinese could manage. Their aim was to deter invasion and prevent the formation of barbarian coalitions. Through trade incentives, gifts, and skillful use of theatrical tactics, China coaxed their foreign neighbors to observe the Chinese norms, while projecting an image of awesome majesty to deter them from testing China's strength. For those who would not obey, China would foster a practical measure: create divisions, using barbarians to check other barbarians, and when necessary, using them to attack others until they could be subdued. Sunzi said that "the enemy must be attacked in such manner as to force an uneven distribution of his troops. In that way the enemy can be divided and conquered with ease."

Historically, the Chinese court was remarkably pragmatic about the means they employed with barbarians. They followed Sunzi's advice of bringing the enemy to them by offering something of perceived value. "If the warlord wins the war without combat, it is because he is a master of deception and guile. He uses things certain to have the effect he wants, such as intoxicating beverages, beautiful women, and expensive gifts that would whittle down enemy resources should they seek to duplicate them. He also uses cunning means to deceive and manipulate the ministers of the enemy state by finding delicate matters to blackmail them with. A capable warlord employing intelligent deception always seeks ways to confuse all known and potential enemies. A fierce warlord must never question his own morality; if he does, heaven will not help him maintain his control and position."

The Chinese are well known for their hospitality—it was pretty much called for by Confucius—but the fact is that they bribed the barbarians and used their demographic superiority to dilute their influence or threat. When defeated, they submitted. This pragmatic approach is illustrated in the "five baits" that a Han dynasty minister proposed to manage the mounted Xiongnu tribes to China's northwestern frontier, showing how close these strategies are to those used today by Chinese in negotiations with third parties:

1. "To give them elaborate clothes and carriages in order to corrupt their eyes.
2. To give them fine food in order to corrupt their mouth.
3. To give them music and women in order to corrupt their ears.

4. To provide them with lofty buildings, granaries, and slaves in order to corrupt their stomach.

5. For those who come to surrender, the emperor [should] show them favor by honoring them with an imperial reception party in which the emperor should personally serve them wine and food so as to corrupt their mind."

Another expression of this tremendous pragmatism was their reaction to conquerors, where the Chinese bureaucratic elite would offer their services, doing so on the premise that such a vast and unique land as China could only be ruled by using Chinese methods, the Chinese language, and Chinese bureaucracy. In this way, the conquerors would find themselves increasingly assimilated into the Chinese order, pursuing Chinese national interests instead of their own. This historical situation is somewhat similar to the one that foreign companies have experienced in China, both in joint ventures and in wholly owned foreign enterprises.

When it comes to managing their companies, the Chinese are also quite practical. They know that management's essence is not in knowledge, but in performance, and that this is verified through results, not logic. So, they show their love, yes, but they know that being warm-hearted, true-hearted, and intimate is a necessary condition to win employees' loyal hearts toward the enterprise, so that their hearts and minds are always aligned with the company's goals. Sunzi said, referring to how to treat the troops: "Give them what they want with regards to the simple pleasures of life. If you do not give this to them, they will seek it elsewhere." The Chinese believe that managers should not be blamed for having low-quality subordinates (if no better are available in the market), but should be blamed for their incapacity to improve the quality of their subordinates.

Referring to the market, Chinese entrepreneurs stress the need to be in constant contact with the market, to focus on clients' demands, not competitors, since in the market they cannot manipulate or overtake competitors, but they can always run ahead of them. They know the importance of modifying their tactics relative to their competitors, and of quickly adjusting to the changing environment to remain competitive in the marketplace. Chinese society is very strong on competition, but very weak on cooperation. In fact, the Chinese are among the world's most individualistic people and possess a dog-eat-dog competitive spirit, even though they are often seen eating, travelling, or having fun together (especially men). In fact, Confucius wanted his disciples to think deeply for themselves and relentlessly study the outside world. Buddhism proclaimed a salvation, which each individual could gain by himself in this world, during his lifetime, without any reference to God or gods.

Chinese entrepreneurs do not just learn for the sake of learning, but in order to apply what they have learned. They always stress that, when a person believes in something, he or she has to execute it, and that it is never enough merely to think about it. Laozi said that: "The way of the sage is to act but not contend." Chinese entrepreneurs roll up their sleeves, perhaps not in the same way that Americans do, but they go about successfully facing the forces in play in the market. Sunzi stated that "the warlord is always in the same place he sends his men. He does not rely on subordinates to explain failure to him, but guarantees his own success by demanding victory of himself. With proper planning, proper organization, and intelligent delegation of responsibility, he takes control of his destiny." And certainly, Chinese entrepreneurs do plan, organize, and manage successfully. They always try to find a solution to a problem and do not stop until they find it, even when the problem looks completely irresolvable. As a result, they often develop innovative solutions. Zhuangzi defended creativity as a fundamental value. Contrary to popular thought in the West, the Chinese are very creative. They are always developing solutions that foreigners might rarely have thought of.

When they undertake a business, they make it a fact of life, going on with it until it becomes successful, no matter what the circumstances are. Otherwise they would have not bothered to start it, or they would have quickly quit in order to do something else—for example, it is common in Chinese cities to see retail businesses that open and close after only six months of operation because they realize it is better to try and persevere with a different approach. The Chinese do not like to waste their time or energy, and they are probably the world's leaders in finding shortcuts—in particular, when it comes to regulations and laws—in order to achieve results more quickly. They do not want to deal with what they do not understand, as they mention when they talk about their dealings with banks. Quite often they stress that "only what you can touch is real. If you cannot touch something and don't understand it, do not get involved with it."

In the same way that Chinese merchants used to show deference and subservience to the Emperor, today China's entrepreneurs pay their respects to the Government. In fact, business leaders in China do participate in politics in their own way. But, contrary to the way this is often interpreted in the West, their approach is merely pragmatic: this is simply the most efficient way to achieve their goals.

Superiority

The Chinese name of China—*Zhongguo* the "Central Country"—and their many years of isolation nurtured a particular self-perception for the Chinese, of being part of a unique yet great civilization, while everyone else is a barbarian, their degree of barbarity being largely determined by their physical distance from China. In fact, for most of history, China has outstripped all other nations. China was for centuries the world's most productive economy and the most popular trading place on Earth. Until the Industrial Revolution, China was far richer than the European states. In eighteen of the last twenty centuries, China produced a greater share of the total world GDP than any Western country.

Despite this history, foreigners came to China, foisted addiction to opium on its people (the British), and slaughtered millions of Chinese (the Japanese), facts the Chinese have not forgotten. In fact, they have been taught from childhood that China was the world's mightiest empire, the best at everything, until the end of the eighteenth century, when foreigners entered their country to exploit their people, even though they had done the foreigners no harm. Moreover, foreigners have historically sought not just to engage in commerce with China, but also to change China, something the Chinese even today strongly resist, and even try to prevent from happening. It is true that Chinese themselves, who thorough history traded with foreigners, occasionally adopted ideas and inventions from abroad. More often, however, they believed that the most valuable possessions and intellectual achievements were to be found in China. Instead, everyone else should acknowledge the sovereignty of the Chinese government, show subservience to the Emperor, and observe the imperial rituals, including the *kowtow*. They offered to treat foreigners humanely and compassionately in proportion to their attainment or appreciation of Chinese culture and their performance of the rituals symbolizing their submission to China.

According to official Chinese records, foreign envoys came to the imperial court to be transformed by the Emperor's civilizing influence. In fact, in 1793, when Lord George McCartney—one of King George III's most experienced diplomats—landed his fleet of British ships on China's northern coast, he brought with him the best goods that Britain produced as gifts for Emperor Qianlong.[11] This was done with the intent of opening China's vast market to British business. McCartney was sent back with a letter to King George that said China (the world's most prosperous and populous nation at that time)[12] had no need for the British goods. The letter cautioned: "You, O King, should simply act in conformity with our wishes by strengthening your loyalty and swearing perpetual obedience so as to ensure that your country may share the blessings of peace." It has been said that for the Chinese, the Promised Land was China and that they were already living in it. The customs of the Celestial dynasty were plainly beyond the attainment of the distant barbarians.

The Chinese have been passing this knowledge about its cultural or national superiority from one generation to the next. They have been taught from childhood that they have to compensate for what the foreigners began doing to them roughly 200 years ago. Even if they remain suspicious about foreigners, by relying on their traditional principles, the Chinese have learned to adapt their suspicions to their advantage in their negotiating tactics and development of business strategies. They have been taught that they have to demonstrate to the barbarians how great a civilization China is and has always been. Without understanding this distinct form of chauvinism, it is not possible to understand the creative force that drives individual Chinese to keep moving ahead, even in the midst of personal difficulties. One could say that they are constantly facing the *yin* of suspicion and the *yang* of arrogance toward the external world, wanting to gain a space where they will always be recognized by foreigners as important and powerful players on the world scene.

The phrase *"Zhongguoren feichang congming"* ("the Chinese are very smart") summarizes their belief in the wisdom they have, in the intelligence they possess that is used in ways we as foreigners cannot or do not—even when, as a negotiating tactic previously discussed, they may play a passive or "dumb" role when engaged in negotiations. This attitude of moral or tactical superiority can be seen today, for instance, in the way Chinese entrepreneurs tend to hide or obscure the fact that their companies are or used to be Joint Ventures (JVs); frequently, this association with a foreign company is where the company obtained their original technology and transfer knowledge. Quite often, instead of referring to the JV, they would simply say that they bought the technology and the training in order to adopt it and use it commercially.

In today's China, everybody recognizes the need to modernize, to advance and to learn from foreign nations. In fact, Deng Xiaoping planted the seed for this attitude, when he said back in 1978: *"We should not act like women with bound feet. If we want socialism to perform better than capitalism, we should learn from other cultures' achievements. We should learn from other countries, including the capitalist developed countries".* But the Chinese also recognize that all this must be done while retaining the essence of what China is. China may be modernizing, but it is not westernizing.

While it may be a prerequisite for the foreigners to follow the Chinese rules when doing business in the China market, or even an obligation to do so when operating, selling, or marketing there, it is quite a different situation when the Chinese are the ones entering or doing business in foreign markets. These markets, particularly Europe and the United States, do not operate according to Chinese rules; as a result, business negotiations with Chinese businesspeople may often lead nowhere. This is an important limitation Chinese entrepreneurs face when investing in operations in foreign countries, and it can also be a competitive advantage, in turn, for Western business people, if such negotiations are well managed. However, in today's global economic and financial turmoil, Europe and the United States may find themselves in a position where, for the first time in history, they may have no other option but to follow Chinese rules when soliciting Chinese investors or business partners for projects in their own countries.

Historically, the Chinese were humiliated by foreign powers, but they have really learned their lessons from that experience. They will not be humiliated again. Now they are learning everything we know, including our culture. In this new stage, since Deng Xiaoping's "reform and opening up" of China, the Chinese government and its people have established the goal of reversing the old rules: they are learning about us (our strategies, culture, and ways of thinking) and continuously updating their information about us, even if we are hesitant or resistant to getting to know China and their culture better. They are learning our technologies, our market rules, our entrepreneurship and business models, and so on, for their own adaptation and use. Conceivably, they can use this knowledge to "conquer" us, in the sense of classical Chinese military strategies and tactics, even though in modern terms this literally means economic or commercial conquest, not military or geopolitical conquest. Effectively, this is what is going on today. We still live in different paradigms, but they increasingly know ours, while we are not that familiar with theirs. Many Chinese have a very clear understanding that they must compensate for the humiliation their country suffered and that they and their companies must strive to be the very best in the world. And they are striving to continue growing and become stronger, in order to win honor for China and the Chinese people.

CHAPTER 3

What Entrepreneurship Is All About. Gao Yu, Rujin

Gao Yu, CEO of *Rujin Kanjian Beijing Shengwu Keji Youxian Gongsi*, is a very atypical Chinese entrepreneur. She is used to working with advisors, a situation still not common in China, where business leaders avoid paying for services because of their intangible nature. Since 2006 she has taken the strategic advice of Professor Liu Deji, a Government's advisor and a well-recognized professional in China. She has five other advisors one each for the following: economic and financial matters, legal issues, products, market positioning and marketing, and social media relationships.

Gao Yu is an entrepreneur in the pure sense of the word. She fears nothing, least of all starting all over again in a new business. Because of this and other reasons such as the way she approaches business and the values associated with sustainable development and its expansion, she is a suitable subject to teach us what entrepreneurship is all about in China.

Gao Yu was born in 1963 in *Cangzhou, Hebei* Province, approximately 180 km away from Beijing and 90 km away from Tianjin. This was a rural place at that time and, with around 900,000 inhabitants, is still pretty small today.[1] This is the place where her father still lives; her mother is no longer alive. Her parents' families were wealthy and used to own a lot of land, but lost everything in 1949. Gao Yu comes from a big family: she has five brothers and two sisters.

In 1981, she moved to live with an aunt in Tianjin because she wanted to study management; there were more opportunities to do so there. To earn some money to support her studies, Gao Yu worked in a bed sheet embroidery factory, doing the embroidery herself.

In 1984, she married a man from Beijing and relocated there, where her husband helped her find a job in a dry bean curd factory where she worked on quality control of packaging. She remained there for over three years, getting a meager salary of RMB 45 a month. Following the Chinese tradition, she gave RMB 20 to her mother-in-law, who lived with the couple, and kept RMB 25 for herself.

With the experience she acquired in Beijing and the knowledge of the embroidery business she acquired in Tianjin, Gao Yu decided to start her own company in 1988—*Hong Mei Gong Yi Ci Xou Chang*—in the Chaoyang district of Beijing. She worked with a company that exported bed sheet sets; this company helped her get embroidery work from factories that needed to have this done before selling their products for export. Her volume of work was thus guaranteed. The company grew to over 50 employees with sales turnover of around RMB 10,000—small, but in line with the business type, until three of her clients from Taiyuan did not pay their bills. Gao Yu was thus forced to close her embroidery business in 1992.

However, this first unsuccessful experience did not prevent Gao Yu from trying again, adopting a pragmatic approach by establishing a joint arrangement with one of her debtors. She got money from her third oldest brother (not an entrepreneur himself) and started a clothing company, selling in Beijing and Taiyuan, fabric she acquired in Shanghai as well as her own branded clothing. These were manufactured in Taiyuan with fabric bought in Shanghai—*Tai Yan Ying Li Da Shang Mao You Xian Gongsi*. More than one hundred people were involved in the manufacturing, which was performed by one of the Taiyuan's companies that owed her money. Most of the clothing production, for men and women, was done for client companies and organizations with demand for her products. Sales turnover was about RMB 6 million in 2002, but Gao Yu saw that the profit margins were sinking; it was time to restructure the business before it was too late. So, she decided to move the manufacturing activities to Shenzhen, where costs were much lower. This was the situation until 2008/2009 when competition also increased there. Subsequently, profit margins were very low.

Seeing this, she got involved in a new business in Shenzhen (her third, but in a completely new sector, wet towels) establishing a company— *Zhongguo Zhongyi Yanjiu Kexue Yuan*. She owns 75% of the capital, with the other 25% owned by a friend of her General Manager (who could not directly participate because of a lack of funds). The products are manufactured and packed by Shenzhen Dworld Industries Co. Ltd. Gao Yu believed that it was possible to develop different types of wet tissues for applications other than hand cleaning (for instance, face cleaning and eye cleaning) to differentiate her products and increase the net profitability of the business. Sales turnover for this business is presently over RMB 2 million, with net profit of around 3%. The business employs over 100 people. About 75% of the employees are located in Shenzhen, and the business has a large distribution network. The General Manager of this company receives a salary plus a performance-based bonus.

Based on the challenges faced by the wet towel business, in 2009 Gao Yu decided to start a new business—her fourth. This was also in the field of hygiene, an area where competition was largely non-existent: feminine hygiene products. She investigated the market and saw that, with social development, women's health concepts had become prevalent in China; the market for women's health products was rapidly growing. In 2008, sales revenue for women's health related products reached RMB 7.755 billion.

The main idea behind this business is that, if women can keep the female parts of their body clean, they will feel well inside. In fact, this is the way Gao Yu's new company—*Rujin Kanjian Beijing Shengwu Keji Youxian Gongsi* www.chinarujin.com ("Beijing Rujin Health Biotechnology Co., Ltd.")—marketed its products using the brand LIVEN (drawn from the phrase *Li Wei*). This was also the main motivation for Gao Yu to be involved with this business: she wanted to help women to feel good about themselves; the desire to make money out of it was secondary for her.

Manufacturing activities began in 2004. While the products have been available in the market since 2006, the previous owners of the business realized that they could not appropriately position the products in the market; they were actively looking for a partner that could help them do so. Gao Yu believed she could help them out, entering the business by buying 51% of the company's capital, which she later increased to 100% ownership. The raw materials and manufacturing are the responsibility of a government owned company, based in Yangsi, Jiangxi province, with which they have a *hezuo*. Thus, this could be said that this is a private-public partnership, in the Chinese version of the concept: manufacturing of a unique product is done by the government, while marketing and distribution is performed by a private company.

With support from the Beijing Reproduction Health Association, the Beijing Yixuantang Chinese Medicine Research Institute, and the Chinese Women's Federation, *Rujin* has been able to form technology cooperation agreements with renowned domestic and foreign expertise, and to create a continuous stream of biotechnology products. Liven Medicine Technology Limited Corporation is one of *Rujin*'s production centers. It is a modern biomedical synthesis business. With government guidance, it focuses on the prevention of women's diseases. It has introduced innovative technologies and cooperated with foreign corporations to develop a series of products, including an anti-itch and infection control vaginal spray, which can not only relieve symptoms, but also prevent genital infections.

According to Gao Yu's market research, the LIVEN products, which regulate the pH in these parts of a women's body, are unique not only in China (where there is no other factory manufacturing them) but also in the world; there is a similar US product, but not convincing so, according to Gao. So, Gao Yu expects to remain for a long time in the market with the LIVEN products, which may not prove easy to copy. Because of this, she expects to be able to keep a net profit of around 10% for quite some time, while simultaneously making the products accessible to a larger customer base.

There are four categories of products to help women maintain their health: for daily use (mainly used after the menstrual period and after sexual intercourse), for vaginal dryness (for cleansing and infection prevention), for use when having problems (to control and relieve the symptoms resulting from vaginal infections), and for use after being in labor (to repair the vagina and vulva). The products are manufactured in the eastern part of Hebei, about one hour from Beijing, using mostly raw materials from Tibet. Gao Yu explains that, because of the altitude and the natural environment, Tibet provides plant materials not available elsewhere in China, and that these are of premium quality, since there is no pollution there.

For sales across China she has mostly been using friends and acquaintances, who have acted as her sales agents. However, she plans on using traditional commercialization means—distributors and products' representatives at three levels (city, district, and neighborhood)—while selling a smaller percentage through e-commerce. Since Gao Yu got involved in the business, demand for its products has continued to increase. This is why she thinks that the wet towel company will eventually merge with the *Rujin* company thereby reducing its marketing and administrative costs and increasing its profitability. Otherwise, she may close down that business and just focus on *Rujin*, as the wet towel business lacks opportunities for innovation while the competition is already brutal. So far, the wet towel business has remained competitive because her company's packaging is convenient for travelling; this has given it a differentiation advantage in the marketplace.

Paralleling the management of her two hygiene-related businesses, Gao Yu has been responsible for the management of an IT services center, *SEC* www.chinajiami.cn (the English name is National Information Security Engineering Center), which belongs to the government. With a staff of eight people, it has taken little of Gao Yu's energy. She is paid a small salary for this work, but the main reason she has been doing it is to keep good relations with the government. On the other hand, the government needs people like her to reach the market.

For Guan Yu to be successful in a business, her leadership has to meet three conditions:

1. As a leader, she has to be extremely good at performing tasks like these. She must have the correct abilities and keep them throughout the time she must lead the business. These abilities are extremely important, since she has to be self-sufficient and can never rely on help from others. Quite often, the problem is that these abilities are lost over time as the business evolves, the market conditions change

or both of them; as a leader, she does not have the ability to keep adapting to the changing situations.

2. She has to remain in contact with the market, leaving her office and observing what is happening in the market and what changes are taking place there, so that she can anticipate the trends in the market and develop a vision on how to best position her company.

3. She must look for new products to commercialize, so that the business can always keep innovating. This is particularly important in China where the competition is so strong and there are always so many people starting businesses, entering the market, trying new approaches, and innovating.

The LIVEN products are of such high quality that, by making them available to a broad range of women, Gao Yu believes they will contribute to their wellbeing and, as a result, the money will follow. She is very happy with the decision she made to get into this new business because she is able to give love to people and help them while, at the same time, making money in an honest way. For Gao Yu, marketing and business development can only be done successfully and in a sustainable way by taking care of people. If entrepreneurs do not care about helping their customers and adding value to their lives, their businesses will not be profitable enough to keep innovating and developing good products; as a result, their profitability will sink.

Gao Yu has published a small, easy to carry booklet, which summarizes *Rujin*'s business culture, based on the Traditional Chinese Culture *DiziGui* book (which basically contains *Standards for being a Good Pupil and Child*). Most of the pages contain drawings; it is written so that anyone, including children, can read it. Its title is *"DiziGui"*, indicating the main idea it contains: to love people and not to cheat them. The first edition published in 2009 resulted in 10,000 copies, which Gao Yu distributed among her employees and business associates to teach them the values behind the Rujin business and how they should behave on its behalf. Since then, new editions have been published.

This booklet is being used as part of their marketing strategy, which emphasizes through several messages how to remain healthy, which she calls "health culture." *Rujin*'s products are just one element to help women remain healthy; they emphasize this in their presentations, explaining that there are other measures that should be taken. This is why they are creating a second booklet, which will summarize all these health culture measures; the second booklet will be distributed with the original "*DiziGui.*" "One day these materials will be translated into English and our products will be exported all over the world, included Europe and the United States," she dreams. She continues: "I have already met with Russian and Indian people interested in our products."

Gao Yu's company is organized into four departments—product/manufacturing, business development, finance, and human resources. She is very happy with her employees, to whom she gives a lot of freedom and responsibility and who, in return, are very good to her. She has always treated her employees as a mother treats her children, and she has guided them by practicing what she preaches. She believes that, when she retires (not in the near future, of course), they will miss her.

Gao Yu is absolutely certain that the culture of a business is based on the values of its leader. In her case, the most important value is to take care of her employees and her customers. But to be followed by the employees, the behavior of the leader has to agree with what she says; otherwise, the employees will distrust her and nothing will come of it.

After having been in business for close to 24 years, Gao Yu still does not feel any need to be successful; instead, she believes that the secret to remaining healthy and keeping a calm mind is that she is and has always been a good person. Over the years, she has seen many entrepreneurs end up with health problems because they are not good people, because they do not practice good values, and because they spend their days in a non-harmonious environment. Therefore, she is absolutely certain that, if an entrepreneur simply cares about the business results and does everything necessary to achieve them, without paying any attention to the morality of her actions, she will end up facing many problems in her business and personal life.

Gao Yu has passed these ideas and values on to her only daughter, who was born in 1986 and graduated in Law in 2010. She works as a teacher of "how to help people," a subject she has been practicing herself all her life. "She is a person that helps everybody. For instance, she has been helping a woman over eighty years old whose hobby is to care for street cats; she has over twenty of them," her mother says. Gao Yu is pretty sure that, if her daughter ends up one day managing, she will do it with these compassionate values in mind.

Gao Yu has not been following the Chinese tradition of working with her family to do business. For instance, her husband has always had his own (small) businesses, nothing to do with hers. For Gao Yu, the familiar and the business sphere must be separated. Otherwise, if problems arise, there will be no solution. What she does, though, is to economically help her family. In particular, she has been helping the brother from whom she borrowed money to start her second business.

The current economy is less favorable and uncertain, but this does not seem to have affected Gao Yu much because she adapted well to market circumstances and always planned accordingly. Moreover, her *Rujin* business had to be developed anyway and has been helped by other circumstances, such as the fact that cervical cancer still has a high incidence rate in China: over 60% of Chinese women suffer from gynecological inflammation, and many of them lack basic gynecological knowledge.

What has affected Gao Yu's business, however, are a number of personal problems she has faced since the autumn of 2009. At the family level, both her father and one of her brothers became sick, the latter with cancer. On another front, in March 2011, she lost a significant amount of the money she invested 10 years earlier in a real estate venture in Hebei. Construction work that was taking place adjacent to the property damaged her building's foundations, causing it to collapse. However, despite the fact that this has significantly slowed the rate of her *Rujin* business' development, she remains energetic, with the same inner-strength as before. In fact, she has not changed her plans to start exporting her products to Africa, while giving a small percentage as a charitable donation. She also has not changed her idea of going public one day.

Gao Yu defines her management style in the following way:

1. She does what she likes, whatever motivates her to keep going. In this way, she feels well, her employees see this and, as a result, they also feel well.
2. She cares for herself, manages herself while also caring for others and managing others, not only her employees, but also her business network.
3. She delegates, that is, she assigns responsibilities to her employees and makes them fully responsible for their execution, making them understand that nobody else will manage the tasks assigned to them.

4. She trains her employees and distributors/representatives on how to follow and use the company's values (the ones summarized in the booklets) to further develop the business, and on the need to work together as a team to grow the business. She started giving this training twice a week, every week, on Wednesdays at 6:00 pm and on Saturdays from 2:00 pm to 6:00 pm. A year later, seeing that most people (around forty) attended the Saturday training meetings, she stopped the Wednesdays' sessions.

5. She constantly studies the market, anticipating and following its trends. Gao Yu truly believes that new business opportunities can be identified, by observing the market.

6. She tries to be her employees' best friend, no matter whether they are men or women, giving them advice—like a sister would do, and joining them in typical recreational activities. She has encouraged all employees to write something about the company and together they have developed a company hymn. Gao Yu believes her style is unique in this respect, since she goes beyond what other Chinese entrepreneurs and leaders do.

FOR GAO YU, IT IS NECESSARY TO KEEP INNOVATING CONTINUOUSLY IN A BUSINESS because otherwise it will not be possible to remain in the market for a long time, as the products will sooner or later be matched.

As for the challenges that she faces in the *Rujin* business, Gao Yu summarizes them in the following ways:

1. To guarantee the products' standard high quality and their packaging: because of this, they changed their packaging in 2011.

2. To communicate the very high quality of the products to a broad range of potential customers, a task to which she has been devoting much of her attention, since the products were practically unknown in the market. They have been using a video describing how in today's life it is easy for women to develop infections of the vagina and vulva, which the Chinese government wants to prevent them from happening (Chinese President Hu Jintao appears in the video). LIVEN products can help; the video is also used for marketing purposes,

when communicating with social media and with the relevant women associations.

3. To develop and establish the means of commercialization; for this task—including training—she is still devoting a great deal of time.

4. To be able to guarantee the supply of products in Beijing and to expand nationally and internationally. Gao Yu believes that, when the right moment comes, it will be possible to start the internationalization process in a parallel way with the national expansion.

5. To keep innovating, and performing new activities, so that the products and the business can remain competitive over time. Gao Yu stated this in Mandarin in the following way: "*xinqi tejue de fangfa shi women fazhang de biaoben*," If they are able to do so, the *Rujin* business can last for a very long time because women are always going to need these kinds of hygiene products.

Gao Yu feels confident about remaining in this business for a long time and is very happy about it because her main hobby has always been working, followed by helping other people and reading/learning. She can practice all three of these at *Rujin* and does so every day, which she appreciates very much.

Gao Yu acknowledges that, since she (together with her husband and daughter) embraced Tibetan Buddhism 10 years ago, her everyday life has become more meaningful: she pays less attention to what other people might say about her or her work; she has increased her awareness of the present moment and gets much satisfaction from helping others. In fact, all the time she carries a Tibetan "*Mala*" (prayer beads) with her and shows a tremendous respect for all types of animals, included the small cockroach that moves with ease around her office when we met again in the autumn of 2012. Buddhism has had such an influence on her, that she has chosen as a final logo for her *Rujin* business, the lotus flower, which also represents the healthy state of the women's vagina. She explains: "The lotus flower's roots are in the ground but, because of its very tall stem, the flower itself always stands high in the air. It is very beautiful and holy to Buddhists. This is why, when showing our logo at the beginning of our DVD corporate presentation, Buddhist religious music is also played."

When Gao Yu gets up in the morning, she feels good just by thinking that she has another day ahead to make a huge contribution to the prevention and treatment of women diseases and to help them live in harmony with life and nature.

A GOOD ENTREPRENEUR IS SOMEBODY THAT:

- *Does what she wants to do.*
- *Starts by being normal and knowing how not to be affected by the ups and downs of life.*
- *Starts small, but is able to manage and control growth.*
- *Knows how to develop a sustainable long-term business, by proceeding step-by-step.*
- *Needs to be successful, but not necessarily become a millionaire.*
- *Plays equal importance to the business results as well as to the integrity of the business.*
- *Knows how to delegate, and never forgets that managing employees is the key to success.*
- *Knows how to become the employees' best friend.*
- *Pays a lot of importance to training employees on corporate values.*
- *Pays vital importance to the quality of her products or services.*
- *Develops and applies the proper marketing tools.*
- *Continuously tracks the market.*
- *Knows the need to keep innovating and adapting as the market changes.*
- *Cares for others and tries to have a positive impact on people's living conditions and wellness.*

CHAPTER 4

The Entrepreneurship Process. Xu Xiaoyu, Bamboo Home

Xu Xiaoyu belongs to what could be named the transitional generation of Chinese entrepreneurs. The transitional generation consists of people recently trained in China who face the new challenges of China's competitive job market. These people most often are not the children of the older generation of entrepreneurs (people over forty-five years old) that has made China's development possible. Xu Xiaoyu was born in 1974; she has been steadily studying and learning new things since her arrival in Beijing where she completed her Master's in Agricultural Management.

In 2007, she decided to start her own business because, based on her working experience, she considered herself too old to find a reasonable management job related to her specialty of agricultural management.

Xu Xiaoyu was born in *Dongbei* (Northeast China), in Liaoning province, in a small village named Linjiatai, 160 kilometers from Dandong, not far from the North Korean border. She does not come from an entrepreneurial background. She has one brother, who is a year younger and is married to an English interpreter. He became an entrepreneur a couple of years before she did and sells video equipment to companies. Xu

Xiaoyu's parents were just employees in Dandong, where the entire family moved in 1980. Her father, a mechanical engineer, used to work in a government-owned refrigerator factory. Her mother, a Chinese language teacher, used to work in a public high school. They both retired from their jobs at the age of 55, when their respective factory and school were closed, but they have continued working since they need the money and consider it to be good for their health. Her father works as an engineer at a private factory, while her mother sells life insurance policies.

Xu Xiaoyu went to Beijing on her own in 1997, when she was 23 years old. She had been working in Dandong, while simultaneously studying, since she was 20 years old. First she worked for a year in a hotel, where she could practice her English while performing a number of tasks in the reception area and in the restaurant. Next, she worked for a company selling construction materials. Though both companies were very small, she did not like the jobs, and did the work just for the money, but she now realizes that the experience she gained in the construction materials company has been very useful to her in her entrepreneurial endeavors.

Xu Xiaoyu came to Beijing with the idea of finding a job where she could use her English in a big company. However, she did not manage to find one right away. After six months of looking for a job, during which time she was also studying English, she was hired by a small advertising company. She started working there in 1998 and remained until 2005, when she began her Master's studies and transitioned to her entrepreneurial life. At first, she did not like the job that she had at that company, but the salary was much higher than she would earn in Dandong, so she decided to remain there. In the beginning, the company only prepared advertisements for other companies. In 2003, as the advertising market became more competitive, the company expanded its services and began organizing agricultural-related events for the Chinese government. Clients included such important corporations as World Wildlife Fund, Siemens, Lenovo, and Kerui Group.

In this single-owner company, Xu Xioayu began performing administrative tasks and doing the editing and set-up of the ads, most of which were for use on television. Later, she began dealing with clients and doing telemarketing to support its business development. In 2002, when the company had grown from three employees to thirty, she became involved in internal management tasks and was promoted to be a Deputy General Manager. However, her remuneration (about RMB 50,000 annually, equivalent to about US$ 8,000 annually) was just a salary and did not include any bonus or profit-sharing.

At precisely that moment, Xu Xiaoyu decided to get formal training in marketing and management, which eventually ended in her undertaking her Master's studies. Xu Xiaoyu remembers this period of her life as stressful, because she was always worried about learning something new and keeping herself updated while preparing for her future challenges in the job market. In particular, she worried about learning everything about her industry before it changed too much and before she became too old to be considered a valuable employee.

Things have changed. Now, despite being an entrepreneur with most of the responsibilities on her side and always being busy, Xu Xiaoyu is quite relaxed. She does not worry about anything, nor does she worry about the future. The reason for this is that now she has faith in God and thinks God will help her overcome any problems that arise.

When Xu Xiaoyu became an entrepreneur, she had already embraced the Protestant faith. She had been baptized the year before. So, her main motivation in becoming directly involved in business was not to earn money for herself but to do it in order to be able to help other people. Her interest is particularly in helping poor women and their children to study and learn, so that they can live their lives in an easier, better way. Her additional motivation is to be able to disseminate the story of Jesus Christ everywhere. This makes Xu Xiaoyu a unique entrepreneur of her generation, since she has from the very beginning approached her entrepreneurial activities with a background mixing traditional Chinese values and Protestant values.

Xu Xiaoyu managed to attract to Protestantism both her own brother, who was baptized when she was, and her two business partners, who were not religious people before joining the business. Another example is that, in 2009, Xu Xiaoyu started reading the Bible regularly in her office to her employees and associates (which is pretty much the Protestant tradition).

Xu Xiaoyu realizes that she has changed a lot since she embraced the Protestant religion; the story for her brother is similar. Her sister-in-law is also a Protestant; her brother met his wife at a Protestant event, in which they participate regularly. Their parents do not really understand what their children are involved with, but they do not interfere. A friend of Xu Xiaoyu first introduced her to the Protestant faith. At that time, she did not know much about Protestantism or Catholicism and she might just as well have become involved in Catholicism instead, but since there are more Protestants in China, it was easier to come into contact with them.

Xu Xiaoyu met her future husband, also a Protestant, through a mutual Protestant friend. They married only a few months later in late 2009. In April 2011, their daughter was born. A divorced American, he had come to Beijing for a six-month assignment to help his client, a technology company, establish operations in China. When he met Xu Xiaoyu at her shop, they fell in love, so he decided to remain in Beijing running his advisory services company. However, he does not speak Mandarin (has not tried to learn it) and does not like to eat Chinese food.

Xu Xiaoyu recognizes that most Protestant Chinese may be reluctant to acknowledge that they follow this religion because according to the way they were raised, there was no place for religion in their lives. In this respect she is different: she feels the need to tell the world that Protestantism has changed her life, including her way of looking at everyday events. In addition, she believes that it is easier today for her and all Protestant people in China than it was before. The Chinese Government has become more open, perhaps because younger people are interested in other things than money and the material things in life. The number of Protestant students in Beijing universities keeps increasing over time, indicating that Chinese Protestants are finding a balance between the material and the spiritual.

When Xu Xiaoyu decided to pursue her Master's in Agricultural Management, she did so for two reasons: agriculture is a sector with a great future in China; and this was the first time that the *Zhongguo Nongye Daxue* (China Agriculture University, a school with an excellent reputation in China) was offering a Master's in *Nongye Guanli* (Agricultural Management). When she started her studies, her idea was not to become an entrepreneur, but to change her job, becoming either a teacher or a professor, or perhaps moving to a much bigger company. She started with great enthusiasm and high expectations, but was later disappointed with the university's teaching style. Instead of participating in interactive learning experiments with classmates, the classes were filled with lectures. She acknowledges that her disappointment stemmed from being exhausted from working fulltime while attending classes all weekend plus three evenings a week. In any case, Xu Xiaoyu believes that Chinese universities need to change to include a much more interactive style, one where someone besides the professor talks, and where the learning environment encourages teamwork.

In 2006, during the course of earning her Master's degree, Xu Xiaoyu realized that a woman of her age would find it difficult to acquire the kind of job that suited her new skills the best. At 30 years old, even if she could find something in the competitive Chinese market, she knew it would be almost impossible to develop a professional career in a big company.[1] She was inspired by the experience of her brother, since he decided to work for himself, and likewise began considering the possibility of becoming an entrepreneur. After realizing what an asset her situation was, lacking any significant financial responsibilities (that is, she was not married and had no children, unlike many Chinese people her age), she told herself that she would not merely think about becoming an entrepreneur, but actually do it.

She turned to a man from Dandong, a good friend from the time she worked at the construction materials company, and proposed they become business partners. This man, together with his brother, had already had a business in Dandong—a milk manufacturing facility—that he had sold because he wanted to start a new business. So, in Xu Xiaoyu's view, he was perfect for a business partnership because he possessed the entrepreneurial background she lacked. He agreed to become Xu Xiaoyu's partner and relocated to Beijing in 2006.

They did not know what kind of business they should develop and started investigating possibilities. It was actually Xu Xiaoyu's partner's idea to get involved in something related to bamboo products. In 2007, after graduating and leaving the advertising company, she and her partner performed a market study of bamboo products, traveling for six weeks to Shanghai, Shandong and Jiangsu to look for products that they could commercialize in Beijing. They focused on four privately owned factories, evaluating not only the quality of their products, but also the companies themselves while interacting and negotiating with the partners. At that time, none of those companies had any representatives in Beijing (but by 2009, all of them did). When the evaluation process was completed, they decided to use TENBRO brand fiber, which they considered the best.

TENBRO fiber, from *Shanghai Tianzhu Fangzhi Xiawei Youxian Gongsi* (Shanghai Tenbro Bamboo Textile Co. Ltd.), www.tenbro.com, is reputed to be the earliest and most professional bamboo fiber supplier in China, and a patent holder of multiple bamboo fiber products. They have been accredited by the State Intellectual Property Bureau, are owned by *Hebei Jigao* (Chemical Fiber Co. Ltd.), and have been engaged in bamboo fiber production for more than eight years. The production lines are believed to use the most advanced machines on the market, with a stable production capacity of 30,000 tons per year of bamboo fiber, and 50,000 tons per year of bamboo pulp. In 2002, TENBRO set up a spinning mill with 90,000 spindles. Most of the machines employed are imported, such as the AUTOCONER 338.

TENBRO bamboo fiber is made from select pollutant-free bamboo from Sichuan Province, where the company has built bamboo plantations to have greater control over the raw material. TENBRO has already passed the organic certification of OCIA/NOP. About 90% of TENBRO's products are exported. Textiles made of TENBRO fiber are characterized by their natural antibacterial and bacteriostatic properties, excellent permeability and coolness, moisture absorption, soft and smooth texture, excellent pigmentation, and ultra-violet-proof properties. In addition, bamboo fiber is a biodegradable material; its decomposition process does not create any environmental pollution. As a raw material, bamboo fiber is a natural, green and environmentally friendly textile. It can be spun purely or blended with cotton, hemp, thin silk, woolens, Tencel, Modal, polyester, and spandex, among other fibers.

For the commercialization of those bamboo products, they established a company named *Beijing Luse Chang Cheng Shangmao* (Beijing Green Great Wall Trade Co. Ltd., www.zhulincaotang.com). They began using the trademark *"zhujing fang"* (Bamboo Home) for their retail shops, the same trademark used by *Shanghai Tianzhu Fangzhi Xiawei Youxian Gongsi*, with whom they have a contract (signed in July 2007) to represent their products in Beijing. Their company was actually the very first that the Shanghai firm signed a representation contract with; as a result, they were eventually able to export 100% of their production. The first Bamboo Home shop Xu Xiaoyu's company opened in Beijing was the first retail shop in the China market offering the products of *Shanghai Tianzhu Fangzhi Xiawei Youxian Gongsi.* The contractual agreement Xu Xiaoyu and her partner negotiated was not a franchise, nor does it include a franchise fee, as it does not provide the franchise's typical services (for instance, the shop's design) except the products themselves. It is a pure product representation contract. Instead, the Beijing shop design was created by her own company—*Beijing Luse Chang Cheng Shangmao.*

Thus, in their shops they can sell bamboo products manufactured by other companies and, of course, bamboo products of their own design exclusively manufactured for them under their trademark *"zhulin caotang"* (Blessing Home). The only condition is that the products must be different from the ones manufactured by the Shanghai company. That was a critical point for both Xu Xiaoyu and her partner since their idea from the very beginning was not only to sell other companies' products, but also have their own brand on most of the products they sell. Their brand helps them differentiate their products in the market and helps guarantee the sustainability of their business. In fact, they have been following this model since 2010.

Product design is the area where they realized they could keep innovating and adding value. Since they performed their market study, they have seen that all manufacturing companies had more or less the same limited range of bamboo products. In fact, the reason they selected *Shanghai Tianzhu Fangzhi Xiawei Youxian Gongsi* for their *hezuo* (partnership) has nothing to do with their range of products, but with their quality. This company had already been in the market exporting to more than twenty countries for nine years, while the others have only been doing so for three years.

When the details of the business were well worked out, Xu Xiaoyu and her partner realized that they were going to need somebody to take care of administration and finance. Xu Xiaoyu contacted a woman she had worked with for seven years at her previous firm and convinced her to join them, giving her 5% of the company's shares as compensation. With this arrangement, Xu Xiaoyu still remained the biggest shareholder, owning over 50% of the shares, while her original partner retains over 40%.

As to the sharing of responsibilities, from the beginning, her partner took care of the logistics and inventory management, while Xu Xiaoyu worked as the Managing Director, which includes almost all the remaining functions (including market research, business development, new product design, contacts with new factories/procurement, shop management, and client service). A function she has devoted much of her attention to is business development with corporate clients. This aspect of the business has been much more affected by the turmoil of the economy than have retail sales (for instance, in 2009 corporate sales decreased by 50%, leading to a 40% decrease in the total sales turnover of the company).

When Xu Xiaoyu got pregnant, she decided to start decreasing her involvement in running the business, so that her two partners could take care of her responsibilities by the time her child was born. She knew this would involve modifying her original business development plans and she realized that the business expansion would suffer as a result, but she did not have the slightest doubt about prioritizing her child's care ahead of her career and business. In fact, she always planned to breastfeed her daughter during her first year of life, at a minimum.

Xu Xiaoyu acknowledges that, since she left her business development responsibilities, none of her partners really took them over; as a result, her business has very few new clients and has not grown. The impact on her company's sales turnover is obvious: it has decreased from the RMB 1.6 Million, in 2009, to the current 1.3 Million. The main impact has been in corporate sales, which have decreased from the previous 60% to the current 48% of their total sales turnover. About 80% of their corporate sales come from the clients she brought on board. Xu Xiaoyu believes that her male partner has no time to devote to business development, since he did not take over any of her previous business functions; her female partner took some over, but her attitude and capabilities were not appropriate. So, all their new clients since she stopped working on business development have simply walked into their business by themselves, not as a result of any active marketing initiatives. However, despite the increase in retail competition in Beijing, her business's annual profits still remain around 20% of the sales turnover. These profits have been continuously reinvested in the company, so that the partners have kept the low salaries they started with—in the case of Xu Xiaoyu, just RMB 100,000 a year. She explains that today becoming an entrepreneur in China is as difficult as it probably is in other places of the world and that people do it not to become millionaires but, in many instances, just as a working lifestyle—to be more independent, and to have the possibility to decide how to manage their careers and businesses.

Xu Xiaoyu acknowledges that her entrepreneurial style is not necessarily the same as that of the previous generation, who normally tended to start their business by themselves or with family members as partners. However, from the very beginning, she realized the importance of starting the business with others (partners she trusted, of course) because she knew that, when a new company gets started, there are many tasks to be accomplished and to be responsible for; too many to be undertaken by just one person.

Apart from the three partners, Xu Xiaoyu's company has three additional employees: one shop assistant; one person responsible for Internet sales (which they expect will grow over time); and one accountant working part-time. The shop assistant is a cousin of Xu Xiaoyu's to whom, following the Confucian tradition, she offered the opportunity to come to Beijing to work in her company.

FOR XU XIAOYU, STARTING A BUSINESS WITH PARTNERS IS VERY IMPORTANT because when a new company gets started there are many tasks to be accomplished and to be responsible for.

They now have two shops in Beijing. One is in *Hepingli*, which opened in autumn 2007; a second shop opened on *Beisanhuang Anzhang Qiao*, about two years later. They are selling Shanghai Tenbro Bamboo Textile Co., Ltd. products as well as their own products, which have been designed with the help of some third-party collaborators. The products include towels, socks, underwear, bed sheets, scarves, and clothing for both men and women. The main difference between Shanghai's products and their own is that this uses better fabric and more beautiful designs and colors. The shop at Hepinli is named *Zhulin Caotang*—their own products' brand—and they have relocated their office close by. The shop at *Beisanhuang Anzhang Qiao*, which still uses the original name

Zhujing Fang (Bamboo Home), was originally run by her staff. However, a year later, in autumn 2010, Xu Xiaoyu decided to pass the shop on to a friend she knew from her Protestant circles; since then, he has served as a distributor of her products, which they sell to him at a 40% discount.

Before Xu Xiaoyu got married and had her child, her business plan included the franchising of their trademark in Beijing and all over China. Because franchising has such a long way to go in the China market, she had extremely ambitious plans: to own ten shops in Beijing and 500 in China. For the design of all the future shops, she was planning to use their second Beijing shop as the model. As was the case with their first shop, all the walls were covered with bamboo stalks, but with a much more modern appearance. However, because of her marriage and the many rapid changes it introduced to her life, as well as her realization of how extremely competitive the bamboo fabric product market was becoming, Xu Xiaoyu decided not to implement her franchising plan, turning instead to e-commerce for her business expansion. This is, in fact, where she will be putting all her efforts when she goes back to business, once her daughter's breast-feeding period and pre-school process are over. She thinks e-commerce has grown steadily in China and has the advantage that people can buy twenty-four hours a day. Xu Xiaoyu acknowledges that to start and manage a virtual shop she will have to find someone to help her. She thinks a partner would have the advantage of providing additional funding for it, but an associate or just an employee could also be a possibility. For the e-commerce website, she plans to use a different brand name than that being used for her physical retail shops, but the products will continue to bear the same brand name, although the e-commerce products will have to be cheaper and slightly different in design. In her opinion, cheaper prices are what customers are looking for when buying on the Internet.

Xu Xiaoyu is happy with the products her business is dealing with because the bamboo fabric offers many advantages over other fabrics; in particular:

- Bamboo fiber is softer than the softest cotton, has a natural sheen to its surface and feels similar to silk or cashmere.
- Bamboo absorbs water three to four times better than cotton, keeping skin comfortable, rather than sticky, in hot weather.

- Bamboo stays two to three degrees cooler in hot temperatures and warmer in cooler temperatures.
- Bamboo clothing is naturally antimicrobial, requiring no added harmful chemicals.
- Bamboo apparel is thermal regulating, anti-fungal, anti-static, and will keep you cooler, drier, warmer, and odor free.
- Bamboo fiber is 100% biodegradable.
- Bamboo is grown without using pesticides or chemical fertilizers.
- Bamboo requires no irrigation.
- Bamboo rarely needs replanting.
- Bamboo grows rapidly and can be harvested in three to five years.
- Bamboo produces 35% more oxygen that an equivalent number of trees.
- Bamboo is a critical element in the balance of oxygen and carbon dioxide in the atmosphere.
- Bamboo is an excellent soil erosion inhibitor.

But most of all, and despite the workload she has experienced over the last few years, Xu Xiaoyu is happy with her life today, not only because she has a happy family, but also because, just as previously she managed to set aside time to go to church, which was extremely important to her, she continues to do that even now. Before having her daughter, she went to church every Tuesday and Thursday evening, going Saturdays to study the Bible and on Sundays for Mass. Now because of her daughter she cannot attend the Bible study group meetings; she only has time to go to church on Sundays. To compensate, she tries to keep as many Protestant habits as possible at home (for instance, to say grace before each meal) and to set aside time to keep reading religious books.

Since Xu Xiaoyu started her own business, she gets up every morning feeling good just by thinking that she has another day ahead to earn money to help other people and to spread the teachings of Jesus Christ and the Bible. Now married and with a baby daughter, she has less time to do this, but she also feels wonderful about sharing Jesus' love with her new family.

THE ENTERPRENEURSHIP PROCESS INVOLVES:

- Looking for the right partners.
- Looking for the best product available in the market.
- Negotiating and signing the most appropriate contract with one's associates.
- Developing and implementing the right business strategy.
- Appropriately sharing the responsibilities among the partners.
- Having clarity from the very beginning about the need to innovate to remain competitive in the market.
- Making the right decisions at the right moments and implementing all needed actions to make them happen.
- Being able to integrate business expansion with one's personal life.
- Not making the business grow at any price.
- Not being in a hurry to become rich. There is time for everything in life.
- Earning money to help others live a happy life.

CHAPTER 5

Entrepreneurship by Innovation in Management. Yang Mianmian, Haier

The origins of Haier date back to the early 1920s, when a refrigerator factory was built in *Qingdao* to supply to the Chinese market. After the establishment of the People's Republic of China in 1949, the factory was taken over and turned into a state-owned enterprise.

By the 1980s, the factory had accumulated a deficit of over RMB 1.47 Million (about €147,000) and suffered from a dilapidated infrastructure, poor management, and a lack of quality control as a result of the planned economic system. Production had slowed to a trickle, rarely surpassing 80 refrigerators a month, and there were mountains of unsold products. Morale was low among the 600 employees and the factory was close to bankruptcy. In desperation, the *Qingdao* government turned to a young assistant city manager, Zhang Ruimin, who was responsible for a number of city-owned appliance companies. He was an avid reader of Western and Japanese business practices and management techniques.

Zhang was appointed managing director of the factory in 1984. He brought with him another addition to the management team, a person who became known over time as his "golden partner." This person was Yang Mianmian, who Zhang Ruimin defined as being "different from the others; while her peers go to buy food, wash clothes, knit and do all kinds of similar things, during working time, she is always involved in serious readings." In fact, she was the only woman in his management team and the first female engineer in the factory.

The oldest of her parents' five children, Yang Mianmian was born in August 1941 in Shanghai. Her father was an electrical machines engineer and her mother was a nurse. Both had management and entrepreneurial abilities, which their children could sense. Since her mother did not like the household chores, they always had a maid at home. Her mother was a very open person, who wanted the children to travel and visit other places. Perhaps because of this, Yang Mianmian's sisters and brother now live in different places (Shanghai, Beijing, Hong Kong, and the United States). Yang Mianmian always felt different from them. She had a strong character and always knew that she wanted to follow her father's example and study engineering. In 1958 she moved to Jinan, Shandong province, to attend the Shandong Industrial Institute (today Shandong University). She graduated in 1963 with a degree in internal combustion engines engineering and never returned to Shanghai. Upon graduation she was sent to Qingdao as a school teacher. She remained there until 1968, except for one year (between 1965 and 1966) in which she was sent to the countryside, to nearby Pingdu. During those years working at the school in Qingdao, Yang Mianmian kept studying. She managed to follow every full week of work with a week off for studying, which was ideal for her, since she just wanted to learn new things. From Qingdao she was sent to an automobile factory to work in engineering and designing tasks, which she found highly enjoyable and interesting. In 1978, she was sent to work in a hospital to perform managerial tasks. By the time Yang Mianmian joined Haier she was the mother of two teenaged girls who, despite their parents' studies in engineering, chose not to follow the same path, instead pursuing other fields which they found more interesting, such as foreign trade.

When Zhang Ruimin took Yang Mianmian as part of his team, she simply thought, "It is my opportunity to help Zhang Ruimin and work side-by-side with him, so I shall be happy." Their goal was to turn the factory around and generate profits in a very short period of time. But she acknowledges today that she did not realize at that time how difficult and stressful the situation would be in the Qingdao refrigerator factory. She also could not imagine that, from such an unpromising state, the company could be reconstructed and developed to become the world leader that it is today.

In 1984, China's economy—and business leaders—were gradually breaking the ice. Yang Mianmian did not have a market economy's management background. Neither did Zhang Ruimin. He began by emphasizing quality and brand development, and by developing an internal culture of entrepreneurship, as prerequisites for the development of a long-term sustainable business. Yang Mianmian immediately became an active promoter of his approaches and strategies and the ideal partner to complement Zhang Ruimin's entrepreneurial and leadership abilities. The history of the Haier that we know today would not have been the same without these two people working together side-by-side, complementing each other, in reshaping the business. Without Zhang Ruimin there would not be Haier's unique corporate culture today. Without Yang Mianmian these cultural principles would have been only theory, and would have not filtered down to pervade the whole organization. She explains it in this way: "our CEO thinks a lot and I help him implement those thoughts. At Haier, we have always thought that strategies can only be and shall be tested in fields and that the essence of management is not in knowledge, but in performance. When I speak, employees began writing down. They know that they shall not just listen, but understand what is being said. They do know that time counts and they shall not lose any bit of it. They do also know that what is important is not just to think, but to act and to act in the right way. They do know the importance of each of them being aligned with the company's goals. As Sun Tzu did, we have always believed at Haier that "victory comes when the team and the leadership do share the same goals. At Haier we know that only if the employees and the customers are successful, can the company be successful." Zhang Ruimin and Yang Mianmian's joint achievements have been described as "*tian yi wu feng*",[1] meaning very skillful and flawless.

Yang Mianmian is today the President and Executive Vice-chairwoman of the Board of Directors of Haier Group Company. She is involved in the formulation and implementation of corporate strategies and in the supervision of the overall management of the Group. She has been in charge of the management of the white goods business since 1984, when she joined the company. She has served as the Chairwoman and an Executive Director of Haier Electronics Company since January 2005. She is the Chairwoman of Qingdao Haier Co., Ltd. (a company listed on the Shanghai Stock Exchange). Although she could have retired long time ago (and is in fact a grandmother since 2002, of two grandchildren), and her husband retired a long time ago, she keeps saying "as long as I am useful to the company, I will keep working. Haier for me is like my third daughter and working makes me feel good." And so she does, wearing every day the company's uniform, as "everybody does at Haier, both at China and abroad," she says.

Fortune ranked Yang Mianmian for three consecutive years—2006, 2007, and 2008—as one of the "World's Most Powerful Women." She is the only Chinese woman to have won such an honour for three consecutive years. Forbes ranked her in 2007, 2010, and 2012 as one of the "World's 50 Most Powerful Women in Business," referring to her as "one of the most influential Chinese business women." Despite having been ranked worldwide and having received so many nominations and awards in China, Yang Mianmian's open and close communication style has not changed. She remains accessible, answers all kinds of questions with an open mind, laughs and makes jokes very often, is full of vitality, seems to feel always happy and relaxed, creates a calm atmosphere around her, and truly focuses on the person in front of her, when this is the task she has to perform. If she could communicate in English, there is no doubt she would have been rated higher in the International rankings, for she is a very unique (woman) entrepreneur and leader. Listening to her describe Haier's evolution and management model, one can feel how much of a first class entrepreneur and strong business leader she really is.

The History of Haier

Brand Building Phase (1984–1991)

When Zhang Ruimin and Yang Mianmian arrived at the refrigerator factory in 1984, they realized that the poor condition of the factory's quality controls was endangering its continued survival. They saw that workers knew how to do things correctly, but that their attitudes were preventing them from proceeding this way. So, upon their arrival, Zhang Ruimin and Yang Mianmian put a stronger emphasis on the development and implementation of procedures than on training. Other tough measures were also undertaken to change workers' attitudes. The most famous action was taken in 1985, when a customer brought a faulty refrigerator back to the factory and showed it to Zhang Ruimin. He and the customer then went through the entire inventory of around 400 refrigerators looking for a replacement. In the process, he discovered that there was a 20% failure rate in the merchandise, 76 refrigerators in total. To emphasize the importance of product quality, Zhang had the 76 dud refrigerators lined up on the factory floor. He then distributed sledgehammers to the employees and ordered them to destroy the refrigerators. The workers were hesitant; the cost of a refrigerator at the time was about two years' worth of wages. Seeing their distress, Zhang said: "Destroy them! If we pass these 76 refrigerators for sale, we will be continuing the mistake that has bankrupted our company." The refrigerators were smashed to pieces. One of the hammers is on display at the company headquarters for posterity and as a reminder to Haier staff of the crucial importance of quality. Haier's "Brand Building Strategy" and the "Zero Defect" quality standards were thus established.

In 1984, Haier had been founded as Qingdao Refrigerator Co. and, with China opening up to world markets and foreign corporations beginning to search for partnerships in China, Zhang Ruimin and Yang Mianmian decided to enter into a joint-venture contract with Germany's Liebherr Group.[2] Under this contract, Liebherr offered technology and equipment to *Qingdao* Refrigerator Co. and refrigerators were manufactured under the name of *Qingdao-Libohaier* (Qingdao-Liebherr). To show the cooperation between China and Germany a mascot was developed: the "Haier Brothers," a Chinese boy and a foreign boy united for a promising joint-future; it has remained Haier's mascot until today. Seventeen *Qingdao* employees were sent to Germany to learn as much as possible about Liebherr technology and management. They received practical training at various levels. Apart from Zhang Ruimin and Yang Mianmian (the only two engineers of the team), there were five engineering university students and ten workers who did not have any degree. Germans treated them very well (Yang Mianmian in particular, because she was different, not simply one more male engineer) and were very happy with them because they could see how diligently the team learnt and also that in the evening, after work, they did not stop to enjoy the place, but kept studying. The team spent a month in Germany, except Yang Mianmian who remained there for a couple of months. During this time, she could see how reliable German technology and people were, how quickly and efficiently German employees would work, and what excellent attitudes they had about their work. This was the confirmation to her that their decision to team with a German company was a good one, and for Yang Mianmian this was an experience she will never forget. "I learned all I could learn about how things work in a company when employees' attitude to work is very good. This is the precious treasure I took with me from Germany. How to manage I learned by myself, but the difference in the attitude to work, this I could have never learned alone, here in China. So, when coming back, all I had to do was to apply what I had learned in our Chinese environment and for this I worked many long hours upon my return, so many that my life just moved around work those days," explains Yang Mianmian.

The installation of Liebherr's equipment and technology was accompanied by a new and rigorous commitment to quality. Zhang Ruimin and Yang Mianmian applied disciplined management techniques and procedures aimed to change employees' work attitude, the constant priority for them, believing that "repeated problems are problems of attitude." With the combination of all these strategies, and in addition to employees' training, the company eventually began to turn around. Yang Mianmian remembers that it was not an easy process, not something that happened from one day to the next, but step-by-step they managed, in a very short period of time, to make their employees transform their previous culture of "*dou keyi*" (that is, "todo vale" or "anything goes") and understand the importance of quality. If the quality of their products was good, there would be no more faulty products returned to them. The work that Yang Mianmian did side-by-side with Zhang Ruimin for this to happen was very important and somewhat unique. In Yang Mianmian's words, "Zhang Ruimin's attractive personality helped us to accomplish our goal. Since those days, we have always remembered at Haier that our team leaders have to create an atmosphere full of vitality." By 1986,

Qingdao Refrigerator Co. had returned to profitability (RMB 1 million profits) and sales growth averaged 83% per year. This growth continued over time so much that, as an example, the RMB 3.5 million sales of 1984 rocketed to RMB 40.5 billion by 2000, a growth of more than 11,500%. With the success of Qingdao Refrigerator Co., the municipal government asked the company to take over some of the city's other ailing appliance makers. In 1988, the company assumed control of Qingdao Electroplating Company, which was making microwaves.

In 1990, after the restructuring of the Qingdao Refrigerator Factory and the diversification of its product line beyond refrigerators, the company adopted a new name: Qingdao Haier Company Ltd. The word "Haier" was taken from the last two syllables of the Chinese transliteration of its German partner Liebherr (*Libo-Haier*, in Mandarin), who permitted the JV company to also use its logo during this early stage of Haier's development. In that same year, Haier exported its first batch of (20,000) refrigerators to Europe, with Germany as the first destination. In 1991, Haier took over Qingdao Air Conditioner Plant and Qingdao Freezer; the same year the so-called "brand-building phase" was completed and The Qingdao Haier Group was established.

By only focusing on refrigerators, Haier was able to accumulate valuable business and management experience, which allowed the company to build a management model that could be used with future business units. Haier was able to transform itself from a small factory operating at an annual loss of nearly RMB 1.4 million into the number one refrigerator brand in China with about 1,000 employees.

Diversification Development Phase (1991–1998)

In the 1980s, demand vastly exceeded supply, with Chinese firms generally setting sales targets based on production capacity. By the early 1990s, however, the situation had reversed, dealing a significant blow to the strategies of the past decade. Many home appliance manufacturers chose to compete on the basis of price, which provided occasional short-term market gains but reduced their capacity for further innovation and corporate development.

Haier observed that marketing was less about beating annual sales quotas and more about winning the hearts of the customers. The reduced demand in the 1990s did not mean the market had reached the limits of its potential, but rather that products were not meeting the expectations of increasingly savvy consumers. So, the company established its "Diversification Strategy" to expand the Haier brand beyond refrigerators, adding washing machines, air conditioners, and other items to its product line. At the same time, Haier did extensive consumer research, listening to its customers and even regarding complaints as a valuable tool for refining corporate strategy, which further bolstered customer loyalty to the Haier brand. While most enterprises became engaged in a price war, Haier gained competitive advantages by adopting for the very first time in China the "zero worry" system, which is "you call, we do the rest of the things."

In its new growth track alone, after breaking the relationship with Liebherr, the company set out to establish itself as the country's leading brand, focusing upon reliability and product quality. Yang Mianmian acknowledges that this diversification process could not have been possible had they continued with Liebheer, so the only solution was to go their own way, since they were convinced that diversification was also going to allow Haier to spread out its risk among various product lines. In 1992, Haier got the ISO 9001 accreditation, being the first Chinese white goods manufacturer to get this. In 1993, its name was simplified to Haier Group—the company's current name—and a logo, containing an English version of the pinyin "Haier," was designed. In this same year, Haier Refrigerator Company was listed on the Shanghai Stock Exchange, and Haier refrigerators and other products entered the Middle East and African markets. In 1995, the same year Haier opened its new factory in Qingdao—"we needed to expand very fast," explains Yang Mianmian— Haier bought out its chief rival *Qingdao* Red Star (*Hongxing*) Electric Appliances Stock Co., Ltd. and took just three months to reshape its extremely poor performance.

In that same year, Haier began to export its products to the United States of America, initially under the name of Original Equipment Manufacturer (OEM), and later with Haier branded products. Haier's move into the United States (US) market was cautious at first; it focused on two market niches: compact refrigerators and electric wine cellars. Both markets were underdeveloped, but Haier believed that they both had growth potential and were being largely neglected. This was, in fact, why they decided to choose this market niche and avoided facing the major US market competitors. The company's sales figures soon proved their belief correct, allowing Haier to firmly establish itself in its US niches. In three years, Haier acquired 30% of the compact refrigerators' market share, combatting competitors by adding new features, such as mini-fridges that doubled as computer desks. As a result, Haier got the attention of major US retail chains, including Wal-Mart and Best Buy.

In 1996, Haier adopted the OEC Management approach (as seen below), which proved to be the key to successful expansion of the business. In the same year, Haier also began its expansion in Asia with the establishment of local assembly plants in Southeast Asia—in Indonesia in 1996, and the Philippines and Malaysia in 1997. In the same year, the company moved into television manufacturing with the acquisition of Yellow Mountain (*Huangshan*) Electronics Group. Haier's entry into the color television industry marks the company's first foray into the brown goods market. Altogether, from 1984 to 1998, Haier acquired 18 companies that were losing, in total, RMB 550 million, and activated the assets with a total amount of RMB 1.42 billion, through restructuring, recapitalization and recovery of idle assets. By introducing Haier's management team and corporate culture into these companies, Haier was able to activate the "shocked fish" (as seen below), helping these struggling firms to maximize their latent corporate potential. Among the companies acquired (apart from the aforementioned) were: Wuhan Xi Dao Industrial Stock Co., Ltd., Laiyang General Household Appliances Plant and Hefei Yellow Mount Television Plant.

In 1984, Haier had only refrigerators; by 1998, when its "diversification development phase" was completed, it had dozens of products in both the white and the brown goods, including washing machines, freezers, air conditioners, televisions, and water heaters. Haier's management strategy of focusing on quality and doing whatever necessary to increase it[3] has already proved to be successful. In December 1998, Haier refrigerators won the first National Quality Gold Medal, the first such award in China's refrigerator industry, which established Haier as the number one refrigerator manufacturer in China. By the end of the 1990s, by using intangible assets to get the most out of the existing tangible assets, Haier had captured a dominant market share in its core white goods division, and was the most recognized brand in China, with products ranging from mobile phones to computers.

Globalization Phase (1998–2005)

Yang Mianmian explains how Haier saw that, in the twenty-first century, globalization provided opportunities for Chinese companies to earn foreign exchange by leveraging lower production costs and functioning as an original equipment manufacturer (OEM), for multinational corporations (MNCs). But Haier also saw that, as China developed economically, rising labor costs were going to mean that China's time as the world's "factory floor" would soon be coming to an end and that many MNCs were going to shift their production facilities to other countries, such as Vietnam, which offered lower labor costs. So, Haier thought that only those MNCs with their own proprietary intellectual property and strong brand identities would be competitive in the world business arena. Faced with this reality and having secured its positioning in the domestic market, Haier knew the time was right to enter the international stage with the goal of building a global brand name. So, it launched the "globalization phase", which lasted until 2005. To achieve this, Haier developed and implemented a three-step globalization strategy: (1) enter the international mainstream markets; (2) utilize main sales channels to deepen market penetration; and (3) establish Haier as an internationally recognized global brand. It also established the strategy that "market development precedes production plants," meaning that a manufacturing facility in a foreign market shall not be built until it has been confirmed that there is enough market demand for it.

With its success exporting compact refrigerators and wine cellars to the US, Haier made further progress in the North American market by moving into the full-sized refrigerator category, bringing the company into direct competition with established American giants such as GE, Whirlpool, Frigidaire, and Maytag. Haier America was established in 1999, and as part of its strategy, Haier decided to build a production facility in the United States at Camden, South Carolina, which opened in the year 2000 (Haier America Refrigerator Corp. Ltd.). It was the first

Haier overseas industrial complex: Haier America Industrial Park. With a design center in Los Angeles, a marketing center in New York, and a manufacturing facility in South Carolina, Haier established its first international "Three-in-One operational framework." In 2001, Haier compact refrigerators had taken the biggest market share. By 2002, US revenues reached USD$ 200 million, still small when compared to its overall revenue of US$ 7 billion and its very ambitious goal of reaching US$ 1 billion and 10% of the US refrigerator market. To show its ambition to the world, in 2002, Haier moved into a landmark building in midtown Manhattan, formerly the headquarters for the Greenwich Savings Bank, a 4,800 m² building built in 1924 in the neo-classical style. The building was renamed the "Haier Building," and Haier America has been headquartered in this building since then. In 2003, Haier's South Carolina plant began producing full size refrigerators, based on the idea that since Haier products were produced and sold in the US following American people's habits and desires, American consumers could see Haier as an American brand. They began targeting, in particular, lower-income young people and college students, who were attracted to the competitive pricing of Haier's compact appliances. By 2005, Haier had 50% of the wine cellars market, 26% of the compact refrigerators market share, and 17% of air conditioners sales in the US.

Yang Mianmian still remembers how many people in China prevented them from establishing in the US and how, when Haier set up its first plant in the United States, an article was published with the title "A Caution to Zhang Ruimin," stating that it was going to be difficult for Haier to make its way into the United States and that others had already failed to do this. The caution was surely out of nice consideration, especially taking into account that it was the first manufacturing facility that Haier was establishing abroad, and that the US had the highest cost of labor. "Why did Haier want to go?" Yang Mianmian explains, "We used to say that it was because of China entering the World Trade Organization (WTO), which we had no choice, which in a way was true for the ambitious goals we have stated for ourselves. But, we have other reasons. We have seen that, when a foreign company established a plant in China, they had everything—except raw materials and cheap labor—which were the only things we had. So, in order to compete with the newcomers and globally, we needed to acquire state-of-the-art technology, fist-class management knowledge, and local financial support. And this is why we decided to establish ourselves in the US market, from where we were particularly interested in learning their management techniques. We also knew that it is the process of localization that makes a brand competitive in the local market and, as result of repeating the experience in other countries, worldwide. We knew that being a national brand was not enough. Time has shown us how right we were in our thinking. To be in the US market helped us a lot to internationally develop our brand and to learn a lot about how we should continue with our International expansion."

In the year 2000, Haier created Haier Europe, and in 2001, it purchased the Italian Menigati Refrigerator Company, which was the first cross-national acquisition by a white goods company from China. With the company's design and marketing centers in Milan, Haier achieved its goal of a Three-in-One Localization (localized design, manufacture, and marketing) in Europe, the second such framework in the world following Haier's success in the United States. Yang Mianmian explains that Italy was selected as the European head office on account of the longstanding tradition the country has in design and in the home appliance sector. The refrigerator plant was located in a geographically convenient area together with many plants from famous manufacturers like Whirlpool, CANDY, and Zanussi, which gave Haier an immediate visibility in the local market, while simultaneously projecting its scope into the rest of Europe. The acquisition provided Haier with a white goods production base in Europe (which included many other products, apart from refrigerators), as well as access to design and technology, local procurement procedures, the local manufacturers' association, and other local information, paving the way to accessing local funds, human resources, and customers in the European market.

In 2002, Haier entered the Bulgarian market as the first Chinese home appliance company to sell its products in Eastern Europe. In 2002, *ERT*, the largest home appliance magazine in the United Kingdom, reported that Haier products achieved an A+ for energy conservation. Haier's refrigerators were among the first A+-rated energy-saving products introduced into the European market. In 2003, Haier's Italian-manufactured products debuted at the two largest chain stores in Romania, after which Haier began exporting products to Bulgaria, Malta, the Czech Republic, Cyprus, Albania, Ukraine, and Russia. From the beginning of 2004, Haier products were present throughout Europe, with branch offices in Germany, Spain, France, and Italy. In that year, Haier home computers were introduced into the French market, making Haier the first Chinese company to export its own brand of computers overseas. Meanwhile, Haier's products continued receiving awards in the European market.

Along with the US and European expansions, Haier continued to enter other international markets as well. In 2001, production facilities were constructed in Pakistan and Nigeria. In 2002, Haier formed a joint venture in Tunisia to manufacture white goods. In 2002, Haier and Sanyo established a joint venture to distribute Haier products in the Japanese market. The Sino-Japanese cooperation invented by Haier CEO Zhang Ruimin and Sanyo President Satoshi Lue has been praised, as the Asian model to follow, by the world community.[4] Haier's products were distributed by the top Japanese retailers, such as YAMADA, KOJIMA, and JUSCO, and widely recognized by Japanese consumers. Also in 2002, Haier established trading companies in Malaysia and Thailand and Haier's products entered the Australian and New Zealand markets. In 2004, a production facility started to operate in Jordan and Haier Electronics Middle East Company was established in Dubai, greatly strengthening its position in the Middle East market. By 2004, Haier had become the number one home appliances company in China.

During the 17-year period from 1984 to 2001, Haier experienced an average annual growth rate of 78%. From 2001 to 2004, Haier Group's annual sales grew 1.7 times (and doubled in the US market), and its total exports more than tripled. By 2005, Haier had a new logo (the one that is being used until today) and had been able to establish a tripartite (design/ production/marketing) operational framework in six key regional markets: North America, Europe, Middle East/Africa, Asia-Pacific, ASEAN, and South Asia.

Global Brand Building Phase (2005–)

Yang Mianmian explains how, by 2005, she and Zhang Ruimin had already seen that there were many cultural differences between China and the markets Haier was already in, as well as other potential markets. It was clear that the best approach was to develop the Haier brand as a local brand in each of the local markets, while simultaneously having additional brands for the distinct local markets. As such, at the 21ˢᵗ anniversary of its founding, Haier announced the beginning of its "global brand building strategy phase." The new stage aims to create a localized Haier brand in each national market, promoting their competitive products and business management to generate win-win profits with their suppliers, and increase customers and users all over the world. The idea behind this developmental stage is to transform Haier from a culturally unitary organization to a multi-cultural one. "In the Globalization Phase, Haier is still based in China, radiating to the world; while in the Global Brand Building Phase, Haier aims to build a local Haier brand in each geographic area all around the world," explains Yang Mianmian. For Haier, the essence of globalization is localization, which means a "Three-in-One" operational framework: complete localization of design, manufacture, and marketing. It also aims to use local financing and employees to become a part of the local community while creating a global brand.

In 2005, Haier (Middle East) Industrial Park opened in Jordan, as the largest home appliance industrial park in the Middle East and Haier's largest overseas manufacturing complex. The industrial park became Haier's operations platform for the Middle East region, providing a base for Haier's products to be sold in surrounding countries including Syria, Lebanon, Egypt, and Palestine. In that same year, Haier Electronics Group Co., Ltd. was listed on the Main Board of the Stock Exchange of Hong Kong. Haier became the number two seller of air conditioners in the US and was ranked by Financial Times as the first of China's Top 10 Global Brands. With all these successes, Haier made a bid to acquire Maytag Corporation, but failed.[5]

By April 2006, the Haier Group had obtained 6,189 patented technology certificates (1,234 for Haier inventions) and 589 software intellectual property rights. In the same year, Haier launched the first high definition television in the US market and signed a partnership with the National Basketball Association, becoming the only global appliance sponsor of the NBA, and showing Haier's determination to become, just like NBA basketball, a part of mainstream American culture. Also in 2006, Haier established a joint venture with Sanyo Electric Co. Ltd., Haier-Sanyo Co. Ltd., to combine Chinese and Japanese values to improve their competitiveness in the global refrigerator industry. In November of that year, the Haier-Intel Innovative Products R&D Centre was established, beginning a new stage in Haier's computers business. In that same month, the Haier Ruba Economic Zone was opened in Pakistan, in the presence of the PRC President Hu Jintao. Also in 2006, Haier's "Casarte" high-end market brand was launched.

In 2007, Haier's cooling and purifying air conditioners obtained a US patent and the company was awarded a €24 million contract to provide 100,000 computers for the Macedonian Ministry of Education, the largest European order ever received by the company. Haier then signed with Cisco, a memorandum of understanding (MOU) on strategic cooperation and a comprehensive strategic cooperation MOU with Intel on the theme "Joining Hands to Create a Prosperous Future." Also in 2007, with the idea of beginning to profit from the rapidly growing Indian market, Haier acquired a refrigerator plant in India. Additionally, Haier (Thailand) purchased Sanyo's refrigerator factory in Thailand, making Haier the second largest refrigerator manufacturer in Thailand. In 2007, Haier launched a series of independent sub-brands, such as the Royal Bo double-door refrigerator, INNOV high-definition TV, and Casarte refrigerators, aimed at the high-end customers' segment.

In China, in November 2007, following the government's trend of beginning to foster national consumption, Haier launched its *Jia Dian Xia Xiang*—"Home Appliance Promotion in Rural Areas"—project, with the aim of developing products and solutions to satisfy rural users' needs. Yang Mianmian explains how Haier saw it as an opportunity to expand its market while serving the farmers' needs and continued resilience, despite the ups and downs of the government program. Under this project umbrella, Haier started to develop and implement products that provide solutions to issues that are specifically relevant to rural areas, such as: washing machines that are not accessible to mice, household appliances equipped to accommodate irregularities in electricity supply and the low safety education of rural customers, energy-saving and environmentally friendly products, solar panels and temperature control devices to be installed in animal farms, mobile phones and computers for self-education, etc. All these products would be customizable for rural customers who, for instance, could choose a particular color for their home appliances (for instance, when getting married).

On January 1, 2008, Haier Group level ERP systems, HGVS (Haier's global value system), arrived on the line, involving 35 divisions and 42 industry and trade companies, covering all product lines to achieve the streamlined "Four-in-One" flow of orders, logistics, information, and capital. Also in 2008, Haier was singled out for the second time, by Financial Times, as one of China's Top 10 Global Brands. Forbes also ranked Haier 13th. Haier was ranked as one of the "Top 600 World's Most Reputable Companies" with a top honor and the highest ranking of any Chinese enterprise. For eight consecutive years, The Asian Wall Street Journal's annual survey of the Top 200 Asian Companies has ranked Haier first among Mainland China companies for its leadership.

Haier was the sole white goods sponsor of the Beijing 2008 Olympic Games. In the same year, it surpassed rival Whirlpool as the world's top refrigerator producer in terms of sales: it sold 12 million refrigerators worldwide, up 20% from the previous year, amounting to a total of US$ 17.8 billion. Its market share reached 6.3% globally and 26.2%, the highest margin, in the Chinese market, where it claimed 30% of the high-end products' market share. In 2008 alone, Haier applied for 912 patents, with 525 of them patents of invention, which amounted to two invention patents per working day. By the end of 2008, Haier had applied for 8,795 patents (2,261 invention patents) and the brand was valued at RMB 80.3 billion.

Yang Mianmian says that in 2009, under the new financial crisis scenario, Haier changed its products' exportation model, which until then followed a 50% domestic market—50% exports approach. The company decided to begin prioritizing the domestic market and set a 60% domestic—40% exports goal for that year. To increase domestic sales and in cooperation with the Chinese government's "Rural Household Appliance Subsidy Program," Haier devoted additional attention to its "Home Appliance Promotion in Rural Areas" program. Meanwhile, Haier continued innovating and progressing in the international market. In the 2009 US market, for instance, Haier launched the new LED high-definition television and, in 2010, the Energy Star line of dishwashers.

Haier also continued developing new products for its "Casarte" high-end market brand and launched the "Casarte Casa Imperial" subbrand. In the autumn of 2011, Haier acquired from Panasonic Corp its Sanyo refrigeration and washing machine business units in Japan and Southeast Asia. This positioned Haier as one of the top five major appliance players in Japan, a market traditionally driven by domestic players.

Haier is today the world's No.1 brand of consumer appliances—representing 6.1% of global sales—and one of China's Top 100 IT Companies. It was selected in 2010 as one of the world's Top 10 innovative companies by USA Newsweek's website. Haier now manufactures home appliances in over 15,100 different specifications under 96 categories. The company has 10 industrial parks (4 of them abroad) and 30 production facilities (24 outside of China), 18 design centers (including the ones in Milan and Seoul), 8 R&D centers (5 outside of China, including Los Angeles and Tokyo), 16 industrial complexes (including the ones in the US, Jordan, Thailand, and Pakistan), 64 trading companies (19 outside of China), and over 240 subsidiaries all over the world. It employs over 70,000 employees worldwide (with over 10,000 of them outside of China), has a sales network of over 130,000 points, and has over 10,000 service centers all over the world. Its products are sold in over 160 countries. Despite the current economic turmoil, Haier's turnover has continued to see growth, increasing from US$ 18.25 billion in 2009 to US$ 26.29 billion in 2012. This has been particularly relevant in the international market, which increased from about 12% of the total 2009 turnover (US$ 2.2 billion) to around 16% of the total 2012 turnover (US$ 4.2 billion). More significant has been Haier's profitability increase, in particular between 2009 and 2010, during which time it grew from 2.8% to 4.5%. Profitability kept growing, though at a slower pace, reaching 4.8%. Yang Mianmian explains how the evolution of Haier's brand value (which rose to US$ 12.6 billion in 2010) is a manifestation of the positive changes introduced to transform it into a services company (as seen below). Apart from its listings in the Shanghai and Hong Kong Stock Exchanges, Haier is an index stock of the Dow Jones China 88 Index.[6]

Haier's global branding strategy aims at positioning the company as a local brand within the different world markets, in conjunction with enhanced product competitiveness and strong corporate operations. Haier's international business framework incorporates a global network of design, procurement, production, distribution, and after-sale services. It aims to provide integrated home appliances to meet the needs of global consumers through continuous innovation, stresses Yang Mianmian.

Haier has six businesses units: (1) white goods (refrigerators, air conditioners, washing machines, dishwashers, vacuum cleaners, water heaters, and kitchen appliances); (2) brown goods and digital and personal products (televisions, home theatre systems, DVD players, mobile phones, computers, and other digital information products); (3) client business solutions (central air-conditioning, integrated kitchen, interior decoration, medical equipment, and intelligent home appliances which include the U-home concept); (4) equipment components manufacturing group (plastic and metal plate production line and electric control integration); (5) retailing, including its own home appliance sales channels with Haier branded stores, franchises, and village-level chain stores; and (6) finance, which also includes its real estate business. Haier has been widely recognized as a leader of nine products in terms of domestic market shares and the 3rd biggest player of three products in the world market, as well as a world-class company in the fields of home integration, network appliances, digital and large scale integrated circuits, and new materials.[7]

Today, Haier is a provider of integrated solutions that include central air-conditioning systems, integrated kitchens, intelligent home appliances,[8] supermarket display cabinets, medical freezers, E-Home[9] and U-Home solutions,[10] and the Mitsubishi-Haier commercial air conditioner. Haier is currently placing an emphasis on E-Home and U-Home integration, while controlling its patent standards and further improving global marketing networks and creating more user resources. Yang Mianmian emphasizes that, particularly in China, it is this integral project approach—spanning from design to installation for entire buildings—that they are intensively promoting. For instance, Haier did this work for the Intercontinental Hotel in Qingdao. Haier's integrated solutions, as well as some of its most relevant products, are all visible in their huge Qingdao headquarters' showroom. Haier's U-Home digital home solution has been defined as an international standard by the International Electro-technical Commission, making it the first digital-home international standard owned by a Chinese company. Yang Mianmian considers this of great significance to the spread of internet usage in the digital home field and stresses how the first Internet-of-things refrigerator[11] was developed by Haier; Haier is on its way to further innovations in the field of Internet-of-things appliances.

In China, Haier's four leading product categories—refrigerators, refrigerating cabinets, air conditioners, and washing machines—hold over 30% of the market share. In addition to high-quality home appliances, Haier is also focused on offering best-of-breed service solutions to its customers. Haier's service system spans throughout the production process, from product design, production, and manufacturing, to pre-sale, sales, and after-sales service. Since 2002, Haier has successfully established a network of over 5,000 domestic professional service suppliers to deliver timely customized service. In China, Haier employs more than 40,000 people (80% of which are between 30 and 40 years old and 30% of which are women) and has 12 industrial parks (with the biggest one located in *Qingdao Kaifa Qu Gongye Yuan*—*Qingdao* Development Zone Industrial Park), five manufacturing bases, and 42 trading companies. It has strategic alliances with Sunning and Gome chain stores, among others. Over the years, Haier has also been significantly contributing to the welfare of Chinese society.[12]

Despite how easy it all looks today, Yang Mianmian still remembers how difficult it actually was. She recalls, for instance, how much the company struggled to get financing to develop the different manufacturing facilities in China. Initially, they acquired funds to relocate their *Qingdao* factory, but then had to wait until it was finished to get the financing for their second one; the same went for building the third one, and so forth. They also needed a lot of capital for the development of new products; they had to do it fast, knowing they could not wait because the market was not going to wait for them, but "we had to struggle to get the required financing anyway," she says, while laughing. She also stresses how the situation in their company has changed since she came on as the sole woman engineer of only two engineers—she and Zhang Ruimin. Today, Haier employs over 15,000 people, a third of which are *waidiren* (Chinese not originally from the place where they are working) living on the corporate premises. Now 40% of the staff is composed of engineers, but only 20% of these engineers are women. In the management team, 25% of the members are women.

Haier corporate headquarters' international department has about 200 employees, 5% of whom are foreigners (older than the average Chinese employee) and 20% of whom are Chinese who graduated abroad, a recent trend that will help Haier's globalization process.

In overseas markets, Haier has established its own home appliance sales channels with Haier branded stores, franchises, and village-level chain stores. Haier products are available in twelve of the top fifteen chain stores in Europe (such as DARTY, KESA, Media Market, and Carrefour) and in the top ten US retailers (SEARS, Lowe's, HOME DEPOT, Best Buy, PC-Richard, Wal-Mart, Sam's, Costco, BrandsMart, and Target). Haier is now approaching its goal of being "local" in American and European markets via localized design, manufacturing and sales processes. Haier has also tapped into the finance and real estate businesses.

Haier America has established successful trade partner relationships not only all throughout the US, but also in Canada, Mexico, and the rest of Latin America. In this region, the Haier Group is directly expanding its activities today; for instance, it has been doing extremely well in Cuba and more recently in Venezuela, where it has entered into a joint-venture agreement with the government. In Africa, Haier has plants in five countries—Tunisia, Nigeria, Egypt, Algeria, and South Africa—and has established a dealer network for the local market in more than 20 African countries, to directly or indirectly provide a full range of cost-effective products. It also has sourcing cooperation agreements with companies such as White Whale in Egypt.

Today, Haier Europe coordinates the marketing and sales of Haier brand home appliances in 17 European countries: United Kingdom, Ireland, Germany, Netherlands, Belgium, France, Luxembourg, Greece, Spain, Portugal, Switzerland, Austria, Italy, Denmark, Norway, Finland, and Sweden. Haier Europe also runs all logistic activities through four distribution centres serving the entire European market, located in Spain, the United Kingdom, Holland, and Italy. More than 96% of the staff at Haier's European operations is composed of local employees. In 2009, Haier Europe decided to move its headquarters from Milan to Paris, where it still keeps a portion of Chinese employees (about 2%) to help coordinate with Haier's corporate headquarters.

Yang Mianmian emphasizes that Haier has long been a proponent of innovation in satisfying the demands of worldwide consumers and achieving win-win situations together with its clients.[13] Haier's patent applications total over 10,000, ranking first among Chinese home appliance firms. Haier has participated in the drafting of 51 international standards, 27 of which have been issued and implemented. It has also been involved in the formulation and modification of over 200 national standards. Haier invests over 6% of its annual sales revenue into R&D.[14] "We are always developing new products," she stresses.

When in 2011 Haier participated in the IFA Berlin trade fair—the world's largest and most important trade show for consumer electronics and home appliances—Yang Mianmian recalls that visitors could see that Haier's products were no longer cheap, and could recognize their innovation. Their prices were comparable to those of traditional world-recognized trademarks, such as Bosch and Siemens. This and the associated higher margins explain why Haier's turnover in Europe grew over 80% between 2010 and 2011. This same trend—higher prices plus higher margins—has been experimented within other markets, pointing to Haier's future growth trajectory.

To illustrate Haier's constant innovation process, Yang Mianmian recalls how in April of 2007, seeing the transformation that the sector was experiencing, Haier launched a 1,000-day information management revolution, which involved restructuring organizational frameworks, processes, and personnel. Haier's design centers, manufacturing bases, and trading companies in over 30 countries have since come together to share global resources through a single information platform. The integration of its global resources will allow Haier to satisfy consumers' needs all over the world. By integrating its centers around the world, Haier created a 1+1+N team without borders. Through tapping the global marketplace of ideas, innovations, and human resources, the company has improved its ability to confront challenges and develop timely, effective solutions.

She also explains how, when Haier launched its "Global Brand Building Strategy Phase", it saw that with the flattening of the world through the development of information technology and ever-faster global economic integration, companies cannot satisfy consumer requirements on their own. Haier believes that no individual, company, or country can survive without the support of a wider community and that finding a way to integrate individual talents is the key to future success.

In the "diversification stage," Haier vitalized the assets by mobilizing its employees to work hard toward the sustainable development of the business. Today in the "Global Brand Building stage," the key is localization.

Haier's Internationalization Strategy

Yang Mianmian states that Haier's internationalization strategy has been unique from the very beginning since they wanted to have access to the best available technology and talent, local financial sources and customers with the most sophisticated demands. So, Haier's strategy was "*xian nan, hou yi*" ("First difficult, then easy"), that is to build first the brand in the developed markets and, afterward, use it to expand the business into developing markets which would be easier to penetrate. This is why Haier started by exporting its products to the quality-oriented German market, back in 1990; it then established its first overseas manufacturing facility in the US, before performing its first overseas acquisition in Italy, Europe.

For Haier's management team, it has also been very clear that in order to be successful in the international market, it was necessary to be very competitive in the domestic one: "without the domestic market, the business is rootless; without the international market, the business is weak," they say. When going abroad, says Yang Mianmian, Haier minded the traditional Chinese philosophy which requires a person to be a sage inside before becoming a king outside, but put it in reverse, saying: "we shall be a king outside before becoming a sage inside; that is, we should first of all have the ambition to forge a world brand and, then, fight for the goal of building ourselves into a sage. We will become a sage only because we want to be a king."

"Haier has experienced a tough time when starting to go abroad and it went through a very steep learning curve,[15] but always had very clear that it was the way to go, that there was no point in remaining in China, 'fighting over the same piece of meat,' because in a very short time only the bone was going to be left," explained Yang Mianmian.

So, Haier set the goal of the "Three 1/3s": 1/3 made and sold at home, 1/3 made at home and sold abroad, and 1/3 made and sold abroad. In order to achieve this, Haier's "three-in-one localization" required technical development centers, manufacturing bases and trading companies to be established overseas to enable localized operations with respect to design, manufacture and marketing. Haier's aim was to integrate funds, intelligence, and cultures to create a world-class brand. Three steps were defined for this: (1) the internationalization of the management system to build up employee loyalty; (2) the internationalization of its service approach to build up customer loyalty; and (3) the internationalization of the brand to build up international competence. Five globalization strategies were also established: (1) the globalization of design; (2) the globalization of manufacturing; (3) the globalization of marketing; (4) the globalization of procurement, which is carried out via Internet; and (5) the globalization of the capital operation.[16] "At Haier we also say "global sourcing, global marketing," says Yang Mianmian.

She stresses that, during the globalization process, the principle of "interaction, development, and innovation" has been applied. The best practices of Haier America are shared with Haier Europe, and the successful marketing of Haier Europe is introduced to Haier Middle East, opening up the way to global marketing. An example of this international cooperation is the development of the Casarte high-end market products. "At Haier, we believe that only when each individual employee is internationalized, can Haier be a real internationalized company," says Yang Mianmian. Also during the globalization process, strategic partnerships have been established with top global suppliers, enlisting their participation in the front-end design of Haier products.

Another principle that Haier applies globally is "Co-option." Haier fully embraces this as the strategic trend of corporate globalization in the twenty-first century. It is based on competency complementation, which aims for win-win cooperation enabled through the exchange of resources. Haier subscribes to the new rule for international businesses today: cooperate or perish. Yang Mianmian remembers that Haier implemented this principle as early as 2002, when announcing the co-option with Sanyo Japan and Sampo Taiwan.

Haier's globalization strategy has been summarized in three principles: (1) go abroad, by going to mainstream markets in mainstream regions; (2) go local, gaining admission into mainstream local channels selling mainstream local products that respond to the needs and habits of the local consumers; and (3) go higher level, continually improving quality to become the mainstream brand.

What Has Made Haier The Success Story That It Is Today?

From its early start as a small collective factory on the verge of bankruptcy, with only this as a blueprint, Haier has succeeded in establishing a global brand, creating its own marketing concepts and earning the approval and trust of customers from numerous countries and cultures, providing them with the highest quality products that best serve their needs and desires at minimum cost. Even tourists visiting Qingdao visit Haier's factory these days (numbering about half a million per year). What is the secret behind Haier's success? "Our management culture! From the very beginning our management approach was different, our CEO's approach was different from others here in China. At Haier we say that 'if a company's capital is the boat, then its brand is the sail; if a company is a human being, then its culture is its soul'. From very early days and over time we have defined important management principles to follow, such as: to always keep in mind that the journey of a thousand miles begins with a single step; to act instead of just perceive; to be cautious all the time, as if walking on thin ice; to remember that management is the art of leverage, that is, it is the amount of resources utilized, not the amount of resources possessed by the enterprise that counts; to seek truth from facts; to act promptly to problems and quickly find innovative solutions to avoid them from happening again; not to forget that yesterday's advantages may be converted into today's disadvantages, that yesterday's success and glory can be tomorrow's obstruction and, therefore, it is always necessary to run ahead of competitors; to keep always focused on clients' demands instead of that of competitors because customer's loyalty is priceless; and many others. And for the team leaders, we established, for instance, that in their absence, the subordinates shall continue normally working and in a synergic manner," answers Yang Mianmian.

As early as 1998, the so-called "Enterprise Culture Centre" was established to interact with employees, visitors, and media. Among other products, they produce what has been named the "Corporate Culture

Brochure of Haier." The front page of this booklet features a smile, and written below it are the words, "I smile because I am Haier." For Haier, "a smile is not only the one that can be seen on the face. A smile means superior services beyond customers' expectations. A smile means 100% acceptable products for the next process. A smile means never say no to customers. A smile means OEC. A smile is the driver of the world-class brand. If the market operation of an enterprise is compared to a smiling mouth, R&D and marketing will be the two corners of the mouth. With rising R&D and marketing, there will always be a real smile."

Yang Mianmian explains the importance of aligning employees with the company's goals: "for years, Haier has been fiercely embarked on a re-engineering process, has introduced new marketing concepts, a new organization structure, and new management ideas. The real challenge was for the employees to gain understanding, adoption, and appreciation of these advanced principles. As the Old Chinese saying goes: 'the real hero is the people.' A tool we have been using for this to happen are the 'Haier's Pictures and Words,' which are drawings and messages created by Haier's employees to show their understanding of and identification with Haier's values. Since the year 2000, several editions of 'Haier's Pictures and Words' have been published. They are the voice of Haier people, the attitude of Haier people, the philosophy of Haier, the culture of Haier. Haier employees identify with Haier culture through these drawings and messages. They represent the everyday values and attitudes that are experienced by Haier people. Using cartoon sketches to interpret corporate culture and management principles, is another innovation Haier has introduced in business management, since it is the very first time this is being used in the world."

Additionally, important concepts and principles of Haier's service oriented philosophy include:

- **The approach of the "floating boat":** when the competition is strong, you have to be stronger to win. In that way, you can have the competitive edge and beat your opponents in the market.
- **"With creative thoughts, there is no fear of off-season or weak market":** at Haier, the objective of business operation

is closely oriented to the market. Efforts are made to explore new markets and new market demands and, thus, to set the trend of the consumer market.

- **The constant rule of the market is a constant change:** accordingly, Haier needs to adapt its strategy to the constantly changing market place. In this information era, competition is cut-throat. Haier has no choice but to shoot "flying targets" in order to gain the advantage.
- **Build a good impression:** to build a good impression is to be fully devoted to work, sparing no efforts to satisfy personalized needs and care for work and customer. This will guarantee Haier's business a bright future with an impressive, cohesive, and innovative global brand image.
- **The customer is always right:** in 1995, Haier put forth the concept of "Star Service" based on the principle that the customer is always right. Haier's business relies on customers for success: only when the customers are satisfied is the business successful.
- **Challenge is the drive of innovation:** to create a market means to discover potential profitable opportunities while covering a market share as large as possible in the existing market. A successful business is the one that is good at making "new cakes" and defines the trend of the market.
- **Never say "No" to the market:** whether people are in the assembly line or in the marketing department, or even in the service centre, it does not matter. Every job is linked to the market. Every employee of Haier should satisfy all his/her customers, and no employee should ever say "No" to the market.
- **A complaint lodged by a customer is the most precious gift:** what a customer is complaining about is what needs to be improved. Only when these complaints are properly handled is the business benefited. When making a buying decision, the customer is focusing much more on the convenience and comfort that the product can deliver than on the product itself. When his/her expectation cannot be satisfied, complaints are unavoidable. But, when these complaints

are properly handled, the business benefits immensely. "The permanent property of Haier's business is customer loyalty." The more loyal customers Haier has, the greater are its assets. Otherwise, assets will turn into liabilities and the business will go insolvent. In this information era, customers are likely to shift. Customer retention is about understanding and satisfying personalized needs. For this purpose, Haier maintains a work environment that facilitates corporate-wide innovations. Employee loyalty will in turn bring about the customer loyalty required for sustainable growth and contribution to the community.

Haier's innovative "OEC," "Market-Chain," "Individual-Goal Combination Win-Win Culture," and "Inverted Pyramid" management models and its "People-Centred Accounting System" have attracted International attention and have been recognized worldwide. In March 1998, Zhang Ruimin was invited to lecture at Harvard Business School on the concept of "Activate Shocked Fish," a Haier corporate strategy of maximizing a merged company's latent or underutilized potential. The case has since been used at Harvard Business School. Subsequently, the University of Southern California, IMD in Switzerland, INSEAD in France, and Kobe University in Japan have conducted research on Haier's "OEC approach," "market chain management," and "individual-goal combination" management systems. Haier's market chain management system is also included in the European Union's case database. Today, thirty of Haier's management case studies have been incorporated at twelve universities around the world.

Haier believes that maximizing profit is one of its business objectives but definitely not the ultimate goal. Haier staff members have an imperative goal: improving mankind's existence and development and aiming for its perfection. Based on this, Haier's staff has progressively established a concept of development and business over the last 25 years that revolves around people. At the heart of Haier's scale of values are customer satisfaction and the greatest aspiration for the company is to win the customer's heart. The customer's heart is the real and most precious market resource. Striving to improve its products to make life simpler and more convenient, and applying its know-how and energy with even greater commitment to create, together, a perfect world is at the heart of Haier's client-centered philosophy.

"We cannot claim to have done everything we wanted to but we are certainly promising to do everything we intend to." With increasingly more customers placing their trust in the brand, Haier's staff do not merely dedicate themselves to the research and development of ever-better products; they pursue the fundamental objective of applying themselves, with increasing energy and enthusiasm, to the know-how, innovation and continuous development of Haier's business, as well as the protection of mankind and the planet.

Haier's main operational idea has always been "get what we want without losing what we have"—in other words, "first, secure what we have before exploring new business in related products; and second, get what we want by becoming the best performer of the new business." Haier's corporate spirit has always been "creating resources and global reputation" together with the guiding principle of "combining individuals with orders" and "acting fast to get success." Today, Haier is gaining market share by the innovation of its business model, and by its innovation in management. Haier today defines itself as "an innovation-driven world-class brand."

"Meeting customers' needs through practical innovation, to give them more sensible options that empower them to live a modern, affordable, and sustainable lifestyle. For Haier, quality begins with a corporate philosophy, the belief that it is important for us to design and produce products that are durable and will provide years of worry-free use. Haier has always held the customer in high regard and has a history of taking our product development cues from them, fostering relevant innovation.[17] The range and scope of Haier's product offerings allow us to do what only a handful of companies can: combine products and services in ways that can uniquely meet consumers' needs with Haier solutions."

Yang Mianmian defines Haier's secret as "having had a leadership that has always been developing new concepts and drawing all employees with them, always ascending new heights on top of achieved developments, always searching for excellence in management and in products' quality." In fact, innovation is the core of Haier corporate culture, which features recognition and participation of all employees—both in China and worldwide—in realizing Haier's ideal to be a globally recognizable brand. When Haier launched the "Global Brand Building" strategy, it emphasized its resolve to "create resources and worldwide prestige" and a working style of "individual-goal combination, swift action and success." Resource Creation is based on innovation; even Haier has fewer resources than its rivals, but it benefits from competitive advantages developed over time through innovation. It is through innovation that Haier shall achieve its higher objective of "worldwide prestige," by meeting the needs of customers from all over the world, which will in turn make Haier a globally recognized world-class brand. "Haier has always been guided by four principles: innovative strategy, efficient organization, creative technology, and market orientation. Since 2002, Haier's development theme has been Speed, Innovation, and Strategic Business Unit (SBU)," says Yang Mianmian.

Speed helps create customer resources. In other words, Haier wants to be the early bird catching the worm. Speed plays a significant role in order acquisition, fulfilment and follow-up service. Fast speed is aimed at realizing zero stock, zero distance, and zero operating capital.

Innovation is to create value by helping customers, provided customer resources are ensured. Fast speed is gained by innovative thinking and spirit. In today's fiercely competitive environment, the market positioning will be lost without innovation. During the innovation process, innovation should be combined with speed. Haier's decentralized organizational structure and its management and production processes are concentrated upon satisfying both the market demands and the innovation needs. Only those who satisfy customers' individual demands and add value to them will be chosen by the buyers.

SBU is the abbreviation of Strategic Business Unit. Haier's principle is that, if not only every division, but also every employee is a SBU. Haier's business strategy will be carried out and shouldered by all employees. At the same time, the innovation of every employee will ensure that Haier's strategy is successfully implemented. A SBU is an instrument to achieve efficient and innovative performance to be able to satisfy the individual customer needs. SBU demonstrates high-speed innovation. With the SBU system, Haier's objective of high-speed innovative production is quantified for each individual employee. As a result, every employee carries out technical innovation and prompt action to satisfy his/her customer. This helps to optimize customized production. For every employee to become a SBU there are four fundamental elements established individually, in-line with the company's goals: market target, purchase order, sales achievements, and market return (award or penalization). For employees, SBU means innovation aimed to create added value for the customers. For the company, SBU means corporate competence, which cannot be copied by competitors if every employee becomes a SBU. For customers, it means loyalty to the enterprise and the brand. If every employee becomes a SBU and carries out innovation, customer demands can always be satisfied. In relation to the SBU concept, Haier has established a one-ticket responsibility system to support its one-stop service through business process reengineering: through one-stop service, a customer may have all requirements met at one SBU that is responsible for the whole order execution process (one-ticket responsibility system).

But, if innovation is a core competency of Haier, so are their employees. "Haier provides every employee with opportunities to develop and demonstrate his/her talents and promotion is based upon excellence, not appearance," stresses Yang Mianmian. "It is not able people, but the mechanism to encourage able people development, which we should be concerned about. The responsibility of a manager is to establish a 'race track,' that is a personal development opportunity for every employee to become a SBU". Haier based this in three principles: fair competition, ability-based appointment, and reasonable job rotation. Employees are constantly evaluated and classified by performances, and the managerial personnel do not work at the same position permanently but rotate regularly. There are regulations established for job performance evaluation, promotion competition, and managers' rotation. This rotation aims to avoid inefficient performance in management due to thought rigidity and creativity shortage after a relatively long period at the same post, and to create opportunities to young managers. "At Haier we say that 'a talent today could become a mediocrity tomorrow'. Haier's human resource management aims to eliminate misconduct in business practice and to stimulate the enthusiasm of its employees, since every one of them can feel the pressure that comes from both inside (including, promotion competition) and outside the company (that is, the market) and convert this pressure into creative mobility. This is the key to success," emphasizes Yang Mianmian.[18]

As early as 1984, Haier made it very clear that "quality products are made by qualified people" and have since stuck to this principle. People are the only productive factor that is both active and creative. Since Haier's management made the tough decision of destroying 76 defective refrigerators back in 1985, Haier has always insisted on quality. Even when there was a great demand even for products of inferior quality, Haier based its brand strategy on quality, both in the domestic and the international markets. Haier believed that there is no way out for defective products other than elimination. At Haier, a defective item has to be rejected. The total quality management system of Haier focuses on people who are the ones that made the quality products. In Haier's factories, 100% of the products are tested for quality (sometimes during days, weeks, or months) and every day the three best products that employees have made are shown to the rest of the team. Also shared with the team are any problems encountered during the day during production. There are general working instructions, which are changed once a month. Haier's cultural philosophies also remind employees about their attitude toward work. Every month the best worker receives the "Employee of the Month" award. Any new product that Haier develops is tested in the market; sometimes it is manufactured in China and tested there before being sent to the destination market, and in other cases it is just the opposite. For years, Haier has been working with the best work suppliers for supply parts (such as GE for washing machines). Yang Mianmian stresses that, since 1984, it has been Haier's culture "*xian zhiliang, hou shuliang*" ("first quality, then quantity") and "*zui hao, zui gui*" ("the best, the most expensive").

By making high-quality products, Haier has always competed on quality rather than price, consolidating resources as soon as possible to best satisfy personalized needs and exceed customers' expectations. Yang Mianmian acknowledges that for Haier it has always been "a value war instead of a price war" and that Haier's brand marketing philosophy has always been "our brand is the sail, our customers the teachers."

But if quality is the essence of Haier's products, reputation is the essence of its business. At Haier, a technically acceptable product is not necessarily a qualified product. Only products that guarantee customers' satisfaction are qualified. For Haier, the point of marketing is buying rather than selling—securing customer loyalty by building a good reputation in the process of selling. Products that fail to meet customer needs are of little marketability and, thus, of little profitability, generating a bad reputation for the company. Reputation is more important than sales volume for Haier. To build a good reputation is to keep a close eye on changes and take proactive actions to satisfy customer needs and exceed customer expectations. Never say "No" to customers.

In the end, for Haier, the core competence does not lie in a single element. It is its outstanding ability to obtain customer resources and loyalty that has made Haier competitive in the market. The key to obtain local customer resources is the localization in design, manufacture, and sales. This is why Haier products have been warmly received all over the world.

Haier's Management Concepts

Yang Mianmian defines Haier's global branding process as combining the best in Eastern and Western management thinking to create a foundation for further innovation. Since its founding in 1984, Haier's unique philosophy has merged the business experience of East and West to become an international model of corporate management, which they have been constantly communicating to their employees. "We do acknowledge Chinese traditional culture and respect it very much, but for our company we needed to develop a more sophisticated management model which also imports elements from the West and builds upon them. This is what we have been teaching to our employees: our unique corporate culture. Just pure Traditional Chinese Culture they can learn in the school and at home," she explains.

Haier's model can be summarized as being focused around customers, guaranteeing that every employee is in contact with the market. Internally, the model stimulates employees' enthusiasm, innovation and competitiveness, while linking each employee to one another, so that disputes among them are non-existent and the specific responsibility of a particular employee contributes to the achievement of the company's goals. In fact, Haier's corporate culture features the participation and recognition of all employees. Haier's decentralized management and organizational restructuring approaches are supported by the use of advanced information and network systems for fulfillment, market chain performance, logistics, capital operation, after-sales service, product inventory, and operational cost reduction.

The following concepts constitute the core of the traditional Haier Management model, together with its new service-oriented business approach (as seen below):

The "OEC Approach"

The "All-around Optimized Management Approach" was Haier's first major initiative in innovative management. First implemented in 1986 and later named the "OEC Approach," this management style incorporates clear and comprehensive control over all company functions and has been the cornerstone of Haier's management culture for about 25 years, helping it to improve its products' quality and employees' efficiency.[19] One of Haier's mottos says that "a world brand begins with OEC."

OEC is an abbreviation of "Overall Every Control and Clear," indicating overall control and supervision of everything done by every employee every day. The purpose of the "OEC Approach" is for every employee to achieve each day's plan, evaluate that plan, and improve upon those daily accomplishments 1% better than the day before: "everyone, everything, everyday." The OEC Management comprises of three systems: objective, daily revision, and incentive. The objective must be established first; daily revision is fundamental to evaluating the objective's fulfillment; as a result of the daily revision, the person is awarded or penalized. OEC scores are used to assign workers' remunerations, awards, and promotions. The OEC approach is the right way "to do the thing right."

"Do the thing right. What's extraordinary? What's challenging?"
It is extraordinary to do an ordinary job well each individual day.

For a job recognized as very simple, it is challenging to do it well in a serious and earnest way.

The "Ball-on-Slope" Theory

As part of implementing the OEC model, Haier developed the "Ball-on-Slope" theory. A company is akin to a ball on a slope. Two forces are needed to move the ball uphill: one to keep the ball from rolling back down the slope (business management) and the other is the one necessary to keep the ball moving upward (the company's objective and capacity to innovate). These two forces are the key to a company's continued success.

The "Ball-on-Slope" theory is used to convey how management is critical for business success, and that consistent efforts should be made to ensure management efficiency, which fluctuates continuously. Management shall also be flexible and adjustable depending on the company's objectives and internal and external conditions. Haier's policy is "to prepare for actual use, not for show."

The "Activate Shocked Fish" Theory

During Haier's Diversification Development Phase, company management proposed the concept of "Activate Shocked Fish." A "shocked fish" is a company with good tangible assets but which has been managed poorly and face bankruptcy.[20] Haier would purchase these companies and use advanced management techniques to realize and maximize a struggling firm's latent potential and turn it into profit. Haier also used mergers with struggling companies to carry out capital restructuring. Haier used intangibles such as its corporate culture and management theories to maximize the tangible assets of the merger target. This also allowed Haier to expand the scope of its business quickly while keeping overall costs low.

Market Chain Management

Haier's Market Chain Management is based on the idea that every employee shall face the market: "market is where you are and what you do."

In 1998, Haier began a process of re-engineering, which continues to this day. The objective of the re-engineering drive is to remove barriers between the company and the market, as well as those within the company between different departments, to build an "end-to-end" market chain process that operates smoothly inside and outside the company, and to turn every employee into their own individual SBU. The end result is that everyone in the company is a master of the corporate marketing objectives.[21]

Market Chain Management is supported by Haier's computerized information system, which is designed to organize the flow of information and logistics and enhance capital performance to realize the "3 Zeros." It is enabled by the speed of synchronous process and the strength of SST.[22] Consistency between employees' individual values and customers' needs is guaranteed by a performance-based salary, which encourages employees to work hard to satisfy consumer requirements with the innovative acquisition and efficient execution of orders.

A critical idea behind Haier's Market Chain Management is the "**Zero Inventory, Zero Distance, and Zero Working Capital**." An order-oriented system means that the products are manufactured under orders to satisfy specific customer needs. The products are delivered on a cash-on-delivery basis, which is how the "3 Zeros" goal is accomplished: Zero Inventory, to eliminate all stock in the warehouse;[23] Zero Distance,[24] to satisfy customer needs in the shortest time, so that products can be shipped immediately after a customer has made an online purchase order; Zero Operating Capital, which is the ability to convert money into tangible goods and then again into money, meaning that there is no operating capital (since the company collects payment from the goods' buyers before paying its suppliers).

"Do the right thing and do the thing right"
There is a distinct difference between doing right things and doing things in right way.

If a very good quality product ("do the thing right") cannot be sold or used, what the worker has done is not right.

Doing the right thing is the basis of doing the thing right.

The management system shall be constantly improved to ensure that every employee is doing the right thing in the right way.

From "Manufacturing" to "Marketing Service-Oriented" Business Transformation

In 2009, the Chinese Government established an initiative to foster domestic demand in rural areas: a 13% subsidies' program for farmers to buy household electrical appliances.[25] Haier responded by accelerating the development and implementation of its "Home Appliance Promotion in Rural Areas" project, through which Haier has been developing products and solutions to satisfy rural users' needs, as an opportunity to expand their market while servicing the farmers' needs.

However, in the midst of the financial crisis, this did not seem to be enough to avoid the decline of Haier's profit margins and market positioning. It was necessary to do something else. Haier's managerial perspective was that crisis brought with it opportunities, and only with innovation would those opportunities be grasped. As Zhang Ruimin said, in 2009: "facing the current crisis, we really have to know not only the way to get through the winter, but also how to swim in the winter time, when the water is extremely cold, instead of hibernating. We have to boldly live through the tough times instead of burying our head in the sand." To survive the winter by repeating what they have done before was meaningless for Haier's management. So, explains Zhang Mianmian, "We conducted a comprehensive check of all our businesses to spot all problems. We found problems; we discovered that we must embrace the scientific development concept to take advantage of the financial and economic crisis and to survive in the fierce competition of the Internet-era. Our answer was that we have to make Haier an information-based company, a service-oriented company and a company with an "individual-goal combination" win-win culture. Through these changes, we are transforming the whole operational model of the company and making sure that every employee pays attention to consumer demands and overall organization performance. We are focusing on large-scale efficient customization instead of massive production. In this way, we will be able to reach our goal of creating a world famous brand, which satisfies the personalized needs of customers with the shortest delay."

Changing To an Information-Based Company

"At Haier we have long believed that everything a company does must be centered on the customers' needs and preferences, because we are here precisely to serve the customers. So, in the internet era, in which market demands are changing rapidly, Haier's information system shall focus on the market and the clients, not on the company. An information-oriented enterprise follows customers' demands via information technologies, versus a corporate information system that focuses on internal processes' efficiency improvement. An information-based company designs all business processes around the customer's demands, which are the ones in the central position. The traditional company-centered model is replaced by a client-centered one. An information-based company is like a mobile phone that can be taken walking into consumers to know their demands and swift actions accordingly, versus just waiting for the incoming call to a fixed-line telephone, which is what happens with a corporate information system. This is extremely important today because every customer has his or her own and unique demands, which keep changing all the time and had to be met in the shortest possible delay [sic]," explains Yang Mianmian.

She continues: "So, the first transformation at Haier is transforming itself into an information-based company to be able to adopt a customer-centered production and operation system. In this way, Haier shall generate value for the customers, providing them with the products and services that they need at the fastest speed to meet their demands."

For this to happen, Haier works out the business mode of "JIT under Zero Stock," which means that Haier will deliver products to its clients immediately, if this is what they need; so that Haier will not have any stock, if clients do not need it. An end-to-end process is formed from market knowledge to product R&D to supply chain to ultimately satisfy clients' demands. When this business mode was put into operation, in the first quarter of 2009, Haier's inventory turnover was shortened to three days, one-tenth of the average inventory turnover of Chinese industrial companies.

Changing To a Service-Oriented Company

When Haier's management team was evaluating their decision to transform the business from a "manufacturing" to a "marketing, services-oriented" one, they asked themselves if Haier was mature enough to leave behind the manufacturing component of its business. Over the years, Haier has developed cost advantages by continuing to innovate on a business model built around manufacturing. Relinquishing their own scale advantages and manufacturing profits[26] to go into the unknown "marketing, services-oriented" approach, focusing on R&D, branding, commercial channels, and services to clients, may be the end of its price competitive high quality products. However, Haier has already had successful experiences with production outsourcing and strategic partners.[27] It has also been following the successful outsourcing experiences of many foreign companies and how it has allowed these companies to focus on product development, brand building, and service to customers. Haier continues to explore new management and marketing approaches, constantly restructuring itself as a result.

Under Zhang Ruimin's new definition of Haier—"a service provider of better life for people, in their current homes"—in a new market scenario, this transformation seemed to be the inevitable path to follow in order for Haier to continue creating differentiated competitive advantages and to safeguard its positioning and profit margins.

Moreover, in this era in which clients need not products, but solutions, Haier's management was sure Haier could know and satisfy client's demands at the fastest speed only by transforming—from a manufacturing business to a service-oriented business, "selling products by services and selling services by products." "We saw that products will be very cheap to buy, but the income will be generated by the services associated with those products sold to customers, that is with the contents that can be incorporated to each of these products (for instance, for the TV, for the computer, for the mobile phone) and with the intercommunication between them. Since Haier has a very wide range of products, we saw that we could do it, that we have this competitive advantage versus other companies that just have one product or some very few," explains Yang Mianmian. This way, Haier could become the most competitive provider of quality living solutions. Customers will just have to think that there is a brand—Haier—which can help them to fulfill and solve all their home appliance needs and issues.

For this to happen, an individual-order combination system had to be established and, with it, the "triangle" straight-line functional structure needed to change to an "inverted pyramid" matrix structure and the capital-centered accounting system to a "people-centered" one. Additionally, Haier established the goal of zero-distance integration between its virtual and physical networks. "By introducing these changes in our business model, Haier can deliver products to clients immediately if this is what the client needs and does not need to have stock if the client does not need it. These changes shall allow Haier to achieve its transformation from a 'selling products' to a 'selling services' organization. Our organizational model will be followed and benchmarked all over the world, I am sure of it," states Yang Mianmian.

Win-Win Mode of Individual-Order Combination

Previously, Haier corporate culture highlighted "quick response and swift," namely meeting consumer demands in a rapid manner. This helped Haier to position itself in the global market where it is today. However, "quick actions are missed targets," says Yang Mianmian. Under the Internet age, the previous mode of mass production has evolved into a mode of mass customization; "producing before marketing" has now evolved into "marketing before producing." In this new situation, the traditional mode of producing-stocking-selling has to give place to the sell-on-demand-mode. Haier's e-age business model is the win-win mode of "individual-order combination" that is being implemented all over the world and receiving worldwide attention, including customers in Africa and Latin America.

"Individual" refers to each Haier employee and "order" refers to the market objective of A-level competence. "Combination" means that every employee is an independent and innovative SBU with the goal of creating value for the clients and achieving primacy in the marketplace. Thus, every employee has his or her own market objective. "Win-win" means that, by creating value for customers, the value of both the company and the employee are achieved and, as a result, both win.

The individual market objective is not prescribed by superiors, but based on the A-level competence of the market he or she is responsible for. The individual income is not determined by superiors either, but depends on the value he or she creates for customers.

To operate in this culture, managers have to shift from "time reporters" to "clock builders," by building the "clock system"[28] that enables each employee to assume his/her responsibilities like the gear of a clock and helping employees to achieve their individual goals via an "individual-order-remuneration" account mechanism. To measure the everyday efficiency of every employee Haier uses the colors red, yellow, blue, and green. In the same way that a company has three financial statements—a balance sheet, a cash flow statement, and an income statement—every Haier employee shall have his or her own personal statements and is asked to report his or her gain or loss on a daily basis and, if he or she is in red, why. To represent the type of problem an employee is facing Haier uses lamps with the problem's color. Every employee becomes accountable for corporate earnings and expenses, and profits will be shared between the company and every individual. The goal is that every employee and function unit's task fulfillment becomes green.

Under Haier's innovated mechanism, the market is divided and allocated to different teams, with each employee focusing on one market segment. Based on preliminary analysis, three levels of competence objectives—A, B, and C—are set up, each of them pointing to a different compensation level, so as to encourage the entities to compete for A-level objectives. Compensation is based on the objectives achieved. Haier calls this method "the thermometer," which is divided into five sections: win-win, bonus, money-earning, debt, and bankruptcy. By calculating the value each employee creates for customers, he or she can find his or her position on the thermometer, under which basis his or her compensation is decided. The border between generating money for the company and wasting its resources is between the "money-earning" and the "debt" sections.

Yang Mianmian explains that in this new Haier model, those employees that cannot accomplish their individual goals will have no other choice but to leave the company. And stresses, once again: "every employee's performance is daily tracked. His or her remuneration keeps constantly changing, according to his or her monthly performance, quarterly performance, and annual performance, combined with the performance of his or her department. An employee will get an above-baseline reward if he or she has fulfilled his or her enterprise profit and market costs."

"This mechanism basically means that each individual should bear in mind his/her goal and receive remuneration, if the goal is fulfilled, or penalization, if the goal is not fulfilled. Employees can figure out the way to increase his/her value, the source where his/her income comes from, the aspects that he/she should be responsible for and the losses, which are related to his/her performance. Everyone has to make his or her own clock to know the time, instead of just remaining passive looking at the time ticking. "Individual-order combination" is our method and "swift action and success" is our target. The market of each SBU should be identified clearly and actions should be taken promptly. In this way, by assigning incentives-based responsibility to staff, the quality of the products delivered to their customers and the on-time delivery are assured and the management can be shift from "afterward analysis" to "beforehand win calculation." As a result, the company can calculate its due profits in advance while, simultaneously, meeting the constantly changing customers' demands," explains Yang Mianmian.

She continues: "It is a totally new culture, which involves not only that every employee's final remuneration is based on results (including factory workers' remuneration) and that employees shall work together, but also that they shall do this as detailed as possible to define products' prices. In this way, Haier will achieve the goal of really manufacturing the products that customers demand with the highest possible quality. The time from the identification of the customer need to having the product in the market shall be reduced from the original 30–35 days, in 2009, to 3 days. When we started thinking about this, in 2008, we knew that for our transformation to end up being a reality, we have to motivate employees to change their ways of doing things, their habits and performances. We set as a deadline for it to happen April 26, 2010, the date the transformation of our information management revolution was completed."

"Our Win-Win Mode of Individual-Order Combination" has changed the role played by Haier's employees: from command-receiver into individual CEO. He or she shall not wait for the direct manager or for the top management to tell him or her what to do. As a result, the slow response problem of the traditional operation mode is overcome. Instead of being told how to act, now each employee operates his or her own business and is self-driven. When we designed this management model, we thought it could be very successful because it is very much in line with the Chinese entrepreneurial spirit. So, we went on with the introduction of two fundamental improvements in our management model: the "Inverted Pyramid" and the "People-Centred Accounting System," explains Yang Mianmian.

Inverted Pyramid

As the traditional organizational structure fails to meet the e-Age customer-centered win-win mode of individual-order combination, Haier reshapes the previous pyramid structure into an inverted one, so that employees, superiors and functional departments are all pursuing the same objective: to create value for customers.

In the "inverted pyramid" organization structure, clients are at the highest level, followed by the first-line managers. Employees face clients and the market directly and are responsible for collecting information from them. All other functions, including management, become service providers for front-line employees. Leaders no longer give orders but provide employees with resources and services, as do the first-line managers in the lowest level. In this way, the original straight-line organization structure is changed to a matrix structure. If all managers in a company become support providers, then everyone's work is centered on creating and meeting consumer demands and the whole company is transformed into a service system. In the "inverted pyramid" organization, the design people in direct contact with the customers are at the highest level, in the middle are the production people, and at the bottom are the sales people. Every employee has responsibility over the people that are above him or her in the pyramid.

In other words, once the "inverted pyramid" matrix organization structure has been established, Haier breaks up the original functional departments and establishes SBU to directly face clients. SBU in this case is a team with the same target, organized by breaking up original functional departments, so as to provide valuable solutions to clients, calculate input/output independently, and realize constant innovation. "How does this work in practice?" says Yang Miamian. "For example, farmers in Northeast China's rural areas complained to our sales representatives there that frost cracks easily appeared in winter in their washing machines, when placed in their backyard (which they often do). Our sales staff there can quickly send the information to relevant managers so that, together with R&D personnel, anti-frost solutions can be worked out."

Haier calls those employees who are close to the market "independent operation entities," because they can work independently to promote (bottom to top) change in the way things are being done—including supply chain management, marketing and business planning—and they can ask different levels of management to provide support for implementing them. "An 'independent operation entity' can be a planner, a salesman, an accountant, and a human resource manager. The smooth operation of Haier's independent operation entity is not achieved by top-down surveillance, but by the creativity of fully emancipated employees. Every employee can access the company's resources and shall increase its value as well as create value for customers. The "independent operation entities" shall sell, first, services along with products and, secondly, products along with services. For instance, Haier mode-card TV set is not only a television set, but it supports learning and game functions via mode-cards. The consumer can shift between different modes by using the cards. A mode-card club is also set up to provide upgrading services to members, both the learning and the game databases can be upgraded. This product potentially changes the lifestyle of our consumers because it is a TV set but also a game console and a learning device. It is a good example of selling services along with products. Going the other way around, a good example of selling products along with services is Haier's leading positioning in China's vast rural market, where we have the largest market share. We have managed to accomplish this because of our extensive delivery network in the countryside—we provide door-to-door services in small villages—and because we have the 'intangible' information networks to provide just-in-time delivery with zero inventory," elaborates Yang Mianmian.

She continues: "new market demands emerge every day and if the frontline employees become 'independent operation entities', then who shall be in charge of strategic decision making and of envisioning new market trends? Those at the bottom of the 'Inverted Pyramid' structure shall shoulder the responsibility. In the new structure, the requirements for the corporate leaders—that is, for us—become higher because they have to follow changing market demands to grasp new opportunities and provide support to materialize them, while simultaneously they shall also decide the company's targets and direction to ensure its sustainable growth. But, by accelerating the decision-making process and its accuracy, this new structure has already improved our performance: compared with the industrial level of 50 days, Haier's inventory cycle has gone down to only 5 days and it has even achieved minus cash flow cycle."

People-Centered Accounting System

Yang Mianmian explains how the traditional accounting system is after-business accounting, focusing on statistics and results, but neglecting duties and causes. By using the independent operation entity as the main body of the accounting system, Haier transforms the traditional financial reporting into three tables: profit-and-loss table, daily checking table, and individual-order compensation table.

Compared with the profit-and-loss table of traditional financial reporting, which calculates profit by deducting costs from gross income, Haier's profit-and-loss table represents a new concept. When calculating income, there is no difference from traditional reporting. However, profit refers to the income generated by creating value for customers under the mode of independent operation entity. The gap between income and profit is the loss which, because of its un-sustainability, makes only a minor contribution in creating value for customers, and must be improved.

The task of the daily checking table is to make up for this gap, focusing on the innovation of the platform, process and mechanism, so that everyday budget and checking are fulfilled.

Lastly, the individual-order compensation table is the one that integrates personal compensation with an employee's performance in creating value for customers.

Haier's new accounting system has aroused the attention of the US Institute of Management Accountants because it integrates personal compensation with the value created for customers. It is thus considered a new solution for future administrative accounting.

Haier's reversed organization structure

Management innovation should ultimately be reflected in the transformation of the business model–the business model in the information age for haier: Zero reserved stock, supply and prompt delivery when demand arises. This would require the organization to have fast response capabilities to meet the market demand.

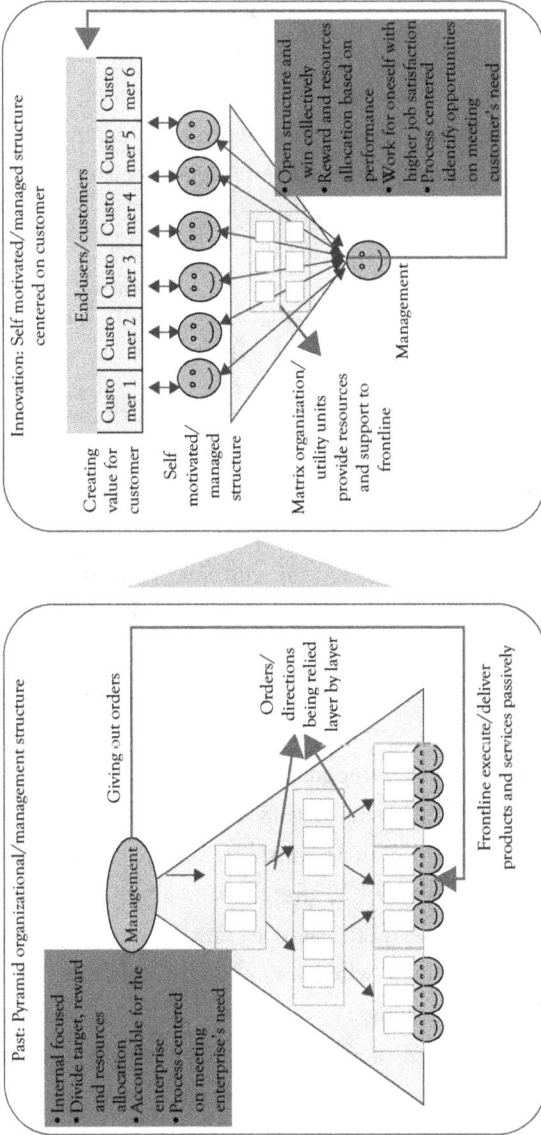

Past: Pyramid organizational/management structure

- Internal focused
- Divide target, reward and resources allocation
- Accountable for the enterprise
- Process centered on meeting enterprise's need

Management

Giving out orders

Orders/ directions being relied layer by layer

Frontline execute/deliver products and services passively

Innovation: Self motivated/managed structure centered on customer

End-users/customers

Creating value for customer	Custo mer 1	Custo mer 2	Custo mer 3	Custo mer 4	Custo mer 5	Custo mer 6

Self motivated/ managed structure

Matrix organization/ utility units provide resources and support to frontline

Management

- Open structure and win collectively
- Reward and resources allocation based on performance
- Work for oneself with higher job satisfaction
- Process centered identify opportunities on meeting customer's need

Organization structure innovation: Convert "Regular Triangle" into "Reversed Triangle" in order to establish self motivated/managed structure to create value to customers, and to achieve Zero distance between haier and customers/end-users.

Haier's reversed organization structure.

Traditional financial reporting is capital-centered, focusing on share-holders' interests, while Haier's three-table-mode is an employee-centered one. By enabling the employee to create value and market resources, under the individual-order mechanism, a win-win situation among the customers, the enterprise and the employee is achieved, and the employee's high performance, high added-value, and high compensation are realized as well. As such, it can be said that traditional financial reporting is capital appreciation-oriented, while Haier's independent operation entity-based three table mode is people-centered and value-centered, "which is a fundamental difference," Yang Mianmian says.

Zero Distance Integration between Virtual and Physical Networks

Haier's virtual network refers to the Internet, by which the to-be-achieved objective is not to promote sales, but to strengthen communication, so that customer viscosity can be formed through the on-line community. "For example," explains Yang Mianmian, "Haier will offer all sorts of on-line air-conditioner solutions and customers can easily find out the best solution for them, simply by inputting their room's area, orientation, decoration, style, and color."

Haier's physical network refers to its marketing network, logistics network, and service network. In China's major cities, Haier has established over 1,000 neighborhood stores, 5,000 county-level specialty stores, 24,000 township points of sales, and 100,000 village-level liaison locations. In over 2,500 countries outside of China, Haier has established logistic centers with over 17,000 after-service stations.

With these networks, Haier aims to satisfy its customers under the principles of "wherever and whenever, on-the-spot delivery and service is forever" and "sell-on-demand."

Based on its win-win mode of individual-order combination, Haier has increased its competence by integrating the virtual and physical networks. This has attracted the attention of some overseas corporate giants, such as GE, that have authorized Haier as their agent for household appliances business in China. Some well-known European and Japanese enterprises have also aligned with Haier for some regional markets.

The Future

Despite the current economic uncertainties, Yang Mianmian is pretty confident about Haier's future. She says: "we just have to keep innovating, developing new products, localizing, and continuing in our transformation from a manufacturing to a service business. We just have to diligently keep working, doing a little bit more every day, keeping improving our individual performance, keep adapting very quickly to the changes in the market place without losing our stability. This is the way to go; we did always have it clear. We did always know we would end up being a very reputed service global company, but we did just have to wait to start making it possible. It is very difficult to implement, it is not an easy way. But, while in 2009 we planned to do it, now we are actually doing it everywhere, not just in China, but also in Europe and the US. Thanks to the Internet, every employee of Haier is in direct contact with the market and can accompany customers all the way from the before-sales phase to the after-sales one, which we have named "Haier's Worry-free Service." Our employees are really attached to their customers, adding value to them. To make this possible, we are using social network groups, such as Facebook, Twitter, Baidu, Taobao, Renrenwan, and Sina.com. Once a customer has become a "Haier's fan" they get a full range of services; for instance, when a couple is about to get married we provide them not just with a set of products, but with a design solution for the whole house.

Haier's fans are in constant dialogue with us. By listening to their needs and providing customized solutions to them, we are winning their loyalty, which is helping us to increase our sales and margins, both in China and abroad. To listen to our customers' needs all over the world is helping us not only to develop the products that can satisfy them, but also to use those cultural differences to develop innovative products. The fact that within the China domestic market itself we do have every culture and every need is also helping us very much in this process. We do have in China extremely rich and extremely poor customers, urban, as well as rural ones and, in a way they do represent the different types of clients that we find all over the world. Moreover, because China is a very young economy, its population are embracing technology and the use of Internet and mobile devices—about 120% of our population use mobile phones, which is providing us with scenarios for developing and implementing technological solutions that afterward we may end using all over the world. Our goal is to generate 30% of our revenue in the international market."

Yang Mianmian explains that Haier's transformation into a service company is pretty much in line with the *lusi jinji*—green economy—concept the Chinese Government is emphasizing these days. As such, Haier is moving from a *hong jinji*—red economy—company to a *lusi jinji* one. This involves targeting customers that are looking for alternative ways of acquiring their home electric appliances and satisfying their needs, in particular the younger population. "We do target the young people, as Apple has done, and do provide them with solutions that not necessarily involve acquiring a product—for instance, a platform for listening to music. When products have to be modified to meet their specific needs, once finished, we deliver them directly to their homes. For these young consumers that want to buy tailor-made household appliances and intend for a simple lifestyle, we are using the trademark LEADER in our domestic market. We have made a big marketing effort in the last two years to build it. Already around 40% of our clients are young people," she says laughing, very happy that they are making it happen.

She continues: "we are in the process of doing this from products to services transformation. However, changing employees' and customers' minds and ways of operating, takes time. It may take us over five years to make it fully happen, but we are striving to be successful. We have already seen the positive impacts of our "win-win mode of individual-order combination" and we are giving customers an incentive to contribute to our products' design: when they design a product that will afterward be used by other clients, we give them a discount of RMB 500 in their own purchase. We are going to be successful; I have no doubts about it. In relevant markets, we may also continue performing some acquisitions, such as the one we completed in the autumn of 2011 to better position ourselves in the Japanese market. In the current fiercely competitive market and uncertain economic situation, only those companies that can adjust to the changing environment and extremely quickly make the required changes can win the battle, that is, remain competitive in the market place. We do have the strong determination to run ahead of our competitors. We will gain market share by the innovation of our business model and will become a new and stronger Haier."

When Yang Mianmian gets up in the morning she feels very good just by thinking that she has another day ahead to help Haier to transform into a service company and to continue, as she has been doing since 1984, contributing to Haier's positioning as a world leader reputed brand.

Haier Is Ocean

Haier would like to be the greatest ocean, which rivers of all origin, size, and path flow into. Be it a brook of no name, a running river that travelled through mountains and plains, or just a torrent of muddy water, the ocean takes them all and it turns them into pure green ocean. Ocean is so indiscriminate and accommodating, as if it has limitless capacity to [accept] rivers of all kinds. The Yangtze River, the Yellow River, and the hundreds of streams along the way are all rushing persistently to it inspite of the long journey and the zigzag caused by the terrain. Where the rivers end, the ocean's immense presence begins in deep green jacket and white gloves. Its everlasting waves are magnificent! It is eternally unrivalled!

Once united together, we have no division in us, but only unity for all. Like the ocean, there is only one direction to march for. Fearlessly, we strive firmly toward a unified target. In so doing, we find the energy and the power to overcome all obstacles, witnessing the miracle of being an ocean!

The most commendable [thing] about the ocean is its unconditional dedication. Year after year, it demonstrates the unselfish philosophy of "live, but not occupy" and "provide, but not depend." While it does not seek rewards, the ocean has reached ultimate eternal existence. This existence provides a lasting environment for all to live in the ocean.

Haier would like to be an ocean. As rivers of all kinds to the ocean, Haier is to take on the talent of every corner of the world to achieve the grand ambition the company has established [for] itself. In addition, Haier shall be furnished with the cleansing power the ocean has to enhance the qualification of its workforce. Haier people are able, adroit, and diligent. The development of Haier depends on the support of its various skilled and qualified employees.

The power of the ocean at Haier lies in the ultimate unity of Haier people. The spirit of Haier's culture—diligence in our work, devotion to our country and pursuit of excellence—is the key to the needed unity. Haier promotes the attitude of being appreciative at the heart and being a team player in action. At Haier, we compete with one another for the contribution to the whole, not for personal gains. It is in our hands to realize the improbable and turn the impossible into reality. At the end, Haier shall launch powerful waves forward, regardless of any obstruction.

We would like to be an ocean for the society and for all people. Haier shall reach the eternal existence, as the ocean has done, when Haier earns the society's continuing recognition for its "sincerity forever" given to the society and the people. Haier people shall receive ample reward for the top efficiency crated for the enterprise and the superior contribution made to the society. Haier people and the whole society shall become one.

Haier is ocean!

Zhang Ruimin, Haier's CEO, March 1998

CHAPTER 6

Entrepreneurship by Using Modern Traditional Chinese Medicine. Wu Naifeng, Tasly

Traditional Chinese Medicine (TCM)— *Chuantong Zhongguo Yao*—has been in use for more than five thousand years. The concepts of this tradition share close parallels with Taoist beliefs, and are largely based on the philosophical concept that the universe is made up of an energy called *qi*. Any state of matter or energy in existence is comprised of this matter. According to TCM, the body is a small universe unto itself that is a complex of subsystems of energy and matter, and these systems work together to maintain a healthy mind and body. TCM's view of the body is not concerned with its anatomical structures, but with its functions—digestion, breathing, aging, and so on. In TCM, the spleen is not a discrete piece of tissue, but an aspect of function related to a process: transformation and transportation. Among the many other differences between TCM and modern Western science is TCM's functional description of the mind and emotions as a result of various internal organs rather than the brain. The characteristics of the operation of the mind/body are described in terms of the five elements (metal, water, wood, fire, and earth), *Yin/Yang* organs, deficiency/excess, emptiness/fullness, hot/cold, wind, dampness, pathogens, internal/external, meridian channels, *qi* (of several different types), essences, body fluids and vessels—TCM perceives health as the harmonious interaction of these entities with the outside world, while disease is interpreted as a disharmony in this interaction. It posits that illness is caused by external or internal factors or both, which disrupt the body's natural processes. Following a "macro" philosophy of disease, traditional Chinese diagnostics are based on overall observation of human symptoms rather than "micro" level laboratory tests. There are four types of TCM diagnostic methods: observing (望 wang), hearing and smelling (闻/聞 wen), asking about the background (问/問 wen), and touching (切 qie).[1] TCM therapy largely consists of Chinese herbal medicine, acupuncture, dietary therapy, and *tuina* massage. The health-promoting aspects of *qigong* and *taijiquan* are also closely associated with it.

With TCM as its basis for developing advanced pharmaceutical products, a company named Tasly was established in May of 1994 in the northern part of *Tianjin*.[2] A "pioneering TCM enterprise," as they define themselves, Tasly's most recognized contribution is the advanced dripping pill technique.[3] Since its establishment, Tasly has made leaps in its development, becoming a high-tech group whose scope of business includes: modern TCM, chemical medicine, biological medicine, healthcare products, hygiene products, functional food, medical management, medical equipment, and medical distribution. The company has also incorporated all associated functions of these endeavors: research and development, planting, manufacturing, and distribution. Its products—such as Cardio Tonic Pill, Nourishing Blood and Cleaning Brain Granule, and Chuanxinlian Lactones Dripping Pill—are all well-known in the TCM market. With 21 high quality medicines and many other health-related products, Tasly is recognized today as one of China's top three pharmaceutical and health products groups.

There are two people behind this success story during China's period of economic reform: Wu Naifeng, President of Tasly Group Co., Ltd. www .tasly.com, and her husband, Yan Xijun, Chairman of the group. They began working together in similar positions in 1979 and have remained together as a team ever since, complementing each other very well.

Wu Naifeng was born in 1952, in Chengde, Hebei province, twenty kilometers northeast of Beijing, which she claims to be a very beautiful place best known as the site of the Mountain Resort, a vast imperial garden and palace formerly used by the Qing emperors as a summer residence.[4] Her parents, originally from Chengde, were both professionals—her mother, a normal employee and her father, a director in a government-owned company. Wu Naifeng is the oldest of six children—four of them boys—who did not share her entrepreneurial spirit, and who worked all their lives for the government. Three of her siblings remained in Chengde, and only one left Hebei and relocated in Wenshan, Yunnan province. Unique within her family, this entrepreneurial attitude radiates from Wu Naifeng, giving her a younger look and providing her with energy that is fully evident in the speed at which her mind executes and functions. She even remembers and eagerly demonstrates the little bit of English she studied at school as a little girl.

Wu Naifeng began working when she was 17 years old. She did not have to go to the countryside, but was sent to Xian to work in an army hospital. While working within that environment, she decided to study pharmacy. At the university she met a classmate, Yan Xijun, an orphan originally from Gansu, who had wished to join the army since his tough teens. He soon changed his name to Xijun (which means "eager to join the army" in Chinese) and after completing six tests, saw his dream come true. In 1976, this tenacious man became Wu Naifeng's husband, and thereafter her longtime professional and business partner. After graduation in 1979, the military couple moved to Chengde to do management work in the medicines department of an army hospital, where Wu Naifeng's husband became her boss. Almost simultaneously, their son was born. In 1990, they moved from Chengde to Tianjin, continuing to do the same type of work in the same positions, this time at *Er-Wusi Yuan* (another military hospital).

While there, they realized that Chinese people needed quality medicines, which were not available in the market. There were several problems with the safety of those medicines that were available. So, they came up with the idea that through intensive R&D, with TCM as the basis, they might be able to develop new medicines and establish their own company to manufacture and sell them. They did not hesitate to put their idea into practice and in 1991, parallel to their work at the hospital, they began developing their first medicine and building their factory. Their first workroom was their dormitory. In 1993, their idea proved to be fruitful; they came out with their first advanced TCM medicine, which became widely recognized as Tasly's Cardio Tonic Pill (also known as "Compound *Danshen* Dripping Pill"): a medicine to help people with coronary and heart diseases, which combines several Chinese herbal ingredients.[5] The medicine is provided in the form of advanced dripping pills, tiny black balls similar to white homeopathic pellets. The advanced dripping pill is a Tasly innovation that has also been used in many other Tasly products. Patients are prescribed ten of these pills, three times a day.

Wu Naifeng clarifies that: "Modern TCM[6] products are made from the same traditional ingredients as TCM, but are packaged in capsules like chemical medications. Modern TCM has abandoned the old TCM's preparation method and adopted new techniques, materials and equipment to make the new preparations. This guarantees the curing effect and stability of these Chinese medicines. We have built up a modern TCM industrial chain with internationally advanced standards covering GAP, GEP, GMP, GCP/GLP, and GSP. Modern TCM technology has enhanced the level of medical production and lays a solid foundation for TCM's international competitiveness. We have been the first company to standardize Chinese medicine ingredients and manufacture Modern TCM, so that manufactured Chinese medicines can be brought in-line with international standards. For instance, Tasly has built the first Chinese GAP-compliant herb base at Shangluo, Shaanxi province, taking the lead in proposing and formulating a new GEP standard on active TCM ingredient extraction, and successfully applying multiple fingerprints to its quality control process. Moreover, Tasly has launched a state-of-the-art modernized TCM manufacturing platform and developed the world's largest digitally controlled dripping pill production line. At Tasly, we have created an integral industrial chain of modern TCM which comprises: good agricultural practice, good extracting practice, good manufacturing practice, good supply practice, and good laboratory practice."

In 1994, *Tianjin* Tianshili Joint Pharmaceutical Company was established, with 70% of the shares in the hands of *Er-Wusi Yuan*—the military hospital they have been working for—and the remaining 30% possessed by the *Tianjin* government. Wu Naifeng explains that they wanted to put their project to work and they could not afford to do it by themselves, so they found this solution appropriate despite the fact that it left them with no shares at all in their own company. Eventually, this situation was reversed in 1999, when the firm was privatized and they, along with their management team, claimed 30–35% of the shares.

Wu Naifeng clarifies that they chose the name "Tasly" because it represented the spirit in which they were planning to build and conduct their business. The brand "Tasly" is the transliteration of the Chinese characters 天士力—*tian shi li*. "*Tian*" stands for heaven or nature; it could also be explained as the forces of utmost importance in Chinese culture, such as the strict and scientific laws; for an enterprise, "*tian*" could also be interpreted as the ever-changing market and the customer. "*Shi*" means, outstanding people. "*Li*" symbolizes power; for an enterprise, it refers to cohesion and the power of innovation. The idea behind Tasly's establishment was to build an innovative health industry enterprise, adhering to the philosophy of pursuing harmonization of man and nature and improving people's quality of life. This is why Tasly emphasizes on environmental protection and natural resources conservation, as well as the creation of customers' value. Wu Naifeng further emphasizes that they have inherited and continued to develop the traditional Chinese ethics and have always tried to support people's welfare and contribute to the creation of a harmonious society.

Wu Naifeng explains that Tasly has always made steadfast efforts in: performing advanced scientific research, expanding its technical management and capital operation, updating its industrial structure and product mix, and introducing innovation in its sales mode—something for which she has been directly responsible. Over the years, Tasly has made constant efforts to promote innovation in scientific research and self-improvement in order to build up core competitiveness. A modern TCM system has taken shape step-by-step, and is composed of: anti-virus medicine, anti-flu medicine, cardiovascular medicine, brain-vascular medicine, anti-tumor medicine, immune system medicine, and digestive system medicine.

Wu Naifeng stresses how all of Tasly's achievements demonstrate a great determination to strive forward on the road toward TCM modernization. Tasly has always kept in mind the concept of creation, and of expanding the market to biomedicine, chemical medicine and the field of healthcare products and services. She says that "creation is the soul of

Tasly; our future development also relies on innovation. On the road to TCM modernization, we adopted the concept of creation and developed the spirit of innovation, in order to make a more fruitful contribution to society."

From owning just one product, Cardio Tonic Pill, at its establishment, Tasly has grown into an enterprise, which manufactures a series of high-tech products. Since 1996, when its second medicine was put in the market, Tasly has continued to develop a new medicine every year, and sometimes two medicines in the same year. In 2009, the company had nineteen medicines, thirteen of which were advanced TCM, and six of which were occidental medicines. Between 2009 and 2011, they have put two new medicines into the market. Wu Naifeng points out that Tasly's Cardio Tonic Pill has become the first modern TCM to gain the American Federal Drugs Administration's (FDA) application approval; it has completed FDA Phase II and is now undergoing FDA Phase III clinical trials. Besides medicines, Tasly has developed many other health-related products such as herbal extracts, teas, cosmetics, daily hygiene products, and medical equipment. Since 2002, the annual sales of Cardio Tonic Pill have continuously reached RMB 1 billion, and it has been the Chinese consumers' first selected TCM brand. Tasly has gradually developed a product family of drugs for the cardiovascular system, the anti-cancer and immune system, and the gastrointestinal and hepatobiliary system, as well as drugs for virus killing and cold resistance.

Following its TCM product innovations, Tasly's internationalization strategy is now well underway. Its major products have been registered in 34 countries and regions and are now being exported to: South Korea, Southeast Asia (Indonesia, Malaysia, and Vietnam), Russia, Mongolia, Cuba, Africa, India, Pakistan, Europe (starting in Holland), and North America. For Wu Naifeng and her husband, entrance into the western medical market was the way to realize their dream of "sharing the joy of health with all the people of the world." In May 2003, the CMC Tasly Group BV www.shenzhou.com was established in Holland, as a joint-venture with Chinese Medical Centre BV[7] to export alternative medicine products. Although no longer active today, this joint venture marked a leap in Tasly's incorporation into the western medicine market. Another important step was back in 2008–2009, when the company started exporting to Canada, three years after it started sales to Russia in 2005. In 2006, Tasly's Cardio Tonic Pill successfully entered the medical markets of Pakistan and India.

It was in 2006, explains Wu Naifeng, that Tasly designed its internationalization strategy for the next 10 years, which is comprised of the following elements: organizing a team of talented people by the way of international cooperation; promoting industrial developments based on technological innovation; setting up a platform for scientific research and development; positioning itself as an technologically advanced international enterprise; and establishing a solid foundation for technical management via industrial management. The strategy involves internationalization of both the products and of the enterprise's capital. For the internationalization of products, Wu Naifeng and Yan Xijun chose a three step approach: first, direct sales, in developing countries; second, in the same countries, distribution through agents (when direct sales are not possible); third, getting the certifications that will allow Tasly products to enter into the mainstream market for prescription medicine in the developed countries. For capital internationalization, they chose three modes: first, making full use of Tasly's brand, technical innovation, and marketing ability to attract more firms from developed countries willing to undertake joint-cooperation; second, conducting strategic investments alone or in cooperation with others to establish an international development platform; third, seeking the appropriate opportunity to enlist the whole Group in an international stock exchange, thus realizing globalization of both capital and assets.

Since then, Tasly has set up two organizing systems of international trade and international direct sales. It has established a global marketing mode of expanding from developing countries to developed ones. Tasly has divided the market into "four regions and one spot." The one spot refers to Russia and the four regions include: Asia (centered in Malaysia and Korea), Europe (centered in Holland and France), North America (centered in the United States), and Africa (centered in South Africa and Nigeria). International direct sales have been promoted in Southeast Asia and Africa. In Africa, sales volume has grown rapidly: in just the first year the number of members reached 220,000, spanning 20 countries. Wu Naifeng explains that to perform global direct selling they created Tasly

International Pharmaceutical Co., Ltd. (formally named Tasly International Co., Ltd until June 2007).

At the national level, Tasly is present in over thirty Chinese cities, having reached every corner of the country from north to south. It has also set up twelve science research parks employing over 350 personnel, including 212 masters and 45 doctors and post-doctors. In fact, R&D has been at the core of Tasly's business model, since its establishment in 1994. Tasly group invests about 5 to 10% of their annual turnover into R&D. Tasly Modern TCM Garden is listed as an exemplary project of the national high-tech industry. Its information project was listed in the Chinese Government's Five Year Plan. The enterprise has received numerous awards, such as "excellent enterprise of Tianjin," "pioneering enterprise of ideological construction," "top 10 industrial enterprises with self-innovation and creation," and many others. For Wu Naifeng, all these honors and awards demonstrate that the Tasly trademark is becoming more and more popular not only in China, but also around the world.

The Technological Centre of Tasly Group, created in 1997 and previously named Tasly Medical R&D Centre, is responsible for scientific research, technical research, and product development. Wu Naifeng explains that, through years of development, it has become a modern technical centre with advanced equipment, rational structure and perfectly functional systems. Two platforms have been established for basic research as well as industrialization research. In December 2002, the Centre was recognized as the 9th national technological research centre. R&D activities performed in the Centre by approximately 250 employees include: development of new products, pharmacological and drug effect research, clinical pharmacological research, extraction of effective ingredients, preparation techniques, and quality standard testing. The Centre is additionally responsible for technical development and specialist education. Over the years, the Centre has undertaken more than 40 key national scientific research programs. Tasly's post doctoral station was approved by the National Ministry of Personnel in 2002. Over twenty PhDs work there to complete their dissertations, conducting research on genetic studies for coronary heart disease, chemical ingredients of natural herbal plants, cell culture and industrialization and the application of biological enzyme engineering in TCM modernization, clinical research on the circulatory system, TCM internationalization, and modern pharmaceutical enterprise management.

Wu Naifeng also considers it relevant to mention the Tasly Institute, which owns a large group of departments of scientific research management and services, such as the: Modern TCM Department, Chemical Medicine Department, Pharmacology and Toxicology Department, Medical Analysis Department, International Medical Research and Registration Centre, Medical Affairs Management Centre, Clinical Medicine Department, Project Management Department, and Logistics and Equipment Management Department, among others. The Institute employs around 130 people, including 22 doctors and 38 masters; senior technicians exceed 65% of the working staff. Researching fields include: Chinese medicine, chemical drugs, biomedicine, healthcare products, and food and beverages.

TCM's compound prescription is a complex system and remains a primary focus of Tasly's research. Many problems are yet to be resolved, including how best to evaluate the effects, and which ingredients play the key roles in releasing the symptoms. Further research on these problems will quicken the steps of TCM modernization and will benefit herbal research around the world. This is why Tasly tries to build up scientific cooperation with famous universities and research academies both at home and abroad, in order to establish "a huge scientific researching system with Tasly's characteristics." For instance, Tasly has made extensive cooperation with overseas scientific research institutes and universities such as Harvard University, Aston University in England, and Baker Medical Research Institute in Australia.

Tasly Modern TCM Garden, in the northern part of Tianjin, houses Tasly's group headquarters, modern TCM manufacturing base, R&D Centre, and Bio-Vaccine and Health Products and Cosmetics Manufacturing Centre. Tasly also has factories in: Huian, Jiangsu (acquired in 2003 as *Jiangsu Diyi Pharmaceutical Co., Ltd.* and the base for chemical pharmaceutical manufacturing), Zhangjiang, *Shanghai* (Shanghai Tasly Pharmaceutical Co., Ltd., the base for biology pharmaceutical manufacturing), Xian (the city where both Wu Naifeng and her husband studied), and Shanxi, where the herbal plantation base is located. In this location, explains Wu Naifeng, the number of employees remains fairly small (less than 200 people), but Tasly remains there because of the higher reliability and quality of the raw materials, a prerequisite for the preparation of their medicines. As such, Tasly places utmost emphasis on controlling the quality of raw materials thorough all stages of preparation: seed selection, supervision of the growing environment, plantation management, harvesting, packaging, storage, transportation, and manipulation. Shanxi is where Tasly first built a state-level Dansen source base. Apart from this province, Tasly has made special efforts in cultivating key raw materials in their herbal bases of Yunnan and Hunan since 2002.

Tasly's location in Tianjin today is different from where Wu Naifeng and Yan Xijun originally started. In 2001, after two years of construction, they moved to the current Tasly Industrial Park, in *Tianjin Beichen* Science and Technology Park. She explains that they have remained in Tianjin for over twenty three years because: (1) the local government has been very helpful and provided them with a lot of support; (2) they are located in an economic development zone, which has a lot of economic and fiscal advantages; and (3) the local environment is very good for business and fosters creativity and entrepreneurship. Although they are buying both in the north and in the south of China, the cost to transport raw materials is small enough that it does not outweigh the advantages of being located in Tianjin.

Tasly Modern TCM Garden receives visitors—including *waidiren* tourists—every day, totaling around 50,000 people per year. Apart from manufacturing, the facilities serve numerous other functions, such as: product showrooms, conferences, business trainings, and cultural exchange. There are six training rooms, each with a different name, offering trainings at a fee—to government officials, for example—or rental space to third parties. The premises also feature the Tasly Health Star Platform, a modern health service website (www.5ijk.net) and call center for clients who may have questions or concerns about a particular Tasly medicine. Wu Naifeng explains that, as is common in China, the complex also provides housing for workers. She also says that they have expanded the complex and it is likely will continue to do so, since the available land is 26,068 square meters. Quite recently they have finished the construction of a new medicine factory, which not only produces Tasly products but packages the products of other firms as well. The huge embossed granite

Chinese medical drawing that stands at Tasly Modern TCM Garden was, in 2001, recorded in the Guinness World Records.

From the original Tasly Pharmaceutical Company, the business has expanded to include a group of 41 companies today. Wu Naifeng describes the process as follows: "In 1998, Tasly Pharmaceutical Company— *Tianshili Zhiyao Gufen Youxian Gongsi*—was privatized; 20–25% of our shares were claimed by *Zhong Yang Yao Yi Gongsi* (a company owned by the *Tianjin* government), 30-35% remained in the hands of our management team [which included Yan Xijiun and myself], and the rest by the people and companies that have nothing to do with our business. Following this, Tasly Pharmaceutical Company was transformed into Tasly Group to allow the business to continue its expansion with a group structure. Since then, we have been creating about 4–5 subsidiary companies per year, which handle all the same functions that we perform.

In August 2002, Tasly Pharmaceutical Co, Ltd.—the company dealing with our original pharmaceutical business—was listed in the Shanghai Stock Exchange. Since then, the company has increased the traded shares from the original 25% to 80%, and has seen a 30% increase in its market value. Tasly was the first TCM company to be traded. The remaining subsidiaries were all participated in by other parties, who normally have below 49% of the shares, since we normally hold a participation of over 50% and, in any case, never lower than 30%. In the company group, we [my husband and me] are keeping 49% of the shares, while the remaining 51% is in the hands of 'the group's team'—a lot of people from *Tianjin* and outside of *Tianjin*, most of whom hold less than 10% participation. Within this group there are two main partners each holding around 10% of the group's shares: *Tianjin Zhongyang Zhiyaochang*—80% of whose capital is in the hands of the Tianjin government—and *Tianjin Zhejian Jianfeng Jituan*—20% of whose capital is in the hands of the Tianjin government. Tasly's market value has been estimated to be around US$ 2.2 billion. Our plan is to list a couple more companies in about two to three years' time."

Wu Naifeng continues, "Going back to our subsidiaries, there are: a R&D firm, 7 products' representation companies, an alternative medicines firm (*Kasly*), a company dealing with packaging, and our new line of skin protection products' firm—which we started selling in 2007.

Among our nonmedicinal products we have: shampoo, body wash, body milk, toothpaste, pills to improve the quality of the skin, and pills to clean the liver—for instance, for people who drink too much alcohol. In the domestic markets we have been commercializing these products first under the trademark *Kasly* and more recently under the *Dilan* one, but for the international market we use the trademark *Tasly*. In 2005 we established a JV hospital in Shanghai with the Woolide Korean hospital: the Shanghai Tasly Woolide Hospital. We do also have a joint-venture with Co-operative group (Co-op) British company: the Co-op joint-venture—*Sheng Te Gongsi,* in which Tasly has 40% of the shares, which was established in 2007 with a registered capital of US$ 18 million. To build the new plant, which began operating in 2010, our investment was in the range of US$ 40 million. On Co-op's side, investments were made by Sants, its medicine wholesale subsidiary. The plant employs 200 people and has an annual production capacity of 200 million pills and 200 million capsules. All the drugs manufactured by the plant are for exportation to the EU market (to Co-op's 600 pharmacy outlets), and eventually, to other EU markets. The factory produces well-established generic medicines as well as newer generic versions of drugs that have recently come off patent. In order for Co-op to have greater control over its supply chain, they approached us with the initiative to establish this JV. However, for us this business is still not relevant, since this JV's sales are not big."

Wu Naifeng explains that the Co-op joint venture is the first that Tasly has established with a large international group, but that the company may pursue more JVs for other markets—for instance, the USA or other EU markets—and even for manufacturing in other countries, if necessary. While the FDA's approval process was being initiated in 1997 (which the management team considered quite a challenge at the time, given the fact that Tasly had been established less than three years earlier), Tasly independently established a R&D company in the United States, in Washington DC. For years, the company remained fairly small—less than ten employees—but considering the high standards of the pharmaceutical system within the US, it was a strategic investment of experience and learning, and management decided to acquire land for establishing a real R&D center with around 100 employees.

In June 2011, it was announced that Tasly Group would invest US$ 40 million in a new 430,000-sq.ft. production facility, training location, and R&D centre for TCM in Montgomery County, Maryland—the largest investment made by a Chinese company in the state. The chosen location is the Shady Grove Life Sciences Centre, where dozens of jobs are expected to be created over the next three years. Tasly will be working in association with Johns Hopkins University in the areas of training and R&D. "We think this is an incredible opportunity for Tasly to develop innovative new products and introduce them to the US market. This also marks an important chapter in the globalization of TCMs, which are famous for their lack of side effects. We will be progressing faster, once we have completed the FDA's approval process," says Wu Naifeng.

Despite how cumbersome the whole thirty-step process has been, Wu Naifeng is certain of the importance of full FDA approval for the Cardio Tonic Pill. Not only will it help Tasly to sell the product in the US market, but it will also be a significant reference in other developed markets—in particular, the EU. She does acknowledge, however, that once the Cardio Tonic Pill gains final FDA approval to be sold in the US market, it will become necessary—in 2015, if all goes well—for Tasly to develop a different structure for US operations. The management team intends to begin marketing to hospitals in the US, but the strategy is still being formulated.

Another move in terms of developed market expansion is the letter of intent Tasly has signed with the Australian company Healthpac International Medical Corporation, on the establishment of an integrated high-level Sino-Australian medical centre of TCM and western medicine.

FOR WU NAIFENG TO BE PRESENT IN THE US MARKET IS VERY IMPORTANT because it has the best quality drugs' system and getting FDA approval is crucial not only for Tasly's sales in the US market, but also to help it penetrate other developed markets.

Tasly's strategy of marketing to hospitals has already proven successful in the domestic market, including Hong Kong where 90% of its products are being sold to hospitals, and the remaining 10% to drugstores. The company does not use any distribution intermediaries to reach target clients; it is done directly, under Wu Naifeng's supervision. Tasly's turnover has grown from the original RMB 5 million back in 1994, and is now over RMB 12.5 billion, 95% of which still comes from the pharmaceutical business and the domestic market. In the same period, profitability has gone from zero to around RMB 900 million per year. Today around 15–20% of Tasly sales are exports, with about 80% of those going to South East Asia (mostly Vietnam) and Africa, (where they are selling in all countries). Export to Africa began shortly after Tasly began doing business, beginning with South Africa and then expanding to Nigeria and other countries in western Africa. Japan is also a successful market, hosting a 100% owned subsidiary there since 2010. Tasly plans to continue selling in these countries and avoid expending excess energy in pursuit of the more competitive European and US markets.

Since 2007 in the domestic market, besides selling to hospitals and drugstores, Tasly also conducts direct sales in its own 200 shops, located mostly in *Tianjin* (where they have 20) and *Dongbei*—the Northeast part of China (mostly in Dalian, Shenyang, and Jilin), where management is easier because of physical proximity. In recent years, they have been promoting the opening of shops in cooperation with a partner, with the partner typically owning less than 51% of the business. Wu Naifeng explains that, despite a percentage of their products being sold in third party shops, the company decided to establish their own shops as the best strategy for direct communication and marketing to final consumers about Tasly products. This proved to be an effective approach for brand development, with the shops themselves are under the trademark Tasly name. There are about 2,000 employees working in the Tasly shops, with about 1,300 of them as shop attendants and an average of 6–8 people per shop. The remaining 700 employees work in subsidiary companies, which are responsible for representing not only their products, but also complementary products from other companies. Wu Naifeng clarifies that without the products of other firms, it would have been impossible to keep the shops profitable with Tasly's twenty medicines. She adds that, over the years, she has come to understand the importance of product quality, and that promotion of the brand depends on the business' ability to offer a well-organized sales service to their customers. "We regard service to our consumers as essential to our business," she adds. In 2011,

Tasly Group began preparing to conduct online sales in the Chinese market for nonmedicinal cosmetics as well as OTC products but has not yet confirmed what percentage of the total sales for those products will come from e-commerce.

"We do have other companies operating in different sectors, as well," continues Wu Naifeng, "such as the one we have in Guizhou province producing white wine—*baijiu*—under the brand *Guotai*. The Japanese university *Qing Ying* performed a comparative test with the famous white wine *Maotai*[8] and came to the conclusion that our *Guotai* is better for health. More recently, we have established a JV in Hebei for the production of red wine. In 2010, with the intention to increase our presence in the international market, we decided to emphasize the expansion of our non-medicinal business and to develop new non-pharmaceutical products—*baojianping*. As such, we established a new trademark—DEEPURE—to be used in two products: instant bio puer tea from Yunnan, and mineral water from *Changbai* Mountain, in Jilin." Wu Naifeng notes that these products are also being sold in the domestic market, but she expects them to sell very well in foreign countries, especially their innovative instant puer tea, in places where the tea preparation culture is not as developed as in China. Unlike pharmaceutical medicine, this product also has the advantage of not requiring extensively bureaucratic processes of official approval for distribution. As such, its sales in the developed countries may grow very quickly. In Japan, for example, Tasly established a company in 2010 and started selling the product in 2011. Europe and the US are the next target markets.

Also in 2010, Tasly initiated the *yangsheng* business, aimed at providing health management services, primarily for the elderly, in association with hospitals. Beginning in their Tianjin headquarters, a Health Management Centre for employees and clients was established. In 2011, these services were brought to Puer, Yunnan, where the puer tea is also cultivated, and offered through hospitals in Tianjin and Shanxi. "In summary, based on our modernized TCM industry, we have made a reality our goal of becoming a Pan-Health Industry leader operating in the areas of: life protection (including modernized TCM drugs, pharmaceutical chemicals, biologics, and special therapies) and health care (including health products, functional foods, cosmetics, biological tea, safe drinking water, and modern liquor)," explains Wu Naifeng.

To better prepare for new market challenges and the further expansion of the business, both Wu Naifeng and her husband decided to do a PhD in economic management, which they completed in 2008. Both felt it was a way to open their minds to new approaches they could apply to their business. She emphasizes that she has never had a problem having her husband as her boss for over 30 years. She has also never had a problem working with her son, who returned to China upon his graduation in international financial investments from Reading University, and who has been working in Tasly Group since 2004. He pursued this subject precisely because it would be useful in supporting the future expansion of Tasly internationally.

TASLY'S BUSINESS DEVELOPMENT STEPS

- First step: Building up the scale of production based on high technology in a relatively short time. This step was realized within the first 10 years.
- Second step: Taking the Great Health industry as a guideline and the pharmaceutical industry as a centre, laying a solid foundation for internationalization. Tasly is now at this crucial step. The objectives for this step are: to develop high-level scientific research, to adopt accurate techniques, to bring up professional working staff, to provide excellent service, and to exploit the prosperous market and powerful industry to set up a comprehensive enterprise. Four rules are being applied to ensure the above-mentioned objectives: brand guarantee, cultural guarantee, financial guarantee, and knowledge guarantee.
- Third step: Establishing an internationalized group to strengthen the business foundation. Six focus areas have been identified for this to happen:
  - Focusing on the concepts of enterprise development strategy and management.

- Focusing all actions on the target of and in the direction toward internationalization.
- Focusing all practical work and industrial programming on the Great Health industry.
- Focusing all data and conclusions on accurate and scientific standards.
- Focusing all principles for action on guaranteeing product quality.
- Focusing all promises to the customers on excellent service.

In recent years, according to Wu Naifeng, the sector has constantly been facing problems of a different nature than before. In 2008, for instance, there were many problems associated with Chinese products' quality, and in 2009, the international market performed very badly, forcing Taasly to turn toward the domestic market. Nevertheless, Wu Naifeng claims that they have not been affected by the 2009 financial crisis, nor by the recent economic turmoil. In fact, their turnover has continued increasing by 20% every year, in accordance with their business plan. The same applies to their investments: between 2009 and 2012 the group invested around RMB 4–5 billion. She states that they are not worried about the short-term evolution of the global economy, since she is confident in their business' trajectory of growth. Moreover, in the medium-term, she is optimistic about the domestic market, since demand will be fostered by the Chinese government, once it begins financing a percentage of medicinal costs, as well as by the demographics, considering the aging of the Chinese population.

Their new 12th five year strategic plan (parallel to the Chinese Government's 12th Five Year Plan) is called "One Core Two Wings," meaning that they will have modern TCM as their core center (including chemical and bio drugs), with the health industry as one wing (including natural botanic products, skin products and cosmetics, modern liquor, bio puer tea, and mineral water), and the provision of health management services as the second wing. It is these two wings that Tasly has been focusing on since 2009. In the health management services' wing, Tasly has implemented standardized special medical treatment, medical rehabilitation, and a health management demonstration park. A specialized, high quality health service and nursing system has been designed, and Tasly aims to establish a professional network of prompt, accurate, efficient, and informative medical treatment and rehabilitation, both in China and abroad. In addition to its own health management centre, Tasly plans to build about five health rehabilitation areas in China. Wu Naifeng explains that "with medical rehabilitation as its core center, healthy living and health management as its medium, and health community as its carrier, the health management industry provides health resource-sharing and a healthy way of living new model in accordance with the different and dynamic demand [sic]. By medical rehabilitation we mean: setting up specialized and comprehensive hospitals focusing on the cardio-cerebral vascular system, metabolic disorders, and senile functional deterioration; setting up photo, bio-chemic, and enzyme checking, analyzing, and diagnostic systems; based on modern diagnostic technology, we include acupuncture, nursing, and other medical treatments. In the area of health management, with the support of the three medical health research centres—John Hopkins University in the US, Beijing University, and Tasly Research Academy, we set up a two-stage health check system. In this way, we can provide not only a high-quality, low-price customized service, but also conduct health evaluation and analysis regularly and track its evolution over time. Finally, with respect to the healthy way of living, relying on the medical rehabilitation and health management system, we bring TCM's characteristic 'preventative treatment of disease' into full play and provide individual service for members. In accordance with members' needs, we provide health management door service and first aid, guaranteeing in this way our first-class service. Finally, we set up a specialized, high-quality nursing and health service system. In summary, we are going to build specialized hospitals and health real estate, health living areas. According to our model, the hospitals provide the health services, based on the living area's demand, the medical treatment, the healthy life style and the health management. The medical rehabilitation offers nursing services: the first 12 months is a mobile service, up to the first 5 years is a regular service, and from the 5th to the 30th year is a staged regular service."

Tasly's goal is to have a turnover of RMB 30 billion in 2013 and RMB 40 billion in 2015, drawing 50% of this from each of its two wings. Its goal is also to have 50% of this turnover coming from the international market, since much effort will be focused in becoming a global company, "a leading brand of the Great Health Industry," stresses Wu Naifeng.

Management of the group is shared by both Wu Naifeng and her husband. He takes care of: exports and foreign market development, the US firm and US market, and the creation and development of new companies. Wu Naifeng is responsible for: marketing and 80% of the products' development. About 50% of the group's employees are under her direct responsibility. In the group company, there are three Deputy General Managers below Wu Naifeng. In the management team there are eight people, all but one of whom are pharmacy graduates; the other's background is in management. The six managers below Wu Naifeng and her husband are responsible for: marketing, administration, finance, R&D (two people), and production. The total number of employees of the group is around 12,000 people, 30% of whom are in Tianjin, 60–65% in the rest of China, and 5–10% abroad. In China, the employees are distributed across the different facilities in: Tianjin, Shanghai, Shanxi, Jiangsu, Yunnan, Jilin, Guizhou, and Hebei. On the board of directors of the group company there are eight people: three people from the group's management team, one person from *Zhong Yang Yao Yi Gongsi*, and the rest representing other shareholders' interests.

Wu Naifeng explains that their business management approach changed significantly after their listing. They realized they needed to quickly adapt and improve their information systems and IT culture, and they knew that listing a company in the stock exchange would help them to quickly introduce the necessary changes into their management culture. The listed company itself has over 2,000 employees and is being managed by a managing director, who is one of the group's Deputy General Managers. Wu Naifeng is the CEO of the company and her husband the Chairman of the Board of Directors, which is comprised of seven people.

As for her management style, she asserts that she wants to establish direct relationships with both employees and clients. She believes that each person has unique abilities and it is very important to help him or her to develop them and show their potentials. At Tasly they have always said that "it is not the word position that counts, but the word abilities." She says that at Tasly "we have always used as a development guideline the saying, 'new thoughts, high technology, high starting point, and rapid steps.' For this to happen, we need a creative team that is capable of keeping constantly learning and improving, developing new products as well as providing new services to better serve our customers. This is what will help us to remain competitive in the market, what will always make reality our strategic conception of being an 'ever-lasting enterprise, ever-improved talented people, and ever-respected brand'."

She goes on to explain Tasly Group's management style, which she defines as being based on assigning clear responsibilities to employees and allowing them to proceed with their execution. Tasly employees' remuneration is based on performance, and promotion opportunities are based on abilities. "People are the most important resources for Tasly, thus employees' training is of utmost importance for us. Since innovation is imperative for us, we stick to the idea of hiring talented people regardless of their nationality. As such, we have been very aggressive in recruiting back to China, talented high-level science overseas Chinese. As a result, in our management and research teams we have masters and PhDs from the US, Canada, and Japan. Our teams combine high technology and traditional Chinese Medicine knowledge, so that our products can be innovative worldwide. We have created a pleasant environment for those talents to work together, and reach mutual recognition; thus the team is able to create values and bring prosperity to the company. Besides, we have pursued the establishment of a professional working team covering technology, management, production, marketing, and academic knowledge. On top of this, something which is very unique to us is our capacity to very quickly adapt to the needs of and changes in the market place and to implement new ways of doing things, always remaining persistent, and holding faith. We have been very successful in making sure that this culture filters down and is being shared by each of our employees. It has been said that Tasly's culture of service to clients has been influenced by the culture of military service in which we—the two founders—as professionals, were raised. In fact each year, the new college graduates joining the group have to take part in the military-style training that they are provided with to be free of any fear of difficulties and so that they dare to fight for the principle of "never step down from the service when the service is over."

She continues: "human beings create history, but inside a company, history is created by the efforts of all its employees. We communicate to our people that they should get along well with each other, coordinate with each other, and unite together to achieve the common targets. We try to provide a harmonious environment where every employee can make full use of his or her potential, exchange information freely, and cooperate effectively. We also advocate the creation and expansion of the knowledge scope, enabling employees to be able to solve problems concerning not only their own jobs, but also of the others'. We have published a book—'Tasly Stories'—where we record the deeds and contributions our people have made in order to spread the spirit of Tasly. Exemplary employees are listed in the book to encourage more and more people to achieve more challenges and dedicate themselves to the development of Tasly. In summary: we advocate healthy habits and positive attitudes toward life and career, we invest in improving the working environment of the employees, we promote communication between employees and the enterprise and—very importantly—we allow employees to hold Tasly's stock, so that they will share the profits from the enterprise.

Our code of conduct comprises five elements: service—serve both the customers and the market; loyalty—be faithful to the company and to his/her performance; execution—be determined in carrying out the firm's principles; cooperation—active cooperation with honest attitude; study—keep learning to allow for promotion. Our objective is that employees are capable of assuming professional and supervisory roles in their departments and can quickly advance in their professional career with us. We promote that employees choose themselves which professional path they want to follow—management, professional skills, marketing, or operations. This creates a win-win situation for both the company and the employee, who can focus on fulfilling his/her personal ambition. To recognize employees' work, every month the 'Stars of the Month'—chosen through public voting—are praised.

By combining Traditional Chinese Culture with modern management culture we have developed our own corporate culture, which we are very proud of. 'Harmonization of Man and Nature' is the essence of ancient Chinese culture and our philosophical concept. 'Improving People's Life Quality' is the management concept of our enterprise in accordance with the central task of the twenty-first century put forward by the World Health Organization. Harmony is the essence of Tasly Group: harmonious relationship between man and nature helps both to achieve mutual development; harmonious relations between body and soul ensure the prosperity of a nation; harmonious business ties expand trading scope; harmonious society enables the good functions of the government and happiness of the people; harmony needs changes, innovations, and advancement with times; harmony means wisdom, erudite in knowledge about China and the outside world; harmony leads to victory, inheritance, and the diffusion of its culture. During the pursuit of harmonious relation with Nature, society, people, and culture, Tasly aims to win the recognition of the whole world, and realize its noble cause of 'sharing modern TCM with mankind.'

Our cultural principles are being summarized in our logo, where one can see two Chinese characters '天' (*tian*—heaven or nature), '人' (*ren*—human), and an English letter 'A'. It means that human and nature are mutually dependent as an organic whole. The characters of '天' and '人' symbolize Tasly's philosophical concept of 'Harmonization of Man and Nature,' and its compromise with sustainable development. The triangular shape is the most stable structure, which embodies the smooth and effective management style of our group. The three A's that can be seen show our target of achievement, that is striving to become a first-class multinational group. The red color represents the vigor and enthusiasm of Tasly people."

TASLY GROUP
天士力集团

Wu Naifeng summarizes the essence of Tasly culture in these three principles: inheriting and promoting the heritage of the ancestors, bringing credit and exemplary service to the customers, and being responsible and realizing personal life values. She confirms that Tasly aims to build up a well-known and long-lasting brand with unique characteristics, expanding the fame of the brand "Tasly" from the products to the corporation, from the pharmaceutical industry to what she calls the Great Health industry, from the domestic market to the overseas market.

Tasly inherits and carries forward the traditional Chinese virtues of helping those in need and taking care of social welfare. For instance, after the 2008 Sichuan earthquake, Tasly donated over RMB 11 million in cash and medicines, for relief and post-disaster reconstruction. Tasly's generosity has received numerous awards such as "Prominent Contributor for Philanthropy," "Philanthropic Star," and "Red Cross medal," and Wu Naifeng has often been directly involved in many of them.

In their business activities, Tasly has always tried to apply the same principles. An example of this is the setting up of the Salvia source base in *Shang Luo, Shanxi* Province, where Tasly invested RMB 6 million, which has greatly benefited local farmers. The herbal source base enlarges the vegetation area and reduces the wind, preventing sand storms and improving the local environment. Furthermore, it improves the economic conditions of the farmers, whose income multiplied by 10 after they began to plant salvia miltiorrhiza. The plantation base has solved the basic living challenges of more than 90% of the farmers in four counties of *Shang Luo*. The construction of this herbal resource base has been useful both for the process of TCM modernization and the development of the western region.

Tasly has also been helping to promote the use of Modern TCM and to increase health education. For instance, in the spring of 2003 when the SARS outbreak spread all over the country, Tasly donated the Bupleuri Dripping Pill and Huoxiang Zhengqi Dripping Pill to doctors and patients in the subsidiary hospital of *Tianjin* Armed Police Medical College. Leaders of Tasly Group also went to the major hospitals in Beijing and Tianjin to offer these pills. Another example took place in April of 2005, when Tasly donated to CCF (China Charity Federation) units of its most successful product—Cardio Tonic Pill—for a total value of RMB 6.7 million. The following year, Tasly made a donation of medicines valued at over RMB 1 million to Tianjin Charity Association—the largest sum value ever received.

Despite being very busy and holding numerous responsibilities, Wu Naifeng seems to have energy left for hobbies, such as: traveling— mostly in China; listening to Chinese traditional music; and reading books—mostly historical ones. For business reasons, she has visited many foreign countries—the US, Canada, the UK, Russia, and the EU—all of which she enjoyed very much. She says she truly enjoys her work, and has not yet thought about retiring. The many awards she has received and the name she has been given as "Heroine of *Tianjin*" do not seem to have affected her spontaneous, quick, and efficient approach to life and business.

When Wu Naifeng gets up in the morning, she says she feels very good just by thinking that she has another day ahead to continue combining ancient Chinese culture with continuous innovation, and to help to create a world-famous modern TCM brand for the benefit of all mankind.

ENTREPRENEURSHIP BY USING MODERN TRADITIONAL CHINESE MEDICINE MEANS:

- *Combining TCM knowledge with modern technology.*
- *Placing R&D at the core of the business and continuously innovating.*
- *Continuing to invest in possessing the best available methods and technologies.*
- *Standardizing TCM ingredients and guaranteeing their high quality.*
- *Using an integral industrial chain, which goes from plants' seeds to products' distribution.*
- *Directly selling to clients as the preferred sales mode.*
- *Constantly educating and serving the client.*
- *Establishing leadership in the domestic market to face internationalization challenges.*
- *Exporting products before conducting international investments.*
- *Starting with the developing markets before entering the developed ones.*
- *Striving to have the best available talent regardless of nationality.*
- *Constantly tracking the health-related needs that may appear in the market.*

- *Constantly adapting to the ever-changing market and customers' needs.*
- *Being very aggressive in recruiting back to China talented high-level science Chinese from overseas.*
- *Making clear to employees that it is not the word 'position' that counts, but the word "abilities."*
- *Motivating employees to get along well with each other, coordinate with each other, and unite together to achieve common goals.*
- *Motivating employees to keep learning, improving, and innovating.*
- *Developing a management system that allows employees to choose their professional paths and to quickly advance in their professional careers.*
- *Advocating employees' healthy habits and positive attitudes toward life and career.*
- *Allowing employees to hold stock in the company, so that they will share its profits.*
- *Cooperating with famous universities and research academies both at home and abroad.*
- *Establishing R&D centers in relevant countries abroad.*
- *Establishing JVs with relevant international companies.*
- *Continually expanding in every respect and in every market.*
- *Going public both to raise capital and accelerate internal cultural changes.*
- *Internationalizing both the products and the capital.*
- *Having very ambitious goals, such as to become a first-class multinational group.*
- *Diversifying around the core business to remain competitive in the market and to achieve the ambitious goals.*
- *Keeping the modern TCM business core in equilibrium by stabilizing it with two health-related wings.*
- *Standing by the principle of achieving the "Harmonization of Man and Nature."*
- *Establishing as an ultimate goal the improvement of the health of humankind.*

CHAPTER 7

Entrepreneurship by Using Traditional Chinese Culture. Liu Kecheng, Dae Joo

Liu Kecheng, the president of *Qingdao Dazhou Yundong Yongpin Youxian Gongsi* (www.daejooleports.com; in English named "Qingdao Dae Joo Leports Co., Ltd." daejoo.en.china.cn), is a Chinese entrepreneur who is worried about preserving Traditional Chinese Cultural values, to which she devotes a great deal of effort. In fact, in 2009, she started providing annual training in Traditional Chinese Culture for university students,[1] which takes place on her company premises for free. In addition to this formal training, on Sundays the students are taken to visit a Red Cross retirement home, located in the western part of Qingdao. They go to practice the values they have learned; in particular, to show their love and compassion to people who need it. Every student receives ten days of training. After the completion of each training session (and always during the students' vacation time), new students are brought in to participate during the next vacation period. Students are lodged in Liu Kecheng's premises during their ten days of training. So far, sixty students have participated per year; 90% of them are from areas outside Shandong province, with 60% of them being females.

Liu Kecheng thinks that, since the twenty-first century is going to be the Chinese century, it is very important for young Chinese (and Chinese people in general) to study and practice the values of Traditional Chinese Culture, which are unique and at least 5,000 years old. She firmly believes and practices what is written outside the Red Cross retirement home, (which she visits every Sunday): "If there is harmony at home, there will also be harmony in the companies and the economy, and the whole country will prosper."

Liu Kecheng also uses and practices Traditional Chinese Cultural values to manage her business. Since 2003, all her employees (including all the manufacturing workers and staff receive ninety minutes of training on Traditional Chinese Cultural values every Wednesdays and Saturdays. In 2007, she introduced the practice of reading some paragraphs from Confucius to her employees; this takes place daily for thirty minutes before work. In 2010, she introduced training on quality management for the managers (who comprise 30% of the staff), which are taught once a week (from 15:00 to 17:30 hours) by outside professional teachers, included some from Taiwan. About 90% of her employees come from the countryside, and she has seen how their attitudes have changed after receiving this training. They face their work and lives with a more positive attitude, which is beneficial both for them and for the business. Liu Kecheng is also in the process of applying these values in her operations, which she expresses by saying "*yong zhonghua quantong zhutui xiandai qiye fazhan.*" She believes that this has a positive impact on the company's image, since clients see the emphasis she puts on the implementation of Traditional Chinese Culture and the distinct way her company does business.

Qingdao Dae Joo Leports Co., Ltd. is located in *Nanwang* Industrial Park, in Licang district, in the northeast part of Qingdao, Shandong province. It was established in 2002 as a *hezi* (joint venture) with a South Korean[2] company-Dae Joo-specializing in the design and manufacturing of all kinds of backpacks, sports bags, computer bags, and luggage. Using the most advanced Japanese and Chinese technology, it manufactures about 3.5 million high quality pieces per year, which are exported to Europe, the US, South-East Asia, and Australia. Only in 2008, in connection with the Olympic Games, did the company sell any of its production in the Chinese market, totaling about 1%. At the end of 2007, the company earned the TrustPass® certificate, which is provided by the China Internet Network Information Centre and Beijing International Business Credit

Evaluation Company, after completing an authentication and verification procedure conducted by a third-party credit-reporting agency. TrustPass® certification guarantees the identity and legitimacy of a Chinese supplier.

Up until 2010, Qingdao Dae Joo Leports Co., Ltd. had many well-known foreign clients: Nike, Adidas, Eastpak, REI, Decathlon, Victorinox, Lowe Alpine, The North Face, and Justsport. However, in that year many of these clients began shifting their production to other Asian countries, such as Indonesia, Vietnam, and the Philippines, so that by 2011 only Eastpak, REI, Decathlon, and Just Sport remained as clients—with all of them having decreased the volume of their procurement orders. This situation would have been disastrous for Liu Kecheng's company if the partners had not brought on board a very good new client at the end of 2009: the Korean company Lock & Lock. Liu Kecheng manufactures home-related products for this new client, including clothing baskets, food baskets, dish cloths, kitchen drapes, among other items.

Nevertheless, because of the very high quality of their products, the company suffered much less than most of its competitors did from the economic crisis; the reduction in product demand and in margins has greatly affected their sector over the last few years. In fact, the worst year for the company was 2008. During 2009, although still just focusing on the foreign markets, they managed to increase sales by over 10%. The fact that they did not depend on only one client or one country or geographical region has also helped them to successfully overcome these new economic challenges. About 60% of their exported production is sold in the US; 20% is sold in Europe (mostly: Switzerland, The Netherlands, Austria, Denmark, Finland, Italy, and Ireland); with the remaining 20% sold mostly in South East Asia and Australia, with some minor sales in Latin America and Africa. Many low-quality competitors were forced to close down in the first half of 2009, or fought to survive, adopting tactics like reducing their products' prices as much as 15%. However, Liu Kecheng's company strengthened itself as it continued to export goods and win new clients. At the same time, its capacity grew as it began positioning itself in the Chinese domestic market, which has been growing and should continue doing so in the years to come.

Liu Kecheng was born in 1960, in *Linyi*, located in the southern part of Shandong province, about a four-hour drive from Qingdao. She lived there until 1978, when she went to North Korea to study business administration, while working at a television station there. She came back to China in 1982 and relocated to Qingdao, where she started work as a manager in a government-owned relaxation and health center. In 1985, she married a public official working for the central government, and continued working at the center until 1994. Between 1990 and 1994, in parallel with her work at the center, she often traveled to South Korea, providing interpretation and translation services to Korean entrepreneurs, a well-paid job at the time.

In 1994, seeing how China was developing and how business people were prospering, she decided to start her own company *Zong Yi*, which was 100% owned by her. At first there were just fourteen employees. It was a difficult period, because of the heavy workload she assumed while her son was still quite young; however, she was so certain of where she was going that she did not place much importance on her workload. Her company started manufacturing bags and backpacks, which were the only type of products they manufactured until they began working for Lock & Lock. She knew she did not have any previous experience in manufacturing or in this sector, but she was sure she could learn by herself. And, since she knew so many Korean people, she thought she could find Koreans willing to help her and become her clients. In fact, the client for whom she had been doing translation and interpretation work was working in the same sector, and he assured her that he would buy her backpacks, which he did.

When Liu Kecheng started, there were already many companies manufacturing these kinds of products in the Qingdao area and exporting them to South Korea, so the competition was fierce. Since she did not have an assistant and had to learn everything from scratch, she worked every day from 5 am to 11 pm, and sometimes close to twenty-four hours a day just before the shipment of an export order. She did everything in the company (including driving the car many times a day) and at home (including cooking); she did so many things that today six people would be needed to undertake all those tasks. Fortunately, her parents-in-law helped her a bit with her only son, who was still very young.

By 2001, the company had already grown to 180 employees with an annual sales turnover of RMB 2 million. All products were exported, which was in line with her original idea and strategy: not to manufacture for the Chinese domestic market, which at that time, was more complicated and exhausting work.

In 2002, when it was time to introduce some changes to the business to continue moving forward, Liu Kecheng's older sister introduced her to the South Korean company Dae Joo. They ended up establishing a joint venture, with Liu Kecheng retaining 40% of the joint-venture's shares, leaving the remaining 60% in the hands of Dae Joo. Because she could communicate in Korean language, this helped her to make the decision to proceed with a Korean partner versus, for instance, Japanese or any other foreign company.

After establishing the joint venture, many changes were introduced in the business including a RMB 25.5 million investment. Liu Kecheng bought the land where the current factory is located, and Dae Joo bought the manufacturing technology. Seven Korean people moved to Qingdao to help with the building of the new plant and the reorganization of the company. Six departments were established: procurement, exports, client services, financial, administration, and human resources. Liu Kecheng created the position of deputy managing director to supervise everyone below her, hiring a Korean manager for the position.

Since then, the situation has changed greatly. Today, there is only one Korean employee based in Qingdao, who supervises the financial management of the company. The company has grown to over 800 employees), 80% of whom are women (as is traditional in this sector) with an average age of under 30 years old. The firm's annual sales turnover is now RMB 150 million, much lower than 2007's figure of RMB 200 million, but still higher than the figures in 2008, RMB 80 million, and 2009, RMB 100 million. Its net profit used to be around 5%, but margins have gone down progressively over the last few years and are now around 1.5–2%. Today, 70–80% of sales turnover is generated by just one client: Lock & Lock. Because of these factors, both Liu Kecheng and her partners want to develop their business in the domestic market. They have also introduced some techniques to increase productivity, such as just-in-time production.

The factory operates six days a week from Monday to Saturday. Normally, Liu Kecheng takes a break on Sundays, but sometimes she works seven days a week. Every two months, she travels to Seoul, South Korea, staying there two or three days. She also travels once a year to the US and to Japan for purposes of studying the market. The US relationships are very close, partly because of the historically close relationship that the US has enjoyed with South Korea. She does not travel often to Europe, but occasionally she visits there (and in other countries) to study their markets. In 2011, she visited eight countries in Europe: Norway, Finland, Sweden, Denmark, Ireland, The Netherlands, Switzerland, and Austria. Previously, she has also visited Brazil, which was a market she did not care for very much.

Until 2001, most of Liu Kecheng's clients were Korean or Japanese. The other markets were developed after 2002. Today, her business development efforts are still largely influenced by Dae Joo and her previous Korean business links. Liu Kecheng acknowledges that she has learned so much by working alongside South Koreans. In her opinion, the South Korean management style is closer to Western companies than her own. However, now that she has assimilated this knowledge while simultaneously practicing Traditional Chinese Culture, she does not much care for Western companies' management style.

In 2003, Liu Kecheng started studying the traditional history of China—Confucianism, Taoism, Buddhism—and enjoyed it very much. The deeper she delved into Traditional Chinese Culture, the more she liked it. These studies have become her hobby and her main interest in life. Her religion is Buddhism, and she has several Buddha statues and many other traditional Chinese objects in her house. In particular, she values the importance placed on taking care of others and showing one's love for them, that is, the central importance of compassion in their teaching. In her view, the drawback of Western companies is that they only seem interested in generating profits for the company, its shareholders, and top management; they do not put any particular emphasis on the well-being of their employees. As a result, she believes Western employees are only worried about making money. As a consequence, she believes they do not pay much attention to their colleagues, their working environment, or, quite often, their private life; as a result, they are not happy with themselves, and their job performance is lower than it should be. By contrast, Traditional Chinese Culture teaches giving love to the employees, taking care of them and their families, helping them when they need support, and generating a sense of community and harmony among them. When this is practiced, employees end up being happy with themselves and in harmony with others—with their colleagues and bosses at work, with their friends, and with their families.

Since Liu Kecheng started studying and applying Traditional Chinese Cultural values, her priority has become her employees. Her company has become like a home, in which all members are given love. To her all people are equal, no matter how low or high their cultural or educational background may be. Everybody has similar thoughts, feelings, and human needs, and everyone needs the same love and compassion. This is even more important when families are far away, which is the case for 80% of her employees, who are *waidiren* (original from other places of China). Liu Kecheng personally takes care of her employees' needs. She organizes birthday parties for them and celebrations for those that cannot return home for the Chinese New Year. Now all her employees call her "mama"; she is very pleased when she hears this. By taking care of all her employees without distinction, she has managed to show them how they were capable of doing things they considered impossible for them at first, helping them to grow both professionally and personally.

FOR LIU KECHENG, WESTERN COMPANIES' MANAGE-MENT STYLE HAS DRAWBACKS because for them, the wellbeing of its employees is not the number one priority and, as a result, employees are unhappy and their performance is lower than it could be.

Liu Kecheng is fairly certain that, without her employees' focused approach, her company would not be where it is today. Nor would it have done so well over the last stretch of difficult years. Many of her competitors, 30 in number, have found it difficult to cope with the challenges of recent years and survive. This is due to several factors. Her company's competitors are significantly smaller (typically with thirty to 200 employees) and have no proper management systems in place. Their corporate cultures are also very different from hers.

Before Liu Kecheng started studying and applying Traditional Chinese Culture and values in her company, her factory workers and operators often fought among themselves, stealing, drinking too much alcohol, and doing things "uncultured" and "uneducated" people often do. But now their attitude is completely different. Now they are happy with themselves and understand the importance of their work. Now they pay attention, for instance, to how they cut the fabric, so that it is not damaged while minimizing remnants.

The attitude of office employees and company managers has also changed greatly. Before, managers did not pay close attention to what she told them, and quite often forgot what had to be done, or did not follow the best way of doing something. Now, by contrast, she does not need to tell them anything; they do everything they are supposed to by themselves, and in the most appropriate manner. Whether she is present in the company or away on a business trip for days or weeks, it no longer matters. The employees take care of everything by themselves so that everything runs smoothly.

The change of attitude in Liu Kecheng's employees has positively impacted her business: production costs have decreased and product quality increased. This, in turn, has had a positive impact on profitability and on the company's positioning in the market. Liu Kecheng is very pleased with these results, and is particularly satisfied by how well the company is adapting to the changes in the market place and building up its competitive advantages.

In 2008, at a women entrepreneurs' meeting that took place in Qingdao, Liu Kecheng shared her experiences with other entrepreneurs. They were so interested that, for two years, she regularly organized training sessions for women entrepreneurs on Traditional Chinese Culture and values and on how to apply them in their companies. The first two training sessions were in December 2008, when 600 women entrepreneurs came to Qingdao for a four-day training session and in May 2009 when, through the Qingdao Entrepreneurs' Association, 1,200 entrepreneurs attended (50% of them male). Professors in the field also contributed, including professors from Beijing University and from higher learning institutions in Taiwan, Hong Kong, Australia, and the European Union. The fees paid for everything (included accommodation) were low, about RMB 1,000. After the four days of training, entrepreneurs began to observe changes in themselves. Very often, these entrepreneurs (and others) would visit

Liu Kecheng's company to observe. The first time she was contacted by a group of entrepreneurs (both men and women) that wanted to visit her company and learn from her experience was in August 2009.

In addition, in 2009, women from different parts of China came to Qingdao on Saturdays—for a full day of training on Traditional Chinese Culture and values, so they can apply these principles in their own companies.

Given how many entrepreneurs became interested in her experience, and because she wants to help other people as much as she can, Liu Kecheng plans to open a school or center to teach entrepreneurs Traditional Chinese Culture and values and how to apply them in their businesses. Her original plan was to do this in 2015, when she thought she would have more time available for the project. However, because of the current difficult market situation, she thinks her plans may have to be delayed. In any case, she is 100% certain that she will open this school, because for her it will again be a way of giving her love to other people. A further step will be to eventually transfer this school model to other countries in which there are a lot of *hanren* (overseas Chinese). A Japanese entrepreneur has already visited Liu Kecheng asking for advice on how to manage his Chinese employees.

Liu Kecheng's love and compassion for others is something she has cultivated at a personal level long before 2003. It is something her parents—both Buddhists—taught her. In 1994, she became interested in Buddhism and read many Buddhist texts. Under her influence, her husband also became a Buddhist in 1997, but not her son, who is still too young to pay attention to any religious faith. Since she became Buddhist, Liu Kecheng has paid much attention to the cultivation of her inner self. She sometimes prays, but what she does most is to practice love and compassion, which she firmly believes is what Buddhism is all about. In 2000, following Buddhist tradition and thinking that it was better for both her health and the preservation of the natural environment, she became vegetarian (but not strictly so, at least not since 2010). Her husband also became vegetarian in 2007 (but not her son). During all these years, she has never forgotten that *yiqie zhongsheng benlai shi fo* ("we all have Buddha nature").

Liu Kecheng does not worry much about the future. She knows that her business will grow and will continue diversifying its client base by developing the domestic market. She focuses on the present, on taking care of her employees, and on training them in Traditional Chinese Culture and values. She knows that by doing so, and by continuing to advance step-by-step, the future will bring good opportunities for her and her business. She thinks that it does not make much sense to worry about what has not happened yet, because what has to happen will happen.

To succeed in China's market, Liu Kecheng believes her company has to position itself in the segment of highest product quality. Their products for China's internal market should be of better quality and more expensive than their products for export. In 2009, she began seriously thinking about developing the internal market for backpacks, travel bags, and sport bags. She registered the following brands: Winner Cool (*Wanku* in Mandarin), the most expensive and targeted at the middle-high segment of the market; *Da Zhou*, the second most expensive; *Xiaoxin Tianxia* and *Dizigui*, less expensive brands; and *Da Zhou Tongxiao*, the cheapest brand. At the time, Liu Kecheng decided to start working in the domestic market with the Winner Cool brand and, little by little, introduce the other two registered trademarks.

But as time passed and her 100% export business began to change, she decided to simultaneously start with the *Dizigui* trademark for children's schoolbags. This line includes backpacks and pencil bags, as well as home-related products, such as clothing baskets, food baskets, dishcloths, and kitchen drapes. The *Dizigui* trademark is used for the children's bags because these products have an educational dimension, including texts from the *Dizigui* book.[3] The Chinese character—*hanzi*—that they are using for the character *gui* of their registered trademark is not the same as the book's name: here it means "guiding," while the *gui* of their trademark means "come back," showing students that Chinese traditional culture will come back. For the home-related products, she created the *Aibao* trademark, targeted at the medium-high segment of the market.

For the distribution of these products in the domestic market, Liu Kecheng decided to use a combination of traditional retailing and local distributors with direct sales to companies and events (business, cultural, and training related). For this purpose, she established a new department in her company, *Guonei Yinxiao*, and placed her son in charge of it. She thinks that, after almost three years of preparation for the domestic market, she will be successful. She believes her company's domestic market business can reach 10–50% of their sales turnover in the short-to-medium term, and could result in much bigger profits than the export business, but when this will happen she does not exactly know. What she knows is that they have to learn how to sell their products in the domestic market, which is completely different from selling them to multi-national companies for export. She also knows that the shrinking export market will bring fierce competition to the domestic market, which means that only companies—like hers—with high quality products, reasonable prices and good after-sales service will be successful.

Though one of her seven sisters is also a successful entrepreneur like herself, Liu Kecheng does not like to work with her family members. This is why she wants her only son, born in 1985, to learn how to start developing a business for himself. This is why she put him in charge of the new domestic market department. Previously, since his return from Australia in 2009, he has been supporting her with the company's trade. He graduated with a degree in architecture from the University of Notre Dame in Australia, where he spent six years. But he did not like Australia or the US, so he decided to return to China. She has taught her son Traditional Chinese Culture and values, which she hopes he will apply both in business and at home. He married in 2010.

When Liu Kecheng gets up in the morning, she feels great about having another day ahead to give love and compassion to her employees, to keep diversifying and growing her business, and becoming a model to help other entrepreneurs apply Traditional Chinese Culture to their businesses.

ENTREPRENEUSHIP BY USING TRADITIONAL CHINESE CULTURE MEANS:
- *Establishing the employees' wellbeing as priority number one.*
- *Managing the company like a home.*
- *Giving all employees equal love and compassion.*
- *Taking direct care of the employees' needs and personal problems.*
- *Helping all employees to grow professionally and personally.*
- *Showing employees that by giving love and compassion they can become happier people.*

- *Showing employees that by working in a more responsible way they can be happier.*
- *Generating a sense of community and harmony among employees.*
- *Generating a culture of mutual responsibility among employees.*
- *Generating a working environment and culture that can easily adapt to changes in the marketplace.*

CHAPTER 8

Entrepreneurship by Determination. Li Lanzhen, Tianyi

Li Lanzhen is the managing director of three companies: *Tianjin Tianyi* Construction Group Co., Ltd., Green Ocean Real Estate Co., Ltd. (www.tianyijianshe. com), and Changye Construction Industry Co., Ltd. Born in Shaoxing, Zhejiang province in 1966, she worked in Shaoxing as a school teacher until 1992, where she was employed as an executive assistant and accountant. She was hired by Guo Zhongchao—a civil engineer, with the highest engineering degree in China (*gao gongchengshi*). He is four years older than her. Guo Zhongchao had been given the assignment to open a subsidiary company in Tianjin for the Shaoxing government-owned construction company he worked for, *Shaoxing* No. 1 Construction Industry Group Co., Ltd. The firm had subsidiaries in Shanghai and Hangzhou and wanted to profit from the many opportunities available in the north, in particular in the city of Tianjin. As such, *Shaoxing* No. 1 Construction Industry Co., Ltd. (Tianjin Division) was established and Guo Zhongchao became its managing director.

In the spring of 1992, Li Lanzhen and her boss Guo Zhongchao—who would eventually become her husband and long-term partner—went north to Tianjin with some ten people, each carrying with them many hopes and dreams. They walked into an unknown but very promising market. They knew no one in the city, but were confident that by working very hard they would manage to comply with the mission they had accepted. They knew they had a long way ahead and would have to proceed step-by-step to show the high quality of work they performed. After trying very hard, in 1993, they finally got their first project: the *Haihua* building, a 10,000 square meter commercial housing project on Xianyang Road with construction costs of RMB 6 million. The nearby rundown *Xiaoyuan* Hotel became the temporary project's office. Both Li Lanzhen and her husband realized that the execution of this project was critical for their eventual establishment in the Tianjin market. Therefore, they made this very clear to each person involved in the project's implementation, everyone from managers to operational personnel. They started working when the sun rose and stopped when the sun set. Although the project was standard, they dealt with every single step carefully and strictly met the various construction standards, to make the project a benchmark in the Tianjin construction market.

The years that followed were extremely complicated for Li Lanzhen and her husband. They still knew nobody in the city and the first contract they had got there, because of its small size, was not enough to give them the required credentials to develop further business. Theoretically there were many big opportunities in the Tianjin market, but they just could not reach them. Finally, after a lot of hard business development work, they got the opportunity to build a university building, but the client gave them no money in advance. In fact, this same situation repeated itself over the next two projects they got. They asked their *Shaoxing* parent company for help but they only received RMB 500,000 to cover their advance costs, both for the university project and the two projects that followed. Despite the many difficulties faced by them, they did not give up. Eventually in 1995, when taking their driving lessons, they met a local person who ended up lending them the money they needed to successfully complete their first *Tianjin* projects.

In 1997, *Tianjin Huayuan* Industrial Group was founded; knowing that the New Technology Industry Park area had to be developed with new businesses and investments, they decided to establish there. The problem was, however, they lacked financing to begin building their facilities. Seeing the opportunity to work for this group, Li Lanzhen and her husband realized they needed to take some risks to be successful. "We basically saw and still see the market as a battleground, and risks exist on every battleground. What is important is to know if a company can dare to take risks because there are possibilities of success," she explained. So, when they were given the chance to build a RMB 2.8 million 16,000 square meter complex of five factories for a project fee of just RMB 150,000—despite the huge difference—they did not doubt their desire to do so.

Challenges did not end with this tiny budget, however. They were only 36 people, and when they arrived at the site they faced all sorts of problems: weeds grew everywhere on the saline-alkali land; water, electricity, and road infrastructure to be used during construction were totally non-existent. On the second day, they found that people had located three tents on the land, bicycles were everywhere, the food was rough, time was short, and the budget was too low. But, instead of giving up, they built all the initial buildings and installations on schedule. This ended up helping the zone to attract further foreign investments. After such an achievement, the leaders of the Park trusted them and "We began our real business and company's trademark building journey," said Li Lanzhen.

Upon completion of that project, they contracted six large projects, among which were: *Houtai*, *Hongzhe* Properties, and the *Xiqing* Building of Politics and Law. In the following years, the business became rooted in Tianjin, benefiting from Tianjin's aggressive development policies and gaining support from Tianjin's municipal government and many other local institutions. Over time, the Tianjin government became an important client for them. In 1999, following the privatization process initiated in the previous year by its parent company, *Shaoxing* No. 1 Construction Co., Ltd., was privatized and became an independent *Tianjin* firm. Li Lanzhen's husband was named general manager, while she took the deputy general manager position.

After all those difficult years since their arrival in Tianjin, in parallel with her work, Li Lanzhen began to study civil engineering. Three years later, she passed all the required examinations to become a civil engineer of the highest level—*gao gongchengshi*. She has continued studying, and from time to time has attended university courses. Having been in a managerial position since 1998, she decided to formalize her practical training by studying for an MBA at the *Tianjin Nankai Daxue*, from which she graduated in 2002. In 2009, she decided to update her knowledge and began an Executive MBA in factory management at *Zhongguo Qinghua Daxue* in Beijing, personally attending courses at the university four times a month. This Executive MBA has helped her to "put the pieces of the puzzle in the right places. Before, I acted on intuition, very often without knowing the implications of what I was doing. Now, I can put things in perspective, which is very helpful," Li Lanzhen explained.

Referring to the facilities they constructed for themselves over the years, Li Lanzhen explains that in October 1998, as the company was known to more and more people and their business kept expanding, they decided to build a villa-style office building. Fully designed and constructed by them, it is "a special building among the construction companies located in Tianjin." In 2002, when the company was significantly developed and had already gained a very good reputation in the Tianjin market, they needed to hire new people and create larger facilities. So, they constructed an advanced equipment residence-style office building in Houtai, Xiqing, which "was unique not only among the construction firms located in Tianjin, but also among those located throughout the country."

In 2004, *Shaoxing* No. 1 Construction Industry Co., Ltd. changed its name to Changye Construction Industry Co., Ltd., leaving management responsibility in the hands of Li Lanzhen and her husband, a situation that has continued until today. Both retain about 25% of Changye Construction Industry Co., Ltd.'s shares.

Also that same year, as the market kept expanding and the business growing, Li Lanzhen and her husband established *Tianjin Tianyi* Construction and Development Co., Ltd., which later on became *Tianjin Tianyi* Construction Group Co., Ltd. The two founders held 19% of the shares while the remaining shares were distributed among ten different shareholders, some of them from Tianjin. Li Lanzhen became its managing director, emphasizing in this way her experience in business development over the years. Her husband became the company's chairman. She explained that, in 2006, the company had reached annual sales revenue of RMB 1.2 billion, a construction area of one million square meters, 600 white-collar employees, and a construction team of 4,000 workers. Then, they realized they needed to change their office premises once again, building a modern office building. In spring 2007, *Tianyin* Group moved to its current location, where they have enough land for further expansion. That same year they intensified their business development activities in Shenzhen and won a construction project for *Xiangang Zhongwen Daxue*, The Chinese University of Hong Kong. It was also in 2006 that *Tianjin Tianyi* earned the *Tianjin* Excellent Creditable Construction Enterprise

Award, "a very important step in the evolution and future development of the group." Over the years, the group has established 100%-owned subsidiaries in: Beijing, Shenzhen, Guanzhou, Zhuhai, Xian, Chengdu, Chongqing, and Inner Mongolia. Currently, Li Lanzhen and her husband hold 10% of *Tianjin Tianyi* Construction Group Co., Ltd.'s shares.

The same year, they started their first real estate project on a piece of land they had previously acquired with the idea of developing a housing project. The initiation of the real estate activities completely transformed the size and profitability of their business. In their first year, they generated sales turnover of RMB 60 million (higher than the RMB 50 million their construction business had after 12 years of hard work) and a net profit over five times higher than their construction business—15% vs. 3%. Since then, the real estate business has provided the group with the highest relative profitability as housing prices have kept increasing; it seems many people want to buy an apartment in Tianjin. In turn, constant rising prices have generated significant real estate investments from local people, who hope tomorrow's prices will still be higher than today's. "But, since the government introduced restrictions on buying real estate, the situation has now changed," explained Li Lanzhen, who also stated that the market has not grown as much as it may have appeared to. She has been managing the real estate business since it started and has about eighty white-collar employees under her responsibility. To separate their construction business from their real estate activities, in 2010 they created Green Ocean Real Estate Co. Ltd. *Luhai Fandichang Youxian Gongsi*, which they are now using for their real estate business activities. Li Lanzhen and her husband have kept full ownership of this company, which has offices located in the Xiqing district of Tianjin, in Zhongbei Town. Its annual development capacity is 800,000 square meters, and it has developed several large projects, which amount to an area of 2 million square meters: Green Ocean Qingxinyuan; Tianyi Modern Classical—located in the center of Jinghai county, in the area between the old and the new city; Forest Valley—located in the center of Bohai Economic Rim and characterized by its ecological approach; Green Ocean Green Belief—located in the core development area of Zhongbei Town, a modern residential area in Tianjin's Xiqing district; and Xincheng Mansion. Annual sales turnover for this company is around RMB 8 billion and its current profitability being 10%.

Despite the high profitability of their real estate projects, Li Lanzhen prefers the construction industry as it requires the development of special abilities that cannot be so easily replicated from one day to the next; over time, these special abilities can transform themselves into competitive advantages. She believes their corporate culture has much to do with their construction background, which forces professionals to keep improving to be winners. She likes that culture. In fact, by listening to her, it is quite easy to observe that she is in love with her civil engineering profession.

FOR LI LANZHEN, THE CONSTRUCTION INDUSTRY HAS POSITIVE FEATURES FOR SELF-DEVELOPMENT AND COMPETITIVENESS because it forces professionals to keep improving to be winners and it requires to develop especial abilities, which over time transform themselves into inherent company's competitive advantages.

As for their construction activity today, they were happy that they achieved: annual production of several million RMB when they first came to Tianjin, while today their aggregate production is over RMB 3 billion. In 1997 their sales turnover was RMB 30,000 and their profitability non-existent, while today their sales turnover is over RMB 2 billion (80% of it generated by the Tianyi group), its profitability around 3% and its capital around RMB 5.9 billion. Since their first building was completed in 1993, they have constructed over 200 key projects, including commercial buildings, schools, universities, libraries, government departments and administrative centers, scientific research institutes, factories, sport centers, offices, and housing, among other projects. Among those that can be mentioned: Tianjin University of Technology; Tianjin Academy of Fine Arts; State Safety Bureau; Tianjin University of Science and Technology; Tianjin Foreign Studies University; Administrative Centre of *Jinghai* County; International Mathematics Research Centre of *Nankai* University; Tianjin International Hall for Light Industries Commerce and Trade; Tianjin Normal University; *Hebei* University of Technology; Tianjin University of Technology and Education; College of Music; College of Physical Education; and Tianjin Talent Technology Mansion. About 75–80% of their clients are governments and government-owned institutions.

For their current business activities, about 60% is pure construction and the remaining 40% real estate. For years, the group has been recognized as "contract focused, credit observed." It is regarded as one of the ten enterprises that have contributed to Tianjin's development. It has been honored with many prizes such as the "*Haihe* Cup" for high quality projects in Tianjin, the "*Luban* Award" for its high-quality national, provincial, and municipal architecture projects, and the "2009–2010 landmark of urban housing in China, Excellent Residential Estate." They have won certificates for quality, environment, and health and safety management systems. They are also in the process of acquiring the right to operate overseas. *Tianjin* Building Committee has listed them as an "advanced construction enterprise" and "quality-trusted enterprise." *Tianjin Tianyi* Construction Group, while 100% privately owned, is one of the 500 largest construction companies in China. It has the I general contracting Grade, the highest ranking a construction company can receive in China, for both its infrastructure and building construction activities. This lets them build very large infrastructure projects and buildings of more than four floors tall.

Over the years, the group has grown by including a large number of the vertical construction industry chain's functions, such as: architectural design; civil engineering; a color-steel structure plant, located in *Zhangwo* Industrial Zone; a plant for plastic steel windows and doors; electromechanical installations, covering a broad range from boilers and air conditioning units to intelligent buildings; decoration, both indoors and outdoors; real estate, mainly residential housing; facilities and property management, or *wuye* in Mandarin, a particularly Chinese concept; city planning; city and ancient garden development; irrigation; and construction labor. They also own a hotel with a restaurant, Old *Xianheng* Hotel, which opened in 2007 as a branch of *Shaoxing Xianheng* Hotel Chain Development Co., Ltd. This hotel combines traditional and modern style, reflecting water's role as an element in Shaoxing's culture. Located beside the group's headquarters, it offers the same menu as the original restaurant, which has operated in Shaoxing since 1894; it has become very popular, attracting many local residents. The figures confirm this as it generates sales turnover of RMB 10 million and net profit of about 10%.

Among their other subsidiary companies are: Tianjin Tianyi Global Trades Development Co., Ltd., Tianjin Yuanzheng Construction Labor

Co., Ltd., Tianjin Tianyue Architectural Design Co., Ltd., which combines cultural backgrounds; Tianjin Yuanzheng Decoration Industrial Co., Ltd., established in 1999; Tianyi Theme Culture Hotel, started in 2009 in Jixian county; Tianjin Guorong Fengye Real Estate Development Co., Ltd.; Tianjin Xinhe Real Estate Development Co., Ltd.; Tianjin Zhongyitiancheng Real Estate Development Co., Ltd.; Tianjin Xingkeyuan Real Estate Development Co., Ltd., established in 2004, which has developed an energy-saving, complete day lighting project with total built area of 62,000 square meters in Qingxinyuan Uptown, located in Yangliuqing town, Xiqing district; and Tianjin Tianyi Scientific and Technological Co., Ltd., established in 2005. Among their subsidiaries there is also a firm providing required after-sales services; a company manufacturing their corporate uniforms, and a wine distribution firm, started in 2006, including white, red, and yellow wines (red wine is from Tianjin—from a joint venture with a French company—while yellow wine[1] mostly comes from Shaoxing.)

Li Lanzhen's group follows common building practices in China, manufacturing every possible component on-site. For instance, all prestressed concrete pillars are manufactured on-site. Their general approach is not only to do their own construction work, but also to finish the units and sell them directly to the purchaser. This is in line with the integration of their value chain that they have pursued over the years. Li Lanzhen elaborates that this is why, for instance, they have a Mechanical Device Management and Logistics Base, which includes more than 2,000 medium and large-sized mechanical devices for all the types of construction projects they work on. She claims that they have the ability to supply one million square meters of building materials at one time. Another example of their integrated value chain approach is the fact that, since 2005, they have been pursuing the technological development of their construction materials through their subsidiary Tianjin Tianyi Scientific and Technological Co., Ltd.

As to the group's organization, Li Lanzhen says that there are four people who report to her in positions equivalent to deputy managing director: two dealing with construction, one with real estate, and one with finance. Because of the origins of the group, 80% of the management team (50% in the case of *Luhai*) is from Shaoxing; they originally came to Tianjin in 1992. As for the staff, all together (including the Tianyi group and the Changye group) they have around 1,000 regular white-collar employees, including

55 middle-level managers, 24% of whom have a Bachelor's degree, and 2.6% of whom have a Master's or PhD degree. As for the age of their employees, 9.3% are over 50 years old, while about a third of them are under 30 years old. About 70% of their white-collar employees work on the construction side of the business. In addition, they have temporary employees and workers for their various projects' sites: over 10,000 in all. The hotel employs another 100–150 people and the count goes on, as they continue adding new businesses to the company. For instance, in 2009 they established a joint venture with *Zhongguo Nongcun Yinhang*, also known as the "Agricultural Bank of China" to provide the bank with a real estate investment assessment service.

When referring to their corporate culture, Li Lanzhen said: "There is a well-known quote from Wang Xizhi's *Lantingji Xu* (*Preface to the Poems Collected from the Orchid Pavilion*).[2] "As for this day, the sky is clear, the air is fresh, and the breeze is mild. High above is the immense universe. Around us are myriads of variety. Stretching our sights and freeing our minds will allow us to fully enjoy the sound and sights. This is really delightful." If applied to a company, this means that: a favorable atmosphere and a warm and harmonious environment will provide limitless space for the company to develop. And this kind of atmosphere is precisely what we have been trying to create in our group. Our core values are: to know what is honorable and what is disgraceful, to contribute sincerely to every task we undertake, to apply self-discipline and to pursue our further development. We seek excellence, cooperation, and mutual benefits. We foster progress, everyday improvement, and precision, and strive to be number one in the marketplace. For us, the clients always come first; we place a lot of attention on constantly communicating with them and providing them with first class service. Our service objective is: "Quality first, and customer first." We consider it to be important to continuously adapt to market trends and take every new opportunity that may become available.

Internally, we are people-oriented and responsibility-focused, placing much emphasis on standards, high efficiency, and perfection. We encourage our employees to: love their work, be industrious, stay in line with rules and regulations, be skillful in business, be progressive in learning, serve the clients warmly, pay attention to efficiency, be friendly to each other, be civilized and polite, and be innovative and work together to achieve the group's goals. We invest a lot every year to build our internal corporate culture. For instance, we built a library, and publish a monthly magazine titled *Tianjin News and Information*—whose main aim is to mobilize our employees; we also frequently organize activities such as quality education, knowledge contests, technical competitions, and cultural and physical entertainment. Our magazine has helped develop employees' participant consciousness and team spirit; it has had a great influence in the creation of our corporate culture. To improve the working environment and living conditions of our personnel, we invested RMB 200 million in the construction of a 260,000 square meter intelligent office building as well as a 3,800 square meter hotel in *Huayuan* Industrial Zone, where we still have plenty of space for expansion.

Because of the nature of our business, for our construction workers— all *waidiren*, we place great emphasis on safety and prevention. We emphasize that preventing accidents is most important, and we have developed and used appropriate systems (included GB/T28001) to guarantee compliance with our safety standards and lower the risks of accidents for our employees. We constantly remind our employees to follow the principle of 'safety first—*anquan diyi*,' but preventing more important incidents from happening even more important." In all our construction sites, we have many signs and messages reminding employees about the importance of safety and prevention, as well as a number of people (from one to five, depending on the project's size) whose sole responsibility is to protect workers' health and safety. At the end of the work day every day (from 17:30 to 18:00 hours), these safety employees or the project manager (a civil engineer) give workers 30 minutes training on safety and prevention.

Because they have no family here and avoid the burdens of a long distance commute in the city, our construction workers live at their respective construction sites. They work eight hours a day.

Given the importance of quality in our business, for many years we have devoted great attention to employees' training at all levels—managers, engineers, technical personnel, and construction workers. The management team has been directly involved, as well as other personnel, in these training activities; we have also invited outside experts to hold lectures. Every employee must pass an examination to verify his or her level of safety knowledge. Excellent performers are given prizes while those who have not passed their exams are given time to succeed; if they cannot pass their exams, we dismissed them.

Over time, we have built up a team with strong cohesiveness and high professional qualifications that has become the main force for our business development. We respect our employees, care for them and they appreciate it. We have created an environment that allows them to fully develop their talents. The development of our group also needs the understanding of our staff's relatives who should value our employees' hard work. We have managed to communicate to them that if we have great and far-reaching ambitions, remain united combining our efforts to build a prosperous future, conduct innovation with firm determination, keep improving, give back to society with sincerity, and show our excellence, we will surely be able to lead today, win tomorrow, and constantly renew the group. We constantly remind them that our corporate motto is: 'Be credible, progress, improve every day, be precise and strive to be the best.' We also tell our group to say, 'people first, with their strong points up front.' The fact that we have senior managers that started with us in 1992 is a positive sign that our management style helps us retain our best employees.

As for her personal management style, Li Lanzhen is said—by those that have known her for many years—to be different from other construction sectors' leaders (who are mostly male). She explains that her style is "First I do, then I give other people a chance to do," so that she can show employees the way to proceed. When employees have problems among themselves or with a particular project, Li Lanzhen is always ready to help solve their problems. She is defined by her management team as: "a good mother who cares about her employees; a person for whom there are no obstacles that can prevent her from reaching her goals; a person with the body of a female, but the inner attitude and strength of a male; *bu yiban de nuren* ('not a common woman')."

She acknowledges that competition in the market is fierce. In particular, in Tianjin, there are many construction companies (most of them private) from all over China, including many from Hebei, Anhui, Henan, Jiangsu, and Shandong. However, she feels confident about her company's future because of their high quality work, and their excellent technology, care for the environment, and service during and after construction. She said they will overcome challenges by continuing to follow the same rules they have followed since the company was started: "The best win and the fittest survive," meaning that they have remained active, taking every opportunity the market has had to offer, and transforming every threat into an opportunity in order to grow stronger. It was by following this rule that they developed from small to large, from weak to strong, from no presence in the Tianjin construction market to becoming a main player in it. It was also following this rule that they completed the successful transition from competing to survival, enhancing their reputation, which is where they stand today. It was because of their reputation and highly competitive bidding proposals that they were given the opportunity to participate in the expansion of *Binhai* International Airport and Tianjin Port Enterprise Cultural Center.

As for the evolution of infrastructure policies implemented by the government since 2007, Li Lanzhen acknowledges that the construction business has benefited from them. An example of these policies is the tax incentives offered for projects on key public infrastructure developments, which have been in effect since January 1, 2008. Real estate prices have not been affected by the global economic turmoil; they respond to market rules specific to China—to be more precise—market rules that are specific to Tianjin. As such, because of government restrictions imposed on the number of houses each family can own, the real estate business has become complicated. "Our Tianjin projects are still quite good, although previous to 2010 we had a profitability of 19–20% whereas today we have only 10%. In this new scenario, we decided not to prepare any new land for housing in Tianjin, but to diversify to other products, such as offices. In other locations, such as Inner Mongolia, housing real estate projects can still be very profitable," explained Li Lanzhen.

With respect to their future plans, she explained that the company wants to continue playing a leading role in China while becoming better known in other countries. For these goals, they will continue with their marketing efforts building a reputable, well-recognized trademark. For this, they will continue using services from third parties, since "the marketing and communication culture is very different from our engineering background." In the domestic market, they aim to participate in demanding large-scale construction projects, as well as to continue expanding in their related business areas: construction design, civil engineering, steel structures, electro-mechanical installations, interior design, and real estate. Seeing the Chinese government's emphasis on using BT (Build Transfer) and BOT (Build Operate Transfer) schemes, in 2011, Lin Lanzhen's group created a new company, *Dongfang Tianyi*, that will perform all functions associated with BT and BOT building projects. This company is 27% owned by her group; the remaining 73% is in the hands of *Zichan Guanli Gongsi*, a company fully owned by the Chinese government. Through *Dongfang Tianyi*, they will not only participate in investment and construction of many government projects, such as hospitals and schools, but also in real estate projects all over China. This is one of the reasons her group has already opened subsidiaries in many different regions in China. Their first BOT project is a hospital in Tianjin, which was begun in 2012. To participate in BT and BOT infrastructure projects, the *Tianyi* group is already in the process of establishing a *hezuo* with a company fully owned by the government—*Zhonghang Guihua Jianshe Fazhan Youxian Gongsi*. Once completed, the name of the new company will be *Zhonghang Tianyi*. The *Tianyi* group's goal is to achieve annual sales revenue of RMB 6 billion and one day be listed, although they are still not clear about the details yet.

In the international market, their plan is to develop their business by following the large government-owned construction companies operating overseas. Li Lanzhen's plan is to provide these companies with what she calls "overseas labor services," that is, to partner with them—*hezuo*—to perform construction activities related to infrastructure and real estate projects that these large companies are financing all over the world, including Africa. To do this, they may use the same *hezuo* investment companies created for the domestic market. She envisions this happening in about three years, once they have completed the process of accreditation as a construction company permitted to operate overseas.

"Our ultimate goal is to create a huge construction group that clients perceive as excellent, that competitors see favorably, and that society trusts. This will be our contribution to society. Looking back to the past, our hard work has generated a rich harvest; looking forward to the future, our efforts will bring us prosperity," Li Lanzhen explained. She truly believes that "a person who seeks success will never give up, because the meaning of life for him or her is to diligently work to generate prosperity. Looking toward the future, challenges will coexist with opportunities, and credit will lie together with honors, but our decisions and great achievements will last forever. In our group, we have always held the florid band flower of *Tianyi* with our powerful hands in order to realize our goals, to become stronger and more powerful, following our innovative steps by improving and never being satisfied. By meeting the rising sun, by sharing our hopeful attitude, we expect new growth. Based on our principle of 'natural, harmonious, creditable, and mutual benefits' we are looking forward to creating a splendid future through cooperating with our friends from every industry."

Li Lanzhen's daughter was born in 2000, and raised thanks to her mother's help, who relocated from Shaoxing to Tianjin in order to take care of her grand-daughter. Her father decided to remain in her hometown because, before he retired, he was seldom there. He is a civil engineer as well. Her parents have two more children, but neither of them (nor anyone else in the family), has an entrepreneurial spirit. Her two brothers have worked in her group for close to 15 years, doing human resources management work. She claims that by including her original family members in her workplace has not been a problem, since her brothers get along quite well with her husband. "They think very similarly," an attribute she considers a prerequisite for avoiding any difficulties with her husband. Li Lanzhen explains that, in managing human resources and implementing corporate culture, she is stronger than her husband, while his strengths are in financing, quality, and safety control.

Li Lanzhen is certainly a person of determination. Her business card does not show any title. She believes that, beneath the chairman's position, every employee is equal, where each individual is just a person with the goal of implementing his or her actions. Thus, there is no need for her to show her title anywhere, although every other employee in the company does so. While in her office, she wears the group's uniform with its logo on display; every employee does the same as her. When participating in important outside events, she may wear a suit with a company logo pin on her jacket lapel; every employee does the same as her. However, despite her rigid and austere appearance, magnified somewhat by her group's uniform (she wears a tie and pants), she is a person with many hobbies, including: reading, singing, listening to music, talking to people, and traveling. She has traveled to Europe and Japan to study the markets, and hopes to make time to travel there as a tourist. For the time being, she works seven days a week: from Monday to Saturdays on daily routines and on Sunday for planning issues. She has developed plans for the group's next five, eight, and ten years, but today she is more relaxed since she has completed her Executive MBA studies. On both sides of the inner stairs of her head-quarters building, all the way from the main hall to the top floor, are arrangements of red flower-pots, helping to generate a pleasing, relaxing environment. It was her idea to put the flower-pots there; they are a clear manifestation of Li Lanzhen's clear determination and hidden sensitivity toward the beauty of life and the well-being of the people around her.

When Li Lanzhen gets up in the morning, she is happy she has another day ahead to continue leading her team toward the expansion and diversi-fication of her business, and to continue working hard to implement her ideas and plans in the industry she loves so much.

ENTREPRENEURSHIP BY DETERMINATION MEANS:

- *Not giving up, no matter how numerous and cumbersome the difficulties.*
- *Having the self-confidence to know that negative situations do not last.*
- *Applying self-discipline.*
- *Working diligently to generate prosperity for all.*
- *Looking for support—wherever it is available—to demon-strate the capabilities and quality of the company's perfor-mance.*
- *Being flexible in one's business approach in order to win the market's confidence.*
- *Executing every project—regardless of its size and nature—with the maximum consciousness and quality, as if it was the dream project every company would want to have.*
- *Seeing the market as a battleground, where risks should be taken when there are strong possibilities of success.*
- *Persisting in taking the market's opportunities, even when they seem unachievable.*
- *Developing and implementing plans and actions without delay in order to profit from the opportunities.*

- *Always keeping in mind that challenges coexist with opportunities.*
- *Transforming every threat in an opportunity in order to grow stronger.*
- *Remembering that quality and clients always come first.*
- *Prioritizing technology and conducting innovation with a strong determination.*
- *Keep expanding and diversifying in order to respond to the needs of the market and clients.*
- *Diversifying with the aim of internally providing all vertical integrated functions.*
- *Developing international business by following large government-owned clients that are operating overseas.*
- *Creating a favorable atmosphere by developing a warm, harmonious environment to retain talent and bring limitless space for the firm to develop.*
- *Investing in building a strong internal corporate culture.*
- *Paying a great deal of attention to the health, safety, and wellbeing of the employees.*
- *Developing and applying thorough, comprehensive standards and procedures.*
- *Remembering that employees are the main force behind business growth and expansion.*
- *Devoting a lot of attention to employees' training.*
- *Uniting employees' efforts to build the business' prosperous future.*
- *Fostering credibility, progress, everyday improvement, precision and perfection to become the top performer in the market place.*
- *Remembering that "hard work generates a rich harvest and that efforts bring prosperity."*
- *Having great and far-reaching ambitions.*
- *Continuing to work very hard to build a high quality trademark that clients perceive as being excellent, competitors approve of, and society trusts.*
- *Improving in order to become winners.*

CHAPTER 9

Entrepreneurship by Intuition. Xing Hui, Laote

If not for anything else, all over the world Qingdao is famous for its beer. Many say it is "the best Chinese product ever made" but its name is forever associated with Germany.

Germany had a presence in China from 1861, focusing on the Qingdao region specifically. In 1897, after the murder of two German missionaries, Germany began its official occupation of Shandong Province and JiaoZhou (Kiao-Chau) peninsula, obtaining a ninety-nine-year lease in 1898. The area then was considered a colony and administered by the German navy. Tsingtao (Qingdao in the new pinyin transcription) was its administrative center.

German settlers brought their architecture, culture, and businesses with them to Qingdao and on August 15, 1903, the *Tsingtao* Brewery Factory (Germania Brauerei), was established. The process, equipment, and raw materials were all German imports. But it was the local water of Qingdao that was the distinctive ingredient in the beer. The spring water used in the recipe was from Laoshan (Lao Mountain),[1] an area dotted with many clear springs and waterfalls. Laoshan's water is known to be rich in minerals and said to be good for people's health. The beer was awarded a gold medal at the Munich International Exhibition in 1906, establishing its way in the international market.

The history of *Tsingtao* Brewery has essentially paralleled the modern history of China. When the country was occupied, so was the brewery. As China embraced Communism, the brewery became a state-owned business. When China opened its doors, Tsingtao was one of the first products to be exported, and new breweries in the Qingdao area began to spring up. One of them was *Qingdao Laote* Beer Co., Ltd., whose slogan is "100% *Laoshan* spring brewing."

Xing Hui, CEO of *Qingdao Laote* Beer Co., Ltd., www.laotebeer .com (*Laote*), was born in 1966 in Huhehaote (*Hohhot*), an Autonomous Region in the province of Inner Mongolia, where her family came from. Her grandparents used to be large landowners in Inner Mongolia, but they lost everything in 1949. Her father was a director working in the army. She has two sisters and a younger brother. She did study to become a qualified electronic components professional, and in 1986, began working in an electronic components engineering company, assisting the engineers. But soon she realized this was not the type of work she wanted to do. She felt she was more creative and had other abilities. She needed more room to put these talents to work, so she decided to become an entrepreneur, establishing a supermarket in 1988. She was successful in her businesses, so much so that in 1989 she was given an award for the youngest successful entrepreneur in Hohhot.

In 1990, Xing Hui opened a hotel with over forty rooms, on land near the supermarket. Almost simultaneously, she became involved with *Qingdao Laoshan* Beer in Hohhot and agreed to represent eight of their products; little by little she did the same with some other *Qingdao* beer companies. She began getting a sense of the beer business while representing the beer companies and intuitively felt that it might be a good business to be in. So, she decided to come to Qingdao to gain the closest contact with the sector.

Xing Hui still remembers very well how she came to Qingdao in August 1994 to visit the Qingdao Guoji Pijiujie (Qingdao International Beer Festival). While there, she confirmed the potential of Qingdao's LaoShan beer business and decided that she, and eventually her whole family, should relocate to this city to start a brewery. She came back soon after to study the market and the feasibility of her project. Her intuition was confirmed by the facts. So on November 8, 1994, she relocated with her only daughter to Qingdao to implement her project. Her husband remained in Hohhot, running the hotel and the supermarket, assisted by Xing Hui's brother.

Xing Hui still remembers quite well how difficult everything was upon her arrival and how exhausted she was at the end of each day. She did not know anybody in the new city, and she was not familiar with the business or cultural atmosphere there. She knew nothing about the beer industry and had no manufacturing background. On top of all this, her daughter was still very young.

However, she did not give up, instead realizing that she needed to team up with some local people from the brewing industry who could provide her with access to the right technology and knowledge on how to establish and operate a brewery. Through her previous direct contacts as a beer product representative, she identified a couple of people who eventually became her partners in Qingdao Laote Beer Co., Ltd. The fourth partner, although still in Hohhot and so not of much help to Xing Hui, was her husband.

The factory was established in the Yanyunjian Laoshan district. The company was named "*Laote*" precisely because: (1) the factory was located in the *Lao* Mountain district (in the eastern part of Qingdao) and water coming from the *Laoshan* springs was going to be used for the brewing of the beer ("Lao") and (2) because she and her husband, the founders of the company, came from *Huhehaote* ("te"). They started with an investment of RMB 4.5 million, increasing it to RMB 12.5 million in 1996, when they decided it was the right time to expand the brewery.

In July 1995, they began brewing beer, but things were still complicated over the next couple of years. Xing Hui had to climb a very steep learning curve, since she did not know the market and had no previous management experience (her previous businesses were more family-oriented). In fact, this industry proved to be fiercely competitive, much more so than she had envisioned. Six companies with six distinct trademarks operating in the same area—included, *Tsingtao, Laoshan,* and HB beers—all competed for the same market with the same marketing message: namely, "100% *Laoshan* spring brewing." They did this because *Qingdao* beer is popular all over the world, because Qingdao is where Chinese beer was first manufactured and because *Laoshan's* water has consistently produced high quality beer. Undaunted, Xing Hui fought for her company's survival, so much so that today only two of those six companies remain (*Tsingtao* Brewery, government-owned and *Laote* Beer); the other four brewing companies were acquired by *Beijing Dao Pijiu*.

By 1997, Xing Hui's company sales had grown significantly with sales turnover of RMB 25 million. However, profitability was close to zero. That was the situation for her *Qingdao* brewery, whereas her businesses in Hohhot were doing pretty well. In fact, the Hohhot businesses were doing so well that she and her husband had increased their investments there. In truth, she did have a lot of misgivings. She knew she could not just leave and go back to how things were before August 1994; she was driven to succeed. Otherwise, there would have been no reason for her to have left Hohhot and work so hard since her arrival in Qingdao. At the same time, she was afraid of failure if she could not gain the consumer support she needed to make her business grow.

In November 1997, Xing Hui decided she needed some time to think, isolating herself for eleven hours in the hotel *Qingwashi*, in the *Laoshan* area. Despite her dedicated brainstorming, she still did not see a way out of the brewery's situation of near zero profitability. A strategic path to success seemed to elude her. However, when she left the hotel she decided she would have to find a solution in the next twenty-three hours. She returned to the brewery, and looking at how much she had already built there, she suddenly realized that the previous two years were only the beginning of her long future in the brewing industry. This was just the beginning of her learning curve, but things were not as strategic or decisive as they had looked to her just a few hours before. She told herself that she needed to continue moving ahead in implementing her plan, but she needed a new attitude, forgetting all the difficulties and stress of the past couple of years. This would be just like starting all over again; she was sure that, looking ahead, things were going to turn around.

The next step for her to take, then, was to improve the quality of her products and the all-Chinese manufacturing technology. For this, she decided to make a new investment—the third and largest since the initial investment in 1995—of RMB 20 million to install foreign brewing equipment. She also decided to begin enlarging the size of their land, since she was sure the company was going to expand; they would soon need more space.

Her intuition proved to be right; all throughout 1998, she could see how impressed her clients were with the brewery's new equipment and products. In April 1999, the business, finally, began to take off and turned profitable. *Laote*'s 1999 sales turnover was RMB 50 million, and its net profit was around 4%.

In 2000, they decided it was high time for Xing Hui's husband to relocate to Qingdao so they closed the Hohhot businesses. Xing Hui's need for immediate help was so urgent that they did not at all try to sell the Inner Mongolia businesses, for it would have taken them too much time. By the end of the year, Xing Hui had built a domestic sales network of about 130 representatives and *Laote*'s beer was being sold in over twenty Chinese cities. In 2007, a new building she constructed required a total investment of RMB 70 million. This plus the RMB 7 million they had invested since 1997 enlarged their land property to its current two *hectare* size. In 2002, Xing Hui's company introduced a significant innovation in the industry: the ability to open their glass bottles of beer (which, along with their cans, are supplied, by manufacturers in Beijing) using pull-tab caps.

Today, *Laote*'s factory covers a total area of about 1,300 Ha, including the original small 5,500 square meter building, still in operation. The company primarily brews three types of beer, "all of which use 100% *Laoshan* water." Xing Hui emphasizes that *Huangpijiu* (blonde beer), the first one they brewed, accounts for over 60% of their sales. *Heipijiu* (black beer), which they started brewing in 1995 soon after *Huangpijiu* and *Ganpijiu* (white beer), which they introduced in 2001, together account for about 25–30% of *Laote*'s sales.

Daily production is about 200,000 bottles, all of which are sold in the domestic market: 30% in Shandong province, including Qingdao, where they sell 10% of their production, while the remaining 70% is sold in the western and southern parts of China that are relatively close to Shandong. "Due to the current logistics situation in China, distance is very important for this business," says Xing Hui. Thus, they have never tried to reach the distant markets, including Inner Mongolia, where they are originally from. The company owns ten trucks, which are used for direct distribution of their products in the local Qingdao market. Xing Hui acknowledges that logistics in China, though changing and improving very rapidly, is still very expensive (20% to 30% of the total product costs), in particular for long distance shipping when they have to use long-distance trucks (instead of rail) for their product.

Laote's current annual sales turnover is about RMB 100 million, but profitability has gone down in the last few years. This is mainly due to fierce competition in the industry that is even greater than before. Not only are they facing a great deal of competition from domestic breweries located all over China, but also from foreign beer companies, whose products' penetration in the Chinese market has been increasing over time.

FOR XING HUI, COMPETITION IN THE CHINA MARKET IS FIERCE because in every sector, there are many domestic competitors and foreign products' penetration has been increasing over time.

Xing Hui's company has over 220 employees, all of them from the Qingdao area; 85% are factory workers. They must comply with the manufacturing procedures of the company, especially the hygiene standards. For instance, before entering the brewery itself, where about 75 people work, they must change their clothes and shoes. Because the distances in Qingdao are so great, and for financial support, the company provides 60% of its employees with affordable housing near *Laote*'s brewery.

Qingdao Laote Beer Co., Ltd.'s four original partners are still there today, though 70% of the shares are now in Xing Hui's hands. The remaining 30% are split among the other three partners, with her husband having the biggest share: 20%. All three of Xing Hui's partners work in the company: her husband is the managing director and the other two partners are responsible for technology and procurement, the same functions they used to perform before joining Xing Hui's project, when they were working at (the old) *Laoshan* company.

In a way, Xing Hui's husband has always followed her in her entrepreneurial activities. He did the same back in 1992, when she was developing her Inner Mongolia businesses. She has never considered herself his boss, just his partner, and this is why she believes the dual relationship has worked so well for them.

In fact, Xing Hui believes that she is a bit different from other people. For instance, she is still the only woman entrepreneur in the brewing industry in China. She knew this when she decided to start the business back in 1994, but she never felt threatened because of it. She never had any problems in getting used to men's business style. For instance, in order to make a lot of *ganbei* (drinking toasts) during business meals, she has gotten used to drinking both wine and beer (mostly her beer, of course, although sometimes other brands as well in order to follow her competitors).

Xing Hui's entrepreneurial and managerial styles have always been based on steady advances, step-by-step. She defines herself as:

- Caring about the employees, since they are the most precious treasure the company has. For instance, she has always allocated time to pay her employees face-to-face.
- Identifying the right product demanded by the market and putting it on the market at the right competitive price, so that the profitability and sustainability of the business can be guaranteed. For this to happen, the only tool she has found over the years is "*nuli gonzuo*" (to work diligently). She has not found any magical easier method.
- Being clear and transparent and not playing any tricks with product quality is the only way to win consumer trust and build a reputable brand. In fact, in the current competitive market, without high-quality products the business could not be sustainable. "A single small mistake in quality can damage the brand image and reputation," she explains.

As for the future, given the uncertain economic situation of recent years, it is not so easy for Xing Hui to envision how things are going to evolve. With respect to the brewing industry in China, she is pretty sure that there is going to be a restructuring of the whole industry; despite many mergers and acquisitions made by the large Chinese brewing players, there are still too many companies in the industry. Her plans do not include being taken over by another company, however. On the contrary, she has the intuition, as she has always had, that no matter how the economic situation and the industry evolve, her company will always find a way to keep its business sustainable. They have up-to-date technology and this will help them. Moreover, they have a very good name for their brand: the word "*Lao*" is synonymous with quality when it comes to beer drinking. And they have put a lot of emphasis, in particular over the last several years, on developing their brand in the markets where they are already established and in those they can easily access, always emphasizing that their beers are "100% *Laoshan* spring brewed." They have guaranteed themselves their supply of *Laoshan* water. To the extent possible, they will also keep introducing innovations, like the one they introduced in 2002 for opening their glass bottles. Xing Hui does not have any plans to go overseas, as she is pretty sure they can still develop their position in the China market.

Xing Hui's family has always remained close despite being separated for several years. They make time to be together, such as traveling together—something they all enjoy—in Latin America and South Africa, sharing ideas, and influencing each other. If she influenced her husband to follow her in her entrepreneurial endeavors, he influenced her to embrace Catholicism. He grew up in a Catholic environment, since his parents and extended family were Catholic; he was finally baptized in 1980. Under his influence, she was baptized in 1989. Catholicism has helped them to remain tied as a family and to overcome whatever difficulties they have encountered. "It has helped me to keep my inner strength in the worst moments of my life," Xing Hui says. Their daughter was baptized when she was born.

Xing Hui's only daughter has a strong entrepreneurial background because of always being by her mother's side from a very young age. After school, she used to spend time in her mother's office, and at home she listened about her mother's businesses. In fact, she is extremely close to her mother. She is getting her PhD in Banking and Finance at the Wharton School at the University of Pennsylvania, and is planning to return to China after graduation to work in the financial sector or perhaps, eventually, she could end up working at her parent's company. Xing Hui is not very clear about this.

When Xing Hui gets up in the morning, she feels very good about the day ahead. She looks forward to continuing to use her intuition, enthusiasm, and energy to develop and manage her business, to upgrade *Laote*'s quality brand, and to keep fighting for survival and success, as she has always done.

ENTREPRENEURSHIP BY INTUITION MEANS:

- *Identifying the right product the market demands.*
- *Confirming, in direct contact with the market, that the ideas about a potential business are correct.*
- *Not being afraid to put your ideas in practice.*
- *Teaming with partners who can provide the background and knowledge you may be lacking in your chosen industry.*
- *Choosing the appropriate physical location and name for the company.*
- *Choosing the right slogans and marketing messages.*
- *Not hesitating to perform as many investments as necessary to provide customers with the best possible quality and price.*
- *Guaranteeing the resources that provide competitive advantages in the industry.*
- *Working very hard to get the customers loyalty needed to make the business sustainable.*
- *Introducing innovations, when possible.*
- *Always keeping one's inner strength.*
- *Always keeping in mind the long-term goal, no matter how many difficulties may be encountered along the way.*
- *Advancing step-by-step.*

CHAPTER 10

Entrepreneurship by Perseverance. Wang Xiuyan, Haidilan

Wang Xiuyan was born in 1955 in the city of Benxi, in Liaoning province, but spent her childhood and adolescence in Keerqin, in Inner Mongolia, where her father—a military man working in a factory—was relocated. Her mother had no problem relocating as she was a housewife. Wang Xiuyan grew up with her two sisters and brother (all younger than her) and remained in Keerqin until she was 17 years old, when she was sent to Changbaishan, in Jiling province, to teach Mandarin.

After a couple of years during which she studied intensely to change her professional path, Wang Xiuyan moved to Wuhan city in Hubei province, where she worked for 20 years managing a factory making police uniforms. When she arrived, the factory was very small, with slightly more than ten people. She designed a uniform that drew her supervisor's attention; the *Chengguan* (City Management Officers)[1] decided to standardize it and assigned Wang Xiuyan full design responsibilities. She expanded the factory, purchasing new innovative equipment, and hired new employees to increase productivity and exploit the many opportunities the Chinese market offered. Sales followed and the company grew to more than three hundred people. She achieved success by focusing on selling products in the Chinese market, while placing no attention on exports.

While in Wuhan, Wang Xiuyan married an air force pilot. He relocated with her to Beijing when she was sent there in 1994 to start a new factory. The new factory was located close to the *Nanyuan* airport in the *Nanyuan Kongjun Jichang* area, Fengtai district, in the southern part of the city. Though she loved Beijing very much, upon her arrival, she was under intense pressure as the factory had to be put into operation in only thirty eight days. The company wanted her to take care of their new *Chengguan's* uniform manufacturing facility located in northern China. Soon, the company began to take orders for uniforms from nearly twenty thousand city managers' units nationwide, covering twenty-seven provinces, 350 cities, and 1,300 counties. Wang Xiuyan worked so hard that in 1998 she was hospitalized for about a year due to overworking. However, despite her hospitalization she continued working, developing three thousand new orders. By 1999, Wang Xiuyan had grown the Beijing factory to over a hundred people and had established *hezuo* agreements with factories located all over China, in particular in Dongbei, Wuhan, Jiangsu, and Guangzhou.

That year the government announced it would privatize the factory, and Wang Xiuyan decided to acquire 100% of the shares. She did not need investments from any third parties or banks (she does not like to deal with banks), nor did she feel the need to look for a partner. She thought that by remaining the sole proprietor, she would have fewer problems. She still thinks so today. In 1999, Wang Xiuyan became the chairwoman and general manager of *Beijing Haidilan Fuzhuang Youxian Gongsi* (www.haidilan.com.cn, in English, Beijing Haidilan Garments Co., Ltd.). The company's central offices and showroom are located in southwest Beijing. They are licensed by the government to manufacture *Chengguan's* uniforms.

Despite the strong competition Wang Xiuyan faced from the beginning in 1999, the company has more than doubled its employees and annual sales turnover, which is now over RMB 80 million. In their factory they produce around 400,000 garments a year, which constitutes half of their total sales. Sales remain focused in the China market, where they sell everywhere, including Tibet. Because of this, and because they control about 90% of the Chinese market for this product category, the influence of the recent economic crisis and uncertainties has been relatively low on them. Over time, they have managed to keep a relatively high net profit rate of around 10%.

Since 2009, they have suffered increased competition from Chinese companies that had previously focused on exporting, which, in turn, has had a negative impact on prices. However, because the *Haidilan* trademark is well known and they have such a big slice of the Chinese market, they are not concerned about small companies or companies offering low prices. When they see this happening during a bidding process, they simply decide not to submit a proposal for it. They can do this because, by working with other factories, they have the flexibility to expand or reduce their sales without their factory's production being much affected by the ups and downs in the market place.

Expanding their client base has helped her company. In 2007, they began producing uniforms for the Ministry of Environmental Protection; sales to this customer have been rising since 2009. While 2009 was difficult for many companies in her sector, Wang Xiuyan's company prospered. This is because roughly 20% of their sales turnover that year came from the clothing sold for the sixtieth anniversary of the founding of the People's Republic of China. The national celebration took place on October 1 in Tiananmen Square in Beijing, with a military parade involving 10,000 troops.

In 2010, Wang Xiuyan's company received authorization to begin producing uniforms for the Ministry of Public Security, the principal police and security authority in mainland China which is ultimately responsible for day-to-day law enforcement. She believes that, in the future, this new client will be important for her business, similar to the role played during the last few years by the Ministry of Environmental Protection, which accounts for 20% of her company's sales turnover today and is projected to grow to about 30%. With over four million people to put into uniform (600,000 of them in Beijing), the Ministry of Public Security's demand could increase her company's sales turnover by 30% or so in a short period of time, about a year or so, starting with Beijing and progressing to other cities to cover the rest of China, as they did with the *Chengguan's* uniforms. Police uniforms are a bit different from those they traditionally produced for the employees of the *Chengguan* and of the Ministry of Environmental Protection (these uniforms are the same as only the logos on the uniforms differ), but Wang Xiuyan is confident they will have no trouble overcoming many of their current competitors already working with this Ministry. However, she has not yet determined what share of this new client's business her company will be able to take.

The second effect of this diversification strategy is that her company's profitability in the last years has increased by about 5%. Wang Xiuyan believes that profitability will not grow much because of the strong competition present today in the China market. Still, she is happy to be in a segment of the garment industry unaffected by international competition, as is the case for mass market garments. As a result, the segment where her company operates has stable prices even when there is so much turmoil in the economy domestically and globally.

Wang Xiuyan is happy she made the decision to fully acquire the factory in 1999. Since then, she has managed the company the way she likes and made every decision without having to rely on the approval of any other parties. She is particularly happy with the way she has managed her 300 employees, having developed a kind of a family-style working environment over the last few years. She now pays great attention to being in direct contact with every employee. She talks to them and spends time getting to know their needs. She visits the factory often and considers every worker and employee a member of her family. When requested, she gives money to help her top-level managers buy homes; she gave them RMB 100,000 in 2006, and RMB 200,000 in 2011. The deputy managing director receives a salary of about RMB 10,000 a month, the department managers get about twice the salary. This salary is linked to results, especially in the case of the department managers in direct contact with clients: about 55% of their salary is variable, or 20–30% in the case of the deputy managing director. When a typical employee gets married, she gives around RMB 10,000. Average employees receive a monthly salary of RMB 2,000–3,000, which is also linked to results, but only by a tiny proportion (about 1–2%). She also pays her employees' medical expenses and sends gifts to their relatives on their behalf. Most of her employees (about 80%) are *waidiren*, that is, people not originally from Beijing, so it is important to take care of them and provide them with free housing and food, since they have no other family members in the city. Employees' appreciation of Wang Xiuyan's efforts is shown by how much they support and respect her, and by the low employee turnover at her company. There are people, for instance, that have been working with her for over 18 years.

FOR WANG XIUYAN, TO BE THE SOLE PARTNER IN A BUSINESS IS VERY IMPORTANT because the entrepreneur is able to manage the company the way he or she likes and make decisions without having to rely in any other party's agreement.

Her management team is comprised of about thirty people, who are organized into seven departments: production (which includes quality control of both their own products and those produced for third parties); business development; design; finance; procurement; client service; and administration. Below Wang Xiuyan, supervising everything, there is a deputy general manager who is also fully responsible for the training of the factory's employees. As is common in the clothing industry, over 80% of the employees are women (90% of whom work in the factory). This is despite the fact that clients in their segment are predominantly male.

With this structure and the required marketing, publicity, and advertising being subcontracted to a marketing company, owned by an old friend of Wang Xiuyan, they have managed to keep the loyalty of most of their clients; they manage to keep adapting to their ever-changing needs. Every three or four years the clients request changes to the design and color of their uniforms, which today are more elegant and of better quality than before. The average life-time use for the uniforms is four years for the winter types and two years for the summer.

When Wang Xiuyan acquired the company, she went to Beijing Daxue (Beijing University) to take a one-year training program in Manufacturing Management to ease the transition from public to private ownership. She had acquired substantial practical experience in manufacturing management, but no educational support.

Wang Xiuyan defines herself as a manager who has kept growing and developing her abilities step-by-step. Since she was young, she could see that she had the abilities to manage people and businesses. As a result, she took every leadership opportunity given to her, including the one to become an entrepreneur. She acknowledges that the sector where she works is very tiring, but she knows the sector and her company so well, every department, every corner of the factory and its people, that she could hardly imagine working in a different situation. Moreover, many of her employees have also remained at the company for a long time.

For instance, the accountant (a woman) has been there for over 17 years; there are many employees that came as trainees and have remained there.

Wang Xiuyan has sometimes thought she would like to enter the hotel and restaurant sector, but she does not know it at all; she has also been told they are also very tiring sectors to work in. She has also dreamed about opening a hospital so that she could help other people, but she does not know the health care industry either, and developing and managing such a business is also very demanding. So, she remains in the same sector where she has been since 1974. She believes an entrepreneur has to focus on a particular sector to be successful, since perseverance always pays.

By having been in this sector so long, she is quite familiar with her clients, as she arranges their transportation to and from airports and accompanies them to dinner and entertainment. She and her employees are good friends of their clients and they are used to drinking wine together, singing, dancing, and socializing. When their clients from all over China come to Beijing to visit their factory and offices, they normally remain in the city for about a week. She makes sure that they are taken care of and has her employees accompany them to visit tourist sites and go anywhere they want. The clients are most often men, so in the evening, after dinner, quite often just her male employees take care of them.[2] Since the relationship with their clients has lasted so long, quite often they are the ones inviting their clients to come to Beijing.

Maybe because of the sector she is in, Wang Xiuyan defines her management style as being pretty much male-oriented. Her boss used to be a man, most of her clients are men, she spends many hours surrounded by men, so she does not see any difference between the style her previous boss had and her own. For instance, she delegates tasks in a way similar to what he used to do. She thinks that she does not resemble women in their tendency to plan in advance or make provisions for eventual contingencies. This is perhaps why the economic uncertainties of the last few years or for the future have not worried her at all. Her attitude is to handle problems as they arise, and not to anticipate those that may never come. She is only a woman when she returns home and stays with her husband; that's how she defines herself.

Wang Xiuyan defines her management style and principles in the following way, which she has also summarized in written form in a book she is putting together on guidelines for managers and entrepreneurs:

- To start from the bottom and keep growing little-by-little, step-by-step.
- To apply the acquired experience for the benefit of the business, the employees, and the clients.
- To do advance planning and prioritize the tasks in order of importance, focusing, when necessary, only on the most important ones.
- To execute whatever she thinks or feels necessary to do. Thinking is not enough; it is necessary to act. And for this to happen, to have a very good knowledge and understanding of the distinct situations is critical.
- To use her head to think and design strategies that others will implement without her getting involved in the implementation phase. The leader should never forget his or her responsibilities by getting too involved with the details.
- To recruit personnel by focusing on their personal abilities, not on age, gender, or years of experience. Finding talent among existing employees is always the easiest and most effective way. In recruiting people, one should not only seek their effort, but also their hearts.
- To delegate responsibilities, explaining to every person what his or her responsibility is all about and that it would be impossible for any one person (meaning, the boss) to take care of everything. She has stressed this in particular since the company was privatized, but she has practiced this all her life.
- To fairly reward employees' work. The ancient Chinese minister *Guan Zhong* said: "A man will know his manners only when he has filled his stomach." To not only satisfy the material needs of the employees, but also the psychological needs, taking care of them as a mother and developing a good friendly relationship with them. To help them solve their problems—including their personal problems—when they arise.
- To communicate to her employees the company's goals and motivations and ensure that her employees fully identify with them.
- To regularly train her employees on how to adapt to market conditions, how to treat clients well, and how to best perform

in their sector. With this purpose in mind, she organizes weekly meetings.

- In addition to training, she also helps her employees develop in their professional paths. It is important to see how the employees work, why they do things right and wrong, as well as identifying the employees' potential, and creating conditions to favor the full development of the employees' potential. It should always be remembered that every person is different and does things differently: "A horse can run, but cannot plough as an ox; a cart can load, but cannot cross the river like a boat."

- To fairly acknowledge employees' work and their contributions to the company, so that they can feel in harmony at work and do not feel the need to look for another employer.

- To always remember that employees are the company's number one priority and that only through great interpersonal relationships can corporate harmony be achieved.

- To be a good model for her employees and stakeholders, so that they will follow her. Otherwise, they would never do so.

- To associate with other people or companies or both, when convenient or when the right opportunity arises.

- To make sure that everybody wins: associates, clients, and employees.

- To always remember that when problems arise, an entrepreneur cannot look for help and cannot remain immobile or cry, but should have the ability to independently overcome all kind of obstacles.

- To have a stable mind, this is important in particular for a woman entrepreneur. A stable mind helps a person to remain healthy.

- To remember every day the importance of being happy and in a good mood, since employees and the clients will see it, and that seeing her is what will motivate or de-motivate them to act in favor of the company.

- To show their love to employees, so that they act with appreciation and not under fear, feeling good by being treated well.

- To keep looking ahead and innovating. Find new challenges and face them with optimism, especially the ones coming spontaneously from the market. Avoid looking back or feeling trapped by past situations. Innovation in products, processes, and post-sales service is critical in her sector.
- To constantly keep in mind that life is a learning process.
- To generate alternative solutions to different challenges, so that success is guaranteed.
- To have clear objectives and make them come true by working hard (in Mandarin, *nuli gongzuo*) and diligently day-after-day.
- To work hard and fight hard to keep her company's positioning in the market.
- To never give up studying and learning.
- To never stop asking questions about the sector, the business, and life itself.
- To always remember that sustainable success is impossible without happiness and that a person's happiness and inner beauty go side-by-side.
- To be good to herself to begin with, so that she can be good to others and make them happy.
- Not to forget that to give love to others helps achieve happiness.
- To be satisfied with what she has. People who need too many things can never be happy.
- To work at what she knows how to do and not pretend to do things she is not prepared for.
- To deal with every day as it is and not worry too much about how the day is going to be or how it has been when it has ended. Always work toward accomplishing the day's tasks, but also know that if something cannot be done that particular day, it will be possible to do it the following day.
- To think that there is always a solution for every problem. What has to be done is to look for it. There are people who tend to think solutions are impossible to find, but this is because they do not make a single effort to look for them.

Without making the effort to find these solutions, success will not be achieved.

- To remember that success can be measured in different ways and that quick success is not necessarily the true success.

- To persevere to achieve success is the only possible way. It is by persevering in the sector that she has been successful as an entrepreneur.

- To keep in mind that success begins with listening, continues by putting it in practice, and ends with accomplishing one's goals and objectives. Success is the compensation for a job done well. Without this, success is simply not possible.

- To rely on both men and women to achieve success, since both are different, yet both have distinct characteristics and ideas and contribute in complementary ways to the business. Contrary to what many people think, Wang Xiuyan believes that today women manage men and not the other way around.

- Not to panic when the market becomes difficult and demanding or margins show a tendency to be squeezed or both situations happen at the same time.

- To never think small. Thinking big and setting ambitious goals always ends up paying off.

When the company was privatized in 1999, Wang Xiuyan never thought about exporting their products. She did not know outside markets or the export world, and she always thought that she would make too many mistakes entering foreign terrain, and that it was much better to focus on the market she knew. Over time, she saw many companies suffer from trying to break into other markets, which only reinforced her original idea. Today, having seen the challenges export-oriented companies of her sector have faced in the last few years, Wang Xiuyan is happy with her decision to focus on the domestic market. This is despite the fact that she acknowledges that companies in her sector are having less trouble in dealing with foreign markets than other textile firms, and that she very much likes traveling abroad, both for business and for pleasure.[3] However, it is her intention to continue with her focus on the China market.

She plans to continue expanding and increasing her sales turnover until reaching at least RMB 10 million. She knows the market conditions are very tough right now and may be tougher in the future, in particular because the entire Chinese textile industry must restructure and competition is likely to increase. But given their positioning in the market, how they have been doing over time, and the fact that she has avoided lay-offs over the last few years, and even to increase her staff by 5–10%, Wang Xiuyan feels confident about reaching her goals. Her plan is to do this by sub-contracting production, as they have been doing so far, which has allowed them to have a production base of about 2,000 people. She has never considered expanding their factory and believes it would not make any sense to do so today. The acquisition of companies to grow her own company is a feasible option today, but she has not given any consideration to it. For the time being, she just considers continuing what she has been doing since the difficulties of 2009 began: to work even harder and be even busier than in previous decades.

She also realized these past few years that she has now become closer to her employees and her clients than she used to be. Wang Xiuyan considers after-sales service to clients—repairing the uniforms and replacing them if they have manufacturing flaws—to be a critical factor today to win the client's loyalty. Their repair service in Beijing and the substitution service both in Beijing and in other Chinese places[4] has been excellent and has contributed to their trademark's good reputation in the market (although these services are seldom needed given the high quality of their uniforms—these services together make up only about 5% of their sales).

Wang Xiuyan does not like to work with her family members who, in any case, do not have an entrepreneurial background. Her grandparents were farmers and her father a military man. Her husband retired in 2007 and does not regularly travel away from home as he did before. He does not have an entrepreneurial attitude, but seems to have had influence on their only daughter, born in 1978, who married a military man and works as a flight attendant. She holds a flight attendants' management position with Air China. Wang Xiuyan thinks she has strong management abilities, because she has been self-sufficient since she was three years old. She greatly resembles her mother in the sense that she has kept growing step-by-step: when she was 15 she started working and at the age of 18 she was assigned management tasks. Wang Xiuyan's daughter also appears as the woman in police uniform in the company's product catalog.

What Wang Xiuyan does, following the Confucian tradition, is to help her family financially. She has always thought that, no matter how successful she is in business, her core value should still be her family. Thus she never forgets the importance of a family. She has given a house to her parents, who now live with her youngest sister in Beijing, and regularly gives them money. Her brother and brother's son do not need help; they are military men and work in a factory, as her father did.

Wang Xiuyan does not spend much money buying expensive things for herself; she likes buying clothes, but does not pay any attention to brands. By contrast, she has an active role in contributing to charity and public welfare and has been donating money, for instance, in disaster areas: after the big Sichuan earthquake of 2008, Wang Xiuyan donated a significant amount of clothing to the affected population.

When Wang Xiuyan gets up in the morning she feels good just by thinking that she has another day ahead to contribute to the welfare of her employees and to add value to her clients, by doing precisely what she best knows how to do: managing her police uniform factory.

ENTREPRENEURSHIP BY PERSEVERANCE MEANS:
- *To start from the bottom and keep growing step-by-step.*
- *To remain in the sector where the entrepreneur has always been and therefore knows well.*
- *To be thoroughly familiar with the market and its actors.*
- *To know the clients' needs well.*
- *To always remember that employees are the number one priority and that corporate harmony is the key to success.*
- *Not to undertake tasks the entrepreneur is not prepared for.*
- *To always celebrate success with a reward.*
- *Not to panic when the market becomes difficult and demand or margins go down or both situations happen simultaneously.*

CHAPTER 11

Entrepreneurship Through Opportunity. Guo Feng, Dicens

Guo Feng, the CEO and President of *Qingdao Disheng Jituan Youxian Gongsi* www.dicens.com.cn (*Qingdao* Dicens Group Co., Ltd.), was born in Xian in 1952, but came to Qingdao with her parents soon afterward. She is the oldest of six siblings; she has four sisters, since, following the Chinese tradition that males are worthier than females, Guo Feng's parents kept trying until they finally had a son. Her father comes from Ningbo, in Zhejian province and her mother from Beijing. In December 1968, when she was 16 years old, Guo Feng was sent to teach physics for two years in the cities of Weifang and Qingzhou, both near each other in Shandong province. Her students were older than her but, because of her performance in school, she was assigned the job, which she diligently performed, despite not liking it much.

In 1971, while in Qingzhou, she started working as a machine operator in a construction metal materials factory, which operated uninterrupted twenty-four hours a day. She was one of the more than 400 employees working there. Seven months after her arrival, based on her performance she was given responsibility for accounting and many other administrative and management support tasks (for instance, driving the corporate car). With so many new duties, she ended up working for about sixteen hours a day, only stopping to sleep. Guo Feng remained in that exhausting job for nine years, during which period she married a man from Qingdao who worked in the same factory; they have one son. When her son was two years old, in 1980, they moved back to Qingdao at the request of her husband, whose parents were sick.

After returning to her hometown, Guo Feng started working in the procurement and sales department of a Qingdao government-owned factory that produced zippers for garments. While the factory was bigger— over 1,000 employees—and its industrial sector was completely different from her previous company, her daily tasks at work were similar, focusing on administrative tasks. Her husband, by contrast, went to work in the design department of the Haier group.

About four and a half years later, in March 1985, Guo Feng started working at *Qingdao Luyou Qiche Youxian Gongsi* (Qingdao Tourism Automobile Co., Ltd.), which owned and managed a fleet of taxis, minibuses, and vans, employing around 40 employees. She began taking responsibility for the management of the fleet, together with another person. In 1986, she was promoted to the position of Managing Director for a subsidiary company of Qingdao Tourism Automobile Co., Ltd., which gave Guo Feng the opportunity to start managing people (and not just deal with administrative work) for the first time in her adult career.

She remained in that position until 1988, when she moved to the parent company Qingdao Tourism Automobile Co., Ltd. to undertake the responsibilities of deputy general manager (although she was not given that job title) over the four subsidiary companies. In 1991, she was formally nominated Managing Director of Qingdao Tourism Automobile Co., Ltd., which was facing many difficulties at the time. In order to overcome them, Guo Feng undertook a number of measures. First, she gave employees the right to share in the ownership of the company, so that the goals of the employees and the company could be better aligned. This was an innovative idea at that time and established a new labor-capital relationship. She also changed the orientation of the company to a much more market-oriented model. Thanks to these management changes she introduced, the company was not only able to reshape its business, but also to diversify into the sea and air transportation services business.

In 1993, Guo Feng attended the *Shandong Shengwei Dangxiao* in Jinan to study economic management. This matched with her management challenges, responsibilities, and her desire to better perform her job while continuing to grow professionally. The program lasted one and a half years but, since she could only attend it part-time, it took her four and a half years to complete it.

She graduated in 1997, one year after she was named CEO of *Disheng Chengsi Keyun Youxian Gongsi* and *Disheng Luyou Keyun Youxian Gongsi*—Qingdao Tourism Automobile Co., Ltd. During this time, she managed make the company grow to over 200 employees and 600 vehicles (570 taxis with vans and minibuses making up the remainder of the vehicles in the fleet.). The company's minibuses have been used to provide regular transportation services, such as minibus service between Qingdao and Yantai. In 2011, to increase the size of *Disheng Chengsi Keyun Youxian Gongsi*'s business, Guo Feng decided to establish a fifty-fifty joint venture—h*ezi*—with a competitor. This increased the fleet size to over 900 vehicles and the employees to 1,900 in total. Sales turnover for the joint venture is RMB 52.6 million with profitability around 8%. After completion of this joint venture, she decided to acquire a competitor's business to quickly increase the size and the profitability of *Disheng Luyou Keyun Youxian Gongsi*'s business. This business expanded from 30 to 120 long-distance tourism buses—*dakache*—which could travel on routes between major cities like Beijing and Qingdao. This enlarged business had over 120 employees, and increased its sales turnover by 150% and its profitability by 30%. These operational steps, taken in 2011, contributed to Guo Feng's group's eventual listing (see below).

In 1996, Qingdao Tourism Automobile Co., Ltd. decided to expand their services to air transportation, establishing *Qingdao Zhisheng Jichang Guanli Gufeng Youxian Gongsi* and *Qingdao Zhisheng Feiji Youxian Gongsi* (Qingdao Heliport Administration Co., Ltd. and Qingdao Helicopter Aviation Co., Ltd.) to offer heliport management and helicopter-based services. The company has five helicopters: an American *Shiwaze*, two Russian Mi–26, and two Russian Mi–171.

In 1997, seeing that no one in the market was providing other kind of services, Guo Feng established *Qingdao Disheng Youchuan Youxian Gongsi*

(Qingdao Dicens Motorboats Co., Ltd.) to provide rental recreational boats, both self-operated and group guided. Today, the company has nine boats—three of them large, for group use—eighteen employees, sales turnover of around RMB 6 million, and net profit of 16%. Fees range from RMB 20 to RMB 60 per person for group trips, and RMB 160 to RMB 860 for renting small self-operated boats. The boats are parked at the *Laixi Luhai Shang Luyou Matou* in Qingdao. Guo Feng said that growing this business is very difficult because tourists are not accustomed to using this kind of service as they normally enjoy other leisure alternatives during the two days they usually spend in Qingdao. In addition, in winter there are not many tourists visiting this city. Because of these factors, this business has been pretty stable, not having changed much in size over the past several years.

In 1998, when Guo Feng was still in her CEO position at Qingdao Tourism Automobile Co., Ltd., the decision was made to privatize the company. She wanted to acquire it, but needed partners as she did not have the capital needed to make the acquisition alone. She took a 30% ownership share in the business, leaving the remaining 70% in the hands of three other partners, two individuals, and a company. Everyone involved are all friends of hers; otherwise, she doubts she would have had the credibility to convince them to make the deal.

Immediately afterward, seeing the low performance of the business and its potential, she took over the CEO responsibilities at Qingdao Heliport Administration Co., Ltd. and Qingdao Helicopter Aviation Co., Ltd., whose sales turnover was just RMB 10 million. Over time, this company became independent from Qingdao Tourism Automobile Co., Ltd. With its three Mi–8 Russian helicopters and a professional team of pilots (with an average of over 20 years of in-flight experience), the company began to offer a broad range of services inland and across borders: including air tours, short-distance air transportation, air shooting, overboard loading, air sports, aerial surveys, airborne advertising, aero-forest surveillance and protection, and emergency aid. Qingdao Heliport Administration Co., Ltd. provides support services to Qingdao Helicopter Aviation Co., Ltd., operating a heliport of about 27,000 square meters in size.

Guo Feng continued her education, enrolling in the two-year economic management program that Beijing University offers in Qingdao.

She did this to better adapt to new business scenarios and to profit more from market opportunities as she increased her management and new entrepreneurial responsibilities. She graduated in 2000.

Meanwhile, she continued expanding her business. In 1999, Guo Feng established *Qingdao Disheng Luxingshi Youxian Gongsi* (Qingdao Dicens Travel Co. Ltd.), a travel agency that offers land, sea, and air tourism services because of its link to other companies in the group. This business is pretty stable and, despite having changed its managing director in 2011, no major changes are envisioned in the future.

One year later, in 2000, Guo Feng decided to create a group company—*Qingdao Disheng Jituan Youxian Gongsi* (Qingdao Dicens Group Co., Ltd.)—to form an umbrella over the existing firms and any future companies they might create. She managed to increase her ownership participation to 48% in the Qingdao Dicens Group Co., Ltd. The remaining 52% was still in the hands of three other partners: the original shareholder company, one of the original individual partners, and a new shareholder company. The main motivation behind creating this group company was the limitations on growth faced by the original company, Qingdao Tourism Automobile Co., Ltd., as it operated in a government regulated sector. So, Guo Feng knew the only way to continue growing her business was through diversification, targeting different groups of clients, both from the public and private sectors.

In the same year the group company was established—2000—Guo Feng saw the opportunity to buy a piece of land in Shandong province. She took this as an opportunity to enter the real estate market. She established *Qingdao Disheng Fangdichan Kaifa Youxian Gongsi* (Qingdao Dicens Real Estate Development Co., Ltd.). Since she was aware of her lack of expertise in this sector, she decided to use advisors to help her undertake her first real estate development project.

The first piece of land Guo Feng acquired was for a housing development, located in Rongcheng, a county-level city located in Weihai, a prefecture-level city. The land purchase was finalized in 2002; construction preparation activities lasted two years, with the construction process beginning in 2005. The project included 322 apartments, which were all sold by 2007. The business' profitability was good: 30% net profit, equivalent to RMB 10 million.

In 2001, Guo Feng saw an opportunity to enter the retail automobile business. She created *Qingdao Yiqi Dazhong Teyue Dishengyuan Gongsi* (Qingdao Dicensyuan Auto Sale & Service Co., Ltd.). The company was established as a Volkswagen (*DaZhong* in Chinese) dealership that included providing the following services: pre-sales information, sales, spare parts sales, after sales service, car maintenance, car accessories, car decoration, and car cleaning. The following car models are being sold under this company: Jetta/Suteng, Golf, Caddy, Bora/Baolai, and Maiteng. This business uses facilities with an area of 6,660 square meters. It also employs 115 people, who receive daily training ranging from 60 to 90 minutes. Annual sales turnover is around RMB 220 million (with sales for the Maiteng model double those of the other models combined; sales for all the other models are more or less equally distributed) and its profitability is over 10%. The business has experienced a 10% annual increase since 2009 and will continue doing so. Guo Feng has no intention of any mergers or acquisitions in this business.

A year later, in 2002, *Qingdao Disheng Qiche Weixiu Youxian Gongsi* (Qingdao Dicens Auto Sale Co., Ltd.) was created to provide repair services complementing the car-related services already being provided. This business, employing 30 people, is very small, with sales turnover of RMB 3 million. So, in 2005, 70% of the shares were sold to a Chinese partner. Guo Feng's plans in 2009 were to sell the remaining 30%. Instead, she planned to open a new, much bigger dealership and vehicle repair shop named *Huang Dao Qu* near a gas station in *Qingdao Jingji Kaifa Qu*. She envisioned this business would have the second largest growth potential in her business group. However, as time passed, the performance of the repair service business improved and her other plans were shelved. Since 2009, this business has increased its annual sales turnover by 15% and its annual profitability by 12%.

In 2003, Guo Feng saw, once again, an opportunity in the market (this time related to her previous companies' activities) and decided to create *Qingdao Disheng Jiashiyuan Peixun Guanli Youxian Gongsi* (Qingdao Dicens Driver Training & Administration Co., Ltd.), a company authorized by the state to provide vehicle driving training. It trains people to pass the three different types of exams required to get a driver's license: a theory exam, to verify that they know the safety rules, and two practical exams, to show that the drivers can maneuver and drive on the street under normal traffic conditions. On an average, people require more than 60 days of training to get their driver's license. Daily classes last over two hours. The company employs eighteen people, and it is only one of its kind whose managing director is a woman. The company uses 34 cars and occupies 43,000 square meters of land, 30,000 square meters of which are used for outdoor training. Its sales turnover is around RMB 3 million and its net profit is 2%. Margins used to be lower with the previous managing director (a male), but the woman that replaced him in 2009 is doing a very good job. She has increased the annual sales turnover of the business by 20% and its annual profitability by 15%, even though competition in the market is very strong. In any case, Guo Feng has no plans to increase the size of this business, since its influence on the group is small.

In 2007, after seeing how successful she was with her first real estate project, Guo Feng looked for a second piece of land, this time in the eastern part of Qingdao, in *Xianggang Donglu Pinghe Dadao*. The acquisition was completed in 2009. Construction of this 65,000 square meter new housing development project started in 2011, after almost three years' preparation. This project includes 500 apartments distributed over eight floors, all for sale. Despite the current situation of the real estate sector in China, the apartments have been selling slowly but steadily, since they are in a very good location. Despite the 20% increase in housing prices in Qingdao since 2009, this project's profitability will be lower than expected, since land costs have rocketed. Her goal with this project is to generate sales turnover of around RMB 800–900 million and profit of 10%, which is much lower than before, but still quite good for the Qingado real estate market.

Apart from these two very relevant projects, Guo Feng has participated in other smaller real estate projects. These projects are all housing developments for sale in the Qingdao area. They are located in: *Laoshan*, *Tailiu* Road (an economically affordable housing project), and *Haier* road.

Guo Feng thinks the recent financial crisis and current economic uncertainties have had a positive impact for her real estate business, since they have reinforced Chinese people's tendency not to trust the banks and to make conservative investments. Government policies to cool the real estate market have had the opposite effect. However, she still believes that if the site is good, real estate projects will still be profitable, not so much as before, but still worthy of investment. It is not clear, though, if in the future she will continue with this business, as it is unrelated to the other businesses in her group.

As for her other businesses, the recent economic challenges have not negatively affected them. Instead of being overly cautious, Guo Feng continues expanding these businesses by taking advantage of the opportunities that she sees in the market.

For instance, in 2009, Qingdao Helicopter Aviation Co., Ltd. bought a Mi–26 and a Mi–171 helicopter from Russia; it did so again in 2010.[1] Each year, the company has invested RMB 60 million in these purchases. These helicopters have been used to transport merchandise to the Sichuan area affected by the great earthquake of 2008. This company is also expanding its business by providing aerial environmental surveillance and protection where is it most needed in China, such as with *Da Xiang An Ling*, in Heilongjiang province. Their client is the Chinese State Forestry Administration, with whom they signed a ten-year contract, providing them with an annual net profit of RMB 10 million. These new contracts are transforming Guo Feng's helicopter business. Until the Chinese State Forestry Administration contract, with just over fifty employees, the helicopter business alone had a sales turnover of RMB 10 million and net profit of RMB 2 million. The replacement of the Mi–8 helicopters— which are very costly to operate—with new helicopter models will significantly improve the profitability of the business. Traditional clients in this business include: electric utility companies, the Institute of Oceanography in Qingdao, the *Qingdao* Television Station, and the Chinese State Forestry Administration (although the work with them has been on a very small scale). With this client, Guo Feng sees many opportunities to continue expanding the business, since environmental surveillance and protection is new in China and they need a lot of help to perform these new tasks. In general, environmental protection—beyond the forestry areas—will generate a lot of demand for aerial surveillance, so much so that Guo Feng is planning to buy more helicopters to fully profit from the market opportunities. She sees this business as the one with the largest development potential in her group, assuming that they can keep buying new helicopters to cope with the growing demand. Since 2009, the sales turnover of this business has grown by 20% and its profitability by 5%. Because of all this, she is not planning to merge with any competitors to increase the size of this business. The business will continue growing by itself, that is, organically.

Despite the regulatory constraints, another company that could grow today is Qingdao Dicens Travel Co. Ltd. Its growth potential is clear because of its links to the land, water, and air transportation-related companies of the group; tourism has become one of the most important industries in Qingdao.[2] However, the company has been stagnant in its level of employees (20), along with RMB 30 million in revenues and a tiny 1% in net profit. Even though this is the easiest to manage of all of her group's businesses, Guo Feng thinks that changes in the management could move the company forward. However, she has not yet attempted to make any changes.

In 2008, during the Olympic Games, Guo Feng's group was one of the transportation services providers for the Olympics Sailing Events. She is very proud of the fact that, by improving the efficiency of its taxi services, the company was able to meet peak demand from passengers in the area throughout the event.

In the transportation services sector, Guo Feng also has a small fifty-fifty joint venture (*hezi*) with a Singaporean company for taxi service in the Qingdao area. This business was established in 1993 and has a fleet of 120 Jetta/Suteng taxis. However, the business has never grown; its sales turnover is about RMB 1 million—and its profitability is sinking—close to zero, since taxi fares were stabilized in Qingdao while the drivers' salaries have kept increasing. This is why she does not really pay too much attention to this company, which she does not see as having much of a future. In the case of her other land transportation business, Guo Feng has been able to keep them profitable by providing minibus and vans tourist related services, which is why she is enlarging their size so quickly.

In any case, the most profitable by far of Guo Feng's businesses has been the real estate business. Profitability has never been below 30% and is normally attained in a short period of time. When thinking about this business, she always remembers the Chinese saying: "Once you have been in the real estate business, all other businesses do not count." She refers to developing real estate for sale, not for rent, which would be a different kind of business that Guo Feng is not interested in.

FOR GUO FENG, SELLING REAL ESTATE IS A GREAT BUSINESS because it is impossible to achieve the same profitability in such a short period of time than with any other business.

As for the future, in about five years' time, Guo Feng plans for her group to put 30% of its shares into the stock market. She has already taken several steps to help make this happen, such as increasing the size of several of her businesses. Today total sales turnover of the group is RMB 350 million with 10% profit margin. Its total number of employees is over 2,400 and its total assets about RMB 350 million. She is considering listing it in Shanghai, since the Chinese economy is doing much better than Western economies.

In the autumn of 2011, Guo Feng took another step toward this listing by creating a media company: *Qingdao Disheng Wenhua Chuanmei Youxian* Gongsi. The idea is to use this company as a vehicle for corporate communications through the media, and also to promote car culture and car history-related events. One idea involves bringing together drivers of different types of cars, so that during an event they can be trained on the history and characteristics of their vehicle or even on the vehicles of other participants at the event. "This way, these drivers may end up choosing to change their car model, which will indirectly help our car dealership to develop new sales and new customers. There are already many opportunities in the market, in particular for imported cars—such as Volkswagen—and we have to take advantage of them now. We also have to take advantage of the organization of these types of events, since it is a business opportunity in itself: car manufacturers are willing to sponsor such events and drivers are willing to pay a fee for attending. Moreover, once we have developed our trademark in this new business, we may be able to organize many different types of events, not necessarily car-related. This way we will realize our dream of being in a non-regulated industry, which we can freely develop our business. All the other businesses we are in are government regulated and, as such, we cannot freely develop them," Guo Feng explained.

With respect to her management style, Guo Feng just refers to it as being based on the establishment of procedures for the delegated tasks and making certain that procedures are followed. To guarantee that there is no communication gap or miscommunication between management and employees, she has developed what she calls the "cohesive force" project. Managers are required to visit their employees on five occasions—these are known as the "five must visits:" in case of hospitalization; at her or his wedding; when they are trapped in a dispute; when they are facing an "abnormal" situation in their job; and at funerals. The "cohesive force" project also includes the "five must talks" that managers should have with their employees in the event of these five occasions: relocation; promotion or demotion; rewards or punishment; frustration; and discipline.

Since the establishment of the group, each of its companies has been run by a managing director, who does not hold any shares in the company, but whose annual remuneration is linked to the company's results. The highest total remuneration they can get is RMB 700,000, with the variable component up to 30% of this amount. Guo Feng thinks that they are very well paid, as indicated by the fact that the highest remuneration for a department manager is RMB 100,000.

Guo Feng has never worked with her family because she does not like the idea. In any case, only her brother has his own business, as a representative of a heating equipment company. The rest of her sisters, except one who manages a supermarket in a commercial center, have never had any managerial or entrepreneurial responsibilities. Her husband is not entrepreneurial; he works as the general secretary of a government-owned telecommunications company. As for her son, he studies computer network security in the United States, which he likes very much, after first starting and then leaving a PhD program in the same field in China. Only time will tell whether he will return to China and open his own business there or not.

With so many companies to manage and always having to keep up with new opportunities emerging in the market, Guo Feng is always busy. She defines herself as someone who doesn't have time for hobbies, leisure travel, or sports. Occasionally, she puts some time aside to play golf. However, she always finds time to involve herself in welfare-related activities, and ensures that her business group undertakes social initiatives such as: providing free shuttle-bus service for students and for veterans with hearing-loss, and giving discounted transportation tickets to pregnant women and the elderly.

When Guo Feng gets up in the morning she feels very good by just thinking that she has another day ahead to continue working, expanding and supervising her business, keeping up with new trends and changes in the marketplace, as well as emerging opportunities that could increase her company's productivity and the value her business contributes to society.

ENTREPRENEURSHIP BY OPPORTUNITY MEANS:

- *To implement the appropriate management systems and procedures in existing businesses, to be prepared to face new challenges.*
- *To constantly survey the market and evaluate opportunities that may add value to the current business or are be very profitable themselves or have both characteristics.*
- *To always remember that there are also new opportunities in the current business sectors.*
- *To have the capacity to raise the capital needed to take advantage of opportunities.*
- *To keep studying and learning to fully profit from each opportunity.*
- *To apply already proven management systems and procedures.*
- *To delegate tasks and make sure they are followed.*
- *To guarantee there is no communication gap or miscommunication between management and employees.*
- *To never panic, just keep responding flexibly enough to adapt to market changes.*
- *To go ahead with implementation of planned strategies, no matter what the scenario is with the Chinese economy and world economy.*

CHAPTER 12

Entrepreneurship by Differentiation. Chen Xiuyun, Zhu Mama

Chinese consume a great deal of pork, which is now more than half the meat consumed on an average and reaches up to 70% in some areas. The demand has kept increasing over time with per capita consumption almost doubling since 1990. Based on estimates from the US Development Agency (USDA) and the US Census Bureau, the average person in China consumed a record 39.3 kilograms of pork in 2011, compared with 19.7 kilograms in 1990. While per-capita consumption is still higher in some nations like Denmark, the Chinese, overall, produce and eat more than half of the world's pigs. The crush of demand for pork has made the supply vulnerable to all sorts of fluctuations, from epidemics of pig diseases to weather changes that affect the price of grain that fattens up the pigs. But a nation that runs on pork cannot afford to run short. That is why a national pork reserve has been a priority for the China government since 2007.[1] Chen Xiuyun envisioned the strategic value of pork for the Chinese population when she decided to start her current business in 1999.

Chen Xiuyun was born in 1962 in Sanming, located in *Youxixian* administrative region, *Fujian* province. The name of her company is actually derived from here: *Fujian Sheng Youxixian Shanyuan Xumu Youxian*

Zeren Gongsi. She remained in her hometown until the first part of 2009, when she decided the business needed to start operations in Beijing. She started her company in 2003.

When Chen Xiuyun was 17, she started to work teaching 10 year old children in *Meixianxiang*, her parents' hometown. Her parents' families had been poor simple farmers, who, previous to 1949, did not own any land. In 1953, her father, then, in the army, was sent to Nanjing where he remained for three years. Upon his return to Fujian, he worked as a farmer. Her mother was a housewife with six children. Chen Xiuyun was the second child, but she later became the oldest child. Since her family was so poor, they had to give up her older brother to another family; that way, it was one less mouth to feed (why her parents chose to give away her older brother, she still does not know; perhaps because he was a healthy boy.)[2] Her childhood was difficult as she had to help her mother raise her younger two brothers and two sisters. Seeing her today, one can sense both her rural background and how hard she has worked all her life. She looks older than she actually is.

At the age of 19, Chen Xiuyun started working in a cement factory in Meixianxiang. Her work involved counting the number of cement units produced. She remained in that job until she was 26 years old. Chen Xiuyun then moved to work in a vegetable oil factory in Youxiaxian as a cook in the canteen until 1995. When Chen Xiuyun and her husband both became unemployed, she realized she had worked enough for others and decided to open her own business.

Since she and her husband had a broad background involving pigs and pork, they opened a small pig products shop. This proved to be a smart decision. All their lives they have been in contact with pigs, before they married into their respective family's homes and, afterward, because they themselves raised pigs at home. They ran their shop for four years, but the sales turnover in 1999 was still pretty small—around RMB 35,000—so they decided they had to develop another business involving pigs, but with more possibilities of expansion and profitability.

So, in 1999 they started their current business, although they did not create *Fujian Sheng Youxixian Shanyuan Xumu Youxian Zeren Gongsi* until 2003. They started with 20–25 pigs with the sole idea of developing a business around pork products that would keep growing year after year and allow them to make money. Chen Xiuyun acknowledges that they did not work out the details of the business. For instance, they did not set a target for the number of pigs they would end up having on their farm. Neither did they think about when they would establish a legal company for the further expansion of their business. In a sense, her successful business story is the result of listening to the market and anticipating its needs. For instance, after the establishment of her company, in 2004, Chen Xiuyun began paying attention to environmental protection issues, recycling all the organic materials generated on the farm and reusing them there. This was an innovative approach to take in rural China, and she has continued keeping her leadership in this environmental protection area.

To start up and develop this new business has been a difficult process. To begin with, her children were still fairly young (7, 12, and 13 years old). Then, to directly take care of all the steps involved in pigs' husbandry was an exhausting and somewhat dangerous task. In 2000, Chen Xiuyun was bitten by a pig, receiving over 20 stitches, and was not able to work for a couple of months.

At the farm, Chen Xiuyun had only her husband and five workers to help, so she took charge of the veterinary-related tasks, such as vaccinations, and gave the pigs their injections. She explains that the accident she had in 2000 would not happen today, because now they have the proper equipment. Currently, they have enough cash to make all the necessary investments and have a modern facility, but in the early days, they did not have sufficient funds.

From the beginning, Chen Xiuyun used her family as support in developing the business, but the business has always remained 100% in her hands. Thus, every family member working in her business does so as a simple employee. This includes her husband, who is the Managing Director of her company. She acknowledges, however, that it was her idea to establish the company and that she is the real entrepreneur of the family. This does not seem to pose a problem to them, since her husband—also from *Youxixian*—seems to accept this situation quite well. The other family members working in the company are: one of her younger sisters—who works in the financial area, the sister's husband, who is a company driver, and her husband's uncle, who manages the canteen where the employees eat. In addition, her older daughter (25 years old), who studied in Xiamen and graduated in 2008 with a degree in events' management, is her *zhuli*—executive assistant. Chen Xiuyun's younger daughter (23 years old), who also studied in Xiamen and graduated in 2010 with a degree in logistics, is helping her with the expansion of the business in Beijing. The only person who does not want to work in the family business is her 19-year-old son. Her husband, two daughters, and son live in Fujian, in Youxixian where her main house is. She also has a house in the clean, well-planned city of Xiamen, but they do not use it often.

Outside of the family, Chen Xiuyun has employed three veterinary surgeons, who graduated in 2008 from *Nonglin Daxue* (Agriculture and Forestry University) in Fujian and then came to work for her. The role played by these people is essential to her business, since they prevent pigs' illnesses from occurring or spreading. At a lower level, there are a couple of employees from Fujian, with bachelor degrees in *zhu humus*—something like "pig breeding"—and perform day-to-day tasks related to the care of pigs (for instance, giving them injections). They come from rural areas so, besides what they have studied, they are fairly familiar with animal husbandry. Additionally, Chen Xiuyun has about 30–35 ordinary workers, mostly from Henan and Sichuan.

When *Fujian Sheng Youxixian Shanyuan Xumu Youxian Zeren Gongsi* was created in 2003, Chen Xiuyun and her husband had to change their management style. They wanted to become bigger and knew they had to invest in technology and equipment to avoid having problems such as the bite she suffered in 2000. Between 1999 and 2003, they invested RMB 1 million, while in 2003, they invested another RMB 1 million. By 2007, just before the veterinary surgeon graduates and the bachelor degree graduates joined the company, Chen Xiuyun's farm had 8,000 pigs, all directly managed by herself and her husband.

In 2008, her company's story appeared on *Fujian* TV in a program called *Fujian Zonghe Pindao Shidaixianfeng Lanmu*. The story was told as a success story of a pig farm that went from around 1,000 pigs in 2003 to about 20,000 pigs in a time span of just five years. Today, Chen Xiuyun's farm has over 25,000 pigs. In 2009, her business was affected not only by the financial crisis but also by the swine flu epidemic. However, she did not stop selling her products, "because people went on eating pork meat," she said. But, between April and June of that year, prices went down significantly (around 34%), and it was only after July that prices began to recover to their previous level. The year 2009 was, in fact, a very tough year: Sales turnover fell to 50% of that for the previous year, and profitability was close to zero. However, Chen Xiuyun's optimism did not decline. She went ahead with her plan of expanding the business in Beijing and having a total of 100,000 pigs by 2012.

The decision to start doing business in Beijing was taken in 2008. By then, they were already selling their pigs' products in: Fujian with over 30% of their sales there (50% in Xiamen), Shanghai with over 60% of sales, and Zhejiang, Guangdong, and Jiangxi together accounting for about 1% of their sales. One of the reasons that motivated Chen Xiuyun's decision to come to Beijing was the success her products already had in Shanghai. The big city's residents have a positive attitude about her product quality, which is a major factor when they make their buying decision.

The Beijing office is located in a street quite close to the Olympic Green site. It has five employees and is run by a manager who takes care of everything, particularly when Chen Xiuyun is not present; she visits Beijing once a month. Her Beijing manager used to be a journalist, but changed his profession in 1999, when he began providing advisory services to large Chinese companies. She met him in 2003 and, since he was familiar with the "pig culture" (because of his family background—he is from Taiyuan) and had lots of media contacts, she decided he was the person to bring on board in Beijing.

Chen Xiuyun's main idea of coming to Beijing was to develop the "*Zhu Mama*" trademark so that, when customers see it in stores or restaurants, they will immediately associate it with quality pork and environmental protection. Chen Xiuyun's idea is, in fact, quite similar to the European use of "denominations of origin" and similar certifications used in the West to differentiate high quality products. Her dream is eventually to develop a network of business-people she could help as a mentor, so they can align themselves with her business concept and trademark and support its development. She believes she has already moved a long way toward her goals, since from 2008 onward nobody calls her by her given name. Instead, everyone calls her "*Zhu Mama*"— literally "mother pig"—identifying her quality brand of pork products she continues to develop.

Of course, the path is not easy, as there are many competitors in the market. Some of them are huge firms, most of which used to be owned by the government. There are also many large private companies that started from scratch. But, *"Zhu Mama"* believes she is unique, as no one else is following the same approach in China—*"wo shi yijia, meiyou ren neng gen wo yiande"* ("I am unique, nobody else can be like me"), she says with total conviction. Her business has two main differentiating features: (1) her pigs are not raised for their meat to be processed; they are raised for their meat to be cooked and eaten, so that their high quality is readily apparent; (2) her pigs' breeding process is very different from her competitors, as the pigs are raised in a very clean and unpolluted environment. This is why her pork's price is higher than her competitors—about 2% more, but she does not worry about this, since she is convinced that there is growing demand for her high quality pork in the cities. She insists that, in the current legal climate, there can only be one company like hers in China, and that hers was the first to achieve this status. This is why she will remain unique. So, she is not worried today about the constant fluctuation in prices— for instance, the increase in retail prices seen in 2011.

Nevertheless, *"Zhu Mama"* wants to differentiate herself as well in her sales model. Today, her meat is sold to slaughter-houses, which sell them to restaurants. In about five years, she wants to begin changing this model, so that she can directly deliver her products to restaurants. This will maximize the profitability of the business, while keeping market prices competitive. She made this decision in 2009 and has been performing all the necessary changes since to make it possible. She also defined Beijing as the main target where she plans to start doing this. One of the reasons to start in Beijing is due to a new expressway, which will simplify the logistics and distribution of her products. To directly reach other cities is not so easy, since she acknowledges that there are still many bottle-necks in China's logistical system.

FOR CHEN XIUYUN, TO ELIMINATE INTERMEDIARIES IN THE DISTRIBUTION CHAIN IS AN EXCELLENT STRATEGY because it allows maximization of profits, while remaining competitive in the market.

Chen Xiuyun is also planning eventually to expand the processed pork product line, since these products will be of higher quality than similar ones currently sold in the market. She is not short of ideas on how to maintain a differentiation advantage in the market-place, she says.

Her company's current sales turnover is around RMB 15 million with profits of roughly 5%. Next year she expects to have sales turnover of RMB 50 million and, in three years' time, RMB 100 million with around 10% profits.

To make her dreams a reality, *"Zhu Mama"* has kept making significant investments in the Fujian facilities since her company was established. Between 2004 and 2009 she invested RMB 30 million; even in the terrible economy of 2009, she invested RMB 3 million. In 2010, the investments needed to expand her farm to accommodate her goal of 30 million pigs amounted to RMB 30 million. Of course, in order to perform such a large investment, she has had to work with the banks. Thanks to the support and backing of "The All China Women's Federation"—*"Fulian,"* however, she has not faced any problems raising the necessary money.

Although she acknowledges that there are not many people in China today that use Taoist medicine practices, Chen Xiuyun does. For instance, from time to time she invites a Taoist monk to visit her home; he takes out the blood that her body is not using—from the arms, the legs, the body, the hands, the feet—to help rejuvenate her blood and energy. She feels that this is a good practice for her health. Following Chinese tradition, she also likes singing and dancing. And, something that is not so common in Chinese women of her age, which shows how this woman has performed such a wide variety of tasks, she likes driving cars, and laughs a lot when talking about it. However, as with many of her peers, she does not have much free time to devote to her hobbies; instead, she uses her limited free time to help other people with their problems. For instance, she visits homes for the elderly, hospitals, and schools. She has also helped jobless people learn stock-breeding technologies and given money to over a hundred farmers to help them become self-employed. In 2009, she gave RMB 1million to the association: *Fuwu Pin Jijin Hui.* She has undertaken many activities over time to improve local development in her region, which has won her admiration from both the local people and the local authorities.

She believes this is pretty much in line with her Buddhist background, which she inherited from her parents. She is also fairly certain that Buddhism has also shaped her approach to life and business. For instance, she describes herself as being a well-balanced individual with compassion toward others. In her company, she has been using these values when managing her employees, constantly taking care of them and giving her love to them. She is totally convinced that this style has translated into strong results for her company, especially when taking into account that 90% of her employees are *waidiren* with no family and no possibility of returning home even for the New Year. Because of the nature of her business, no one at her company has a vacation—not a single day during the year, not even herself or the younger veterinary surgeons. So, by providing her employees with lodging and food at the farm and paying close attention to their material and affective needs, Chen Xiuyun has been able to keep them productive and satisfied with their everyday lives. She is also convinced that her workers are very good to her because she has been very good to them. She repeats: "*wo xing hao, wo dui yuangong hen hao*" ("I have a big heart, I am very good with my workers.)"

As for her management style, Chen Xiuyun likes to delegate responsibilities; since 2008, her high school graduate employees have developed written procedures to facilitate everything. Now life is easier in a way for "*Zhu Mama*," since she does not have to pay attention to every single detail of the business. The high school and college graduates she hired have let her manage the way she had always wanted to, which gives her more time to devote to other aspects of the business. Her employees with management responsibilities receive remuneration, which includes a variable component based on company performance. For instance, in 2009, since the business conditions were so bad, no one received their variable payment.

Chen Xiuyun's husband is helping her with the implementation of her ideas. They complement each other quite well, but his character is not entrepreneurial. By contrast, she thinks that her three children have inherited her entrepreneurial character and that they will all end up helping her significantly in the expansion of the family business. Her husband is also a Buddhist though, like her, he does not follow the rites, but just puts its philosophy and values in practice. As such, her husband also applies Buddhist values to his management style and his relationship with the employees.

When Chen Xiuyun gets up in the morning, she feels good just by knowing she has another day ahead to continue creating greater differentiation in her business and to realize her dream of begin recognized across China as *"Zhu Mama,"* the mother of the best pork products in the country.

ENTREPRENEURSHIP BY DIFFERENTIATION MEANS:

- *Producing products of very high quality.*
- *Paying attention to the production process and the minimization of its environmental impact.*
- *Developing a trademark, that is synonymous with unique high quality products.*
- *Building a high quality trademark, that is associated with the entrepreneur behind it.*
- *Positioning the products at the highest end of the price range.*
- *Correctly marketing the products and communicating with the media to educate consumers about their differentiation advantages.*
- *Targeting consumers in urban areas that have a positive attitude toward product quality and may prefer her products to the alternatives in the market-place.*
- *Eliminating intermediaries in the distribution chain.*
- *Continuing to perform all the necessary investments that can guarantee her differentiation advantages.*
- *Incorporating the necessary work talent as the business expansion proceeds.*
- *Linking management remuneration to the company's results.*

CHAPTER 13

Entrepreneurship by Joint Venture. Chen Yulan, Jifa

The seed company of *Qingdao Jifa* Group Co., Ltd. was established in 1955 in Jimo,[1] north of Qingdao, under China's first Five-Year Plan. It was set up by seven farming family members as a small manual workshop to produce wigs for export. The total assets of the company were as low as RMB 1,500. Today *Jifa* has over 15,000 employees, assets of over RMB 2.7 billion, and RMB 31.8 billion in annual sales, 90% of which are exports. It is also one of the top 500 export companies in China today. As such, it is considered a "miracle of the Chinese industrial revolution" and has received much recognition for its "incredible economic contribution and social benefits to China."

The Jifa brand is famous in China. Its underwear, sport and casual wear products, woven fabric, knitted apparel and garments, and high quality hair products are well-known. China's Ministry of Commerce has historically given the brand export priority, so *Jifa*'s products are free from both national and export inspections. *Jifa* has received a gold medal as one of the 100 large national export enterprises and one of the 10 most famous brands in China's textile industry.

The transformation and development of this successful enterprise in the post *Deng Xiaoping* era would not have been possible without the female entrepreneur that made it happen: Chen Yulan. Chen Yulan, President of *Qingdao Jifa* Group Co., Ltd. (*Jifa*) www.chinajifa.com, was born in 1941 in Jimo. Between 1954 and 1955, she worked in the fields as a farmer. From 1955 to 1963, her work involved knitting apparel. There were roughly 250 women doing this kind of work in Jimo. In 1963, she joined the *Jimo Fazhipin Chang* (*Jimo* Hair Products Factory), as an entry-level employee, doing administration and warehouse management work and managing just a couple of other workers. In 1964, she was made head of the financial department, having responsibility of over 15 people. She remained in that position until 1974. During that period, despite *Jifa*'s poor equipment, its products gained recognition all over China. In May 1968, to highlight *Jifa*'s achievements, the National Hair Products Conference was held in Jimo. Chen Yulan was provided with training in manufacturing management and, in 1974, she was designated deputy managing director of the factory. She communicated very well with her boss, so managing over 250 workers in her new position was not a burden to her. During that period, Chen Yulan discovered she had the ability to manage people effectively and she enjoyed working in the managerial role very much.

In 1981, after her boss retired, Chen Yulan was named *Jifa*'s President. She was excited at the opportunity and extremely happy with her management team, which was of outstanding caliber. Together with the team, she decided to diversify and expand the business. She wanted, in particular, to increase the range of their textile related products, where she saw plenty of export opportunities for both men and women's products. Next, Chen Yulan went to Japan to learn more about the latest production technologies and techniques. Upon her return, she transformed the factory by introducing knitting manufacturing technology. This change made it possible for the company to increase their number of export products by 1984. She also returned from her visit to Japan with the idea that, in order for *Jifa* to grow rapidly and exploit all potential market opportunities, the best strategy would be to establish Joint Ventures (JVs) with foreign companies; this would provide *Jifa* with outstanding technology as well as foreign clients. To facilitate the implementation of this new strategy, in 1992, *Qingdao Jifa* Group Co. Ltd. was created. This was soon followed by the establishment of *Qingdao Jifa* Import and Export Co., Ltd.

Previously, there was only one export-oriented enterprise they owned, *Jifa* Hair Products Company, which exported 100% of its products.

Although the Group established two more JV hair products companies (as mentioned later), *Jifa* Hair Products Company has not subsequently sought out or teamed up with any JV partners. It has also maintained its original leadership position in the China market. It produces men's and ladies' wigs, toupees, doll wigs, training wigs, and mannequins, hair pieces, hair extensions, hair nets, hair-dressing aprons, and all kinds of hair accessories. Today, 20% of its production is sold in the domestic market, a shift made since the beginning of the financial crisis of 2009.

Continuing with her expansion plans, in 1994 Chen Yulan established *Qingdao Jifa* Garment Sales Co., Ltd., a JV with a Japanese partner. This enterprise produces and markets *Jifa's* high-quality textile products abroad, and also develops its own brands and retail shops for the domestic market. This company produces and markets underwear, sports and casual clothing for both men and women. Exports still constitute about 90% of its sales, which mostly go to Japan, France, and the US. Step by step, Chen Yulan grew the exports of her companies' hair and textile products to a level that, for nearly 20 years, made *Jifa* the most important Chinese textile exporting company of that period.

In 1998, *Jifa* Group was privatized; a process which was accomplished in two phases: first, a 50–55% share was taken by Chen Yulan and her management team (she took a slightly bigger percentage) and, later in 2000, the remaining 45–50% share was split among a great number of its employees, so that many of them could also participate and be motivated by sharing in the companies' profits. That same year *Qingdao Shiji* Hair Product Co., Ltd. was created as a JV with a Hong Kong partner, to produce high-class toupees and other hair ornaments exclusively for export. It was in the late 1990's, when *Jifa* was facing fierce competition, that Chen Yulan decided to accelerate the process of bringing in new technologies from other countries mostly from Japan—and to invest RMB 1 billion in developing the *Jifa* Industrial Park.

In 2002, *Qingdao Huasheng* Socking Co., Ltd., a JV with a German firm, was created to produce high-quality cotton socks mainly for the export market (90% of its sales were exports). However, the JV was terminated in 2005, due to communication problems with its German partner and clients. Chen Yulan affirms that the German culture was very different from her own and from the other companies they had previously partnered with in JVs. In her opinion, this is the only JV which has failed. She acknowledges that her company has teamed up most often with Japanese companies, and that her companies generally use Japanese technology because there are fewer communication problems. Since 2005, *Jifa* Group has controlled 100% of the shares in this factory, which has an annual production capacity of 16 million pairs of socks. Sales have recently been shifting to the domestic market, where they now sell 30% of their production.

Jifa's investment in new technology allowed for the diversification of its product base, so that it not only kept its leading position in the textile industry, but also developed nine other businesses, which today constitute around 50% of *Jifa's* sales and profits. Chen Yulan also dedicated a lot of effort to the expansion of the company's export markets, reaching over 20 countries, included the USA, Japan, and many European countries. By 2004, *Jifa's* exports amounted to US$ 200 million.

To favor export expansion, in 2004, *Qingdao Huayun* Hair Products Co., Ltd., another JV with a Hong Kong firm, was created to produce high-class toupees and other hair ornaments for the export market. In the same year, after a mission of the *Shandong* government to Romania, *Jifa* established *Qingdao Huamian* Washing Co., Ltd., a JV with a Romanian company, which controls 40% of the shares. It uses Japanese technology and can dye and finish 18,000 tons of knitting fabric annually. About 90% of its production is exported to Hong Kong, France, Japan, and Romania. The annual sales turnover of this company is RMB 4.5 billion.

Encouraged by her achievements, and wishing to increase *Jifa's* credibility in the market, Chen Yulan saw further opportunities for vertical integration in manufacturing. In 2005, she decided to develop *Jifa Longshan* Industrial Park. At the same time, she decided that *Jifa's* Group should develop numerous new JVs with international companies—six of them Top 500 corporations—to diversify its product range and become more vertically integrated. International advanced yarn spinning, dyeing and finishing, printing and garment equipment from Japan, America, Italy, Switzerland, and other countries, were all installed. The list of

"JVs established by us is too large to mention them all," acknowledges Chen Yulan. Some examples are provided in the table below.

These JVs proved to be a smart strategy that not only gave *Jifa* access to the best available technology, but also to new management techniques and new clients abroad. Today *Jifa* Group has more than 40 subsidiaries— some 100% owned and some JVs with foreign companies—operating in its three main lines of business: hair products, knitting wear, and tatting garments. *Jifa* usually has between 18% and 55% participation in the shares of its JVs, with just a few exceptions. The company and its subsidiaries occupy over 30 buildings, including all their factories and warehouses, which are located in the *Jifa* and *Longshan* industrial parks.[2] Total sales revenue is over RMB 6 billion, and their combined exports are over US$ 470 million. Chen Yulan regrets, however, that their mean profitability is very low—less than 2%—and has been decreasing over the last few years. Profitability is a bit higher for its hair products—about 2%—with annual sales of over RMB 300 million.

Leaving aside its traditional hair products, in the textile industry the range of *Jifa*'s today products is very large, including many different types of fabric, and many finished products: underwear (*Jifa*'s largest production volume and the products that originally built its reputation), outerwear (which today offers the biggest potential for *Jifa*, particularly, in the domestic market), sportswear, casual wear, swim wear, baby clothing, shirts, socks, gloves, scarves, and other garment accessories. *Jifa* also produces embroidery needles and (apart from its own use) can provide other vendors with textile related services such as spinning, knitting, bleaching, dyeing, printing, finishing. Some of the finished products are directly sold in the domestic market in their own-brand retail stores. They mostly use the brand "*Jifa*" for their mid-range products, and "*Jasfeel*" for their high-end underwear and garments. There are "*Jifa*" and "*Jasfeel*" shops in Beijing and "*Tianjin*" and "*Jifa*" shops in Shanghai. Their "*Jasfeel*" flagship store is located in Qingdao.

This expansion has all been financed by local branches of the national banks, with whom they have traditionally kept a very close relationship. Interest on loans is now higher than in 2008 or earlier years, but they have managed to continue obtaining affordable loans. This easy access to financing made it possible for *Jifa* to own their huge premises; it even encouraged Chen Yulan to go into the real estate business, where they established *Jifa* Real Estate Development Co., Ltd. Among its projects are "*Jifa* Sunlight City", "*Longyuan*," and "*Runfa* New City."

Qingdao Jifa Longshan Dyeing and Weaving Co., Ltd., a successful JV, established in 2005, with Daiwabo Corporation, Sojitz Corporation, Toyota Tsusho Corporation, and Tomen Corporation. Its annual production capacity is 100 million meters and today 50% of its sales are sold in the domestic market.

Toray *Jifa* (*Qingdao*) Co., Ltd., a JV with Toray Corporation. It produces polyester/cotton blends and 100% cotton woven fabric; other processes include spinning, knitting, dyeing, and finishing.

Qingdao Shuangfa Garment Co., Ltd., a JV with the Japanese firm Sojitz Corporation, which produces mostly shirts and other clothing items. Its annual capacity is 2.4 million pieces.

Qingdao Lifa Knitting Co., Ltd., a JV with Toray (Hong Kong) Group and Toray (China) Group, which produces knitting underwear and outerwear. It uses Japanese technology and has an annual production capacity of 5 million pieces.

Qingdao Guihua Knitting Co., Ltd., a JV with Japanese Itochu Corporation's Roy-Ne Company. It combines the knitting, bleaching, and dyeing processes together with scientific innovation.

Qingdao Jifa Huaxin Printing Co., Ltd., a JV with Japanese Kaneoshi Co., is a knitting printing factory with an annual capacity of 40 million pieces. It has an advanced photo stencil system and is the largest table-printing factory in China.

Qingdao Zhongmian Knitting Co., Ltd. is a JV with Nimichen Corporation (which holds 50% of the shares) and a *Qingdao* government-owned company (which owns 32% of the shares). This company uses Japanese dyeing technology, and is the first in its sector in China that used a computer management system, including automatic chromatography and advanced testing and detection instruments.

Qingdao Jifa Hua Hong Knitting Co., Ltd., a JV with Marubeni Corporation, produces underwear. It uses Japanese technology and has an annual capacity of 9.6 million pieces.

Qingdao Jifa Huajin Garment Co., Ltd., a JV with Japanese Marubeni Corporation and Toray (China) Investment Co., Ltd., produces medium and high-quality shirts and other garments. Its annual production capacity is 2.4 million pieces.

Qingdao Jifa Xuchang Garment Co., Ltd. is a JV with Morrow Corporation, a Japanese firm. It has an annual capacity of 1 million pieces of high-quality swim wear which are supplied to several world-famous brands.

Qingdao Yihe Knitting Co., Ltd. is a JV with a Japanese company where *Jifa* retains 90% of the shares. It uses Japanese technology and has an annual production capacity of 16,000 tons of high-quality knitting fabric, which is used by other *Jifa* companies and also sold in Japan and in the domestic market.

Qingdao Jifa Nekoshima Embroidery Co., Ltd. is a China–Japan JV which uses the famous Japanese Tajima embroidery machines and the advanced DG/ML pattern making system. Its annual production capacity is 12 billion stitches.

Another slightly different company that Chen Yulan established is *Jifa* International Commodity Exhibition and Business Co., Ltd., a 25–75% JV with a US company, located in the Qingdao Special Economic Zone (SEZ). It combines the functions of commodity exhibitions with business, economic, and technology cooperation. It provides services to other firms, including consulting, investment advice, and financing. Its customers can benefit from the favorable policies of free trade with no licenses or duties, which the Qingdao Special Economic Zone provides.

In the services sector, *Jifa* owns *Qingdao Jifa* International Freight Agent Co., Ltd., which provides a variety of freight transport related services. The list continues in the company's domain of diversification/vertical integration in the services sectors, where *Jifa* owns a business

center—*Qingdao Jifa* Business Centre—and a water treatment plant—
Jimo Water Treatment Co., Ltd., with a capacity of 60,000 tons/day—to
treat the water used in some of their manufacturing processes.

For Chen Yulan, the key to *Jifa's* long-term achievements under her
leadership has been innovation. She has always taken a market-oriented
approach and has kept innovating in the technologies used and in her
business model. Particularly since 2000, she has kept introducing innovative technologies and worked very hard to develop *Jifa's* brand. In order
to earn customer confidence in *Jifa's* products, she has always emphasized
the importance of quality control, no matter whether the products are
for the domestic market or for worldwide exports. She has made certain
that *Jifa's* products meet tough quality control standards. At the same
time, *Jifa* has aggressively invested in new product development (achieving a new product ratio of 30% of the total products) and has registered
many patents for its new products. Today, *Jifa* has become one of the key
government supported enterprises in China. Chen Yulan has shared her
success' story with other Chinese entrepreneurs, and helped more than
one thousand companies improve and progress toward their own success
stories.

In 1996, Chen Yulan built the first National Industry Technology
Center in China—*Qingdao Jifa* Group's Technological Center. The Center
is the core institution behind *Jifa's* technological development, employing
over 200 people and qualifying both as a national-level enterprise technology research center and as a certified laboratory. The center conducts
research in the following fields: new textile fibers, new technology, fine
chemical products, printing and dyeing technology, membrane material
research for textiles, and new materials for synthetic hair products.

Under Chen Yulan's initiative, *Jifa* has also invested more than RMB
10 million to set up a National Research Laboratory—*Qingdao* Textile
Testing Center—that can conduct more than 300 different textile and
clothing material tests, following standards established by China, the US,
Japan, and the European Union.

Jifa's research on medical protection fabrics and garments has received
the first prize of Qingdao advanced technology. In 2003, the scientific
results from its research on "sea fiber chitosan textile products"[3] received
the second prize for National Technology Progress. Chitosan fiber is, in

fact, a unique fabric *Jifa* is producing. Chen Yulan emphasizes that it is a special product, which has given *Jifa* competitive advantages in their underwear products; they have also been marketing it as such.

Applications of Chitosan fiber are being developed through *Qingdao Jifa* High-Tech Material Co., Ltd., whose manufacturing processes start from filature, through spinning and weaving, to dyeing and ready-made garment production. The company carries out control and inspection of the various raw materials and fibers. It can manufacture Chitosan products to different specifications, including: Chitosan fiber, Chitosan plied yarn, 100% Chitosan yarn, Chitosan knitted fabric, Chitosan woven fabric and Chitosan terry cloth. The firm can also supply medical dressings, such as artificial skin, hemostatic cotton, hemostatic gauze, and Chitosan wound plaster. It can also manufacture filtering and membrane materials. *Jifa* possesses a national invention patent for the use of Chitosan in the textile industry.

Another important step to competing through investments in innovation was the creation in 2007 of *Qingdao Jifa* Tech Co., Ltd., the first Chinese firm to undertake ePTFE membrane[4] research and manufacturing. The company not only manufactures ePTFE membrane, but also laminates it with a diverse variety of substrates. *Jifa*'s ePTFE membrane and PTFE fiber can be engineered to different specifications. The membrane, with its laminated fabric, can be used in different application including apparel, filtration, medical, safety, architecture, upholstery, and military use. *Jifa* can process all kinds of blended fabric and meet the demands for different products.

Chen Yulan has always reminded her employees that *Jifa*'s long-term success can only be achieved by "relying on its capabilities, depending on quality, and developing through innovation." "Capabilities" since those were the only real assets workers had when the company was established, back in 1955. "Quality" because without their clients' support it is impossible to build a sustainable business. "Innovation" because without it, no company and brand can survive in today's fiercely competitive market.

Beyond these factors, Chen Yulan's priorities today are on talent and human resources management. She still believes her management team is composed of excellent quality people. Their numbers have been increasing over time, from the original six people to the current ten people—five of them being women. As for the rest of the 12,500 employees, 98% come from *Jinan,* and 65% of them are women. Before joining *Jifa,* they were all farmers. So, Chen Yulan believes that her group has really contributed to the welfare of her employees.

Chen Yulan manages her employees in a "very traditional way," she says. She uses procedures and rules, as well as training, to guarantee the quality of their manufactured products and their logistic activities; for instance: there are signs about quality, safety, and innovation posted all around the shop floors; and there are daily quality and quantity controls at the factory level. But she also uses the heart, meaning that she likes to keep in close contact with the factories' employees, to establish personal relationships with them, to help and support them and make them know that they can rely on her whenever necessary. She has gone so far as to tell them that she is their best friend and they all should support her. She has established standard motivation techniques, such as the "employee of the month." Finally, to compensate them with a reasonable salary and incentives (particularly as many of the employees are also shareholders in the company), this serves as a way for Chen Yulan to motivate the employees to develop their abilities, act innovatively, and operate in line with the corporate goals.

The company is also structured in a traditional way, with a large number of manufacturing departments. In addition to these, there are some additional departments, all under Chen Yulan's direct supervision: exports, warehouses, administration, and finance. Horizontally, there are two other functions: quality control and priority projects. Above these departments and directly depending on her are the managers responsible for the domestic market and the domestic retail shops.

Since the financial crisis, Chen Yulan understands that attention has to be focused now on the domestic market, where they have to create a new brand for their outerwear production, using the innovative ePTFE membrane they produce. In fact, she has had this idea in mind since 2007—the year they established *Qingdao Jifa* Tech Co., Ltd.—but they did not begin thinking about it seriously until she realized they could no longer be 100% dependent on exports, since that would make them vulnerable over the long term. "A strong outerwear domestic brand being sold in its specific retail shops will provide *Jifa's* business with bigger stability," she believes.

Another strategy Chen Yulan would like to implement to reduce *Jifa*'s strong dependence on exports is the acquisition of an excellent foreign brand they could use later on to sell their manufactured products all over the world, using that brand's distribution channels. She thinks that developing their own brand "from scratch" in the international market is impossible. So, the only way to change their current business model has to be through acquisition.

FOR CHEN YULAN, TO ACQUIRE A FOREIGN BRAND IS A GOOD STRATEGY because it is the only way to quickly leverage a globally famous brand and access its distribution channels.

Chen Yulan acknowledges that the transition to the new business model is not easy, and it implies that they need to incorporate new capabilities—for instance, to tackle the domestic market properly, which will be totally different from the capabilities they have been using for their export-oriented business model. However, she believes that they should be able to overcome the new challenges, in the same way as they did when transforming from the original company to the large group they have today, given how much the group has contributed to the welfare of *Jimo*'s population.

Jifa originated in a rural community, and it grew there; most of its employees are also from this same rural community. The company has kept evolving, following the trend of economic and social development in China. So, Chen Yulan regarded the contributions made to this rural area as a kind of social responsibility. *Jifa* has contributed over RMB 3 billion in taxes over the past 30 years. The processing fees for its local sub-contractors reaches about RMB 200 million every year and it increases RMB 200 per capita, annually. Under her leadership *Jifa* has not only contributed to local economic growth, but also invested its profits in improving public welfare, aggressively participating in charity and rescue activities. Over the years, it has donated over RMB 10 Million, including RMB 2.7 million for the Sichuan earthquake and RMB 3.16 million for the *Jimo*'s Farmers Healthcare Project.

After more than 55 years of steady growth, *Jifa* Group is considered vital evidence of China's economic revolution, serving as a role model of savvy business management, a "miracle" performed by Chen Yulan.

However, this experience does seem to have changed her natural and modest attitude. For her, everything she has done and achieved at *Jifa* Group is not important. She says that she is not like Yang Mianmian— Haier's President (mentioned in Chapter VI), who is only six months younger than her and attended the same school (although they did not meet each other until the end of the 1980s). Chen Yulan feels she is not an important person, and that she is not like Yang Mianmian, who is a symbol of excellence. Chen says she would have liked to be trained by Yang Mianmian; "Yang Mianmian is a model [*bangyang*] for me."

Chen Yulan is married to a man who is also originally from *Jimo*, someone who used to work for the government but is now retired. Her daughter pretty much resembles her father, works for the government and lives in Qingdao with her husband and young son. Chen Yulan thinks that she resembles her mother's character greatly, although her mother never worked outside of her house. Her father was one of *Jimo*'s farmers. Although she has travelled on vacation (for instance, to Europe in 2005), Chen Yulan does not like travelling. Her only hobby is her job.

By the time this book is published, Chen Yulan would have retired. However, for nearly five decades, she has woken up in the morning feeling good just by reflecting that she had another day ahead to continue making great efforts to maintain the leading position of *Jifa*'s products in the international market, and to implement *Jifa*'s new strategy for developing the domestic market.

ENTREPRENEURSHIP BY JOINT VENTURE MEANS:
- *Proceeding from the ground up.*
- *Establishing the company's group structure.*
- *Keeping full control of the group company.*
- *Not necessarily holding majority of shares in its JV companies.*
- *Foreseeing when the incorporation of new technological advances is needed to remain competitive in the market place.*
- *Understanding that foreign cooperation also means easier access to foreign markets.*
- *Continuing with the implementation of strategy, even when failure occurs.*

- *Choosing partners that have a culture compatible with their own.*
- *Using the JVs to implement whatever is necessary (for instance, product diversification, vertical integration) to be able to profit from emerging or existing market opportunities.*
- *Making innovation the key for long-term success.*
- *Not being afraid to enter new fields when the right opportunity arises.*
- *Keeping overall control over the group's strategies.*

CHAPTER 14

Entrepreneurship by Leveraging Projects. Gong Min, Keying

Beijing is not only the political capital of China, but it is also recognized as the cultural capital of China. It is, therefore, the place to be for a company operating in the cultural industry, which is what Gong Min has been doing since the end of the last century. Gong Min is the Chair-woman and Managing Director of *Beijing Keying Guoji Jiying Shi Cehua Youxiang Gongsi*—Beijing Keying International Movie and Television Design Co., Ltd. The company is located in Haidian district, which is well known for its prominence in the media, events management, and advertising industries. It provides the following services: design and production of movies, television programs, and special subjects films; VCD and DVD marketing materials for companies; design, organization, and implementation of large social and group events (including performances), for companies, associations and other similar organizations. Its brochure states that the firm has the acceptance and trust of the nation-wide mainstream media.

Gong Min was born in Beijing in January 1960. Her parents were also from Beijing. Her father—an engineer, now deceased—used to be a top leader in a government-owned construction company. Her mother—still alive and living with a maid—was also a leader at a government-owned textile factory. Gong Min has an older brother and sister, and a younger brother. All of Gong Min's siblings work for government-owned organizations, so their spirit is different from Gong Min's entrepreneurial profile. Neither did she inherit her entrepreneurial spirit from her parents or from her parents' families. Her father became an orphan when he was two-months old, and her maternal grandparents were farmers near Beijing. Gong Min's father was sick, and her mother cared for him for many years, spending much time with him at the hospital before he died in 1989. Gong Min has a daughter in her mid-twenties, who recently moved to Beijing. Her daughter worked in Shanghai between 2005 and 2010 as a director in a government-owned company. Gong Min is very proud of her daughter, who she defines as "very responsible and independent"; she likes singing and dancing, "like the women from our generation."

Gong Min started working in 1980 with *Wengong Tuan*, a large, well-known cultural group belonging to the Ministry of Culture, which included the artistic company Wenyi Tuanti. She decided to work there, since she wanted to practice what she had studied after finishing school. She really liked the work environment, which cheered her up. She was assigned to do management work at *Zhongguo Tielu Wengong Tuan*, administered by both the Ministry of Railways (the agency that financed it) and the Ministry of Culture (the agency that managed the cultural performances). In that group there were 800 people who, among other artistic activities, did: *huaju*, a spoken stage drama (usually performed by men); *gewu*, singing and dancing; *zaji*, acrobatics; and *shuosheng*, a kind of word play using traditional sayings that is performed on stage (and usually performed by men). Gong Min remained in that line of work until 1999, when she decided to start her own business.

During the many years she was there, her work content did not change much, but her professional skills and abilities grew a great deal. When she began, she needed people to teach her how to do things while, in her last years in the organization, she was the one teaching other people. Between 1983 and 1985 in parallel with her work, she took lessons at *Zhongyang Meishu Xueyuan* to learn stage design and the design of stage costumes. She did not earn any degrees doing this, but she wanted the knowledge so she could apply it in her daily work.

In 1986, Gong Ming married a man who worked in middle management at a government-owned camera factory. This company eventually closed down in 1990 and the couple divorced in 1992, when their daughter was five years old. Gong Min never remarried. Life after the divorce was very tiring for her, since there were performances every evening. Having no one to stay with her daughter; she had to take her to the theatre located in the front of their building in *Muxidi: Erqi Juchang*, or the *Erqi* Theatre. The group often traveled throughout China, which further complicated her life. She thinks it is precisely because her daughter spent so much of her young life with her in theatres, that she likes singing and dancing so much; her daughter even studied piano professionally for five years.

When Gong Min looks back on those days, she is sad; with the advent of TV, video, and so forth, cultural troupes have lost their importance in China, and her old organization no longer performs. In fact, most of its members have already retired. About 200 former members are still on the Ministry of Culture's payroll. In principle, they are still active, as they are still being paid, but they do no work at all. This change in demand for the group's performances is what motivated the change in her business approach.

While working at *Wengong Tuan*, Gong Min learned by observing and adapting to new situations. She learned many things in particular from well-known professionals working in the cultural industry. She had the opportunity to meet many famous people, which she could not otherwise have done. She also developed a special inner-strength, a feeling of not being afraid of anything, which grew over time. Little by little, she was convinced she could perform the same tasks she did at *Wengong Tuan* in her own business, and that she had the capacity and desire to do so. She also saw how much China had developed since its economic "reform and opening up" in 1978, and how many opportunities were going to arise in the cultural industry.

So in 1999, she started a business to provide a complete set of theatre and cultural performance related services. She handled everything from stage preparation and design to clothing design and hairdressing. With the cultural industry in the hands of the government, she established an association with it to make her dream of becoming an entrepreneur real. Gong Min acknowledges that this association has proven useful for the gathering of both information and materials but not for financing her projects, because the government usually does not give any grants and, when it does, it is very small.

FOR GONG MIN, ASSOCIATING WITH GOVERNMENT INSTITUTIONS IS BENEFICIAL because of the contacts and information the institutions provide that can be transformed over time into competitive advantages for her business.

Observing the market trends and proceeding step-by-step from there, she moved into the media-related activities that her company continues with today. She started by doing documentaries and educational programs. Her first project was the development of eight video advertisements shown on China Central Television (CCTV) for the petroleum company *Zhongguo Shihua*, part of *Zhongguo Shiyou Shihua* (China Petroleum and Chemical Corporation, better known as Sinopec). Similar projects and TV movies followed year after year, including: *Happy Events Do Not Trouble People*, whose main character is the famous actor Pan Changjiang, shown on CCTV in 2000 and 2001; *The Last Hostage*, shown on CCTV in 2002; and *Armed Heroes*, a twenty-episode TV mini-series, produced in association with Beijing Television (BTV), Shanghai Television (STV), Shanghai *Wenguang* Company, and Beijing Forbidden City Movies Company to celebrate the seventieth anniversary of the founding of the People's Liberation Army (PLA).

Gong Min acknowledges that the network of actors and professionals she developed while working at *Wengong Tuan* has been very useful in building her business. She often involves them in her projects, although she has continued expanding her network since 1999. Over time, she has found her previous contacts at TV channels to be highly useful. These business relationships have made it possible for her to show programs on 150 of the more than 2,400 Chinese TV channels, included the major ones like CCTV. One strategy she has been following with great success is to associate with (*hezuo*) the big cities' TV channels (there are 150 of these in China), such as BTV (Beijing) and STV (Shanghai).

Between 2003 and 2006, she invested over RMB 4 million, recording 26 TV serial-episodes (25 minutes in length each) to teach the Chinese population how to behave in an emergency situation after a major natural disaster. She named the series "Emergency Aid," and it covered all types of issues related to natural disasters, including the performance of rescues, the provision of help, and restoration of the disaster area. The series was produced in cooperation with the China International Committee for Disaster Reduction and the Administration Department of the People's Republic of China. Interestingly enough, Gong Min states that she undertook this project because, as a Buddhist, she told herself that she had to do something good for the society. She saw that nobody was paying attention to these issues in China and that the Chinese population needed this kind of education. So, after receiving the financial backing (for 50% of the funds needed) from a government-owned company, Gong Min decided to go ahead with her project.

Her intuition about the demand for such an initiative proved correct. The series was shown between 2006 and 2008 on over 150 educational series produced by major TV channels, such as CCTV, BTV, STV, Sichuan TV, Zhejian TV, Jiangsu TV, Guizhou TV, and Yunnan TV. On over 70 of the channels, the series was shown twice, both before and after the 2008 Sichuan earthquake. By 2009, the program had been shown on over 400 TV channels and had been seen in schools, relevant government departments, and relief associations all over the country. That same year, she published a book on the subject, which includes a CD. Both the book and the DVDs of the series can be purchased at Xinhua bookstores nationally. There are several editions of the book and the CD; 80,000 copies of the book have been sold. The main difference between the book and the TV series "Emergency Aid" is that, in the original TV episodes, real people gave their explanations at the actual physical locations, while the book merely uses drawings to illustrate the situations.

Gong Min explains that she recovered her initial investment and ended up making a profit on that project. She did this by selling to third parties the free ad placements that she received from the TV channels. A portion of this free ad time went to the government-owned company that had co-financed the project. This free ad placement was the only compensation she received from the TV stations for carrying her series. They did not pay her any money for the rights to broadcast the series, but by selling the free ad time she made a profit of RMB 1 million that was equal to 25% of the amount she had invested. From the books' sales she gets a 10% commission on the book's price of RMB 28. So, on average she has earned around 30% return on investment, which she considers to be quite good.

Upon completion of the "Emergency Aid" project in 2006 and anticipating its success, she started a new project: the development of an educational television cartoon series: The project called for 300 episodes, each 13 minutes long for a total investment of around RMB 20 million. The first 100 episodes were produced using RMB 4 million worth of investment that she had recovered from her previous project. The second 100 episodes started at the beginning of 2010 and were scheduled to be finished in 2012. These were mainly financed with the income generated from the first 100 episodes. Upon completion of the second portion of the programs, she will start on the final 100 episodes, which will be completed by 2016. The title of the series is *Xi You Xin Zhuan*, which loosely translates as "A New Journey to the West." The series is a collection of traditional Chinese and contemporary stories that deal with current situations and explain current issues.

The initial launch of the first 100 episodes of "A New Journey to the West" was in Beijing, but the episodes have since been shown all over China. They began airing in June 2009 on three major TV channels: Guangdong TV, Jiangsu TV, and *Zhongguo Jiaoyu*. Later, they were aired on an additional twenty TV channels. Every day, one or two episodes are broadcast after school-lunch time, so that children can watch them during the school day. Although the main target group was originally children under 13 years old, the episodes have been seen by around 400 million students of all ages. The reason for broadcasting them in schools is because the content refers to many questions that students pose to their teachers every day at school. The questions cover a diverse range of topics including: happiness, law, security and personal safety, home safety, school safety, traffic safety, health, sexual education, the prevention of sexually transmitted diseases, helping others, emergency prevention, emergency management, and safe travel, among others. Since mothers typically pay greater attention to their children's education, in 2007 Gong Min signed a cooperation agreement with The All China Women's Federation, which has proved useful for marketing reasons.

The financing of this latest education project has followed a different model than the emergency aid project: instead of getting free ad time from the TV channels to resell to third parties, Gong Min decided to sell the episodes directly to the TV channels. The price paid by each channel varies with the audience size. Contracts with the various TV channels were signed for two years (initially 2010–2012); after that the contracts could be renewed. The profit target she set for this project was 40% higher than for her previous project. From the beginning of this project, she envisioned additional income sources, in particular: book and CD sales, commissions, plus merchandising revenues from small reproductions of the main characters, keyrings of the main characters, and such. Gong Min has already sold 200,000 copies of the book containing the first portion of the cartoons, at a price of RMB 12 per copy. For the CDs, she envisioned selling a complete set of 100 episodes, which children could later watch at home on their computers. As for the merchandising, her idea is to test this line of business on this project so that, in future, she may use and expand on it in different ways.

Gong Min affirms that there are not many companies like hers that can provide these kinds of products at the same level of quality. This is why every time she has started a new project and invested a significant amount of money in it, she has always been positive of its success. One example of the project's success is that upon completion of the first part of "A Journey to the West," the government helped finance her company's work for the second part. However, she claims this is not so important in terms of the money but instead for the prestige, since such financing is only given to extremely high quality companies and products.

Building on this financial support and her company's previously successful cartoon production background has helped Gong Min borrow money from the bank to help with the financing of the second part of this project. She explains that she decided to use the banks this time to speed project development and the marketing of the main characters. This way, she can move forward when she feels the market is ripe for her idea of merchandising the main characters. Upon completion of the third part, if she sees that there is a market to further expand the project, she will go ahead and get government approval to develop a fourth series of episodes.

From the first day she started with the second portion of cartoons for this project, Gong Min had the idea of eventually exporting the series. So, upon completing the first part, she began working on exporting the program to other parts of Asia. She already has an association with a company that will take 30% of the income in return for generating sales in the international market.

Her company has sales turnover of over RMB 3 million and around 40 employees working in four departments: design; movie and television; special subjects; and marketing. The younger employees are not like her, trained on the job; usually they have university degrees specializing in TV media. The increase in the number of employees has moved in parallel with the firm's growth: in 1999 they were fewer than 10 people, in 2001 over 20 people and in 2003, when they started their first special project, over 30 people. After the completion of the "Emergency Aid" project and the initiation of the cartoon series, her staff grew in number to its current figure. Over 50% of Gong Min's current staff are working on the cartoon project, but she has also hired a couple of sub-contractors to help out.

The design department is the only one led by a senior woman, who Gong Min got to know a long time ago. She has been doing this kind of work for most of her life. The design department takes responsibility for the design, organization, and implementation of large social events for various companies and institutions. It can mobilize famous actors and actresses nation-wide, since the company has had long experience working with them. It also has close connections with major media nation-wide. Among the projects produced by this department are: the New Spring Festival celebration for the Chinese Mining Industry Federation; the "Secret War Notes" ceremony designed for the National Safety Department, the large-scale press conference organized for Anwante Crop Tech (China) Co., Ltd., and a large-scale spring celebration designed for Andisheng Safe Automation Co., Ltd.

The movie and television department is responsible for the design, shooting, and production of movies and TV programs, as well as corporate advertisements, VCDs, and DVDs. It is run by a male manager, 30 years old. Apart from the special projects and films previously mentioned, this department has also produced (among other projects): a corporate VCD for Pengda Group; a marketing film "*Plant Kingdom*" for the Botanical Garden; a TV movie "*Man of 40*"; and three training films for Paili Sales Company—"Profesional Dealer Functions", "Service to Customers," and "Sales Abilities Retail Personnel Should Have to Face Customers."

The special subjects department is the only one led by a person under 30 years of age. This department is responsible for planning and shooting films dealing with special subjects. Because of Gong Min's previous contacts in this sector, this department can collaborate with famous directors and professionals to create unique high quality products. Before undertaking the two major projects, "Emergency Aid" and "A New Journey to the West," between 1999 and 2003, the department produced films for many famous national companies and organizations. Among these are such titles as: "Repay society and serve the people," "Seek a development base for agriculture," "A red duck rush into capital," "Our intimate people," "*Tsinghua Tongfang*, science and technology made by us," "Change your way of thinking and develop great plans," and "50 splendid years," which was produced for the fiftieth anniversary of China University of Geo-sciences.

The marketing department is responsible for the publication (in Mandarin Chinese) of the magazine "Chinese Market Conditions for Sales and Supply: the Situation for Chinese and Foreign Enterprises," as licensed by the National Publication Office and sponsored by the Chinese World (Asia) News Agency in co-operation with other national units. It is targeted at entrepreneurs, managers, and high-level white-collar workers in China and abroad. This is a means for communicating the capabilities and services of Gong Min's company to the broader market, as well as to keep alive her contacts in the media industry and relevant government institutions.

Apart from these main areas of work, Gong Min's company also provides business services to help other firms develop their brands, such as creating elaborate corporate brochures and associated CDs. They have done such work, for instance, for Inner Mongolia *Huanggang* Mining Industry Co., Ltd. It is an area that does not generate much income, but it is a complement to her other businesses and indirectly benefits their development.

Despite her company's relatively small size, Gong Min has not hesitated to emulate her much bigger peers and invest her profits in diversifying her sources of income (even if at a tiny scale). She has a restaurant— *Hong Ren Fang*—in the sub-urban Fengtai district of Beijing. She has also made real estate investments in rental housing, which she directly manages. As is usual in China, she owns her office premises. Finally, she is planning to start an entertainment business to organize large performances both in China (where her company is authorized to do so) and abroad.

With respect to her management style, Gong Min says that her employees call her "*laonian*," meaning she is like their "old mother," and that they are very good to her. She explains that most of her employees are not from Beijing, where they came just to study or work. So, she pays great attention to them and makes sure their needs are satisfied, since they do not have any family in the city. One of her employees is responsible for human resource management. Once a month, this person organizes the company's internal meeting to make sure that the staff understands the corporate principles and goals and sticks to them. Sometimes, Gong Min attends these meetings but not very often, since she is normally away from the office. This is partly because she is directly responsible for external relations, in particular those with TV stations and relevant stakeholders, such as the Ministry of Education for the cartoon project, and her clients' advertising agencies.

As for her business model, Gong Min's explains that she has always followed the model she systematically applied in her two special projects. The model is: (1) invest up to a limit she can afford; (2) recover the investment and earn a profit; (3) reinvest in a new project the investment she has recovered from her most recent project; and (4) invest the profit in a new line of business. She combines this with the completion of "normal projects" executed to clients' demands, so that she can generate the monthly income needed to cover the company's fixed expenses. As for special subject projects, the only exceptions she has made to this model were the first films she produced when she started up her business. These were acquired by the TV stations or co-financed by them, in those cases where they were collaboratively produced.

She acknowledges that in starting up her business she had to use this alternative business model, since she did not have the required reputation or level of contacts to get free ad time from major TV stations, or co-financing from third parties or from banks, or both. Although this model was less profitable—around 20%—the references she earned from executing those projects opened doors for her preferred business approach. In any case, she states that her main concern since she started her company was not to lose any money, as opposed to making a lot of money. And she is proud of herself as she has not only managed to achieve her goal but also to keep increasing her profits over time. She explains that this is probably because she is making a reality of the message she communicates to her clients and partners, namely, "If you cooperate with us one time, we will cooperate with you for a lifetime. Cooperation once, friendship for life!"

Gong Min claims that her business has not been affected by the 2009 financial crisis or the ensuing global economic turmoil. This is because her business activity is focused on the domestic market. Also, in recent years, the Chinese government has begun promoting many of the programs on which she collaborates, in particular, the special subjects programs. She explains that the only economic problem she might face would come from not being able to generate enough advertising income. However, she does not see this happening, since there are so many companies—domestic and international—operating in so many sectors wanting to win Chinese consumers that she finds it difficult to imagine demand for advertising declining in the near future. Besides, she has already combined this model with the new model of selling her cartoon series directly to TV stations. Moreover, thanks to her strategy of associating with government institutions, she has created competitive advantages for her business, such as access to higher-level people in the organizations and companies she works with. An additional competitive advantage her company has is, knowing in advance what the government's needs are. Other firms in her sector have younger, better-educated leaders but they cannot compete on the same basis. So, by smartly using her company's competitive advantages, she plans on continuing to develop the reputation of her company and its brand.

Gong Min has been a practicing Buddhist since 1997. At that time, she had many problems and stress. Her daughter was still very young, her mother was sick, and she was working two jobs to earn enough money to support herself. Her second job was designing uniforms for hotel managers. To cope, she turned to Buddhism and it has helped her greatly over the years. She learned to feel good about herself and became more relaxed. She keeps a statue of Buddha in her office, but she keeps this private. She does not want to be photographed with it. Despite the many future business plans she has, she would like to be able to have a more peaceful life before she reaches the age of 60. Ideally she would like to work as a consultant for other companies in the cultural sector she knows so well, and have free time to spend with her daughter and, eventually, her grand child. These are her personal dreams.

When Gong Min gets up in the morning, she is glad that she has another day ahead to continue contributing significantly to the educational needs of Chinese society while expanding and generating advantages for her business.

ENTERPRENEURSHIP BY PROJECT LEVERAGE MEANS:
- *Being located in the place where support for leverage can be generated.*
- *Not being afraid of facing any challenge.*
- *Being totally convinced that the project will succeed.*
- *Foreseeing market opportunities.*
- *Proceeding step-by-step.*
- *Teaming with relevant stakeholders that can enhance the brand's image and provide competitive advantages.*
- *Smartly using these competitive advantages.*
- *Developing a broad high quality network of collaborators and business contacts.*
- *Working hard.*
- *Implementing the project with maximum quality and delivering the best products.*
- *Developing a business that will generate enough income to cover the company's fixed costs.*
- *Investing in each particular project up to the limit of affordability.*
- *Recovering that investment and earning a profit.*
- *Re-investing the amount investment in a new project.*
- *Investing the profit earned in a different business area.*
- *Repeating the same cycle with each new project.*
- *Continue to generate new ideas to increase the project's profitability.*
- *Maintaining flexibility to shift the business model approach temporarily when necessary.*

CHAPTER 15

Entrepreneurship by Consolidation. Zhang Ziqin, Sinolgis

After many years of successful Chinese economic development, logistics still present many challenges, comprising what has been termed the bottleneck of e-commerce in China. In order to cure what many people have called its "chronic disease" in logistics, in August 2011 and August and December 2012, China's State Council issued new guidelines offering fiscal and administrative incentives to logistics enterprises.

The new guidelines cover nine areas: reducing tax burdens on logistics enterprises, providing favorable land policies for the industry, promoting convenient transport of vehicles, accelerating reform in logistics management, encouraging integration of logistics resources, boosting the innovation and application of logistics technologies, increasing investment in the logistics industry, prioritizing the development of agricultural product logistics, and strengthening coordination among government departments. The new guidelines put forth specific measures to solve the long-term problems in the industry, including the issues of transportation and taxation—major concerns of many logistics businesses.

Prior to the new guidelines, the State Council had already issued the "Plan on Restructuring and Developing the Logistics Industry" in March 2009. Since the release of the document, China witnessed a rapid growth in logistics. Compared to 2008, the industry's value-added reported a net increase of RMB 700 billion in 2010. However, experts recognize that current policies lag behind the actual needs of the industry, which has restricted further development of the sector.

In the area of transportation, the main problems are high road tolls, inordinate fines, limitations on the number of vehicles from certain cities and regions, and truck-targeted regulations such as stopping upon entrance into the city or interference with off-loadings.

Statistics show that road tolls accounted for nearly one-third of the operating costs of logistics enterprises, which not only weighed on the companies' profit margins, but also reduced efficiency. To solve these problems, China vowed to cut fees and road tolls by gradually eliminating tolls on secondary roads, reducing toll gates, and restricting the number of toll ways, according to the guidelines.

Tax is an important leverage for regulating the economy. Unbalanced business tax rates and repeated taxation in the industry are considered the main restraints on China's logistics development. The guidelines mandate relevant government departments to work on standardizing business tax rates for all the different links within the logistics sector. It is anticipated that, in the future, the business tax rate for the industry will be 3%.

In an attempt to tackle the land issues, the country will make plans for developing national logistics parks, which, according to the guidelines, are likely to enjoy preferential policies. The guidelines also support the use of old factory buildings and warehouses for the construction of logistics facilities.

In addition, the guidelines support logistics enterprises in going public, encourage large logistics firms to boost business through mergers and acquisitions, and buttress small and medium-sized enterprises to forge alliances for common development.

Local governments are required to invest more in the construction of logistics infrastructure and provide necessary capital support to key logistics companies.

In a move to further boost its logistics industry, China is now allowing, between January 1, 2012 and December 31, 2014, that land occupied by a logistics enterprise's self-owned commodity warehousing facilities (both for self-use and for leasing) only pay 50% of the ULUT originally required, based on related regulations.[1]

The guidelines also signified the importance of technology innovation in the logistics industry. Experts have said that the new guidelines are indeed comprehensive, but acknowledge that they may not be fully carried out in practice. Furthermore, the guidelines may be implemented much slower than people expect, due to the fact that logistics are involved in so many government organizations, such as commerce, taxation, customs, and quality inspection.

Nonetheless, China's logistics industry remains promising, and it will still have to go through a number of new reforms before it reaches maturity. This is the prediction of Zhang Ziqin, Chairwoman and CEO of *Beijing Huachu* Logistics Co., Ltd. (Sinolgis is its trademark: www .sinolgis.com).

Zhang Ziqin is originally from Taiyuan, Shanxi province, which has a long tradition of entrepreneurship: between the fourteenth and the nineteenth centuries, *Shanxi* people were in contact with the Jewish and the Venetians, among many other traders. They were the first to trade tea, and during the seventeenth and eighteenth centuries they exported it both to Russia and to Europe. The first bank in China—*Rishengchang*[2]— was opened in this province, in Pingyao,[3] in 1823. It began to develop its financial strength in the seventeenth century, during the Ming Dynasty, and achieved its full expression during the Qing Dynasty, in the nineteenth century. Pingyao was the financial center of China.[4] For the purpose of producing and printing checks, the world's most advanced printing technology at that time—the "watermark" method—was introduced in Taiyuan, Shanxi's current capital.[5]

Zhang Ziqin is very proud about the background of her home province. In fact, her company has a small office to receive clients in the *Jinshang Boguguan*, which is a kind of cultural and business center for *Shanxi* entrepreneurs with operations in Beijing. It opened in 2008 to profit from the Olympics.[6] She has been the Vice-President of the *Shanxi* Chamber of Commerce in Beijing since 2007. Zhang Ziqin was born in 1972 and, from the very first moment she answers the phone to every single detail of how she behaves (for instance, she always drives her own car) it is easy to see that she belongs to a slightly younger generation of entrepreneurs. The cultural gap between her and her over-50 year-old peers is easy to see in her case, more so because she remains more than

100% Chinese (despite having studied abroad—mentioned below), is a self-made woman and entrepreneur (like her older peers), and does not feel confident speaking in English to foreigners—she prefers to use Mandarin (as do her older peers). She has two sons: one born in 2002 and the second one at the end of 2010. Her older son studies in a private boarding school and, for many years, was coming back home only once a week, during the weekend. This seemed to be a good solution for Zhang Ziqin and her husband, who did not have the time to be with him, and for the child, who enjoyed living there. When this situation changed and he began coming back home every day after his youngest brother was born, Zhang Ziqin decided to devote more time to her family.

Zhang Ziqin's parents live in Taiyuan. She has three older brothers, all public officials who moved to Linfen (also in Shanxi province), to live with her father's older sister when Zhang Ziqin was 13 years old. Since that time she remained in Taiyuan alone with her parents and her paternal grandmother. Her paternal grandparents used to be small entrepreneurs who came to town to sell their farm products. Before 1949 they used to own a lot of land, so much that they even exchanged money for land. They also had a broad culture, but all this changed with the communist regime. Her maternal grandfather started working when he was twelve years old in the *Shanxi* Railways Company; he worked very hard and did a number of different jobs, since life was very complicated there with the Japanese in the country and the other special circumstances of that time. Her maternal grandmother was a housewife, and for the rest of her life remembered how she had to prepare a meal for a group of Japanese soldiers who would otherwise have killed or raped her.

Despite her brothers' frequent visits home, Zhang Ziqin remembers the situation after her brothers left as a very difficult period of her life. Her parents were deaf-mute, worked as manufacturing operators (his father in a wood factory and her mother in a power machinery facility) and earned extremely low salaries. So, they were very poor and lived in very basic conditions. For instance, she still remembers how old their TV was and how they wanted to buy a DVD player, but could not afford it. She wanted to earn money to help them by developing her own enterprise. This is how in 1994, upon her graduation in foreign trade from the Taiyuan University, she started working for the *Shanxi Weishi Jiaoliu*

Fuwu Zhongxin in Taiyuan to make her first earnings. This allowed her to help her parents (she gave them 50% of what she earned) and to save the rest to establish her first business. It also allowed her to make her dream of travelling a reality: in three years she travelled to more than 30 countries, visiting some of them more than once. In her work she established a large network of Shanxi business people who wanted to do business abroad, or with foreign companies, or both.

So, seeing the opportunities ahead, in 1997 she started her company *Shanxi Qiao Du Shangwu Xinxi Jiaoliu* to help Shanxi companies do business with foreign companies, and in particular to help them with the establishment and implementation of Joint Ventures. Clients trusted her and were very satisfied with the opportunity to leave these responsibilities in her hands for a service fee, while they could use that time to take care of their core business. Clients generally belonged to the following sectors: coal (split 50–50% between private and government owned companies), steel, forest, machinery/equipment, construction, and the logistics industry. At that time she had many associations with the Shanxi Foreign Commercial Service, and although her only relationship with the logistics industry was through her clients, these contacts would become very useful when she began her direct operations in this sector.

In the year 2000, she went to study in the US and in 2002 completed her MBA, with a major in logistics, from the University of Northern Virginia. After her first year in the US, however, she had to return home for a heart operation. While in China, she met her husband, who is from Beijing, seven years younger than her, and studied actors' characterization at *Beijing Linghe Daxue. He* is today the Managing Director of *Huachu* Group. When she returned back to the University of Northern Virginia for her second MBA year, she was already married and expecting a baby. Upon her graduation, she did not want to remain in the US, which she does not like and does not consider her home, so she returned to China. Prior to the establishment of her new and current business, she evaluated a number of other options, including the IT and the automobile industries, but disregarded them because they required huge investments.

Her logistics business was started in November 2002. Today it provides comprehensive logistic services, including: cargo transportation, land-sea-and-air combined freight transportation, and global cross-border dispatch services. The group has subsidiaries in: Beijing, Shanghai, Guangzhou, Hong Kong, Tianjin, and Haikou (Hainan). The headquarters were moved to Beijing in March 2008 (when Zhang Ziqin relocated as well), but used to be in Shanghai, where operations started in 2004 and where turnover is still higher than in Beijing. The same applies to the companies in Guangzhou and Hong Kong, which have been in operation since 2005–2006 and have higher turnover than the Beijing location. In Hong Kong there are no logistic activities; the company there only operates as a financial center and to help with import-export issues. Close to Beijing is their Tianjin company, where they have a sizeable glass-manufacturing client—*Tianjin Nanbo Yuxian Gongsi*—and a very important location from a logistics point of view. In fact, they have been considering moving the Beijing warehouses to Tianjin, where land is cheaper. "To do this kind of business in Beijing is very difficult," says Zhang Ziqin. Every company has its own Managing Director who does not have any shares in the subsidiary company, except in the case of the Guangzhou location, where the Managing Director holds 49% of the firm's shares. In the case of Haikou, the company is managed by Zhang Ziqin's older brother, but the day-to-day operations are run by her brother's friends, since he is simultaneously taking care of his real estate sales business—50% of the apartments acquired in Hainan by people from Shanxi have been sold through Zhang Ziqin's brother; this is why the activity of her *Hainan* subsidiary has been pretty much linked to the construction materials industry. About 60–70% of its turnover comes from the Shanghai (30%) and Guangzhou (30–40%) subsidiaries, while Tianjin is generating 20%, Beijing 10% and Hainan 5–10%. Zhang Ziqin's logistic premises altogether amount to 10,000 m² and are in close proximity to logistics parks, but they themselves have not built any, and have no intention of doing so.

In Beijing, the company has warehouses in two different locations: one in the south-east part of Beijing 5th belt, in Yizhuang (where they started with an area of 1,500 m² and have built their offices), and another one in the south-west part of Beijing, in Liangxiang (where they have built 10,000–15,000 m²). About a third of this total space is being leased to other companies. There they also have training facilities that they use for training both their employees and other associated logistic companies. For this training, between 2003 and 2005, they were associated with

Qinghua University, but now they are directly managing it themselves. Since 2009 they have a Master in Supply Chain and get approximately 10% of their Beijing turnover from these activities. An additional 10% of their turnover comes from providing services in the area of logistics standards and another 20% comes from their company *Beijing Fangshan*, which provides truck rentals (truck drivers included). The remaining 60% comes from the provision of pure logistic services.

The group's total turnover went down from around RMB 100 million to RMB 70–80 million in 2009, and has not significantly changed since then. The average net profit is around 7–8%, lower by about 2–3% with respect to 2009. With respect to their clients: 30% are from Shanxi (all government-owned companies), 40% are JVs, 30% are foreign companies—mostly from Korea and Japan, and a few European, and about 20% are government-owned companies. About 95% of Chinese clients are middle-size companies that operate in the domestic market. On an average, in about 70–80% of the situations, their provision of services is limited to the domestic market, which has helped them to keep their business in recent years. Their clients' sectors of operation include: automotive, publishing, electric components and communications, elevators, glass, hospital equipment, and lighting. Among their main clients are big groups such as: Otis, *Ming Xin Dian Lan* (in Jiangsu), *Nanbo* (in Tianjin, Guangdong, Guangzhou, and Wujian), *Xi Lai Jian* (a Korean hospital equipment company), *Zhong Guan Cun* (a magazine in Haidian), *Hao Jing Motou* (an automobiles company), *Zhang Tian Dian Xin* (a communications equipment company, in Hainan), and Beijing *Liantong* (a mobile communications group with a lot of subsidiaries). *Huachu* group (for which the trademark Sinolgis is used) has acquired recognition over time from foreign customers and local authorities and has won the Innovation Contribution Award from the United Nations. To remain competitive in the marketplace, *Huachu* has always been anticipating trends and innovating. As an example, in 2009, the group expanded its logistics business into the high-tech industry, in particular to merchandise transportation tracking and products' tracking. For the route from Beijing to Tianjin they have 300 trucks equipped with RFID equipment with support from the government. Through an association with a software expert company, they have also developed software for internal use, which they have been using in the green agricultural products' industry, as well as other sectors.

FOR ZHANG ZIQIN TO HAVE CLIENTS THAT OPERATE IN CHINA'S DOMESTIC MARKET IS A GOOD STRATEGY because it helps to keep the sustainability of the business, when the economic situation in foreign markets is uncertain.

Zhang Ziqin has about 100 employees. She also manages people from other companies, such as those responsible for packing and driving the trucks. Employees working in the warehouses—mostly security employees—are provided with housing and have all other daily expenses covered, since they are *waidiren* with no family in their place of work. At the group level, below her is her husband—the Managing Director—and below him are two Deputy Managing Directors, whom other directors follow. The top management—six people in total—is provided with a company car. Before she has her second child, Zhang Ziqin used to supervise everything, even though her husband has always held the title of Managing Director. However, since she decided to have a second child and to devote time to him and to her family, she has been playing a clearer Chair-woman and CEO role, focusing her attention more on investments and external issues, while her husband has been paying attention to the internal dimensions of their business.

In 10 years' time, Zhang Ziqin would like to be the number one company in China in her sector. Like Chen Yulan, she mentions that she wants to be "like Yang Mianmian, my *bangyang*—model." Following the market trends, she does not envision expansion of their warehouses area (at least not in the same proportion as their business expansion), since companies are demanding to apply just-in-time approaches. She expects the business will continue growing and acquiring new clients as it has been doing in the last few years, despite the economic turmoil. She expects, though, to continue seeing a much more competitive market with falling prices, since many of their competitors have been facing a lot of trouble in the last years, and because their clients—export-oriented businesses—have been too. Partly because of this, Zhang Ziqin has recently been putting an emphasis on acquiring domestic clients with a lot of growth potential, such as the ones linked to the green economy (for instance, organic products and environmental protection product-related clients);

they are beginning to provide logistic services which go far beyond the provision of warehouse space to these clients. Because of the potential of the green industries and the emphasis the Chinese Government is putting on them, Zhang Ziqin is planning to do a video and write a book on the logistic-related aspects of them; she will most likely do this after finishing her Dissertation.

In any case, Zhang Ziqin believes her plan has to be successful since her main strategy is to grow by consolidation, taking on board all those very small companies that have been in the market for over 15–20 years without significant changes or growth and which constitute about 95% of the logistics industry in China. There are over a million of these companies in China, while the large Chinese companies operating in the sector are not private (for instance, China Postal Service—*Zhongguo Yuzheng*, the biggest logistics company in China—COSCO) and, together with the International companies, cover 5% of the sector. Her business approach is very different from those of these big actors,' and she wants to help to build a specific Chinese logistics industry. Toward this goal, her group organized an event in Beijing in 2010—*Zhenxing Zhongguo Wuliu*—and she intends to design an "information-dissemination and training round China" event that may start in Haikou (Hainan) and move afterward to other places in China, ending six months later in the same place it began. The event will be co-financed by Zhang Ziqin's group together with sponsors, so that there will be no participation fee and attendees will only have to pay for their travelling, accommodation, and living expenses. That round China event—*Zhenxing Zhongguo Wuliu Wanlixin*—will be designed to convince small logistics companies to join Sinolgis, so that afterward they would be provided with training and operational rules and procedures. The idea behind this event is to establish a group of companies all sharing the same trademark—Sinolgis—and operating under the same procedures ("pretty much like in the franchise model"), says Zhang Ziqin. She has had this idea since returning from the US, but needed some time—until 2009—to begin thinking about how to implement it. And like her older peers, she is completely sure that, even if her goal is not easy and will involve a lot of hard work, she is going to achieve it. "We have already gone very far since we started and nobody else has begun doing this in China," she confirms. However, her original

2009 plans have slowed somewhat since she became pregnant with her second child. Moreover, and because it involves a very big investment of time, money, and effort, her husband is not very fond of this consolidation idea, so she will be pretty much left alone in this endeavor. But for Zhang Ziqin, increasing the size of her business is a necessary step to remain competitive in the market place. She explains, as an example, how they have been facing unfair competition from the big government-owned companies such as China Postal Service which, were it a private company, would have been bankrupt long ago, since they have continued to experience losses of around RMB 400 million year after year.

Zhang Ziqin's business is also intent on growing the logistic services they provide to e-commerce companies (such as products' storage, delivery to the final client, and payment of the product to the selling company upon the client's reception of it), the development of which is very much conditioned by logistic constraints in China. Precisely because of this, and to properly manage the expansion of her business, Zhang Ziqin realized that she needed to further study and started doing her PhD dissertation at *Zhongguo Dizhi Daxue*. Her dissertation deals with the exploration of new management strategies and the development of standards for e-commerce: *Zi Yuan Xincheng Shizhuan Xinzhong Wuliu Changye de Zuoyong*. Since beginning her PhD work, she has been sleeping between four and five hours a day. She believes it has been worthy, though, since she has already prepared materials for the development of the standards that China will need to use in the industry: *Meijian Guowu de Wuliu Biaozhun*. She has already developed a standard on "the requirements for media shopping logistic services," which was passed to the Government in 2011. This standard pertains to all media—internet, mobile, TV, radio—and covers every aspect of virtual shopping, from payment and goods' tracking to indemnity and after-sales' service. Zhang Ziqin has been the very first woman to author standards for the Chinese logistics industry. She spent over two years writing them up, but was paid very little—just RMB 35,000; so, she was not motivated by the money to do this. These standards are aimed at guaranteeing the products and service quality in e-commerce transactions by way of an intermediate company. This company is between the seller and the buyer and is responsible for: receiving the money when a client performs the virtual transaction, checking the quality of the product before delivery to the client, sending it to the client (or back to the e-commerce company in the case of sub-standard quality), and paying the seller once the merchandise has been received by the client. Zhang Ziqin explains that this e-commerce transaction model (*wuliu jinrong*) will be the future model in China, but that it is still not used very often. For instance, her company performs this kind of intermediate role for only 10% of its e-commerce clients. She thinks it initially has the highest potential in big cities such as Beijing, Shanghai and Guangzhou.

However, much effort she is devoting to it, this development of commercial standards is only a small part of Zhang Ziqin's dissertation, which deals primarily with how the logistic industry could help cities to reshape their economies, particularly those which have been too dependent on just one sector (for instance, coal). She is, for instance, exploring the use of logistic services to take advantage of the new green economy's opportunities, and exploring which kind of training services will be required—both to local public officials and private entrepreneurs—to help this happen. She says: "going on with the same coal example, in the past, they used logistic services in their coal industry and now they have to rethink how to use those services to deal with other products for which there is demand in the market—for instance, green agricultural products."

Zhang Ziqin's business evolution will be influenced by her personal life, and especially the fact that both she and her husband want their two children to study in the US. Their plan is to send her older son, together with his four grandparents, to Los Angeles, when he reaches the age of 10. Then, she and her husband will visit him and his grandparents every couple of months. So, she may ultimately complete a PhD in the US, she says, adding that this is just a possibility today.

Although she belongs to a younger generation, Zhang Ziqin is still more traditional than many of her older peers. In Beijing, she is living in the house of her husband's parents. Among her hobbies are *chufa* (handwriting), playing the *weiqi*, and *bangzhu ren,* that is helping people (for instance, sick people without families). She also likes swimming and travelling, but claims to have only time for helping people and giving to others. She says that she even takes her son to visit sick people and that in her company they do say that they practice "*aixin wuliu*" ("logistics with *love*") and return to society part of the profits they make. She has also set up the "Harmony Logistics Association," based on the concepts of "Love Logistics, Green Logistics." And she is using *Chuantong Wenhua*—Traditional Chinese Culture—in her business management style, claiming, "of course, all of us use this culture when managing our companies." Zhang Ziqin was raised in a Buddhist environment, since all members of her family were Buddhists. However, it was not until she went to the US that she began seriously thinking about religion and recognizing how all religions embrace similar values—'*wan yao gui yi*'. Today she claims "I do believe in every faith, including the Christian religions."

When Zhang Ziqin gets up in the morning she feels very good just by thinking that she has another day ahead of her to help develop standards for the logistic industry in China and to advance her dream of creating a powerful, privately owned Chinese logistics trademark.

ENTREPRENEURSHIP BY CONSOLIDATION MEANS:

- *Convincing small companies to operate under the umbrella of a recognized trademark.*
- *Training those small companies.*
- *Providing those small companies with operational rules and procedures.*
- *Giving constant support to those small companies' operations.*
- *Supervising the quality of those companies' services.*
- *Keeping those companies updated on every new regulation or change in the market.*
- *For the umbrella company to directly contribute to the development of standards for the sector.*
- *For the umbrella company to keep anticipating trends in the market and innovating.*
- *For the umbrella company to constantly invest in marketing to increase the visibility of the trademark.*
- *Not to be in a hurry, to do things step-by-step, making it compatible with the evolution of one's personal life.*

CHAPTER 16

Entrepreneurship in a Highly Regulated Sector. Huang Ying, Bank of Beijing

Huang Ying is the President of the Bank of Beijing's Pinggu branch (www.bankofbeijing.com.cn). Pinggu lies at the extreme northeastern end of Beijing municipality, in a beautiful mountainous area, bordering Tianjin municipality. Named "China's Hometown of the Peach," Pinggu is one of the main agricultural bases in Beijing. Agricultural products include peaches, persimmons, and seedless watermelons. Because the Bank of Beijing's Pinggu branch is about eighty kilometers northeast of Beijing, Huang Ying often drives herself to Beijing for meetings.

The Bank of Beijing

The Bank of Beijing—*Beijing Yinhang*—was established with that name in January 1996 and has developed as a listed bank with a Sino-foreign strategic partnership. Over the past 15 years, the bank has followed its mission to create "value for its clients, return for its share-holders, a future for its staff, and wealth for the whole society." Relying on the booming domestic economy, the bank has passed several bench-marks, including introducing overseas strategic investors, publically listing itself, and setting up regional operations in Beijing, Tianjin, Shanghai, Xian, Shenzhen, Hangzhou, Changsha,

Nanjing, Jinan, and Nanchang. The bank also initiated the establishment of *Yanqing* Village Bank, set up representative offices in Hong Kong and Amsterdam, and initiated the Bank of Beijing Consumer Finance Company—the first consumer finance venture in China. The Bank of Beijing has also established an insurance joint venture called BoB-ING Life Insurance (the 50% stake held by ING Group recently acquired by BNP Paribas Cardif), becoming the first small/medium-sized bank operating in that field.

As of the end of 2010, the Bank of Beijing's total assets balance, total deposits balance, and total loans balance was RMB 733.2 billion, 557.7 billion, and 334.7 billion respectively. Net profit realized was RMB 6.8 billion, with year-on-year growth of 20.75%. NPL (non-performing loan) balance and ratio further declined to RMB 2.32 billion and 0.69%. Provision coverage ratio, CAR (capital adequacy ratio) and core CAR reached 307%, 12.62%, and 10.51%, respectively, all of which are at high levels. The bank has achieved balanced sustainable development of both scale and structure as well as of pace and quality.

As per the latest list issued by *The Banker* on World Top 1000 Banks, the Bank of Beijing ranks number 145 in terms of Tier 1 capital; on the list of Asian banks' competitiveness, the bank ranks number 13, or number 7 in China; on the aspect of brand value, the bank ranks number 9 in China's banking sector.

With its outstanding performance and excellent products and services, the Bank of Beijing is highly appraised by the public. The bank received several honors such as "Best regional bank," "Best Chinese city commercial retail bank," "2009 Top10 listed Asian banks," "Top100 Chinese listed companies," "Outstanding Chinese companies for social responsibility," "Listed companies with most sustainable investment value," and "National civilized units" among others.

The Bank of Beijing has placed great attention on the development of its logo, so that it combines both tradition and modernity. Its meaning is explained as follows:

1. The main graphic of this logo borrows its meaning from the Temple of Heaven (symbolizing harvest) in ancient China, indicating that

the Bank of Beijing was born and grown in Beijing, and that it will develop its future toward the whole country and the world with Beijing as its center.

2. The logo's design reflects the harmonious unity between Traditional Chinese Culture and modern social development. The round red seal, which symbolizes integrity, contains the moral characters of valuing credit and complying with commitments of Traditional Chinese Culture. The design feature of ancient Chinese coins inspires the design concept, so that it is in the same style as China's ancient financial culture. Moreover, modern elements of current social development have also been added into the design—the logo is similar to an "@" shape, reflecting the new image for the Bank of Beijing in the internet and information age.

3. The whole design employs both activity and motionlessness, catering to Chinese tradition while balancing it with a modern flavor. It is smooth but strong, like Chinese calligraphy, signifying the sound management system and operations of the Bank of Beijing. It is also indicative of Beijing's peoples' effective executive ability and extraordinary courage.

4. The letter "B" in the logo represents the English name of the Bank of Beijing. The red color indicates the Bank of Beijing's promising future.

The administrative structure of the Bank of Beijing is shown below.

Huang Ying and The Bank of Beijing

Huang Ying joined the Bank of Beijing back in 1993, when the name of the bank was different and after having worked in another financial institution for about 16 years. She was born in 1956 in Beijing. Her ancestors have been in Beijing for many centuries; they were originally Manchu people.[1] She claims that her family tree is linked to China's historical evolution, since it can be traced back to the times before China's disintegration started; it is also linked to the imperial court. For instance, her maternal grandfather was the chef of the imperial court, until it disappeared; then, he went to work in a hospital, where he prepared food for American people. This is the reason her parents and parents' family ended up working in that same hospital. At a young age, her mother used to work as a nurse, but eventually began performing hospital management tasks, as did her father. Huang Ying is the youngest and the only girl of a family of four children. Her brothers all remain in Beijing. She has been married since 1984; her son was born in 1986. In 2009, her son graduated in psychology from the University of Toronto. After graduation, he remained there for a year to work. Upon his return to China, in 2010, her son began his MBA at Tsinghua University, and eventually developed his own business in China.

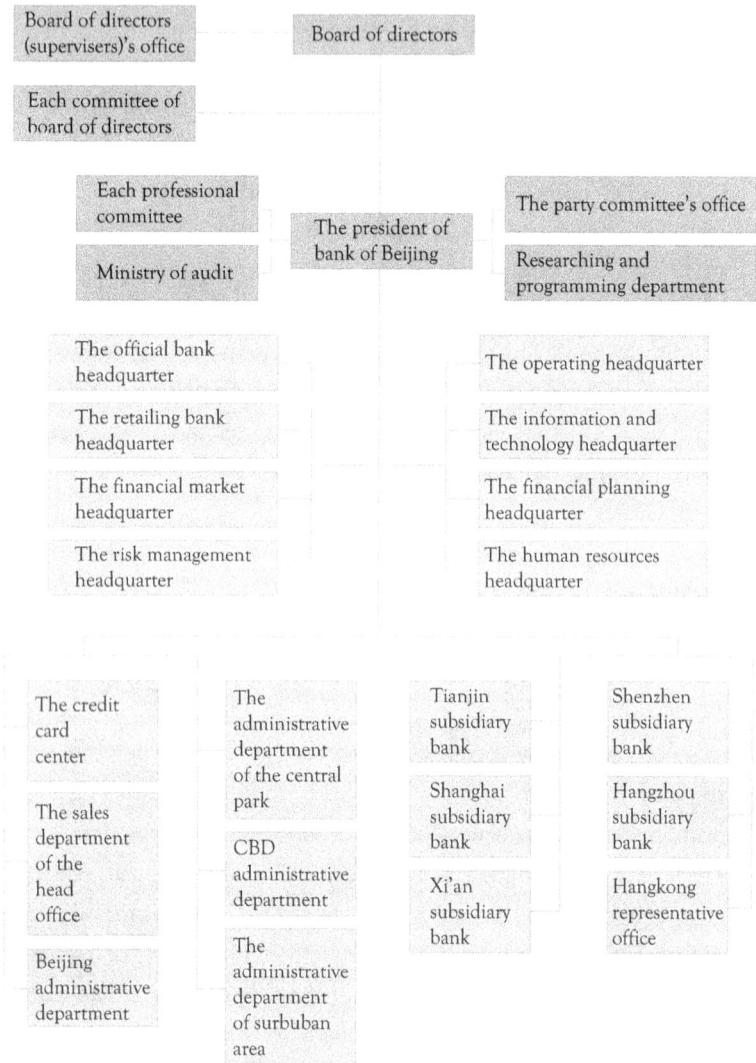

Board of directors (supervisers)'s office		Board of directors		
Each committee of board of directors				
Each professional committee				The party committee's office
		The president of bank of Beijing		
Ministry of audit				Researching and programming department
The official bank headquarter				The operating headquarter
The retailing bank headquarter				The information and technology headquarter
The financial market headquarter				The financial planning headquarter
The risk management headquarter				The human resources headquarter

The credit card center	The administrative department of the central park	Tianjin subsidiary bank	Shenzhen subsidiary bank
The sales department of the head office	CBD administrative department	Shanghai subsidiary bank	Hangzhou subsidiary bank
Beijing administrative department	The administrative department of surbuban area	Xi'an subsidiary bank	Hangkong representative office

Administrative structure of the Bank of Beijing.

In 1975, Huang Ying was sent to work in the country-side, about seventy-five kilometers away from Beijing. She remained there for a couple of years, working on a team of over fifty people, all around her age. Despite work being very hard and not having any chance to study while there, she does have good memories from that time.

Upon her return, in 1977, she passed an examination and went to work for *Zhonguo Renmin Yinhang*—People's Bank of China (PBC or PBOC)[2]—in Beijing, where she remained for 32 years, 12 of those working in the insurance area. She started her professional career there in the credit department, dealing with companies that needed money to expand their businesses. She performed this kind of work until 1981, when she was transferred to the insurance business area where she remained until 1993.

It was during this period when, not receiving any training from the bank, but still desiring to increase her knowledge, Huang Ying attended university. She earned her bachelor in 1985 in *Zhongguo Wenxue*—Chinese literature—and graduated in banking in 1987 from *Shoudu Shifan Daxue* (Capital Normal University). She eventually continued studying all her life because, as she puts it, "I like studying a lot." Between 1988 and the year 2000, she earned a Master's in finance at the *Zhongguo Shehui Kexueyuan* (Chinese Academy of Social Sciences). Between 2002 and 2005 she took a two-and-a-half year Master's program on Manufacturing Management at *Macao Shengyi Xuexiao*, business school. She also earned a Master's degree in Manufacturing Management from *Shoudu Jingmao Daxue* (Capital University of Economics and Business). In 2008 she decided that she needed to start her PhD. She started not just one, but two simultaneously: at Malaysia *Da Keyi Daxue*, Golden Key University, dealing with manufacturing management; and another dealing with psychology and the importance of people, a concept known as "*shiyong xingli xue*." She claims that she likes studying so much, that it does not present a burden for her, and that she cannot stop doing it. Besides, she always thinks that, one way or another, it may prove useful for her work.

In 1993, after realizing that what she really liked was the banking sector, she decided it was time for her to go back to work in banking. The People's Bank of China was a very large government-owned institution, with ongoing changes—including having been split, things were a bit mixed-up there. So, she went to work for a smaller but less bureaucratic bank owned by the city of Beijing. Over time the bank opened to private national and international investors: *Beijing Chengshi Xinyong shi*. She was sent to work in the central branch office, which became known as the Hongxing branch in 1996. The management culture she found in the central office was completely different from the one she was used to. It fit her entrepreneurial spirit much better and she was encouraged to implement the many new ideas she developed.

She began with the same kind of work she performed when she first joined the People's Bank of China—corporate loans—but everything was easier there, and she quickly began undertaking management tasks. There were many opportunities for business expansion and professional development. She was named Deputy Managing Director of the office, and had responsibility of over 100–150 people (out of the total of several thousand employees the bank had) and 50–55 branches. The bank's deposits amounted to a total of RMB 500–600 million.

In 1996, the name of the bank was changed to the Bank of Beijing and the process toward its privatization began. Today, 89% of the bank's shares are in private hands and the bank has around 150 branches (still small, since the biggest banks in Beijing have between 1,000 and 1,500 offices).

At that particular moment, when the bank's name changed, Huang Ying's work changed as she began working in the bank's branches, which are coordinated by the bank's management department manager, a second-level management position. First she was the director of the Jiangguo branch, where she remained until 2000. She was responsible for 50–55 employees and multiplied the deposits amount from the RMB 100 million to a total of RMB 400–500 million by the time she left, generating a profit of RMB 10 million. Next, she moved to the Jiuxiang Qiao branch, where she remained until 2008, managing 70–75 employees and multiplying the deposits amount from 200 million to RMB 2–2.5 billion, generating a profit of RMB 10–15 million. In 2008, having seen her positive performance and entrepreneurial attitude, the bank transferred her to the Pinggu branch, a newly opened branch.

Although she started from scratch, just eight months after her arrival loans amounted to RMB 2 billion with a profitability of RMB 30 million. The Pinggu branch opened mainly to serve the local rural business community, which included farmers who had begun projects that needed financial backing to succeed. In the area there are also government projects that required financing and have, therefore, contributed to the branch's growth. Although about 98% of the Bank of Beijing's clients are big companies with sales turnover over RMB 100 million, to develop Pinggu branch Huang Ying decided to take all types of clients on board, from big government companies (for instance, dealing with building infrastructure) and medium-sized companies to very small businesses and private people. For instance, she has given credit to: children, to afford school; to university students, to continue their studies; and to unemployed people. She has given credit to rural women to improve their lives through increased economic activity. These credits were backed by the All China Women's Federation (ACWF). She has also given credit to farmers to improve their quality of life, including building a new house, eating better, and even going on vacations. The farmers' credit were given as part of the *Zhongguo Xin Nongcun de Shifan Cun*, a program supported by the government to help farmers change their life styles by directly providing money and assisting with bank loans. The people participating in these programs are called "new farmers."

Huang Ying relates how many life-changing initiatives are available today to assist farmers. In particular, the government allows them to rent their land to third parties. Farmers who are doing this are also named "new farmers." Huang Ying cites as an example the project she established with the Chinese government and a large Thai agricultural company to help farmers by renting their land. Since she arrived in Pinggu, she developed several initiatives to help farmers. In particular, the initiative helped extremely poor people (around 2,000–2,500 people) and handicapped farmers (around 200–250 people). She stresses that the Chinese government is paying a good deal of attention to farmers, and she herself is doing the same now.

Among the many project investments, there are many government-supported ones in the Pinggu area, including: solar energy parks and installations of solar panels; wind energy parks; renovation and building of street lights; upgrading water and road infrastructure; and employment generation (around 3,000–3,500 jobs per year). Huang Ying's branch has given credit for all sorts of projects, normally to large government-owned companies undertaking these big projects. In fact, she maintains that it is thanks to these large companies that she has been able to grow the branch so rapidly. Huang Ying emphasizes that by opening their doors and working with all different types of clients in the local community, the bank has localized itself and become the landmark credit institution for the local community. Finally, the fact that in Pinggu competition is less than in other areas of Beijing has helped them to grow very quickly, even in the difficult year of 2009, her first year at that branch.

The policies and projects implemented by the government since 2009 have been quite positive for the Pinggu branch's growth. It is true that interest rates have fluctuated: for example, in 2009 the rates were successively cut five times, but her branch still remained profitable. Moreover, the fact that the Chinese, especially the younger generations, are changing their attitude toward banks is also a positive influence, since the public is beginning to use credit to meet their living needs. This is why Huang Ying has always had a positive attitude toward the future of her branch and of her bank, which aims to become the first private bank in China. By the end of 2011, Pinggu branch had 30 employees, credit of a total of RMB 3 billion and profitability of RMB 100 million, the highest of any Bank of Beijing branch. Half of the RMB 3 billion in loan capital is funding for government infrastructure projects, while 40% of it goes to private companies that execute local government-related projects (for instance, public parks, schools) with the remaining 10% financing local farmers' initiatives. Interest rates have been increasing since Huang Ying was transferred to the Pinggu branch, from the 6–7% in 2009 to around 8% in over two years period.

Huang Ying acknowledges that to achieve such positive results she has had to work very hard, because she could not bring her previous clients with her to her new branch; her Beijing government contacts also all needed to be replaced. However, since she arrived in Pinggu she transformed her challenges into opportunities for being creative and growing faster. This is how she grew her client profile, and designed and implemented new strategies for attracting clients and generating new projects. Some of these new projects are in association with the government and other actors such as the big Thai group. The bank acquired other projects just by being in direct contact with the farmers, the rural people, and the local companies. In 2010, she started a RMB 600 million investment project for a chicken farm with a capacity of three million animals. The project employs over 2,000 people, 500 of whom are handicapped. Another project Huang Ying is very proud of that she also initiated in 2010 is a RMB 250 million investment in a private factory that manufactures 1.5 million solar panels a year, which are sold in the local market—in Xinjiang and Qinghai—and exported to Europe. The Pinggu branch has also given a credit of RMB 3 billion to help make school buildings earth-quake resistant. Last but not the least, Huang Ying is also proud to have loaned over RMB 100 billion to restore the *Wangmu Senlin* public park.

Huang Ying says she is the kind of person who wants to employ every plan she thinks of and implement it successfully. "I am not afraid of any-thing," Huang Ying said. "When a person is afraid of trying things, he or she just gets paralyzed and does nothing," she adds. She is not afraid, for instance, of her branch not recovering the loans that have been made; however, she acknowledges that the government has to increase its IPR (intellectual property rights), product safety and regulations and control over business insurance. "The bank cannot ex-ante take care of all those things," she explains.

In her attitude toward life, Huang Ying is very different from the rest of her family and from her husband, none of whom have her entrepreneurial spirit. Her husband also works in the banking sector at *Zhongguo Yinhang*, Bank of China. He is responsible for the management supervision depart-ment, which is a position slightly lower than the one she has. They knew each other since they were 11 years old, when they were classmates—noth-ing at all to do with the banking sector. In 1972, he was sent to work outside of Beijing and could not come back until 1987, by which time they not only had married, but also had a child. Huang Ying thinks that, although they both work in the same sector, their personal relationship has not really been influenced by this, nor do they do talk about any business issues at home. Since her position is slightly higher than his, she avoids talk-ing any business there. They complement each other quite well at home, where it is her husband who takes care of everything. Huang Ying claims that she is always busy and does not have time to take care of the house. Besides, she does not like to. She and her husband also did not have a prob-lem raising her son while she worked and he went to school because the boy lived at school, first in kindergarten and then at boarding school, coming home only on weekends. This is why she could work and study so much.

When she began her real career in the banking industry back in 1993, there were very few women in the banking industry, but the situation has changed a lot since then. Now about 50% of employees are women; this is the same at the managerial level. However, the average age of female manag-ers is lower (30 to 35 years old) than the age of the average female employees (40 to 45 years old).

With respect to her management style, Huang Ying bases everything on paying a lot of attention to her employees, a concept known as *renxin huan de guanli*. Like many of her peer entrepreneurs, she claims that she takes care of them as if they were her children, giving them a maternal kind of love. So, things run smoothly with her team, so much so that she is frequently seen as being a human resources person; she often performs many functions covered by that department herself. She believes the boss has to trust his or her employees, assign precise responsibilities to them, but let them work by themselves. When the employees feel trusted and have the freedom to perform, they work diligently and deliver good results. For Huang Ying, it is also important to make sure her employees have a harmonious personal life; she believes if there is something wrong at home, this will have a negative impact on the employee's performance. She communicates her management principles to her direct team, so that they can also apply them with the teams they are responsible for. She believes her teams are very well organized. She makes sure that her employees are properly trained and, when appropriate, she herself gives the training. Huang Ying acknowledges that her management style is not something that she learned from a book, from other people, or from any of the degrees or training she has received. Instead, it is the result of her work and managerial experience and of what she has been learning and developing over the years. She feels that she is simultaneously the head of her employees, and their friend and mother. She helps her employees by providing them with ideas and supporting them in implementing her ideas as well as those that they develop themselves.

FOR HUANG YING IT IS VERY IMPORTANT TO TRUST THE EMPLOYEES because when they feel that they are trusted and have freedom to perform, they always work very diligently and deliver good results.

Huang Ying not only applies a special relationship style with her employees, she also uses it with her clients. Since she has so much experience in the sector, particularly in the loan business, she gives her clients advice on how to proceed. When they are paralyzed in the midst of problems because they are afraid and do not see a way out, she helps them to find a solution and overcome their fear to act. For her there is not so much difference between giving love to her clients and giving love to her employees. She feels compassion for them both and is always ready to help every one of them overcome his or her life's burdens.

She is very interested in the Buddhist philosophy and has read some texts, which have provided her with highly useful ideas. She would like to read more, but doesn't because she finds it very difficult to understand the complicated philosophical texts. Beyond all the time she has spent studying, she really enjoys reading for pleasure, making time for it every morning at 5:30 am. She also enjoys traveling; she has visited Europe several times and has also visited Japan. She likes speaking in public and swimming, though she does not have much time for these activities currently. However, she does find time to relax herself by letting her body follow the rhythm of melodious traditional Chinese music; she has been practicing this for over six years.

Speaking in public, training, and communicating with other people provides Huang Ying with so much joy that she thinks she may end up one day—for certain after she retires—training people and giving lectures. This training would focus on advising people on how to open their inner-selves and how to better manage their money and their lives. She will do this as a business, that is, advising CEOs (her target group) on aligning their business performance with their personality and inner strengths, and on using the "give love to receive love" strategy when managing their employees. Additionally, Huang Ying will train people for free, as a contribution to society, to help them feel better about themselves and to improve their relationships with others.

When Huang Ying travels she generally visits natural sites and tries to interact as much as possible with the local people. She does it now only once or twice a year, but she thinks that, when she retires, she will devote a significant part of her life to this kind of travel. In this respect, she claims to be different from her peer entrepreneurs, for she has always had a very special relationship with nature since she was a little girl. "I think quite often that I may have been a bird or flowing water or some other natural element in another life," Huang Ying says. She has felt very happy in Pinggu, in an environment that is surrounded by nature, mountains, trees, water, and birds.

By the time this book is published, Huang Ying would have retired from the Bank of Beijing and would be back working in Beijing, running her own financial advisory services business. And, as she has done for nearly 35 years, she will get up every morning feeling good about how she has another day ahead to think about the joy of nature, and to professionally perform at her best, helping her employees and clients overcome any burdens they may have with their lives.

ENTREPRENEURSHIP IN A HIGHLY REGULATED SECTOR MEANS:

- *Working in a smaller more flexible and dynamic company.*
- *Working in a company where there are possibilities for constant professional development.*
- *Working in a company that has undertaken a serious privatization approach.*
- *Finding a position outside headquarters.*
- *Changing positions if there is no possibility for further growth and development.*
- *Being assigned to a position where the business has to be built from scratch.*
- *Rethinking the company's business model and adapting it to the new business' particular circumstances.*
- *Showing positive results in order to proceed with the changes introduced.*
- *Motivating employees to be creative and productive.*
- *Marketing to clients in an innovative differentiated way: becoming their friend.*
- *Developing mechanisms to take full advantage of the opportunities available in the market place.*
- *Working hard.*
- *Generating new ideas and putting them to work.*

CHAPTER 17

Entrepreneurship by Transforming Traditional Chinese Culture into a Business. Tian Yu, Handelin

Secluded from the chaotic and noisy traffic of Beijing and its never ending activity is the *Zhonghua Handelin Zhihui Nuxing Xiuyang Xuetang* (which has been translated in English as "Chinese Handling Intelligent Female Resting Institute"), a haven of peace in the east side of Beijing, not far from the Pingguo area (www.zhchina.com.cn). This *xuetang* (the exact translation for this Chinese word is study center or study hall) is owned and managed by Tian Yu and her husband.

They began in 1999, in the west side of Beijing, and moved to the current location in 2004. The couple started this new venture from scratch in a new city and in a sector they were not previously familiar with. Prior to their new business, the two ran an everyday clothing business for men and women in Changchun, Jilin, where they had a manufacturing facility and a retail shop and employed over 20 employees. Their production was being sold through their own shop as well as through a third party's retail points.

Tian Yu considers herself originally from Changchun, where her family moved when she was still a baby, although she was actually born in a small village in Shandong. Had her parents been still alive they would be over 90 years old. Her father was a policeman. Tian Yu was born in 1968, the youngest child of a family of nine children—six girls and three boys.

In the mid-1990s, Tian Yu and her husband—Zuo Dawen—began to observe what was happening around them and decided they should do something to help improve the situation that well-off families were facing in the booming Chinese economy. They saw that they themselves and their friends had managed to make money—and some of them quite a bit—and could afford to buy almost everything, but were unhappy and were experiencing a lot of new problems, such as overstress, insecurity, health-related problems, problems with their children, and problems in couples' relationships which many times ended in divorces. Tian Yu and her husband thought that these problems were the result of having an imbalanced professional-personal life, in which attention to the family and the house-hold has been neglected. They thought there should be an answer to handling life in a much more equilibrated and harmonious way, and that eventually this answer could be found in the Traditional Chinese Culture.

So, in 1995, Tian Yu and her husband embraced Buddhism and began to study for themselves, simply through reading, the so-called Traditional Chinese Culture (TCC) *RuDaoFo*:[1] Confucianism, Taoism, and Buddhism. It was not an easy task, since at that time there were not many books available on these topics, particularly on Buddhism, and they could not go to Qufu to study Confucianism, but they managed. After 2004–2005, these kinds of books became more readily available in China. Now many of them have even been translated into English, since the main message of TCC is to be content with one-self, to live a happy life and, as Tian Yu acknowledges, everybody wants to experience this: it is a universal human beings' desire.

She and her husband complemented these readings with others from the Christian culture, since they wanted to reconfirm that all spiritual paths end in the same summit and all share the value of compassion and love to others. They did find a fundamental difference between the Western and the Chinese approaches, however in the Occidental approach, religion is most often mixed with spirituality and values, but in the Chinese tradition these are not the same. The TCC puts the emphasis on developing an equilibrated mind and the rest will be taken care of as a result of it. In the Western world, the emphasis is placed on the technique to perform the action. For instance, "to manufacture a cup, you need to know how to do it, while in traditional Chinese thinking we do not care about this, we just think that if our mind is fine, we will be able to find a way to manufacture the cup," explains Tian Yu.

In this process of learning, the TCC by themselves, Tian Yu became convinced that, in the new scenario of unhappiness among well-off Chinese, women were suffering much more than men, and if they were to have the ability to manage their professional and personal life in a balanced way, relationships at the household level would be smoother and household members would keep the close ties they used to have. So, she decided that along with her husband, she would do something to help those professional women to re-equilibrate their lives and the lives of their family members. Tian Yu was convinced that the secret to this could be found in the Traditional Chinese Culture. They decided to initially focus on women, because they considered women as being more important in maintaining the harmony within the household and society. Women support a bigger burden both at home and in the business world, and they have traditionally had a bigger impact than men at the house-hold level.

In 1999, Tian Yu and her husband left the clothes business and Changchun and moved to Beijing to begin their new dream. Rather than selling their previous business, they simply decided to close it, because their approach to customers had always been very personalized. They knew it would not be easy to find an entrepreneur who could overtake their business to provide that kind of service, which involved a lot of personalized design and sub-contracting.

They thought of relocating to Beijing, since it used to be the center of the Traditional Chinese Culture. Starting this new business, however, proved to be a real challenge. Back in 1999, it was quite easy to earn a lot of money in the clothes business they had been running, but to sell the kind of services they were providing through *Zhonghua Handelin Zhihui Nuxing Xiuyang Xuetang*, and to generate income from them was extremely difficult at the beginning.

However, Tian Yu and her husband were fully convinced that, if they had been previously successful helping women to look fine from the out-side, now they could manage to also be successful by helping women to feel fine from the inside. Tian Yu told herself many times that, in the same way that she helped women to look beautiful with her clothes' designs—which is what she studied at *Changchun* University—she could help women to look beautiful on the inside with her studies of Traditional Chinese Culture. She understood that clothes cannot change how people feel deep inside and that no matter how beautiful their clothes, they have no value at all if the person wearing them feels very unhappy deep inside.

Tian Yu and her husband also knew they could work very well as a team, since they had studied together and had always been working together without any trouble. Upon graduation, Tian Yu thought that it would be much better to start her own business rather than work for the Government and her fiancé (at the time) agreed, so they simultaneously became entrepreneurs and partners. However, even at that time, they felt that they were different from other business people. They have always had a different approach to things, in those days before they were married, and now. Moreover, their evolution over time, as professionals and as people, has always been quite parallel.

The goal of *Zhonghua Handelin Zhihui Nuxing Xiuyang Xuetang* (*Handelin*) is to help women entrepreneurs and leaders to develop the abilities they need to manage their lives. This goes beyond the manage-ment of their business or even their children; it is to help women to feel good about themselves in the first place: to be calm, to love themselves, to be healthy. Only by achieving this, can women continue being successful in business while simultaneously having a happy balanced life. The word *handelin* used in their company's name is related to *huandi* ("emperor," in English) and, as such, is linked to the first word of the name *Zhonghua* ("Traditional Chinese Culture" in English). *Zhihui*, the third word of the name, is related to illumination, extraordinary intelligence, and wis-dom. *Nuxing* are women. *Xiuyang* means doing everything with ability. Translated into proper English, the name of Tian Yu's company would be something like "School to develop the abilities of women to achieve wisdom, through the use of Traditional Chinese Imperial Culture."

As for their logo, it combines the elements of earth (represented in yellow on both sides) and water (blue in the middle). The earth represents women (*"di xian muqi"* in Mandarin) and the water represents the intelligence (both intellectual and emotional). So, *Handelin*'s logo represents the emotional and intellectual intelligence of women—"the interior beauty of women," says Tian Yu.

About 90% of *Handelin*'s clients are women entrepreneurs and leaders, while the remaining 10% are husbands and sometimes children of those women, who are brought in by the women clients. Sometimes there are also male entrepreneurs and leaders that come to *Handelin*'s by themselves the first time and, afterward, they bring their wives and children. Customers vary in age from 20 to 75 years old, with most of them being between 30 and 50 years old. Only about 20% of their customers are from Beijing, but many of them live in the city or visit often. Tian Yu believes that today it is not only women needing the kind of services she provides, but also men, and that the Chinese Government is aware that the Chinese society of today needs to bring back the so-called Traditional Chinese Values. Tian Yu is responsible for the technical aspects of the business and gives instructions herself, while her husband plays the role of a General Manager and is less involved in the day-to-day operation of the business. They have around 30 employees (most of them university bachelors or graduates) and also use advisors (to assist in communications with the government, for example) and over 40 professional instructors (who include university professors and governmental employees) to address the different client groups, as well as the distinct personal profiles of individual clients. Since men and women are different and have distinct interests, and since every person is unique, everyone has to be treated in a different way, which both Tian Yu and her husband acknowledge to be one of the main challenges of the business.

Tian Yu and Zuo Dawen also use music in their training. Music calms the mind; it helps to develop the necessary vision to deal with each particular problem. It is good for health and for the different organs of the body. Tian Yu and her husband have recorded their own music that they call *"Handelin Yue Liao"* (*"Handelin*'s Music Therapy"), which summarizes about 2,500 years of Traditional Chinese Culture, and they disseminate it by including it as part of the training set they give to their clients. "*Handelin Yue Liao*" is a collection of 54 CDs organized around five elements: *Di* (earth), *Shui* (water), *Huo* (fire), *Feng* (wind) y *Kong* (void).[2] To represent each of these elements, different musical instruments are used. For each of these elements, except *Huo* (which has only 10 CDs), there are 11 CDs which contain a total of 538 musical pieces, each of which lasts for an average of 50 to 60 minutes—so altogether there are around 30,000 minutes of music. The package includes an additional CD which contains an introduction of the musical product. Tian Yu explains that through developing this music, *Handelin* has brought together the traditional Chinese music—*liyue*—with those five elements. The project was technically coordinated by Yue Housheng, a monk living in the *Zhongnan* Mountains.[3] They spent two years investing their creativity and money into the project and consulting with a team of experts to assist with their own compositions and with the selection of the other classical Chinese music pieces, before launching the set of CDs in January 2009, which is when they started using it in their training activities. The collection is provided for free to its members (as mentioned later) and can be acquired by other people at a cost of RMB 11,800 which Tian Yu acknowledges is not cheap, while affirming that it is very unique music that cannot be acquired in any other place.

The music of China dates back to the dawn of Chinese civilization, with documents and artifacts providing evidence of a well-developed musical culture as early as the *Zhou* Dynasty (1122–256 B.C.E.). Some of the oldest written music dates back to Confucius's time. Early Chinese music and poetry was influenced by *Shi Jing* (the "Book of Songs"),[4] and the Chinese poet and statesman *Qu Yuan*.[5] It was based on percussion instruments, which later gave away to stringed and reed instruments. The first major well-documented flowering of Chinese music was for the *qin* or *guqin* during the Tang Dynasty, although the instrument is known to have been prominent before the Han Dynasty.

Chinese civilization regards music as an educational technique, in close connection with rite and etiquette, embodying the positive and negative interaction and harmony of all things. The innermost feelings of humans are expressed by sound, and rhythmic and melodious sound is music, which can inspire the minds of people in new ways. Chinese culture deems that moderate, peaceful, melodious, and righteous music should be pursued to enhance the moral level of the people.

Tian Yu defines *Handelin*'s Chinese music as having therapeutic properties and being different from other music available around the world. She says: "it incorporates the five elements (earth, water, fire, wind, and void) of China Buddhist music with the harmonious co-existence of the universe. It is a sentimental, therapeutic, and healthy music, which follows the five sentimental and therapeutic notes of Traditional Chinese Medicine, as well as the temperaments and lives of people. The music embodies the positive and negative interaction and harmony of all things, helping to perceive the emotional colorful world, penetrating into the harmonious and peaceful universe. Its therapy is aimed to cure different syndromes in distinct ways. It can also enable people to face the distinct facets of life with ease. It ultimately aims to avoid attachment and to forget both life and death, reaching a void and spiritual and comfortable frontier of life. *Handelin*'s music can cure the fatigue accumulated in the body, mind, and spirit over a long time and enable the body and mind to really understand the unity between nature and people, as well as to understand the spiritual perception between the realistic world and nature. The music enables people to directly perceive the rise and fall of human life, as well as the sacredness of "mother nature." After merging the body, mind and spirit into the music, people suddenly become aware that there are too many unknown things in the world waiting for them to explore and seek, and that there are too many mysteries waiting for them to uncover. *Handelin*'s music calms and relaxes the mind. It makes people understand that human life is just the transient life of grass and that the facets of life are in the spiritual world, which they have been yearning for. It makes them understand that what is important is acting, doing it and never giving up, despite the recognition that success may not be possible. *Handelin*'s music helps to erase the stains from our mind which, despite being clear as a mirror where all things can be reflected, it is often covered with a shadow and a distorted image of reality. Once our mind has been cleaned, it becomes lively, natural and free from lusts and worries, full of vitality everywhere. Just like a clear spring in the mountains, music can wash and clean the dirt in our mind."

Tian Yu and her husband approached the recording of their music and its application to help women and men to feel better, remembering that today the role of Chinese women in society has nothing to do with the subordination, which Confucius assigned to them. Today men and women are equal in China, and Tian Yu always stresses that it is very important to keep this in mind when referring to the application of Confucius' culture in today's world. By listening to their music, not only will people feel better, but they will eventually have a more balanced, happy, and harmonious life.

Tian Yu believes that in the current Chinese society both men and women have to make changes in their approaches to life, so that both their professional and personal lives can be successfully managed. She believes that not only should a woman stop behaving as the company leader when she arrives home, where she should just behave as a wife and mother, but also that a man should just behave as a husband and father upon arriving home. Society needs the professional/business and the household levels. Both are complementary and need each other. Like the *yin* needs the *yang*, the sky needs the earth, the day needs the night. Should both women and men have peace of mind and remain calm with their hearts wide open, they themselves would realize the truth of this. Traditional Chinese Culture can help them to find this peace of mind. Tian Yu is very confident that, by communicating these values and telling people how to practice them, they can be of service to society. "Those men that are just focused on making money to spend it with their friends dining, drinking, in karaoke, with *nupengyou*, and so forth, do this because they do not know any other way to be happy. But, sooner or later, they will realize this is not enough. Should they deeply know and practice Traditional Chinese Culture's principles, their behavior would be different. They think happiness comes from giving themselves a lot of material things and pleasures, but they are absolutely wrong. The middle-way is the way to go," says Tian Yu.

Handelin training activities include: lectures, listening to music, drinking tea (green, oolong, pu er, black, since every kind of tea has a different impact in the bodies and minds), exercising the body, discussing how to deal with everyday issues such as children, household management, etc. All this helps attendees to understand that there are many more healthy approaches to life and that they shall introduce changes in their current daily habits. *Handelin* opens every day from 8:30 am to 5:30 pm to give introductions to visitors of its activities and approaches. Formal training activities are organized on an average of once a month in different premises and quite often in The Reclining Buddha Temple of the beautiful *Xiangshan* ("Fragrant Hills"), where accommodation is provided for people outside of Beijing. The monthly activities normally last a couple of days, occasionally two and a half to three days.

Occasionally training is also provided outside of Beijing, in places such as *Hangzhou, Qufu,* and *Chengdu,* where they have associated with local partners to make it possible. So far, they have been focusing on places that have something to do with Traditional Chinese Culture and that are in very beautiful and historic settings.

In their courses they have on an average, 40–60 regular students, most of whom are *Handelin's* members. Every year, there is a two day course dealing with *Chan* (Zen) meditation. The fee varies with the content of the training, but *Handelin's* members can attend those courses for free, having only to pay for accommodation and long distance transportation costs. There are two membership categories: standard members and VIP members. Membership fee for standard members is RMB 59,800 and grants the member rights to attend all training activities for free. VIP members pay a fee of RMB 198,000 and have the right to participate in the training activities with their whole family (3–4 people in total) and can meet with *Handelin's* people, whenever necessary, to get advice on how to handle their lives. They now have a few hundred members. Non-members attending their activities pay the pertaining fee. The cost of those individual activities varies between some hundred RMB and some thousand RMB, being cheaper if the person has been introduced by a member.[6] Once a year they organize a special four-day event, each year in a different location in China (for instance, Hangzhou, in 2012), which is attended by over 100 people. For members, participation in this activity is also free.

According to Tian Yu, this membership approach has proven much more practical to them from a business standpoint and much more in line with their conceptual approach than having to look for new individuals for each new activity they undertake. When signing for *Handelin's* membership, members receive *Handelin* music's CDs set—55 CDs altogether—and many books and other written materials and bibliographies.

Moreover, activity participants receive some books and bibliographies, which are related to each activity's content. For relevant books that cannot easily be found in bookstores, *Handelin* buys those books themselves and makes them available for sale to their students. When getting a set of CDs of *Handelin*'s music, the members are told how they shall listen to the music but they do not receive any other special training on it, since "the music to be heard by every person varies with the person's preferences, feelings, needs, and particular circumstances of their present moment," says Tian Yu. She also says that to listen to their music it is not necessary to stop doing other things to just concentrate on this, but on the contrary, it can be listened to while working in the office or undertaking a domestic task at home. "Our music is a kind of company that helps people to remain calm and centered while undertaking everyday activities," she explains.

To manage their company, Tian Yu and her husband apply Traditional Chinese Culture and values. They directly provide training to their employees. Every morning, the employees have to study some teaching from one of the Chinese culture's masters. The profile of their current employees—all with university degrees—is completely different from those of their previous business, so they find it easy to communicate their corporate values to them. Over time, they have seen that employees value working in an organized and harmonious place. They feel more at ease with themselves and, as a result, perform their tasks in a more conscious way. To Tian Yu the fact that the majority of her employees are women—about 90%—makes things easier. She has found that overall it is much easier to work with women than with men, not only as employees but also as customers. Most of their employees are *waidiren* and therefore, to avoid the waste of time in travelling the long distances of Beijing, they are provided with accommodation in close proximity to their training center.

Earlier, to publicize their activities and increase their customer base, Tian Yu and Zuo Dawen used to do a lot of advertising, in journals and magazines, but they do not do it anymore because it is extremely expensive. Instead they are using other marketing techniques, such as their website, telemarketing, and the distribution of brochures. By far their most efficient marketing technique is word-of-mouth praise from their students. In fact, this word-of-mouth advertising often generates the interest of journalists from all over China as well. Journalists come to interview Tian Yu, and then publish articles and interviews in their magazines and journals for free, which is a much more effective technique than direct advertising.

Thanks to all this, selling their services is becoming easier than it used to be. When they started, nobody knew them; so they could not use word-of-mouth. Moreover, since their business is service-oriented, potential customers found it very difficult to understand what those intangible services were all about, and whether to trust them. They saw the advertisements, but did not understand why they would need Traditional Chinese Culture's training and how this could help to change their lives. So, from 1999 to the year 2007, the business grew very slowly. Since then and thanks overall to their students' word-of-mouth referrals, the business is growing at a much faster peace. Nevertheless, Tian Yu's idea was never to grow very quickly, but to do it step-by-step, paying attention to the solid grounding of the business, which is what in the end will allow for its sustainability and steady growth.

It is this same approach that they are following in a new dimension of their business: *Handelin Su Chifan*, a chain of very high quality small vegetarian restaurants, of around 100 to 200 m² each. The first one opened in 2010, in the Suitongyou district, east of Beijing, but moved to a much more centered location in Xidan in 2012. Their idea is to eventually keep opening restaurants both in Beijing and in other places in China, following the franchise model. The first restaurant outside of Beijing is planned to open in the Yangji mountain, in Jiangxi province, not far from the city of Jinjiang, "a place associated with Amitabha Buddha[7] and Lao Tze," says Tian Yu. Tian Yu expects that, after those openings, approximately ten more owned and franchised restaurants will open in Beijing as well as in other places in China, where some of their members have already shown an interest. *Handelin Su Chifan* restaurants are being thought of not only as places to eat very healthy vegetarian food, but also as places where people can go to drink tea and peacefully listen to *Handelin*'s music. They can also be used for hosting some of *Handelin*'s activities. For this new restaurant business, Tian Yu and her husband have created a new company named *Handelin Beijing Canyin Wenhua Yuxian Gongsi*, which is being run daily by their employees, so that they can focus on the management of *Handelin Beijing Wenhua Fazhang Yuxian Gongsi*. Tian Yu affirms that the restaurant business is taking shape step-by-step and that it is not so difficult to run since it is relatively small. "In any case," she affirms, "If you want to do something you have to really go for it."

Tian Yu believes that it was their persistence, which has brought success to their business. Traditional Chinese Culture is to do things little-by-little in a solid way, always keeping ahead and not running away when difficulties arise. Without their persistence, *Handelin* would have not survived. But Tian Yu and her husband knew where they were going. They knew they could not plan ahead for everything and they could not control all situations, but they knew that by going on with their dream, sooner or later success would show up.

Mainly through their Mainland China students and some other people from Taiwan and Hong Kong who often spend time in Beijing and attend *Handelin*'s activities, the company is beginning to be known abroad. In China, the model Tian Yu and her husband want to follow is the opening of centers through local entrepreneurs, but always under their direct and constant supervision and follow-up since their corporate mission may otherwise get distorted. They already have people interested in opening branches of *Handelin* in Wenzhou (through one of her students, the wife of an entrepreneur), Shanghai (through a couple, who are very good friends and have studied with them) and Guangdong (through a man, who also is their friend), but have not opened any yet. Tian Yu and her husband have also received demands from overseas Chinese who would like to open centers in Hong Kong, Australia, and Canada. Of course, they would like to profit in the future from these opportunities, but their priority number one today is the consolidation of their Beijing center and of their restaurant business in the national Chinese market, the original motivation for going into this business. In the future they may team up with their stu-

dents to open around 10 to 20 centers in China, since many of them are becoming interested in opening such a center in their place of origin. FOR TIAN YU, IN A PERSONALIZED SERVICES BUSINESS' EXPANSION PROCESS, THE FOUNDERS' DIRECT INVOLVE-

MENT IS NECESSARY because without constant supervision and fol-low-up, the corporate mission may get distorted.

Tian Yu has always thought it would be highly beneficial to have teaming arrangements with her best students, since they would share the same values and ideas. She is confident that in the coming years there would be students who are ready to communicate *Handelin*'s cul-ture, values, and teachings to other people. She has seen the changes that she and her husband experienced themselves after beginning to study Traditional Chinese Culture. Now she has a clearer understand-ing of who and where she is: her home, the people around her, and her life. Her relationships with her very close family and friends, as well as with other people, have transformed in every respect; now they are more responsible. All three Masters—Confucius, Lao Tsé and Buddha—have had an impact on her current attitude and approach to life, but it is Buddha who has had the greatest influence on her, on her ability to face the world with love and compassion. She has been to India and Nepal to feel the place where Buddha came from and how Buddhism disseminated to the neighboring countries. She has also been to Taiwan, where the Traditional Chinese Culture has remained more intact. Tian Yu claims that she has gained such an internal peace after following these teachings that it is very difficult to describe with words how she feels. She is happy today just by reading books, listening to music, and drinking tea; she does not need anything else to feel at peace and does not need any material possession. She is seeing how day after day in today's China, people are becoming more and more interested in Bud-dha's teachings. For instance, her young son—born in 1992—is greatly interested in those teachings and in the Traditional Chinese Culture, and has already learned a great deal of it. Tian Yu has had time to intro-duce it to him, because she has always had somebody at home helping her with the household chores. As a result, when Tian Yu's son joined the university, he decided to pursue a degree to become a teacher of Traditional Chinese Culture.

It is precisely the changes that Tian Yu and her husband have expe-rienced over time which are making *Handelin*'s business unique in the market place, and giving it a great deal of competitive advantage com-pared to other people, who may eventually try to replicate their business model. When they started, back in 1999, they were the very first ones to think about going into this business. Today, they are still unique, but they are beginning to see people interested in opening similar training centers and attempting to do what they have done. What they have not really seen is those people having made the effort to invest in developing their inner-self, which they considered totally necessary to be able to manage and develop this kind of business with integrity and, even more importantly, with their inner heart. In fact, the people who have already tried to open similar training centers have all failed (including some of their students, who attempted to do so on their own). The fact that they have been the very first and that they are unique has also given them advantages in the eyes of the government, which itself is interested in the dissemination of knowledge about Traditional Chinese Culture, both in China and abroad, and has been very supportive of their work.

Tian Yu explains how they have also been the very first in China to open a chain of vegetarian restaurants, and how their products are very unique: "our *suijiao*—vegetarian *jiaozi*—for instance, are extremely healthy and delicious." Another idea that they have in mind is to eventually build a Traditional Chinese Culture Center—similar to the spiritual centers that can be found in many Western countries—where people could not only receive training, but also eat and sleep, but this is today just a project in their minds and will take quite some time before it can take real shape.

With their unique approach, Tian Yu is certain that they will accomplish much, and may eventually build a profitable business. However, since the beginning, their motivation has not been money-based; what they wanted then (and still want today) was to be able to help as many women and men as possible to have a happy life. They both believe that, in the twenty-first century, the need to apply Traditional Chinese Culture's values in people's daily lives is perhaps greater than ever before, both in China and abroad.

When Tian Yu gets up in the morning she feels very good just by thinking that she has another day ahead to run her business with her inner heart and, together with her husband, move a step further in her endeavor to help women and men to have a happier everyday life.

ENTREPRENEURSHIP BY TRANSFORMING TRADITIONAL CHINESE CULTURE INTO A BUSINESS MEANS:

- *Starting by one-self to learn and apply the Traditional Chinese Culture-RuDaoFo.*
- *Truly transforming the inner-self before starting the business.*
- *Fully understanding that only when the mind has reached its equilibrium stage can the business be successfully developed.*
- *Having as a primary motivation the desire to help people to have a happy life.*
- *Teaching people to face life in a much more equilibrated and harmonious way.*
- *Teaching people to feel good with themselves in the first place: to be calm, to love themselves, to be healthy.*
- *Treating every customer in a different and personalized way.*
- *Eventually, developing unique training support products.*
- *Communicating and applying Traditional Chinese Culture and values when running the business.*
- *Creating a well-organized and harmonious working environment.*
- *Using customers' word-of-mouth as the main marketing technique.*
- *Advancing slowly but steadily.*
- *Managing and developing the business with the inner-heart.*
- *Being persistent to follow the business dream.*

CHAPTER 18

Toward a Twenty-First Century Entrepreneurship Approach

The need to achieve Great Harmony and a harmonious society can be considered the main goal of Traditional Chinese Culture—*RuDaFo*. It is at the core of all Chinese strategies and actions. Chinese political and business leaders often refer to this as their ultimate goal. In fact, the extraordinary ability that Chinese entrepreneurs have to contextualize and adopt a holistic approach to their affairs is associated with their prudence in carefully considering how their actions on one particular issue might affect the entire equilibrium of the system. This reflects the moderation and peace embodied in natural harmony. In fact, the history of China—starting with the Yellow Emperor and continuing with Confucius and Lao Tzu (Laozi)—reflects the attempt to reinvigorate the principle of harmony that existed in a previous "golden age," but was lost due to political chaos.

China is a traditional society,[1] with Confucianism,[2] Taoism and Buddhism at its core. Traditional Chinese Culture's principles and values (as reflected recently in the revival of religion there, to a certain degree, at least) provide the basis for China's progress from its backward situation at the end of the 1970s to becoming the second largest economy in the world in only three decade's time. These principles and values lie at the root of Chinese entrepreneurship and the business management style in China; in some cases it could even be said to lie at the core of their businesses. In particular, their pragmatism, work ethic, and desire to keep learning and innovating reflect the principles and values of Traditional Chinese Culture. Learning was the key to advancement in Confucian society. Deng Xiaoping called for education and study and certainly, the Chinese population has followed his advice; not only have they sent their children to study in the best universities abroad, but they have also themselves continued to learn and improve.

The self-made entrepreneurs of this book are no exception in this respect, and they explicitly acknowledge it. They have combined their intuition and practical experience from their hard work with formal academic training. They have also been successful in their combination of inductive and deductive reasoning. Most often they have added what they have learned formally to their base of intuitively derived knowledge, which is largely tacit, rooted in philosophy, epistemology, cognition, and culture. In doing so, they have developed and applied new business models, and new patterns, approaches and categories for decision-making and strategy implementation—the case of Haier included here being a prime example. These may differ from leading management theories that have been generated and applied in the context of the Western corporate world. However, in an increasingly global economy in which China plays a leading role, and with the traditional capitalist model currently in crisis, these Chinese practices should not be overlooked. Because of the great difficulties Westerners face in understanding Chinese behavior, the communication of business culture has largely been one-way until recently: the Chinese know nearly everything about Western business models and strategies and have learned how to get the best from them, while Westerners know relatively nothing about China and still assume that their own models are universally applicable. Chinese entrepreneurs' approaches to management are creative and innovative and, without doubt, contain elements to help a company differentiate itself in the market place, renew itself and continue growing, all activities that are very much needed in the West.

A striking feature of Chinese entrepreneurs is how they all seem to go with the flow of things, how they seem to easily accept what has happened as the only thing that could have happened, and how they seem to easily accommodate to the ups and downs of life and to learn from them. To them everything has aspects of both *yin* and *yang* and is regulated by their everlasting interaction. So, they are not afraid to face risks or to start all over again (even if they have no previous experience in the sector); they also do not panic when adversities arise. They seem easily to understand that everything, every thought and every manifestation of life is in constant flow, never static, always changing. As such, success will always follow adversity, so one has to be well prepared for either and remain serene no matter what. Chinese entrepreneurs are certainly influenced by the idea that all worldly phenomena are manifestations of a basic oneness, emptiness, or Tao, not a thing in itself, but rather a background: the world is an infinitely open "space" that allows for anything to appear, change, disappear, or reappear; as such, the world is a place where anything is possible. This makes them creative and able to persevere, willing to try what for others may seem impossible or simply unrealistic. They are brimming with a unique inner strength, self-motivation, and in self-control. They remain indifferent to others' opinion and constantly strive to become stronger. They fend for themselves and do whatever is necessary to accomplish their goals and stay ahead of their competitors.

One thing one can expect of the Chinese is their tremendous emotional intelligence, and their ability to deal with all types of relationships and situations. They are always fully present, self-aware of one's self and of one's impact on others. As such, they place great emphasis on the well-being of their employees. Traditional Chinese Culture teaches them to give love to their employees, to take care of them and their families, to help them when they need support, and to generate a sense of community and harmony. Chinese entrepreneurs know that, when this is practiced, employees end up being happy with themselves and in harmony with others, including their colleagues and bosses at work, and their friends and families at home. They know that, only in this way will their employees: love their work, be industrious and skillful, have a desire to keep learning, serve their clients warmly, and pay attention to efficiencies while being innovative. In fact, most Chinese entrepreneurs invest a great deal of their time every year in the management of their employees— *Renxin huan guangli*—and in building their internal corporate culture, which they regard as the soul of their business. They think that a favorable atmosphere, that is, a warm and harmonious environment, will bring better results and limitless space for the firm to develop. And they know that for this to happen they should also love themselves, feel good about themselves, remain calm, keep their good health, and maintain harmony at home (a point on which the younger generations are devoting more time—the cases of Xu Xiaoyu and Zhang Ziqin are good illustrations of this. Chinese entrepreneurs truly believe and apply the philosophy that success comes when the team and the leadership share the same goals. Thus, in large groups, they are developing systems to identify when this is not happening, so that those employees that fail to accomplish their goals may end up leaving the company as the ultimate step. By so doing, they are generating tremendous internal competition and using it to increase their efficiency, to act promptly to emerging problems and quickly find innovative solutions to avoid them from recurring.

Chinese entrepreneurs always hold a positive and pro-active attitude. Even in the difficult economic period covered in this book, 2009–2012, they all affirmed they were fairly certain that they could find a way to survive the crisis and grow after it is over. The fact that they are facing a significant number of challenges—including fierce competition, a squeeze in profit margins, brand development and positioning, the relocation of sourcing activities to other lower cost countries, and the resulting transformation of their sectors and their business models does not seem to worry them too much. They know that only those companies that can adjust to the changing environment and quickly make the required changes will remain competitive in the market-place; the rest will simply disappear. They know that even state-owned companies face strong domestic competition, particularly now that the export market is shrinking. But they are well prepared, since the way forward was never easy for them: to operate in the Chinese market quite often has been like operating in the global market, not only because of its size, but also because every foreign company has also wanted to compete there. They know that only innovative companies that can offer high quality products or services with reasonable prices and good after-sales service will be successful. For Chinese entrepreneurs, the market is like a battle-field and risks exist in every one of them, but it is important to know if the company will take risks when the probabilities of success are high. When the competition is strong, they know that there is no alternative but to compete effectively in order to win. For them a crisis is also an opportunity[3] to improve and learn, to focus on working hard and being efficient today in order to succeed tomorrow. Zhang Ruimin, the Haier CEO, made a quote in 2009 that exemplifies this: "Facing the current financial crisis, we really have to know not only the way to get through the winter, but also how to swim in winter time, when the water is extremely cold, instead of hibernating. We have to boldly live through the tough times instead of burying our heads in the sand." Chinese entrepreneurs do not worry too much about the future. They believe that what will have to happen will happen. They remain calm and have clear-thinking in the face of pressure and uncertainty. They know that what is critical is to keep innovating and improving and to retain the capacity to adapt to market conditions quickly, before it is too late. What counts is today's performance and efficiency. What is important is to keep acting, advancing step-by-step. They always keep in mind that "a journey of a thousand miles begins with a single step."

Chinese entrepreneurs recognize the importance of being cautious all the time, "as if walking on thin ice," says Yang Mianmian. They pay great attention to never losing the stability of their business in the (for them) extremely important process of building and positioning their brands. They know that focusing on clients' demands—not on competitors—and being able to anticipate them is the key: customers are at the core of the business. They know the importance of being clear and transparent to win customers' credibility. For them, the loyalty of their customers is price-less. They know that tenacity and perseverance always pays, even if at the beginning there are many difficulties and the results are not good. In fact, they have ambitious goals and seem to be specialists in transforming small family firms into big businesses. In doing so, they have Chinese business leaders as role models, such as Yang Mianmian, an individual much admired by everyone. In fact, the efforts of Haier's leaders building a globally-known brand are remarkable. The same is true of Tasly, which wants to "conquer" the world, and of Tianyi, which aims at further diversifying and expanding all over the world. However, these entrepreneurs never seem to get dizzy with success. Their original motivation was not to make money, but to implement the business ideas they had in mind in order to improve the well-being of society.

Chinese entrepreneurs say that a person who seeks success will never give up, because the meaning of life for him or her is to work diligently to generate prosperity. Looking toward the future, they see that challenges coexist with opportunities, credit coexists with honor, but decisions and great achievements last forever.

A GOOD ENTREPRENEUR IS SOMEONE THAT:

- *Does what he or she wants to do.*
- *Knows his or her weaknesses, failures, and vulnerabilities, as well as his or her strengths and successes, and knows how to best deal with them.*
- *Has the self-confidence that he or she is not going to fail.*
- *Proceeds from the ground up.*
- *Behaves like a very normal person and knows how not to be affected by the ups and downs of life.*
- *Recognizes the importance of the physical location and the name for the company.*
- *Is able to lay-out and implement the right business strategy.*
- *Starts small, but is able to manage and control the growth of his or her business.*
- *Knows how to develop a sustainable long-term business, by proceeding step-by-step.*
- *Is not in a hurry, recognizing that sometimes one should allow him or herself time for things to happen.*
- *Knows that what is important is not advancing quickly, but doing so steadily.*
- *Understands the importance of equanimity and inner-strength to develop the business successfully.*
- *Recognizes the importance of knowing operations well and of remaining cautious, not undertaking any tasks he or she is not prepared for.*
- *Knows that hard work, self-discipline, and persistence are the key to achieving success.*
- *Seeks truth from facts.*
- *Never stops studying, learning, and improving.*
- *Is always generating new ideas and putting them to work, while simultaneously remaining focused on the business' goals.*
- *Keeps a positive attitude and is not afraid of risks, since there is always a possibility of success.*
- *Gives prime importance to his or her company's reputation in the market.*

- *Places customers at the center of the business, acknowledging the fact that they are always right.*
- *Is constantly tracking the market and anticipating the client's needs.*
- *Is continuously educating and serving the client.*
- *Recognizes the need to link employees to the market in order to keep innovating and adapting to the client's individual needs.*
- *Recognizes the necessity of doing whatever is necessary to stay ahead of competitors.*
- *Makes the right decisions at the right moments and implements all needed actions to make them happen.*
- *Is flexible enough in their business approach to make changes, if necessary.*
- *Does not panic when the market becomes challenging and demand, or margins, or both simultaneously shrink.*
- *Continues with implementing the strategy, even if failure occurs.*
- *Learns from mistakes (included complaints from clients) and uses them as a source for improvement.*
- *Has very ambitious goals—such as being number one in the market—and works diligently to achieve them.*
- *Is persistent in pursuing long-term goals, no matter how many difficulties may be encountered along the way.*
- *Has sufficient self-confidence that negative situations do not last.*
- *Works diligently and applies self-discipline.*
- *Develops and applies thorough and comprehensive standards and procedures to maximize the organization's efficiency.*
- *Applies Traditional Chinese Culture when running the business.*
- *Understands that the performance of a company is the result of the efforts of all its employees.*
- *Pays great importance to training the employees on corporate values.*
- *Creates a well-organized and harmonious working environment.*

- *Strives to have the best available talent regardless of nationality.*
- *Knows how to delegate, and never forgets that managing employees is the key to success.*
- *Makes clear to employees that capabilities, not the corporate position, is what matters most.*
- *Communicates to employees that they are trusted and have the freedom to perform, to do what they feel most inclined to, so that they can work diligently and deliver good results.*
- *Motivates employees to keep learning, improving, and innovating.*
- *Generates a culture of community, harmony, and mutual responsibility among employees to achieve the common goals.*
- *Shows employees that, by working in a more responsible way, they can be happier.*
- *Motivates employees to execute every task or project—regardless of its size or nature—with the maximum consciousness, quality, and efficiency.*
- *Makes an effort to allow employees to choose their professional paths and advance in their professional careers and personal lives.*
- *Advocates employees' healthy habits and positive attitudes toward life and career.*
- *Takes direct care of the employees' needs and personal problems, giving them all equal love and knowing how to act as if they were their best friends.*
- *Generates a working environment and culture that favors the possibilities for continuing professional development, allowing for the retention of talent and easier adaptation to changes in the marketplace.*
- *Guarantees that there is no communication gap or miscommunication between management and employees.*
- *Links employees' remuneration to the company's results.*
- *Eventually allows employees to hold stock in the company, so that they will have a share in its profits.*

- *Places R&D and innovation at the core of the business.*
- *Foresees when the incorporation of new technological advances is needed to remain competitive in the market-place.*
- *Keeps investing to possess the best available methods and technologies.*
- *Co-operates with famous universities and research academies both at home and abroad.*
- *Establishes R&D centers at home and, when going global, in the relevant countries abroad.*
- *Knows the convenience of performing associations and joint ventures with the appropriate partners both at home and abroad.*
- *Acknowledges the importance of choosing partners that have a culture compatible with his or her companies' culture.*
- *Understands that foreign cooperation also means easier access to foreign markets.*
- *Performs as many public-private partnerships as necessary at home, with the aim of also eventually operating abroad.*
- *Knows how to split responsibilities appropriately among the partners.*
- *When necessary, teams with stakeholders and looks for support—wherever it is available—in order to have the opportunity to demonstrate capabilities, quality, and performance.*
- *Is able to negotiate and sign the most appropriate contracts.*
- *Pays vital importance to the quality of his or her products and services.*
- *Develops a brand that is synonymous with unique high quality products.*
- *When appropriate, thoroughly explores the possibility of acquiring a globally known brand as the most efficient path for accessing international distribution networks.*
- *Aims to position products in the market at the possible highest level.*
- *Develops and applies the right marketing techniques and promotes the brand to the market appropriately.*

- *Communicates the product's (and the business') differentiated attributes with the media.*
- *Acknowledges the importance of segmenting and appropriately targeting customer segments.*
- *Knows the importance of using customer word-of-mouth as a marketing technique.*
- *Foresees the possibility of eliminating intermediaries and working in direct contact with clients.*
- *Sees the importance of marketing and working with clients in innovative differentiated ways.*
- *Acknowledges the importance of developing a broad network of high quality collaborators, business contacts, and clients.*
- *Applies modern information technology to manage these networks and transform market inputs into actual products and services.*
- *Is always open to facing new challenges on top of what has been already achieved.*
- *Never forgets that new challenges should be faced without sacrificing what the company has already achieved.*
- *Keeps expanding the business to respond to market and clients' needs.*
- *Knows the importance of his or her direct involvement in the expansion process.*
- *Knows the importance of looking for opportunities in the current sector as well as diversifying out of the core business, thus remaining competitive and achieving the company's ambitious goals.*
- *Is not afraid to enter new fields when the right opportunity arises.*
- *When applicable, seriously studies the possibilities of consolidation or franchising to profit from the market opportunities quickly.*
- *Persistently takes market opportunities, even when they seem unreachable.*
- *Always keeps in mind that challenges co-exist with opportunities.*

- *Transforms every threat into an opportunity to grow stronger.*
- *Cleverly knows how to use and keep the company's competitive advantages.*
- *Has implemented the appropriate management systems and procedures in his or her existing businesses so they are prepared to face new challenges.*
- *Positions his or her business as a leader in the domestic market to face the challenges of internationalization.*
- *When operating in other markets, starts by exporting products, but only with the intention of eventually making international investments.*
- *Recognizes the importance of having clients in the domestic market to keep the business sustainable when the economic situation in foreign markets is uncertain.*
- *Does not hesitate to perform all the investments necessary to provide customers with the most competitive high quality products and services.*
- *Knows that it is critical to earn a return on every investment profitably, and to re-invest it in a new project.*
- *Knows the importance of going public both to raise capital and to accelerate internal cultural changes.*
- *When going global, knows the importance of internationalizing both the products and the capital investment.*
- *Acknowledges the importance of moving from manufacturing to services—to increase margins and guarantee the business' sustainability, and takes the necessary steps to make it happen.*
- *Goes ahead with the implementation of the planned strategy and does not stop, even in situations of economic turmoil.*
- *Pays as much attention to the business results as to the integrity of their business.*
- *Knows that, at the end of the day, the leader has to count on himself or herself to face the challenges.*
- *Manages and develops the business with their inner-heart.*
- *Needs to be successful, but not necessarily to become a millionaire.*

- *Is able to integrate business expansion with one's personal life.*
- *Cares for others and wants to end having a positive impact on people's living conditions and wellness.*
- *Practices philanthropy.*
- *Abides by the principle of achieving the "Harmonization of Man and Nature."*

One way or another, all the entrepreneurs mentioned in this book and the many others I have met over the years share the approach above as to what a good entrepreneur is. This includes Yang Mianmian. Since its founding in 1984, Haier has a unique philosophy merging the business experience of East and West to become an international model of twenty-first century corporate management. Haier's most innovative features are its "inverted pyramid" matrix structure and the related "people-centered" accounting system, both supported by a market-focused and client-focused information system. Haier's vision of its need to transform itself from a goods-based to a services-oriented business is praiseworthy. Their intuition that its physical products will all be cheap to buy and that the differentiation should be in (1) the features that can be incorporated into them and (2) in the associated services, is remarkable. Their goal to become the most competitive global provider of good living solutions is worthy of praise. In Haier's "inverted pyramid" organizational structure, employees directly face clients and the market, and they are responsible for collecting information from them. They can accompany customers all the way from the before-sales phase to the after-sales phase—this has been named "Haier's Worry-free Service." All other functions, included management, become service providers for front-line employees. Leaders no longer give orders but provide employees with resources and services, as do the first-line managers at the lowest level. This way, the original straight-line organization structure is changed into a matrix structure. Since all managers in the company have become support providers, everyone's work is centered on creating and meeting customer's demands; the whole company has been transformed into a service system.

Haier's "people-centered" accounting system uses employees—called "independent operation entities"—as the focal point of the accounting system, transforming the traditional financial reporting into three tables (profit-and-loss table, daily checking table, and individual-order compensation table) which allows the integration of personal compensation as well as the value created for customers.

Haier's management model stimulates employees' enthusiasm, innovation, and competitiveness, while linking employees to one another, so that disputes among them are non-existent; as a result, the specific responsibilities of each employee contributes to the achievement of the company's goals. In fact, Haier's corporate culture encourages the participation of all employees. Haier's progressive management concepts have attracted International attention and have been recognized worldwide. By combining Chinese management culture with Western management concepts, Haier has been able to develop a management model that incorporates the elements that are considered essential for successful management in this century.

Haier is not unique among Chinese companies. For instance, the youngest generation of Chinese entrepreneurs has been trained in the Western management models and techniques (though many of them were raised learning the traditional Chinese management approach from their parent-entrepreneurs). Today, they are figuring out ways to integrate and optimize these foreign ideas in their local companies. They know that directly applying foreign companies' business models is not viable—even for high technology companies. In the same way, they know it would be short-sighted for them to restrict themselves to the traditional Chinese management approach. There are so many highly-educated, diligent-working Chinese, so many minds continuously thinking about and generating new ideas, so many young entrepreneurs that, at the end of the day, they will for sure come up with innovative management approaches. When Chinese entrepreneurs make a strategic decision to obtain something, they will end up getting it for sure, as they have already proved in the last decades.

This leaves Western entrepreneurs and business leaders with only a solution to remain competitive in the market-place: to question whether the (Western) models they have used previously will continue to bring success to their businesses in the future, and to invest time in understanding how Chinese entrepreneurs are grounding, managing, and expanding their businesses (pretty much along the same lines that Chinese entrepreneurs have taken with Western business approaches). Entrepreneurs in the West should understand that, in the near future, Chinese SMEs may become their competitors in the global market, because of—among other reasons—their ambitious goals and the encouragement to internationalize they are receiving these days from government officials. Western entrepreneurs should recognize that to innovate rapidly in every dimension of their business—as the market requires today—they need to understand how Chinese business leaders work and learn from their approaches to management, in particular from their hard work and perseverance.

The world order as we knew it is changing, and China is becoming the leader of it. Chinese entrepreneurs truly believe that the twenty-first century is going to be China's century. Today, China aims at regaining its place as the wealthiest country in the world, to become not just a foreign trade leader, but also a world business leader, showing the world how superior they are, reminding the world how superior they have always been, for millennia. And they want to do this by keeping their distinctive traditions and ways of operating, and turning the rest of the world to submit to the Chinese paradigm. It is this motivation that is strongly pushing every single Chinese entrepreneur to act.

Western entrepreneurs often take a different approach to business problems from their Chinese counterparts, not realizing that their own approach is not the only one and perhaps even not the best approach. Indeed, the richest solutions come when ideas from different perspectives are blended. The value of accepting divergent ideas as a fact of life can be used to enhance the world in which we all live and work. This is a domain in which the Chinese have advanced so much further that we have in the West.

In the West, we often say that our companies cannot compete with the Chinese because the government subsidizes them and supports their efforts. But how much do we know about the role that large private companies and entrepreneurs at small and medium sized enterprises (SMEs) have played in the remarkable development of the Chinese economy? How much do we know about the exemplary efficiency of Chinese state-owned enterprises (SOEs)? And how much do we know about the intricacies of the highly efficient public-private partnerships in China? Are we aware of the fierce competition Chinese companies (included SOEs) have continuously faced in their domestic market? When Yang Mianmian arrived at the Qingdao refrigerator's firm back in 1984, her company already faced very strong competition in the Chinese market. The situation has not improved since then, as China continues to be a market in which nearly all global companies want to operate. But while similar companies are disappearing, why has Haier become the success story it is today? The answer is simple: because of its remarkable entrepreneurship and management approaches, incorporating useful elements from the West. China is a huge, but extremely competitive market, in which survival and success are not simply the result of having some government support; instead, it is because of: excellent business vision and strategies, impeccable implementation, appropriate and efficient management of resources (in particular, employees), innovation, persistence, flexibility and extremely hard work. It is easy to do nothing but blame the competition, as we sometimes do in the West, but this is exactly the opposite of what the Chinese are doing. A better solution for Western entrepreneurs and business leaders would be to act, introducing radical changes in the way they think, and bringing innovation to their entrepreneurial and management approaches. This innovation might simply come from asking the question of "what has to be done to increase our sales?", which is the question Chinese entrepreneurs are constantly asking themselves.

In the West, we often overestimate the role the Chinese government has played in the Chinese economy, and end up blaming our Chinese competitors for it. But, once again, instead of just continue to blame others in this fashion, what we have to do is to try to understand the facts. Since the 1978 "reform and opening up" of the Chinese economy, the Chinese have managed to maximize their competitive advantages by smartly playing off the interactions between the public and the private sectors, and by smartly complementing state-owned enterprises' functions with those of private firms. Government-owned companies (SOEs) have proved to be fairly efficient and the relationship between SOEs and private firms is often very close, and also relatively unique. These "Chinese Public-Private Partnerships" exist all around China, whether in a JV form or as pure associations, merely complementing each other's functions. Through their use, Chinese entrepreneurs have already been able to achieve, in many instances, global leadership. This is illustrated in the various chapters of this book and incorporates many lessons that could prove useful to non-Chinese entrepreneurs and business leaders. If we could manage to apply these lessons in our own systems, this could help us transform our own economies and help us operate our own businesses more efficiently. Instead of listening to Western business people's complacent litanies on what they perceive as China's essential imperfections, they should seriously focus on what they could learn from the nuances of Chinese entrepreneurial and business management approaches.

An additional aspect that non-Chinese tend to overlook are the great sacrifices Chinese entrepreneurs have made at the personal level, especially the generations of Chinese entrepreneurs over 40 years old. They often work long hours, in some cases physically separated from their families—for instance, when the husband and the wife are taking care of different businesses. Despite what we non-Chinese may think, the Chinese economy has been pretty much been developed on the shoulders of individuals who were willing to take a risk and build the Chinese dream. Are we ready in the West to renounce our comfortable life, in the hope that the government will solve all our problems, and begin fending for ourselves? Most of the stories in this book are not those of global businesses, but of SMEs, using entrepreneurial approaches that are particularly relevant to the West today. Outside China, we will increasingly see new entrepreneurs (the self-employed as well as micro-entrepreneurs) entering the market-place just because—after graduation or after becoming unemployed in middle age—they could not find a proper job and have no other option but to create their own business venture. By default, this kind of entrepreneur will aim to build a world where their future depends on their own personal capacities, resilience, and hard work. They will have to learn—as the Chinese have done—how to fend for themselves, without counting on assistance from the government. Even large corporations may have to stop using the traditional employee recruitment and incorporate, as part of their emerging organizational structure, communities of freelancers and entrepreneurs, which will better suit today's business environment and improve dynamism in their own businesses. In the twenty-first century's economy, only those who are able to adjust, who can do a lot with little, and who understand that it is never too late to start all over again will win. Chinese entrepreneurs are already world leaders at this approach, and we should learn from them.

It is true that in today's increasingly interconnected world, the Chinese need us (even if only as consumers), perhaps just as much as we need them. Collaboration too is a necessity these days, learning to work together and support each other. In fact, many non-Chinese companies are designing their products specifically for China's domestic market. But these foreign companies will face fierce competition from Chinese companies that need to keep or expand their business by selling their own innovative quality products in their domestic market. Without making an effort to understand "The Chinese Paradigm" and how to operate in it, however, foreign companies and entrepreneurs may not be able to benefit from the new opportunities that are available to them today in the Chinese market. One example, for instance, is the acquisition of Chinese companies in highly fragmented industries where there are many opportunities for firm acquisitions, or industry consolidation, or both (for instance, fast food). Another opportunity may lie with Chinese SMEs that may find it difficult to go on developing on their own.

From the mid-nineteenth century—with the decline of the Qing dynasty—to the expulsion of the Japanese after the Second World War, most Chinese believe that China suffered national humiliation from their collective lack of knowledge or understanding of the Western world. They were humiliated once, but learned their lesson; they also want to avoid any repeat experience in the future. Deng Xiaoping's famous statement in 1978 is the best illustration of this perspective: "*We should not act like women with bound feet. If we want socialism to perform better than capitalism, we should learn from other cultures' achievements. We should learn from other countries, including the developed capitalist countries.*" Since then, China has launched itself into multiple collective efforts: a massive translation (from their original English version) of business related books; joint ventures with knowledge transfer as the norm for foreign companies wanting to operate in the China market; educated Chinese families sending their children to study to the best world universities; and, more recently, Chinese buying Western companies. The result today is that many Chinese have learned and continue to learn everything we know—including our entrepreneurial and managerial culture—while we in turn know relatively little about them or their culture. We still live in different paradigms, but they know ours, while we do not know theirs. Chinese entrepreneurs have big goals. They want to show to the world what China and the Chinese are capable of achieving. They are striving to continue growing and becoming stronger to win honor for China. Whether they decided to start with the most challenging developed markets (as is the case for Haier), or with the under-developed markets (as Tasly has done), or simply followed their government-owned associates or clients as they went abroad to do business (which is Tianyi's aspiration), the goal remains the same: to one day become premier global companies. They know they will have to adapt, eventually to localize to achieve their goal. But they also know that, by means of business and commerce, they can once again bring China to the center of the world.

Not only is commercial or geo-political leadership shifting to China, but also intellectual leadership. In the years to come, we will see a new type of creativity, not the kind associated with pot-smoking, sandal-wearing counter culturists from the US West Coast—or those who have already shaped our present world, but a new kind originating in East Asia. As those people did, the Chinese also imagine a world not yet in existence, a world where they are the ones who will define the rules. Chinese entrepreneurs not only perform well, but they do so following models based on principles and values that have been shaped over millennia, but which most foreigners are not deeply familiar with. By combining these principles and values with their own innovative approaches, Chinese entrepreneurs are in a position to begin feasibly conquering the world. Today, Chinese entrepreneurs are striving to be successful world leaders. They are fully determined to gain global market share through their innovative efforts in creating new business models.

In 1977, Apple's "Think Different" advertising campaign spoke of "the people who are crazy enough to think they can change the world are the ones who do." Chinese entrepreneurs are crazy enough to think they can turn the world around and re-establish the order that for over 18 centuries placed them at the center of the world. And so they probably will, even if they have to go "beyond reality" or to exceed others' expectations in order to achieve it. It is only a matter of time to see the "Chinese Dream" become true. By learning from Chinese entrepreneurs' achievements, we should be prepared for it.

Notes

Preface

1. As an example, the World Bank "China 2030" report encourages China to promote innovation, competition, and entrepreneurship as a means of economic growth, rather than allowing growth to be primarily government engineered. It states bluntly that the Chinese government has not "expressed an interest in becoming a bastion of free market capitalism."

2. According to a study conducted by the advertising agency TBWA, the appeal of traditional values such as loyalty, moderation, and respect for elders made a comeback between 2002 and 2009. Two examples illustrate this re-emergence of interest in Traditional Chinese Culture: Professor Yu Dan's lecture "Confucius from the Heart," broadcast nationally on China Central Television (CCTV), had a record audience. Also popular was *Golden Marriage*, a television series extolling commitment as the "secret sauce" of love.

3. To Confucius, the functions of government and social stratification were facts of life to be sustained through ethical values. *Junzi* was the term he used to describe his ideal human. *Junzi* literally means "lord's son." As the potential leader of a nation, a son of the ruler is raised to have a superior ethical and moral position while gaining inner peace through being virtuous. Despite its literal meaning, any righteous man willing to improve himself can become a *junzi*. The *junzi* enforces rule over his subjects by acting virtuously himself. It is thought that his pure virtue will lead others to follow his example. The ultimate goal is that government behaves much like family. Thus, at all levels, filial piety promotes harmony and the *junzi* acts as a beacon or exemplar of this piety.

4. However, it has been said that the CCP's efforts at gender equality have not been fully realized, even today. Female representation in the highest levels of the CCP is sparse—for example, since 1949 there have only been two female Chinese governors of any province or municipality.

5. In April 2010, Philip Morris picked Jennifer Li, chief financial officer of Baidu—the Chinese online search company, to join its board as an independent director. She was the fourth Chinese executive chosen to serve as a director for an S&P 500 company and the first woman from China. It was said that her appointment reflected the rise of a new generation of Chinese managerial talent, bringing the country's corporate sector closer to the standard of its international peers.

6. On July 1, 1997, the British returned Hong Kong to China, which became a Special Autonomous Region (SAR) of China. Hong Kong SAR has 50 years of autonomy guaranteed (except for issues related to defense and external affairs), operating under the principle of *"one country, two systems,"* as Deng Xiaoping himself stated it.

7. Chinese women buy twice as much luxury products as males in China. About 30% of the Maserati vehicles sold in China are bought by women, while in Europe they represent only 2–5% of those sales. Diageo has reported that the number of women drinking "Johnnie Walker whisky" in China is also significantly greater than in Europe.

8. Although around 50–60% of Chinese women entrepreneurs have obtained ISO 9000 certification and 15–20% of them ISO 14000 certification, over 7% of women entrepreneurs have had their export efforts cease because their products were not up to international standards.

9. In fact, recent Chinese graduates find it very difficult to accept that, due to the tremendous job competition in China, it is almost impossible to find the "ideal" well-paid job and that there is little employment security. For undergraduates, the situation is even more troublesome, as they typically end up working as executive or administrative assistants—*zhulis* or *bangongshi fuzhuren*—and more and more often in inferior jobs, such as a waiter or waitress.

10. The companies' English names have been left as they appear in those entrepreneurs' business cards and (when available in English) websites, even if sometimes the translations are a bit odd. For the Mandarin names, *pinyin* has been used.

11. The rate of JV failures, in particular among Western companies, is very high, however.

12. Chinese are so practical that a few of the women entrepreneurs found it difficult to understand why, when they had provided so much information in 2009, a second round of in-depth interviews was necessary to produce this second book.

13. In the case of non-public companies, Chinese normally do not provide precise figures—sometimes they provide no figures, for areas like sales revenue (sales turnover) or profitability. This has to be respected, in particular when these figures are not that relevant to the themes this book aims to communicate to the readers.

14. This has been shown to be the case, even for the figures of Chinese companies that are traded on American stock exchanges. On June 9, 2011, the US Securities and Exchange Commission (SEC) issued an investor bulletin, cautioning investors about investing in reverse mergers, and pointing out that these types of companies may be prone to fraud and other abuses.

The bulletin also gave a list of reverse merger companies, whose US trading had been suspended in the previous few months, including a few Chinese names such as Heli Electronics Corp., China Changjiang Mining & New Energy Co, and RINO International Corporation.

15. In the case of the large groups, it was not only their structure which was not clearly explained, but also the many varied business areas in which they have diversified, which in most cases have little or nothing to do with their core business.

16. It has been suggested that corruption in fact supported the CCP by acting as a "transaction tax that distributes ill-gotten gains among the ruling class."

Chapter 1

1. This was the case in the Song Dynasty (960–1279), when China led the world in nautical technology, and also in the early years of the Ming Dynasty (between 1405 and 1433) when China sent Admiral Zheng to travel the world with a fleet whose size and technology dwarfed that of the Spanish Armada (which would not be created for another 150 years).

2. Kissinger, Henry. "On China"; see Bibliography.

3. It is not a coincidence that in Beijing's Forbidden City there is a hall named the Hall of Supreme Harmony.

4. Wade-Giles was the predominant system used for transcribing Chinese terms in most English language publications until the wider adoption of China's pinyin system after 1979.

5. Martial arts were widely practiced before the introduction of Buddhism, both by the civil population and by the monks. It is proved, for instance, by records of the discovery of arms caches in the monasteries of *Changan*, during government raids in A.D. 446.

6. *Taijiquan*, a form of martial art, is often described as the principles of *Yin* and *Yang* applied to the human body. Wu Jianquan, a famous Chinese martial arts teacher, described Taijiquan as follows: "Various people have offered different explanations for the name *Taijiquan*. Some have said: "In terms of self-cultivation, one must train from a state of movement toward a state of stillness. *Taiji* comes about through the balance of *Yin* and *Yang*. In terms of the art of attack and defence then, in the context of the changes of full and empty, one is constantly internally latent, not outwardly expressive, as if the *Yin* and *Yang* of *Taiji* have not yet divided apart." Others say: "Every movement of *Taijiquan* is based on circles, just like the shape of a *Taijitu*. Therefore, it is called *Taijiquan*."

7. It is worth mentioning that, according to the tradition, the birthplace of the Yellow Emperor is believed to be in Shou Qiu, at present on the outskirts of the city of Qufu in Shandong Province.

8. TCM is largely based on the philosophical concept that the universe is made of an energy called *qi*, which can be any state of matter or energy in existence. It believes that the body is a small universe unto itself, that is, a complex of subsystems of energy and matter, and that these systems work together to maintain a healthy mind and body. The main aspects of the TCM's concept of the human body, health, and disease are: *YinYang*, the Five Elements (五形 *wǔxíng*), the organs (脏腑u*zangfǔ*), qi, blood (血, xue), meridians and the Six Exogenous Pathogenic Factors (六淫 liuyin–literally, "Six excesses").

9. Reflexology (zone therapy) is an alternative medicine, a complementary or integrated medical treatment method involving the physical act of applying pressure to the feet and hands with specific thumb, finger, and hand techniques applied without the use of oil or lotion. It is based on what reflexologists claim to be a system of zones and reflex areas that they say correspond to an image of the human body superimposed over the physical structure of the feet and hands. The underlying premise is that such work effects a physical change to the corresponding section of the human body. In China, the practice of acupressure using the fingers also evolved over time into the practice of acupuncture using needles. The belief in the reflex points still existed, but the practice was taken in a new direction with a new theory involving the use of meridians. The Chinese concept of meridian therapy is a fundamental part of the philosophy underlying reflexology today.

10. The application of object placement inside and outside the house is known as *Feng Shui*. Because it is rooted in Yi Jing's binary language, the original *Feng Shui* is extremely technical. It developed from the Daoist systems of astrology, *YinYang*, and the five elements (fire, Earth, metal, water, and wood). The ancient Daoists developed *Feng Shui* from their understanding of the subtle interplay of energies that make up the universe. *Qi* is the most important component in *Feng Shui*; *Qi* encompasses everything and holds together all the different aspects and factors involved in *Feng Shui*. *Qi* cannot be seen, heard, or felt; it cannot be perceived with any of our senses. It's the virtual energy and force that flows all around us. Although frequently criticized by the students of Confucius, the application reached deeply into people's everyday life. The palaces and tombs of the royal families built in the Tang dynasty (618–907) and all the following dynasties strictly followed the prescriptions of *Feng Shui*. When Buddhism reached China, it soon absorbed the *Feng Shui* principles, combining them with its own practices, as can be seen in their temples–most of which are located on famous Chinese mountains.

11. Theravada, literally from Pali "The Teaching of the Elders" or "The Ancient Teaching," is the oldest surviving Buddhist school. It was founded in Nepal. It is relatively conservative, and generally closest to early Buddhism. It is

often named the "Small Vehicle," since it considers monastic life as a supe-rior method of achieving Nirvana. Nirvana refers to the path of seeking complete enlightenment for the self.

12. "Traditionally, a bodhisattva is anyone who, motivated by great compas-sion, has generated *bodhicitta*, which is the spontaneous wish to attain Buddhahood for the benefit of all sentient beings. See Wikipedia entry for "bodhisattva".

13. In Vajyarana Buddhism, Amitabha is "associated with the western direction and with the *skandha* of *saṃjña*, the aggregate of distinguishing (recogni-tion) and the deep awareness of individualities". Amitabha possesses infinite merits resulting from good deeds over countless past lives as a bodhisattva. "Amitabha" translates as "Infinite Light," "hence Amitabha is often called "The Buddha of Infinite Light."" See Wikipedia entry on Amitabha.

14. At a later date, the Pure Land teachings spread to Japan and slowly grew in prominence. Today Pure Land is an important form of Buddhism in China, Korea, Japan, Taiwan, and Vietnam.

15. There are indications that Huike, who practiced martial arts, may have been a military man before retiring to the monastic life. Martial arts traditions in Japan and Korea, and Southeast Asia cite Chinese influence as transmitted by Buddhist monks.

16. Most Zen (*Zen* is the Japanese form of the word *Chan*) lineages throughout Asia and the rest of the world originally grew from or were heavily influ-enced by the original five houses of *Chan*. From China, Zen spread south to Vietnam, as well as east to Korea and Japan.

17. *Gongan* (*koan* is the Japanese form of the word) are paradoxical statements meant to trigger enlightenment. Answering a *Gongan* requires a student to let go of conceptual thinking and the logical way human beings normally order the world so that, like the role of creativity in art, the appropriate insight and response can naturally and spontaneously arise in one's mind. In the late twelfth century Lin-chi was introduced to Japan, where it became known as Rinzai Zen.

18. This school was introduced to Japan in the thirteenth century, where it became known as Soto Zen.

19. One of three sects of Zen in Japanese Buddhism.

20. Many *Chan* teachers today trace their lineage back to Hsu Yun, including Sheng-yen and Hsuan Hua, who have propagated *Chan* in the West where it has grown steadily through the twentieth and twenty-first centuries

21. "The Art of War" is an ancient Chinese military treatise attributed to Sun Tzu, a high ranking military general and strategist, who lived during the late Spring and Autumn period. Composed of 13 chapters, each of which is devoted to one aspect of warfare, it is said to be the definitive work on

military strategies and tactics of its time. Sun Tzu emphasized the importance of positioning in military strategy. The decision to position an army must be based on both objective conditions in the physical environment and the subjective beliefs of other competitive actors in that environment. He thought that strategy was not planning in the sense of working through an established list, but rather that it required quick and appropriate responses to changing conditions. Planning works in a controlled environment; but in a changing environment, competing plans collide, creating unexpected situations. "The Art or War" is still read for its insights on the role of positioning in military, and business settings and in undertaking negotiations with other parties.

Chapter 2

1. Pew Research Centre, Pew Global Attitudes Project. It is interesting to see that the second country on the list is also Asian: India, where 85% of its population stated that they approach the future with hope.
2. In the autumn of 2011, for the first time in its history, China's urban population surpassed its rural population.
3. There was more than one Great Wall of China, as a Chinese archaeology team has discovered. Several portions of the wall are actually double, triple, or quadruple walls running closely parallel to one another. This was a common feature in many ancient fortifications because it made the position easier to defend. Often the troops would be garrisoned between the walls for protection against surprise attacks from the rear. The land between the walls also offered a protected area for flocks and farmland to provision the troops. The Chinese team found that the main wall was larger than the others. The investigation continues.

   Several walls were originally built starting in the fifth century B.C. or perhaps earlier. Under the Emperor Qin Shi Huang in c.220 B.C., the earlier scattered walls were linked together to make a continuous fortification protecting China from nomadic tribes to the north. The Great Wall was lengthened, added to, and rebuilt several times in later centuries. During the Ming Dynasty (1368–1644) there was a major expansion with 5,650 km (3,511 miles) of wall built. A recent survey found the entire wall, with all of its branches, runs for 8,852 km (5,500 miles). This figure is being reassessed now that parallel walls have been found.
4. Within a month of ThyssenKrupp closing a steel mill in Dortmund (one of the largest in Germany), a Chinese company bought it with the idea of disassembling the entire mill and taking it to China, near the mouth of the Yangtze River. Soon after this Chinese company bought the mill, 1,000

Chinese workers arrived in Germany to begin the process of taking the plant apart and bringing it to China. The Chinese worked seven days a week for 12 hours a day. The Germans started to complain, so the Chinese, in deference to local law, took one day off. In the end, the Chinese dismantled the mill in less than one year—a full two years ahead of the time ThyssenKrupp initially thought it would take. Over 5,000 miles away, the Chinese rebuilt the steel mill exactly as it was in Germany. Altogether, 275,000 tons of equipment had been shipped, along with 44 tons of documents that explained the intricacies of the reassembly process. Doing all of this was still cheaper (by about 60%) than building a new mill. In China, the demand for steel was such that the mill could immediately start producing steel at full capacity.

5. *Weiqi* (*go* in Japanese) is a Chinese board game, which uses the concept of strategic encirclement to achieve victory.

6. This is not in contradiction to the Chinese proverb *bu da bu xiangshi*, which means that without a fight, we do not get to know each other.

7. "El Gran Teatro del Mundo" ("The Great Theatre of the World") was published by Spanish writer Pedro Calderón de la Barca in 1655.

8. Zhuangzi was an influential Chinese philosopher who lived around the fourth century B.C.E. during the Warring States Period, a period corresponding to the philosophical summit of Chinese thought—the Hundred Schools of Thought. He is credited with writing—in part or whole—a work known by his name, the *Zhuangzi*. He ranked himself as a follower of Laozi, so that, of the more than ten myriads of characters contained in his published writings, the greater part are occupied with metaphorical illustrations of Lao's doctrines.

9. Kowtow, which is borrowed from *kou tou* in Mandarin Chinese, is the act of deep respect shown by kneeling and bowing so low as to have one's head touching the ground. In Chinese culture, the kowtow is the highest sign of reverence. It was widely used to show reverence for one's elders, superiors, and especially the Emperor (it was part of the Imperial Protocol), as well as for religious and cultural objects of worship. In modern times, usage of the kowtow has become much reduced, and is almost exclusively limited to the religious sphere.

10. The Great Wall was a reflection of this basic vulnerability, though it rarely proved a successful solution to it.

11. It took ninety horses and three thousand coolies to transport McCartney's gifts to the emperor. There were rifles, cannons, telescopes, horse carriages, a twenty-five-foot-tall clock, mountains of the finest woollens and a hot air balloon, complete with pilot.

12. Chinese maps of the world in that day took the form of five scrolls hung side-by-side displaying a huge landmass labelled *Zhongguo*, surrounded by tiny islands labelled "England," "Germany," "France," "America," "Russia," and "Africa."

Chapter 3

1. By Chinese standards.

Chapter 4

1. It is very interesting to stress here how those "two Urban Chinas" live side-by-side today: the one where the generation that made the transition possible keeps working until 70 years old or even older, and the one where the people over thirty or thirty five years consider themselves very old in the market. There is an additional "third Urban China," the one where the people that have just graduated from Chinese universities cannot find a well-paid stable job and need to perform two jobs to be able to pay the monthly bills.

Chapter 5

1. During *Tang* Dynasty, there lived a handsome young man named Guo Han who was famous for his knowledge and good character. He lost his parents at an early age and lived alone in a big house. One summer night, it was so hot and stuffy in his room that he couldn't fall asleep. So he carried his bed out of the room and put it in the courtyard. Lying under a bright moon and watching the twinkling stars, he felt cool and placid. Just before he fell asleep, the breeze wafted along a tender fragrance which fought off all his drowsiness; he looked up at the sky, seeing a beautiful lady flying down from the sky. In an instant, she alighted upon the ground, and stood beside his bed. Guo Han was awe-struck, and couldn't utter a word. The lady told him she was the "Girl Weaver in Heaven." Guo Han continued to stare at this Weaving Goddess. He noticed that her white dress was one uncut piece of natural work, without the slightest sign of sewing. He couldn't help asking: "Why is it that your dress bears no trace of needle work?" With a graceful smile, the lady said: "I'm an immortal from Heaven. Clothes for immortals are never sewn with needle and thread. How can there be seams?" From that story comes the expression "*tian yi wu feng*," used to describe a well-conceived plan, the very skilful and flawless handling of things. It can also be used to indicate a perfectly written poem or other literary articles.
2. www.liebherr.com
3. Apart from the original JV Liebherr, Haier had imported freezer air conditioner production lines from Derby, Denmark and Sanyo, Japan and had established JVs with Mitsubishi in Japan and Merloni in Italy.
4. Haier home appliances were distributed in Japan through Sanyo's sales channels, at prices similar to that of Japanese leading brands, while at the

same time, Sanyo batteries were sold in China through Haier's distribution network.

5. The bid was for US$ 1.28 billion, or US$ 16 per share, topping a previous offer of US$14 per share made by Ripplewood Holdings. It was backed by private equity funds Blackstone Group and Bain Capital. In the end, Maytag was bought by Michigan based Whirlpool Corporation which offered US$ 1.7 Billion in cash and stock, or US$ 21 per share, plus assumed debt.

6. Although under partial public ownership, Haier is still technically a "collective" company, meaning that it is theoretically owned by its employees. However, its actual ownership situation is not clear; the employees receive no dividends and do not know how much they own in reality.

7. Although Haier is not so diversified as other similar state-owned groups, it owns companies that deal with other products and services, in particular: Qingdao Haier Real Estate Development and Investment Company, Haier Pharmacy (founded in 1996), Qingdao Haier Qingda Software Company (established in 1998), Haier Logistics (founded in 1999), Qingdao Haier Insurance Agency (created in 2001), and Haier Group's Conference & Exhibition Division. Moreover, Haier has made its way into the finance industry, having invested, for instance, in the *Qingdao* Commerce Bank and in *Chang Jiang* Securities. It is also running a life insurance joint venture and a finance firm.

8. Haier engages in the research and development of chips for intelligent appliances, digital frequency conversion, wireless high-definition technology, audio and video decoder, network communications and technologies of UWB, Bluetooth, RF, electric power carrier wave within an integrated global resource network. In addition, Haier has established joint development laboratories with several multinational corporations to provide innovative solutions including the smart home system, remote medical diagnosis and treatment, online grocery shopping, fault feedback intelligent security systems, and the smart hotel.

9. Haier launched the third generation of networked home appliances (networked digital home solutions), called "Haier E-home", in 2005. Haier deploys "Haier E-home" using a technological system based on proprietary intellectual property rights, such as home network system structure and home network communications technology. The home network is divided into a main network transmitting high speed information, and a sub-network transmitting low speed information. Haier E-home can enable remote access to home appliances and the interconnection of appliances through the Internet, PDA, mobile communications network, cable TV network, and fixed line networks.

10. Haier launched the U-Home product in 2006 and established U-Home Labs to provide the end-user with new products and innovative network

services. The U-Home is regarded as the trend for future home appliances. "**U**" stands for "ubiquitous," which means anytime and anywhere. In other words: If you are at home, U-Home can connect you to the world; when you are in the world, your home travels with you. U-Home integrated refrigerators, air conditioners, washing machines, use the Internet, mobile communication, and fixed phone networks to allow customers to communicate with their home appliances anytime anywhere and allow customers to control their home appliances and retrieve information remotely. The Haier U-Home system includes home appliance controls, lighting curtain controls, multimedia entertainment, visual talks, security alarms, environmental monitoring together in the world's first wireless-controlled network home appliance system. Using this same concept, Haier also provides comprehensive solutions for communities, hotels, supermarkets, office buildings, factories, and urban security departments, and delivers a series of intelligent products, such as digital video phone systems, security monitoring systems, anti-burglary alarms, environment control and access control systems.

11. The Internet-of-things refrigerator is a very innovative product, which cannot only store food, but also connect with the internet, so that communication between the food of different refrigerators, between the refrigerator and the food in the supermarket and between the refrigerator and the humans can be achieved. The Internet-of-things refrigerator is also equipped with various utility and amusement functions like video-telephone, information browsing, and video playing, making it an entertainment center as well.

12. When the May 12, 2008 Sichuan great earthquake occurred, Haier made a first donation of over US$ 10 million to the disaster area. Afterward it took responsibility to finance the building of fifteen hope primary schools and a hope middle school. By the beginning of June 2008, Haier has donated funds and materials for a value of over US$ 3.8 million to the disaster area. In August 2008, at the opening ceremony of the Beijing Olympic Games, Haier launched the scheme of "one gold medal, one hope primary school," by which, for each Chinese gold medal, Haier would build a hope primary school and name it after the Chinese Olympic champion. At the closing of the Olympic Games, Chinese athletes had won 51 gold medals and Haier promised to build 51 hope primary schools to bring the Olympic spirit to the children attending those schools. Over the years, Haier has assisted in the building of 129 hope primary schools and is producing the 212-episode children's science cartoon Haier Brothers.

13. As examples of innovations introduced by Haier in the market in this century can be mentioned the following: In 2001, Haier launches Patriot I, China's very first large scale integration digital television MPEG-II decoding chip for commercial use; in 2002, Haier invents the world's first double-drive

washing machine, the fourth type of washing machine design after the top-load, front-load, and agitator models. Today China is integrating mobile communications to, for instance, programme the air conditioning or heating of the house to have the desired temperature when arriving at it, programme the lighting of the house to avoid robberies when there is nobody home, etc.

14. An example of Haier's patented technology is NuCool. NuCool combines the best features of current cooling systems for compact refrigerators to create a brand new technology that achieves temperatures as low as 37°F (based on 70°F ambient room temperature), which was not possible with prior refrigerant-free models. NuCool has no compressor and runs whisper-quiet with low-power consumption.

15. For instance, when Haier America was established back in 1999, the entire American team, except for the accountant, was comprised of employees sent from Qingdao.

16. By having 50% shares of Haier Electronics Group, a company listed in Hong Kong, Haier believes to have laid a solid foundation for further movement into the international capital market.

17. Today Haier is connecting with consumers online through interactive brand marketing with the goal to demonstrate, educate, and motivate consumers. Haier is on Facebook, Twitter, and YouTube, and also maintains a 24/7/365 phone customer service, where customers can receive personalized attention. Additionally, Haier e-commerce System is supported by advanced information technology for network management, marketing, service, and procurement.

18. Haier has always stood by the three principles of Technical Innovation, Intellectual Property Rights (IPR), and OBM.

19. In 1993, the then Chinese Vice premiers Zhu Rongji and Li Lanqing, together with the then secretary of the CPC Shanghai Municipal Committee, Wu Bangguo, signed a joint-directive to promote Haier's "OEC Approach" nationwide.

20. According to Haier's "Activate Shocked Fish" Theory, international acquisitions involve three scenarios: (1) "Big fish eat small fish," namely big enterprises merging with small companies; (2) "Fast fish eat slow fish," namely new, technologically powerful enterprises merging with traditional companies; and (3) "Sharks eat sharks," which is normally called "strong uniting strong." In China, a living fish, whether it is small, slow or a shark, is not allowed to be swallowed. The fish's death is bad. So, the only choice available in China for Haier was to deal with the "shocked fish."

21. Haier's operational restructuring based upon the Market Chain was carried out in three phases; (1) integration of internal resources to structure the

Market Chain system; (2) receipt of valuable orders from the Market Chain system, emphasizing satisfaction of customer demands and establishing a global supply-chain to improve corporate competency; and (3) integration of human resources to make every employee an individual SBU.

22. SST is the pinyin initials of three Chinese characters that stand for: claim compensation (*SuoChuo*), claim payment (*SuoPei*), and stop if there is neither claim for compensation nor a claim for payment (*TiaoZha*).

23. Giving up the traditional product-oriented development pattern, Haier adopts the user-oriented large-scale customization of "on demand manufacturing and delivery," realizing "zero inventory" and "zero accounts receivable." On the basis of working capital zero loans, Haier's cash conversion cycle reaches minus 10 days. To achieve this goal, Haier uses the "3-JIT" mechanism: JIT purchase—buy only what is needed; JIT distribution—a warehouse is just a transit station from which all incoming materials should be distributed to the manufacturing facilities within 7 days, with the exception of parts stored in 3D automated high-bay warehouses, which should be distributed within only 3 days; JIT delivery, by which Haier can deliver its products wherever they are needed.

24. Haier has enormous marketing network advantages in China. With the use of the internet, it developed the competitiveness of catering to the demand of consumers in the quickest time via "zero-distance virtual and practical network combination." "Virtual network" refers to the internet, which forms customer loyalty through online communities; "practical network" refers to the marketing network, logistic network, and service network, which helps realize the quickest delivery. Thus, numerous world-renowned brands commission Haier to manage part or all their sales in China. In the meantime, Haier utilizes their channels overseas to sell its products. With resource exchanges, Haier speeds up the pace of entering the world market.

25. According to the Chinese Ministry of Commerce and the Ministry of Finance statistics, financial subsidies for farmers for household appliances reached RMB 10.4 billion in 2009.

26. During its transformation to a service-oriented company, the first step that Haier put on the table was to begin negotiations with a Taiwanese home appliance manufacturer to establish two joint-venture manufacturing plants; afterward, Haier gradually withdrew from these JVs to ultimately achieve a "manufacturing services mode" status.

27. For instance, in the computers' business, Haier had worked with Foxconn, So-Seok, Quanta, and other Taiwan manufacturers. In home appliances, Haier established in 2003 a long-term cooperative relationship with Sampo Corporation.

28. "Clock system" means that Haier shall build a system of self-operation like a clock, according to which each employee works around a market goal.

Employees mix with employees and SBUs mix with SBUs, like the gear of a clock, to ensure that the concerted efforts of the employees are in line with Haier's operations. Employees can drive, operate, adjust, and innovate on themselves to make the Haier's business last forever.

Chapter 6

1. The pulse-reading component of the touching examination is so important that Chinese patients may refer to going to the doctor as "Going to have my pulse felt."

2. Tianjin is one of the four of the municipalities that are not part of provinces, but independent entities whose leaders report directly to Beijing. It shares this status with: Beijing, Chongqing, and Shanghai.

3. Dripping pills are formed in the following process: solid medicine is melted into hot solution, which later flows through a burette with fixed caliber into condensate liquid without mixing. This preparation enjoys the advantages of fast discharge velocity, high bioavailability, and instant effect in a small dose. Dripping pills have great medical stability and are hard to dissolve in water and oxygen. Due to the shaping process within a liquid environment, the medicine remains unpolluted by dirt. Tasly's automatic dripping pill production line employs an advanced computer expert platform to conduct management. It includes a production management system, supervising system, alarming system, logistic code management system, and dynamic equipment management system. This includes the online collection of production data, supervision of quality standards, all-process management of logistic information, and equipment status analysis. The automatic production line for dripping pills has been developed exclusively by Tasly with proprietary intellectual property rights. It has been renovated four times and is the biggest equipment for dripping pill production in China.

4. In 1703, Chengde was chosen by the *Kangxi* Emperor as the location for his summer residence. Constructed throughout the eighteenth century, the Mountain Resort was used by both the *Yongzheng* and *Qianlong* emperors to avoid the summer heat. It reached the height of its grandeur under the *Qianlong* Emperor from 1735 to 1799. The elaborate Mountain Resort features large parks with lakes, pagodas, and palaces ringed by a wall. Outside the wall are the Eight Outer Temples, built in varying architectural styles from throughout China. One of the best-known of these is the *Putuo Zongcheng* Temple, built to resemble the Potala Palace in Lhasa, Tibet. The resort and outlying temples were named a UNESCO World Heritage Site in 1994.

5. Compound Danshen Dripping Pill (also referred to as Cardio Tonic Pill) contains the extract of the root of Chinese salvia (Salvia miltiorrhiza—known

as *danshen* in Chinese), the extract of the root of notoginseng (Panax notoginseng—known as *sanchi* or *tien-chi ginseng*), and synthetic borneol, an active ingredient that replaces the more expensive natural borneol found in cardamom (Elettaria cardamomum var. cardamomum), ginger (Zingiber officinale), and other spices. According to Tasly's information, the pill is sold as a prescription drug in China, Vietnam, Pakistan, South Korea, India, and the United Arab Emirates and is taken by about 10 million people every year to treat angina and coronary heart diseases. International annual sales are around US$ 148 million. *Danshen* has been used in TCM for many years to improve patients' circulation and to treat cardiovascular diseases. The oldest documented record of *danshen* as a medical agent is found in *Shen Nun Ben Cao* (The Divine Husbandman's Classic of the Materia Medica), dated at about 200 A.D.

6. Tasly refers to Modern TCM in this way: "Modern TCM industry adopts new technology to promote traditional industrial technology, establishes the ability for TCM innovation, settles the pharmaceutical technique bottleneck, and forms rational development mechanisms. Modern TCM enterprises set up professional manufacturing and organizing systems, exemplify comprehensive techniques of automatic control on production and improved technique and apparatus, and heighten the level of technology. Meanwhile, Modern TCM also accelerates industrialization of cultivating elite seeds of herbal plants, expands standardized agricultural areas, and develops professional techniques for extraction, separation and preparation. With the development of modern technology, the TCM industry has made great achievements in China and become one of the advantageous industries possessing international competitiveness."

7. Chinese Medical Centre BV was founded by Dr. Dong Zhi Lin in 1986. It has been referred to as the largest TCM centre in Europe, encompassing TCM medical treatment, TCM education, and international sales. The centre has been honored for its outstanding contribution as a European Pilot Organization in the international exchange and development of TCM in Europe. Nevertheless, as time passed, Tasly decided not to sell its products there.

8. Maotai is a Chinese liquor produced in the town of Maotai, in the city of Renhuai, Guizhou province. It is believed that the town of Maotai possesses a unique climate and vegetation that contributes to the taste of the drink. It is classified as "sauce-fragranced" (jiangxiang) because it offers an exceptionally pure, mild, and mellow soy sauce-like fragrance that lingers after it is consumed. Maotai is distilled from fermented sorghum and now comes in different versions ranging in alcohol content from the standard 53% by volume down to 35%.

Chapter 7

1. Since 2008, the Chinese Government has introduced Traditional Chinese Culture courses in the universities.
2. Because of the proximity to Qingdao, South Korea has been performing a lot of investments in the Qingdao area since the opening of the economy. As an illustration, it shall be pointed out that it takes about an hour to fly from Qingdao to South Korea, almost the same time that it takes to do it to Beijing.
3. *Dizigui* is an ancient Chinese book written during the reign (1661–1722) of the Qing Dynasty Emperor Kangxi by Li Yuxiu. Translated into English, the words *Di Zi Gui* mean standards for being a good student and child. In ancient China, this book provided moral instruction to children before they entered school. The original title was *Xunmengwen*—"Elementary text on compliancy." It was compiled according to the essay *Tongmeng xu zhi*— "What small kids have to know"—by the Southern Song period (1127–1279) Neo-Confucian philosopher Zhu Xi. In four chapters, the book explains the behaviour of a Confucian scholar: filial piety at home, brotherly obeisance outside, reverential and trustful, broad-minded, and kind hearted to all people. "The rest of his physical and mental forces are dedicated to learning." Confucius believed that moral principles, virtues and discipline should be the very first lessons taught to a child, that children need to practice them daily and that without moral principles, the learning of all other subjects would be futile.

   Although *Dizigui* is based on Confucian teachings, its fundamental principles encompass the Three Teachings: Confucianism, Taoism, and Buddhism. At the end of the nineteenth century, the *Dizigui* became a textbook in elementary schools and was widely read. *Dizigui's* underlying moral principles are still valid today. In the recent past, *Dizigui* has been experiencing a revival, since both parents and teachers have come to realize that they need guidelines to teach their children moral behaviour, so that the children will grow up to be law abiding citizens with a strong sense of ethics.

Chapter 8

1. *Huangjiu*—literally "yellow" wine, is a type of Chinese alcohol beverage brewed directly from grains such as rice, millet, or wheat. Unlike *baijiu* (white wine), such liquors are not distilled, and contain less than 20% alcohol, due to the inhibition of fermentation by ethanol at that concentration. These wines are traditionally pasteurized, aged, and filtered before their final bottling for sale to consumers. The various styles of *huangjiu* may vary in color

from clear to beige, yellowish-brown, or reddish-brown. *Huangjiu* is either drunk directly after being cooled or warmed, or used in Chinese cooking.

2. The *Lanting Xu* is the most famous work of calligraphy by Wang Xizhi, composed in year 353. Written in semi-cursive script, it is the most well-known and well-copied piece ever. It describes a gathering of 42 literati—including Xie An and Sun Chuo—at the Orchid Pavilion near Shaoxing, Zhejiang province, during the Spring Purification Festival to compose poems and enjoy the wine. The gentlemen had engaged in a drinking contest: wine cups were floated down a small winding creek as the men sat along its banks; whenever a cup stopped, the man closest to the cup was required to empty it and write a poem. In the end, twenty-six of the participants composed thirty-seven poems. The preface consists of 324 Chinese characters in 28 lines. The character *zhi* (之) appears twenty times, but no two look the same. It is also a celebrated work of literature, which flows rhythmically. It is a piece of improvisation, as can be seen from the revisions in the text. The good company and the strong wine put Wang Xizhi in such a happy mood that he took up his brush and, there and then, wrote the *Lanting Xu* as a prelude to the collection of poems. It is said that Wang Xizhi tried to reproduce the Prelude nearly 100 times several days later, but he was never able to match his spontaneous calligraphy of that day.

Chapter 9

1. *Laoshan* is located on the shore of the Yellow sea, about 30 kms east of Qingdao. Its highest peak has an altitude of 1,133 meters. Overlooking the sea, the mountain is characterized by its: many clear springs and waterfalls, imposing canyons, odd shaped stones, undulating peaks, imposing cliffs, caves, and shrouding mists. *Laoshan* is the highest mountain along China's 18,000-kilometer-long coastline, as well as the only mountain with a peak of over 1000 meters along China's coastline. In the book of *QiJi* (478–221 B.C.), there is a statement saying that "along the Yellow sea, the Tai mountain is not higher than *Laoshan*," which does not refer to their actual heights but to how impressive *Laoshan* is. Over history, *Laoshan* has been said to be home of some "Supernatural Spirits." In the Qin Dynasty (221–206 B.C.), the first emperor *Qin Shihuang* once came here to visit these "supernatural beings." In the Tang Dynasty (618–907 A.D.), the great emperor *Lee Longji* also travelled there to find herbal medicines for eternal life. Over the course of history, many other famous scholars visited *Laoshan* and wrote poems and essays about the mountain. *Laoshan* area was the home of the second largest *Quanzhen* Group of Taoism in history. At the height of its prosperity, there were 9 palaces, 8 temples, and 72 nunneries. The Taoists from *Laoshan* were

well known for their religious knowledge, legendary skills, and stories. Also, the Buddhists appreciated the place: In 412 the Chinese Buddhist pilgrim *Faxian* landed at *Laoshan* on his return from India.

Chapter 10

1. *Chengguan* are similar to "City Management Officers," but not exactly this. Today they belong to a government agency called City Urban Administrative and Law Enforcement Bureau (commonly shortened to *Chengguan*), a local government agency that has been established in every city in the People's Republic of China. "City Management Officers" are in charge of the keeping the city in discipline and of the urban management of the city. This includes: local bylaws, city appearance bylaws, streets safety, environment, sanitation, work safety, pollution control, health, and can involve enforcement in planning, greening, industry and commerce, environment protection, municipal affairs, and water in large cities.
2. For an explanation of this, read "China's New Leaders," which is listed in the bibliography.
3. She has travelled to many countries outside of Asia, such as several the US, Argentina, Chile, and several in Europe. She has always enjoyed what she has seen, but eating Western food has always been a challenge for her.
4. Because of the great distances, they cannot provide a repair service to clients located all over China.

Chapter 11

1. Ideally, the four helicopters should have been all acquired in 2009, but it was necessary to wait a full year until the Russian factory could supply the additional two units.
2. Because of its beautiful scenery, facing the sea and surrounded by green and rocky mountains with elegant forms, Qingdao is called "The Eastern Switzerland."

Chapter 12

1. In 2007, the government decided to establish a national pork reserve, reasoning that a backlog of frozen meat could be used to make up for shortages and stabilize prices when necessary. In practice, a strategic pork reserve has problems. Frozen meat does not keep for more than about four months, and live animals must be fed and constantly replenished to keep the reserve

stable. In Shaoxing, a large city in coastal Zhejiang Province, the local government keeps a virtual reserve of pork by paying farmers a subsidy of RMB 20 per pig to keep their herds at a set level. Experts have said that, in only five years, China has built a livestock and meat industry which is the equivalent of the United States' industry; however, it took the United States 50 years to build it to its current size.

2. In rural China, in most families, boys are still considered more precious than girls.

Chapter 13

1. *Jimo* takes its name from *"Jimo Lu* market" in the "old town," a place to buy souvenirs, clothing, pearls, watches, and similar items. *Jimo* is about 45 minutes' drive from Qingdao and is famous for *Jimo Lao Jiu*, a type of rice wine that is best served warm, much like Japanese sake. *Jimo* has grown from a village to a city of over 1 million inhabitants today.

2. In *Jifa* are located the *Jifa* Industrial Park, *Huamian* Washing, *Huacheng* Dyeing and Finishing, and *Huamei* Printing. In *Longshan* there are three areas *Longshan*, *Longshan* 2, and *Longshan* 3.

3. Chitosan fiber is extracted from shells gathered from deep waters off the US state of Alaska. It is widely used in textiles thanks to its: beautifying, anti-aging, anti-bacteria, deodorized, anti-static, and decomposition properties. Underwear made from this fiber can prevent bacteria from spreading and eliminate odor because Chitin as a material is unique given its positive ionic charge. Usually bacteria and viruses have a negative ionic charge, so Chitin can neutralize or kill bacteria and viruses by deforming their internal structure. Chitin fiber can also biologically or naturally decompose, which is both sustainable and environment friendly. Chitosan fiber can remain in equilibrium with the body's energy, and can efficiently protect the skin from such environmental forces like the sun's ultraviolet light. Chitosan has also superb moisture management properties, better retaining body warmth and providing comfort when compared with other fibers.

4. ePTFE (expanded polytetrafluoroethylene) is made by expanding polytetrafluoroethylene resin into a microscopic web-like structure that is amazingly thin—about 10 microns thick. This process creates billions of microscopic pores, which allow air to pass through easily. The ePTFE membrane offers superior performance compared to most other plastics in terms of chemical and biological inertness, temperature range, UV resistance, porosity, and heat insulation properties. ePTFE is naturally water repellent (hydrophobic); it repels rain and snow, while water vapor from

the body can permeate through the membrane, which makes it an ideal liner for *outerwear* garments.

Chapter 15

1. China started implementing its latest "Interim Provisions on ULUT (State Council Decree No. 483)" in 2007. While the actual ULUT rates are determined by provincial governments, Decree No. 483 stipulated the ranges of annual ULUT rates applied in different types of cities:
   - Major cities: RMB 1.5–RMB 30 per square meter
   - Medium-sized cities: RMB 1.2–RMB 24 per square meter
   - Small-sized cities: RMB 0.9–RMB 18 per square meter
   - Counties, towns, industrial and mining areas: RMB 0.6–RMB 12 per square meter.

2. The *Rishengchang* Exchange Shop, in the nineteenth century, at its peak, controlled almost half of the Chinese economy, and its branches were widespread throughout China's big cities and capital, Beijing. In some western and southeastern countries, *Rishengchang* also owned its branches and offices. During those times, there were as many as 20 financial institutions within the *Pingyao*, comprising more than half of the total in the whole country. *Rishengchang* controlled almost 50% of the silver trade when its scale reached the top in the whole *Qing* Dynasty. The exchange shop is now a museum.

3. After its heyday Pingyao fell into poverty and, without the cash to modernize, its streets remained unchanged. In 1997 it was inscribed as a UNESCO World Heritage Site.

4. During the late Qing Dynasty, a new development occurred: the creation of *piaohao*, which were essentially banks that provided services like money transfers and transactions, deposits, and loans. After the establishment of the first *piaohao* in *Pingyao*, the bankers in Shanxi dominated China's financial market for centuries until the collapse of *Qing* Dynasty and the coming of British banks.

5. In 1824, *Rishengchang* set up a branch in Taiyuan. The main business was checks or drafts which were called "tickets" in Chinese. The secrecy of the production and writing of the "tickets" had very strict rules, and workers were never allowed to make mistakes. At that time, Taiyuan was the base camp of *Shanxi* businessmen's distribution and maintenance of goods. In order to work efficiently, *Rishengchang* introduced the world's most advanced printing technology at that time—the "watermark" method. So *Rishengchang* used this method to produce and print the "tickets." Additionally, each "ticket" was stamped with a seal in the key parts. The amounts and recipients of the "tickets" were strictly controlled. When the Shanxi traders went

to other provinces and the frontier border transaction station, they always brought the drafts which were written by the professional official in Taiyuan *Rishengchang* using an ink brush. The handwriting would be simultaneously bulletined and sent to the other 51 branches of *Rishengchang*. Specifically, the drafts were executed with codes—using Chinese writing to replace numbers and regularly changing the password method to prevent the disclosure of confidential information. The fact was that in Taiyuan *Rishengchang* history, the matter of the money being falsely claimed never happened. This fully embodies the intelligence of *Rishengchang*'s operators.

6. The centre has about 30,000 m² of built space and can accommodate between 100 and 150 offices of *Shanxi* companies. In Beijing there are about 10,000–20,000 *Shanxi* entrepreneurs.

Chapter 16

1. Manchu people are a *Tungusic* people who originated in Manchuria (today's northeastern China) and one of the 56 ethnic groups of People's Republic of China. During their rise in the seventeenth century, with the help of the *Ming* dynasty rebels (such as general *Wu Sangui*), they came to power in China and founded the *Qing* Dynasty, which ruled China until the *Xinhai* Revolution of 1911, which established a republican government in its place. For centuries, the Manchu ethnicity has acculturated with the majority *Han* ethnicity of China. Most Manchu today speak Standard Chinese, while the Manchu language is only spoken by elderly people in remote northeastern China and a few scholars. In recent years, however, there has been a resurgence of interest in Manchu culture among both ethnic Manchus and *Han*. The number of Chinese today with some Manchu ancestry is quite large— 10.68 million people. Manchu is the 3rd largest ethnic group in China after the *Han* and the *Zhuang*. Recently, the adoption of favorable policies toward ethnic minorities (such as preferential university admission, government employment opportunities, and exemption from the one child policy) has encouraged some people with mixed Han and Manchu ancestry to re-identify themselves as Manchu.

2. The People's Bank of China (PBC) is the central bank of the People's Republic of China with the power to control monetary policy and regulate financial institutions in mainland China. The People's Bank of China has more financial assets than any other single public finance institution in world history. It was established on December 1, 1948 based on the consolidation of the *Huabei* Bank, the *Beihai* Bank, and the *Xibei* Farmer Bank. The headquarters was first located in Shijiazhuang, Hebei, and then moved to Beijing in 1949. Between 1949 and 1978 the PBC was the only bank in the People's

Republic of China and was responsible for both central banking and commercial banking operations. In the 1980s, as part of the economic reform, the commercial banking functions of the PBC were split off into four independent but state-owned banks and in 1983, the State Council promulgated that the PBC would function as the central bank of China. Mr. Chen Yuan was instrumental in modernizing the bank in the early 1990s. Its central bank status was legally confirmed on March 18, 1995 by the 3rd Plenum of the 8th National People's Congress. In 1998, the PBC underwent a major restructuring. All provincial and local branches were abolished, and the PBC opened nine regional branches, whose boundaries did not correspond to local administrative boundaries. In 2003, the Standing Committee of the Tenth National People's Congress approved an amendment law for strengthening the role of PBC in the making and implementation of monetary policy for safeguarding the overall financial stability and provision of financial services.

Chapter 17

1. The term *RuDaoFo* refers to the philosophical aspects of Confucianism, Taoism, and Buddhism, by contrast with *RuDaoSi*, which refers to their religious dimension. *Ru* means "scholar;" the terms *Rujia*, *Rujiao*, and *Ruxue* are used to refer to "Confucianism" (strictly speaking, there is not just a term in Chinese which directly corresponds to "Confucianism"). *Dao* is "Tao" from Taoism. *Fo* is Buddha. *Si* means "temple."

2. These elements shall not be mixed with the traditional five elements of the I Qing and the *RuDaoFo*: *Jin* (metal), *Mu* (wood), *Shui* (water), *Huo* (fire), *Tu* (earth).

3. The Zhongnan Mountains, sometimes called the Taiyi Mountains or Zhounan mountains, are a branch of the Qin Mountains located in Shaanxi Province. Zhongnan Mountains have been a popular dwelling-place for Daoist hermits since at least the Qin Dynasty. Buddhist monks began living in the mountains after Buddhism's introduction into China from India in the early first millennium A.D. The Complete Perfection Sect, one of the largest branches of modern Taoism, was founded in the Zhongnan Mountains by Song Dynasty Taoist Wang Chongyang. Due to the mountains' close proximity to the ancient capital of Chang'an, officials who incurred the imperial court's wrath often fled to these mountains to escape punishment.

4. *Shi Jing*, translated variously as the "Book of Songs" and the "Book of Odes," and often known simply by its original name The "Odes," is the earliest existing collection of Chinese poems and songs. It comprises 305 poems and songs, some from as early as 1000 B.C. It forms part of the Five Classics. The "Odes" first became known as "Jing" or "Classic," in the canonical sense, as

part of the Han Dynasty's official adoption of Confucianism as the guiding principles of Chinese society around the first century A.D.

5. *Qu Yuan* (340–278 B.C.) was a Chinese scholar and minister to the King from the southern *Chu* during the Warring States Period. He is regarded as the first author of verse in China. His works are mostly found in an anthology of poetry known as *ChuCi*. He is said to have waded into the *Miluo* river, in today's Hunan Province, to commit ritual suicide, as a form of protest against the corruption of the era. His friends threw rice into the water as a food offering to distract the fish away from his body. However, late one night, the spirit of *Qu Yuan* appeared before his friends and told them that he died because he jumped into a river. He asked his friends to wrap their rice into three-cornered silk packages to ward off the dragon. These packages became a traditional food known as *zongzi* (although the lumps of rice are now wrapped in reed leaves instead of silk). The act of racing to search for his body in boats gradually became the cultural tradition of the "Dragon Boat Festival," which is held on the anniversary of his death every year.

6. Much more precise data on members and fees was not provided by Tian Yu and her wish shall be respected.

7. Amitabha is a celestial Buddha described in the scriptures of the Mahayana school of Buddhism. Amitabha is the principal Buddha in the Pure Land sect, a branch of Buddhism practiced mainly in East Asia. Amitabha is known for his longevity attribute and the aggregate of distinguishing (recognition) and the deep awareness of individualities. According to these scriptures, Amitabha possesses infinite merits resulting from good deeds over countless past lives as a bodhisattva named Dharmakara. "Amitabha" is translatable as "Infinite Light," hence Amitabha is often called "The Buddha of Infinite Light." According to the Larger Sutra of Immeasurable Life (Mahayana Amitayus Sutra) Amitabha, after accumulating great merit over countless lives, finally achieved Buddha-hood and is still residing in his land of Sukhavati, whose many virtues and joys are described.

Chapter 18

1. China is so tied to its history and tradition that, as an example, the Yellow Emperor was used by politician Deng Xiaoping in his arguments for Chinese reunification with Taiwan, expressing that Taiwan is rooted in the hearts of the descendants of the Yellow Emperor. The Yellow Emperor was also used by the People's Republic of China when Taylor Wang—a Chinese American Astronaut—travelled space, acclaiming that he was the first of the Yellow Emperor's descendants to travel in space.

2. American poet and philosopher Emerson felt that "Confucius is the glory of all nations around the world." In 1988, after 75 Nobel laureates met in Paris, they issued a joint declaration stating that "if humanity is to survive in the 21st century, it must look back to 2,500 years ago, to the wisdom of Confucius."

3. The Chinese word for crisis is made of two characters: one is danger (危), the other is opportunity (机).

References

Armstrong, K. (2000). *Buddha*. USA: Viking Penguin.

China Association of Women Entrepreneurs, The Research and Consulting Center of China. (2009). *The development report for women entrepreneurs of China: Overcoming the crisis and following the path of sustainable development.* Jianguomen Dajie, Beijing: Women's Foreign Language Publications of China.

Chunli, Q. (1996). *The life of Confucius*. Beijing, China: Foreign Language Press Beijing.

Confucius. (1979). *The Analects*. USA: Penguin Books.

Crissold, T. (2004). *Mr. China*. London: Constable & Robinson Ltd.

Dan, Y. (2006). *Confucious from the heart. Ancient wisdom for today's world.* Beijing: Zhonghua Book Company and Macmillan.

Fairbank, J. K. (1968). *The Chinese world order: Traditional China's foreign relations.* Cambridge, Massachusetts: Harvard University Press.

Goleman, D. (1997). *Emotional intelligence*. USA: Bantam Books.

Goleman, D. (2007). *Social intelligence*. UK: Arrow Books.

Hua, Y. (2009). *Brothers*. New York, NY: Pantheon Books.

Isaacson, W. (2011). *Steve Jobs*. London: Little, Brown Book Group.

Jäger, W. (2000). *Die Welle ist das Meer. Mystiche Spiritualität.* Germany: Verlag Herder Freiburg im Breisgau.

Kase, K., Slocum, A., & Zhang, Y. (2011). *Western management looks East again.* UK: Palgrave Macmillan.

Kynge, J. (2006). *China shakes the world. The rise of a hungry nation.* London, UK: Orion Books Ltd.

Kissinger, H. (2011). *On China*. USA: The Penguin Press.

Lao, T. (2009). *Tao Teh King*. Spain: Editorial Sirio S.A.

Lee, J. Y. K. (2009). *The piano teacher*. London: Harper Press.

Lee, L. (2009). *Shanghai girls*. London: Bloomsbury Publishing.

Man, J. (2008). *The great wall. The extraordinary history of China's wonder of the world.* USA: Bantam Books.

McGregor, J. (2005). *One billion customers: Lessons from the front lines of doing business in China.* New York, NY: Wall Street Journal Books.

Menzies, G. (2002). *1421. The year China discovered the world.* USA: Bantam Books.

Menzies, G. (2008). *1434. The year a magnificent Chinese fleet sailed to Italy and ignited the Renaissance.* New York, NY: Harper Collins Publishers.

Mingyur Rinpoche, Y. (2007). *The joy of living.* USA: Harmony Books.

Mingyur Rinpoche, Y. (2009). *Joyful wisdom.* USA: Harmony Books.

National Intelligence Council, NIC. (2008). *Global trends 2025: A transformed world.* USA: US Government Printing Office.

National Intelligence Council, NIC. (2012). *Global trends 2030: Alternative worlds.* USA: US Government Printing Office.

Nye, J. (2011). *The future of power.* New York, NY: Perseus Books Group.

Pérez-Cerezo, J. (2009). *Emprendedoras Chinas.* Spain: LID Editorial.

Pérez-Cerezo, J. (2010). *China's new leaders.* USA: LID Publishing.

Pérez-Cerezo, J. (2011). Las Mujeres en China. El Desconocido Motor de su Economía. Chapter IX of the co-authored book *Siglo XXI. El Siglo de Oro de las Mujeres.* Spain: Editorial Universitas, S.A.

Pye, L. (1992). *Chinese negotiating style: Commercial approaches and cultural principles.* Westport, CT: Quorum Books.

Redding, S. G. (1991). *The spirit of Chinese capitalism.* Berlin, Germany: de Gruyter.

Rose, S. (2009). *For all the Tea in China.* Hutchinson: Random House.

Shane, S. (2010). *Viewpoint: If you want to see entrepreneurs, go to China.* USA: Bloomberg Business Week.

Shane, S. (2011). *Preparing children to be entrepreneurs.* USA: Small Business Trends.

Spence, J. D. (2007). *Return to dragon mountain: Memories of a late ming man.* USA: Viking Penguin.

Tzu, S. (1988). *The art of war.* Boston, MA: Shambhala Publications, Inc. (translated by Thomas Cleary).

Tzu, S. (1996). *The art of war.* Oxford, UK: Tuttle Publishing (by Stephen F. Kaufman).

Weber, M. (1904). *English translation 1930. The protestant ethic and the spirit of capitalism.* USA: Penguin.

YingShih, Y. (1967). *Trade and expansion in Han China: A study in the structure of sino-barbarian economic relations.* Berkeley: University of California Press.

Index

OTHER TITLES IN THE ENTREPRENEURSHIP AND SMALL BUSINESS MANAGEMENT COLLECTION

Scott Shane, Case Western University, Collection Editors

- *Growing Your Business: Making Human Resources Work for You* by Robert Baron
- *Managing Your Intellectual Property Assets* by Scott Shane
- *Internet Marketing for Entrepreneurs: Using Web 2.0 Strategies for Success* by Susan Payton
- *Business Plan Project: A Step-by-Step Guide to Writing a Business Plan* by David Sellars
- *Sales and Market Forecasting for Entrepreneurs* by Tim Berry
- *Strategic Planning: Fundamentals for Small Business* by Gary May
- *Starting Your Business* by Sanjyot Dunung
- *Growing Your Business* by Sanjyot Dunung
- *Understanding the Family Business* by Keanon J. Alderson
- *Launching a Business: The First 100 Days* by Bruce Barringer
- *The Manager's Guide to Building a Successful Business* by Gary W. Randazzo
- *Social Entrepreneurship: From Issue to Viable Plan* by Terri D. Barreiro and Melissa M. Stone
- *Healthcare Entrepreneurship* by Rubin Pillay
- *The Successful Management of Your Small Business: A Focus on Planning, Marketing, and Finance* by Pat Roberson-Saunders

Announcing the Business Expert Press Digital Library

Concise E-books Business Students Need
for Classroom and Research

This book can also be purchased in an e-book collection by your library as

- a one-time purchase,
- that is owned forever,
- allows for simultaneous readers,
- has no restrictions on printing, and
- can be downloaded as PDFs from within the library community.

Our digital library collections are a great solution to beat the rising cost of textbooks. e-books can be loaded into their course management systems or onto student's e-book readers.

The **Business Expert Press** digital libraries are very affordable, with no obligation to buy in future years. For more information, please visit **www.businessexpertpress.com/librarians**. To set up a trial in the United States, please contact **Adam Chesler** at *adam.chesler@businessexpertpress.com* for all other regions, contact **Nicole Lee** at *nicole.lee@igroupnet.com*.